ISLAM, RELIGIOUS LIBERTY AND CONSTITUTIONALISM IN EUROPE

For centuries, since the Roman Empire's adoption of Christianity, the continent of Europe has been perceived as something of a Christian fortress. Today, the increase in the number of Muslims living in Europe and the prominence of Islamic belief pose questions not only for Europe's religious traditions but also for its constitutional make up. This book examines these challenges within the legal and political framework of Europe.

The volume's contributors range from academics at leading universities to former judges and politicians. Its 19 chapters focus on constitutional challenges, human rights with a focus on religious freedom, and securitisation and Islamophobia, while adopting supranational and comparative approaches.

This book will appeal not merely to academics and law students in the UK and the EU, but to anyone involved in diplomacy and international relations, including political scientists, lobbyists and members of NGOs. It explores these contested relationships to open up new spaces in how we think about religious freedom and co-existence in Europe and the crucial role that Islam has had, and continues to have, in its development.

Islam, Religious Liberty and Constitutionalism in Europe

Edited by
Mark Hill KC and Lina Papadopoulou

JEAN MONNET CENTRE OF EXCELLENCE

European Constitutionalism and Religion(s)

With the support of the Erasmus+ Programme of the European Union

•HART•
OXFORD • LONDON • NEW YORK • NEW DELHI • SYDNEY

HART PUBLISHING

Bloomsbury Publishing Plc

Kemp House, Chawley Park, Cumnor Hill, Oxford, OX2 9PH, UK

1385 Broadway, New York, NY 10018, USA

29 Earlsfort Terrace, Dublin 2, Ireland

HART PUBLISHING, the Hart/Stag logo, BLOOMSBURY and the Diana logo are trademarks of Bloomsbury Publishing Plc

First published in Great Britain 2024

A catalogue record for this book is available from the British Library.

A catalogue record for this book is available from the Library of Congress.

Library of Congress Control Number: 2023940035

ISBN: HB: 978-1-50996-695-0
ePDF: 978-1-50996-697-4
ePub: 978-1-50996-696-7

Typeset by Compuscript Ltd, Shannon

ACKNOWLEDGEMENTS

Many of the chapters in this volume are derived from the texts of presentations given to the XXXI Annual Conference of the European Consortium for Church and State Research convened in Thessaloniki, Greece, in September 2021, under the title 'Islam and Human Rights in Europe'. The national reports for the conference were subsequently published by Comares.

The Conference was the product of a collaboration between the Jean Monnet Centre of Excellence, coordinated by Professor Lina Papadopoulou and the Faculty of Law and Faculty of Theology of the Aristotle University of Thessaloniki. The Conference was dedicated to the memory of Professor Charalampos Papastathis (1940–2012), Professor of Ecclesiastical Law at Aristotle University, and this volume similarly stands as a tribute to skill of his scholarship and the warmth of his friendship.

Additional chapters from a range of scholars were commissioned to augment the core from the Conference, to expand the political, sociological and territorial coverage and to give greater depth and nuance. We are grateful to Hart Publishing, and particularly Verity Stuart, assistant editor, and Kate Whetter, senior commissioning editor, for their unremitting enthusiasm and support.

This book is produced within the framework of the Jean Monnet Centre of Excellence 'European Constitutionalism and Religion(s)' funded by the Erasmus+ programme of the European Commission. However, the opinions expressed are those of the contributors and not the Commission.

Professor Lina Papadopoulou wishes to record her thanks to her assistants, Stefanos Katsoulis and Silia Gounari, for their administrative support in the execution of this project, and to Lydia Papagiannopoulou for her constant support. The editors are also grateful to Loukia Tremma and Elias Canal, law school graduates and trainees at the Jean Monnet Chair for European Constitutional Law and Culture, for their work in organising the manuscript, and to Andrew Hendry, David Anderson and Daniel Webber, for effecting linguistic revision to the chapters of non-native English speakers.

The final debt of gratitude is to Andrew Scarafile of the University of Notre Dame, who curated the disparate contributions into a composite end product.

CONTENTS

Acknowledgements .... *v*
Contributors .... *ix*

1. *Islam, Religious Liberty and Constitutionalism in Europe: An Introduction* *1*
   Mark Hill KC and Lina Papadopoulou

PART I
CONSTITUTIONAL CHALLENGES

2. *Religious Freedom for Muslims: A Challenge to the Historical Foundations and Resilience of European Constitutionalism* *17*
   Evangelos Venizelos

3. *When History Cripples the Future for Muslims in Europe: The Struggle between Two Notions of Constitutionalism* *31*
   Ali Rashid Al-Nuaimi

4. *European Values and Islam* *43*
   Maurits S Berger

5. *Old and New Islam in Europe: A Methodological Approach* *57*
   Konstantinos Tsitselikis

6. *Constitutionalism, Populism and Islam in Europe* *73*
   Andrea Pin

PART II
RELIGIOUS FREEDOM AND OTHER HUMAN RIGHTS

7. *Respecting Human Rights by Reconciling the Rights of Muslim Communities and State Policies* *85*
   Francis Messner

8. *Equality and Difference: Muslim Religious Practice, Religious Tribunals and Muslim Women* *97*
   Samia Bano

9. *From Foreigners to Citizens: Freedom of Religion, Education and Policies for Social Integration of Muslim Minors*..........111
Enrica Martinelli

10. *Regulating Islam: Limitations on Freedom of Religion in Denmark*..........123
Niels Valdemar Vinding

PART III
SUPRANATIONAL AND COMPARATIVE APPROACHES

11. *Islamic Headgear: The Case Law of the European Court of Human Rights*..........141
Vincent A De Gaetano

12. *Hunting Grounds for Religious Slaughter: A Case Study from the Court of Justice of the European Union*..........153
Wolfgang Wieshaider

13. *Reasonable Accommodation of Islamic Practices: Europe and America Compared*..........167
Ioannis Papadopoulos

14. *Divine Command and Religious Liberty: A Theological Reflection on Islamic Constitutionalism*..........187
Mahan Mirza

PART IV
SECURITISATION AND ISLAMOPHOBIA

15. *Muslims in Europe: Religious Freedom and Security*..........199
Agustín Motilla

16. *The Legal Treatment of Islamophobic Speech in Europe*..........209
Lina Papadopoulou

17. *Security and Liberty in the Shadow of Islamophobia in Europe*..........225
Merilin Kiviorg

18. *The European Debate on Restrictions on Foreign Funding of Islam*..........241
Zoila Combalía

19. *Islamophobia, Xenophobia and Religion in the European Union: A Quantitative Analysis*..........257
Anastasia Litina and Konstantinos Papastathis

Index..........273

CONTRIBUTORS

Ali Rashid Al-Nuaimi is a Member of the United Arab Emirates Federal National Council for the Emirate of Abu Dhabi and chairman of the World Council of Muslim Communities.

Samia Bano is Reader in Law at the School of Oriental and African Studies, University of London.

Maurits S Berger is Professor of Islam and the West at Leiden University and Director of the Leiden Islam Academie.

Zoila Combalía is Professor of Law and Director of the Laboratory of Freedom of Belief and of the Masters Programme on Religious Pluralism, Law and Society at the University of Zaragoza.

Vincent A De Gaetano is a former Chief Justice of Malta, and a former Judge and Section President of the European Court of Human Rights in Strasbourg.

Mark Hill KC practises at the Bar in London and is Visiting Professor of Law and Distinguished Fellow at the University of Notre Dame London Law Programme.

Merilin Kiviorg is Associate Professor in International Law at the University of Tartu, School of Law and a member of the Chancellor of Justice's Human Rights Advisory Board in Estonia.

Anastasia Litina is Assistant Professor at the University of Macedonia in Thessaloniki, Greece.

Enrica Martinelli is Associate Professor of Law and Religion at the Law School of the University of Ferrara, and a member of the Scientific Council of the Inter-University Center of Culture, Religions and Rights: International Forum of Law & Religions (FIDR).

Francis Messner is Emeritus Director of Research at the French National Centre for Scientific Research and Professor at the University of Strasbourg.

Mahan Mirza is Executive Director of the Ansari Institute for Global Engagement with Religion and Teaching Professor in the Keough School of Global Affairs at the University of Notre Dame, USA.

Agustín Motilla is Professor at the Faculty of Law of the University Carlos III of Madrid.

Ioannis Papadopoulos is Professor of Modern and Contemporary Political and Legal Philosophy and European Policies, and Director of the Centre for Research on Democracy and Law at the University of Macedonia in Thessaloniki, Greece.

Lina Papadopoulou is Professor of Constitutional Law at the Law Faculty of the Aristotle University of Thessaloniki, Greece, and holder of a Jean Monnet Chair for European Constitutional Law and Culture.

Konstantinos Papastathis is Assistant Professor at Aristotle University of Thessaloniki and an external researcher at Leiden University.

Andrea Pin is Professor of Comparative Public Law at the University of Padua and Fellow of the Center for the Study of Law and Religion at Emory University.

Konstantinos Tsitselikis is Professor of Human Rights Law at the University of Macedonia, Greece, and Dean of the School of Economic and Regional Studies.

Evangelos Venizelos is Professor of Constitutional Law at the Aristotle University of Thessaloniki, and former Deputy Prime Minister and Minister of Foreign Affairs of the Hellenic Republic.

Niels Valdemar Vinding is Associate Professor at the University of Copenhagen, and leads an Independent Research Fund Denmark Starting Grant on Producing Sharia in Context.

Wolfgang Wieshaider is Professor of administrative law, law of religion and culture at the Law School of the University of Vienna and permanent Visiting Professor at the Law School of Charles University, Prague.

1

Islam, Religious Liberty and Constitutionalism in Europe: An Introduction

MARK HILL KC AND LINA PAPADOPOULOU

I. The Landscape

Europe's legal, political and cultural architecture has evolved over a long time both in the light and under the shadow of Christianity, whose doctrines and morals have left an imprint on European societies. Fundamental categories of law and political theory (such as the concepts of personhood, human dignity and equality, sovereignty, representation, and subsidiarity) derive from theological notions. As Venizelos succinctly puts it, Christianity fed the Enlightenment prior to clashing with it.[1] The process whereby European societies distanced themselves from Christian morals has been and remains difficult, sometimes even painful, and often meets with resistance both from Christian churches themselves and from parts of those same societies. This deeply rooted historic legacy of Christian tradition and inheritance undoubtedly informs the unease experienced by European governments and societies today when faced with the beliefs and practices of those of its citizens, together with refugees and immigrants, who are drawn from outside the Christian tradition. This is particularly the case with inhabitants of Europe who practise the Muslim faith.

Muslims now represent almost six per cent (and projected to become eight per cent by 2030) of the population of Europe. This growth coincided with a rise within modern Europe of secularism and religion retreating into the private sphere, divested of much of the soft power it had previously exercised. The increased prominence of Islam poses questions and challenges for traditional European norms and values. There is, however, a tendency within the European academic world to problematise Islam and foster a 'them and us' narrative, a

[1] In ch 2 of this volume.

matter rendered more complex by indications of a reversal in the established tendency of limiting religion, in some instances, purely to the private sphere.[2] This tendency is enhanced by acts of terrorism committed by radicalised minorities within European Islam. These isolated terrorist acts are then exploited by nationalistic and far-right, populist parties, which harvest societies' reactions to them and the expanding flows of migrants and refugees (which reactions they themselves cultivate, as Vinding demonstrates with regard to Denmark).[3]

The problematising of Islam featured prominently in the concluding remarks delivered following the conference of the European Consortium of Church and State Research in Thessaloniki in September 2021 on Islam and Human Rights in the European Union.[4] The difficulty lies in white European commentators, largely of Christian extraction and predominantly male, expressing views on Islamic practices and traditions.[5] In this volume, we have endeavoured to invite the voice of Muslims to be heard, so the holders of Islamic beliefs become a part of the conversation, rather than Islam simply being its subject matter. As Ali Rashid Al-Nuaimi reminds us:

> [T]he rise of nation-states has pulled modern Muslim societies away from the Islamic empire of the past; and the expansion of globalization has encouraged Muslims to migrate across the world, especially towards the West, seeking better life and career opportunities.[6]

The peaceful coexistence and equal treatment of all religious communities is one of the principal objectives of the modern human rights regime, of which freedom of religion is a principal strand. The distinct character of religious liberty is based on equal dignity and the enjoyment of equal freedom of all, irrespective of their religion or other identifiers, which collectively contribute towards the often-derided

[2] See for example, C Calhoun, M Juergensmeyer and J van Antwerpen (eds), *Rethinking Secularism* (Oxford, Oxford University Press, 2011).

[3] See ch 10 of this volume.

[4] See L Papadopoulou, *Islam and Human Rights in the European Union* (Granada, Comares, 2022). The published proceedings comprise national reports from European Union Member States and from the United Kingdom, in response to a common framework questionnaire. This volume contains a number of additional papers which were delivered at that conference, together with others specially commissioned, on the much broader theme of Islam, Religious Liberty and Constitutionalism in Europe.

[5] A similar sense of unease was experienced at the Vienna Conference of the European Consortium for Church and State Research in 2001, whose proceedings were subsequently published in R Potz and W Wieshaider (eds), *Islam and the European Union* (Leuven, Peeters, 2004). See also the observations in M Hill, 'Access to Social and Cultural Rights: The Impact of Covid 19 on the Enjoyment of Religious Liberty by Migrant Communities' in V de Gaetano, *The Impact of Covid-19 on Migration and Migratory Flows: New challenges in tackling cultural and religious diversity* (Granada, Comares, 2023, forthcoming).

[6] See also de Gaetano (ibid), in which evidence emerges as to the effect on Muslim relocation within Europe of the COVID-19 pandemic, which closed well-established humanitarian corridors out of the Islam world through and into countries of the European Union; and Russia's war on Ukraine, which gave rise to massive numbers of non-Muslim migrants heading eastwards to escape the brutality of Putin's expansionism.

European 'vivre ensemble'.[7] Within this normative context, informed by (but not limited to) Europe's Christian traditions, Muslim communities and believers often seek sanctuary from injustices condemned by international human rights instruments, but find themselves confronted with intolerant, sometimes hateful, attitudes and discrimination. This can affect the balance between social integration on the one hand and preserving their religious identity on the other. The chapters in this volume have not held back from confronting these challenges. Together, these essays make a critical analysis, from a range of disciplines and viewpoints, of these perceived tensions in the prevailing constitutional settlement in Europe, with particular regard to law, history, politics and sociology.

II. European Values

In his chapter, Evangelos Venizelos refers to the constitutional settlement of Europe being less of a Christian construct than it is generally considered to be. He considers that Christian values have been supplanted by what he identifies as European values, writing that:

> [T]his acquis is not about a Christian Europe but a Europe of liberal democracy, the rule of law and human rights. It concerns European values which, irrespective of their religious, philosophical, historical, political, social, economic or legal origins, have now become a European constitutional acquis within which the religious aspect operates.[8]

In a similar vein, Messner agrees that 'the values commonly shared in Europe are now being underpinned by human rights, not religious principles'. It will be a matter for debate and discussion, of course, whether Christian values have indeed been superseded by this acquis identified by Venizelos and Messner. Values do not simply emerge overnight. To the contrary, they are the product of a slow process of assimilation and consensus over centuries. So, it would be unsurprising if, notwithstanding the absence of cultural and ethnical homogeneity, the laws and practices of the nation states of Europe, which collectively contribute to a pan-European constitutionalism, contain vestiges of Christian beliefs and practices which have been nurtured and promoted over generations. The choice of Sunday as the traditional rest day throughout the European Union (EU), considered sacrosanct in some countries, is a telling example. The presence of images of the Christian God and of crucifixes in classroom or courtroom, as validated by the Grand Chamber of the European Court of Human Rights (ECtHR), is another.[9]

[7] See *SAS v France* (Application no 43835/11), 1 July 2014. A rather more nuanced and ambitious call for the promotion of human dignity is to be found in the Punta del Este Declaration on Human Dignity for Everyone Everywhere (2018).

[8] See ch 2 of this volume.

[9] See the ECtHR decision in *Lautsi and Others v Italy* App no 30814/06 (Grand Chamber, 18 March 2011).

Thus, constitutional morality not only 'strove to impose itself gradually on Christian and every other religious concept', as Venizelos rightly observes, but it is still striving to do so. In this sense, the justifiable liberal doctrine to which he aspires, namely the pre-eminence of religious equality and autonomy fundamental to constitutional morality (although remaining a noble goal) lacks any *purely* secular character.

Whereas Venizelos insists that the 'pursuit of social cohesion and inclusiveness … cannot be achieved at the expense of the values and institutional acquis of European constitutionalism', Maurits Berger interrogates the very concept of European values. First, Berger observes, rightly, that the values of Muslims are not necessarily different from European values, as believers do not necessarily share all the values of their religion. He submits that most Muslims in Europe embrace the notion of 'separation of religion and state', a precondition for religious freedom.[10] Monotheistic religions generally do have a weak theological and historical record on issues such as gender equality and democracy, as Berger observes. In cases where Muslims are bearers of European values and not antithetical to Islamic values, there is no tension that would raise concerns. Equally, there is arguably no tension between Islam itself and European constitutionalism, since, as Al-Nuaimi observes, 'Islam by its nature is a religion open for independent reasoning (*ijtihad*), with a multiplicity of diverse ideas and interpretations'. What is more critical is Berger's second objection: that European values are not clear. They fall into two separate categories: political–legal values enshrined in laws, treaties, and principles; and cultural–religious values that emanate from local and national traditions. Berger argues that controversies with Muslims arise when states refer to political–legal values to enforce principles that are of a cultural–religious nature. This concept of many 'Europes' and 'Islams' is also highlighted by Tsitselikis,[11] while Messner places Muslim divisions into 'different – sometimes doctrinally antinomic – streams' and considers this heterogeneity something which renders it more difficult to find optimal solutions to when problems arise. This same pluralism within Muslim communities may equally be seen as a positive and dynamic element that allows for contestation and change of Sharia itself, as suggested by Bano with regard to Britain.[12]

Furthermore, Berger detects a bias against Islam, when cultural–religious practices, such as handshaking or dress, are treated as if they were part of human rights. But is it a subjective matter to regard the refusal of a man and a woman to shake hands as an issue of gender equality? It is a matter of personal choice, and

[10] European Union Agency for Fundamental Rights, 'Second European Union Minorities and Discrimination Survey (EU-MIDIS II): Muslims – Selected findings' (EFRA, 2017); Gallup, 'Special Report: Muslims in Europe' (Gallup, 2007).

[11] In ch 5 of this volume. See, also, R Hudson, 'One Europe or Many? Reflections on Becoming European' (2000) 25 *Transactions of the Institute of British Geographers* 409.

[12] See ch 8 of this volume, referencing J Eekelaar, 'Law and Community Practices' in J Eekelaar and M Maclean (eds), *Managing Family Justice in Diverse Societies* (Oxford, Hart Publishing, 2013).

not attributable to unwanted gender segregation, argues Berger. The latter involves an implicit assumption that the decision of a Muslim who refuses to shake hands with a person of the opposite sex (and is therefore denied citizenship) is due to their Islamic beliefs.[13] In relation to Muslim dress, Berger comments that 'calling the wearing of the headscarf an act of intolerance without providing an explanation of what exactly constitutes this intolerance, gives the impression that the judges were guided by preconceived notions rather than by legal rationalism.'[14]

Although for Berger, the burqa ban is usually upheld on the culturally biased argument that 'this is not the way we do things here' in Europe, Vincent A de Gaetano, a former judge of the ECtHR, roundly rejects any suggestion of actual bias. Not only is there no conscious bias, but the situation is also far more complex and fact-sensitive. As he explains: 'There is, in reality, no one, fixed or definite position taken by the Court in Strasbourg on the wearing of religious clothing and symbols, be they Christian or Islamic or associated with, or appertaining to, any other religious denomination.' Each case is decided on its own facts, and there is no single practice of universal applicable to the entire continent of Europe. While France, based on its doctrine of *laïcité*, seems to adopt a more uncompromising and harsher approach, as Andrea Pin demonstrates, in the United Kingdom, for example, religious dress, such as the Islamic headscarf, may be worn in the public square and the private workplace, unless there is some overwhelming reason to the contrary, such as personal safety in an industrial workplace.[15] On the other hand, some countries seem to exhibit overtly illiberal policies where Islamic practices are concerned, as the chapters by Wolfgang Weishaider and Niels Valdemar Vinding demonstrate in the case of Austria and Denmark respectively.[16]

But to the extent that European values can be identified, be they Christian in origin or of a more contemporary genesis, contrasting them with so-called Islamic values tends towards a false opposition, or allows some commentators to consider Muslim populations, even ones who are historically embedded, as not essentially 'European'.[17] The theological reflection in the chapter of Mahan Mirza is strongly

[13] See some relevant cases in the media: 'Muslim couple denied Swiss citizenship over no handshake' (18 August 2018), available at www.bbc.com/news/world-europe-45232147; 'German citizenship denied for refusal to shake woman's hand' (17 October 2020), available at www.dw.com/en/man-denied-german-citizenship-for-refusing-to-shake-womans-hand/a-55311947. See also 'Muslim Woman Who Refused Handshake And Then Suffered Discrimination Wins Court Case' (16 August 2018), available at www.npr.org/2018/08/16/639239165/muslim-woman-says-she-refused-handshake-received-discrimination-swedish-court-ag, in which a Swedish labour court ruled that a translation company had to pay a Muslim woman discrimination compensation, after her job interview was terminated upon her explaining she would not shake a male worker's hand for religious reasons.

[14] See ch 4 of this volume.

[15] See ch 6 of this volume; see also M Hill et al, *Religion and Law in the United Kingdom*, 3rd edn (Alphen aan den Rijn, Wolters Kluwer, 2021) paras 346ff.

[16] Andrea Pin has similarly forthright observations in respect of Belgium, France and The Netherlands in ch 6.

[17] See Tsitselikis in ch 5 of this volume.

suggestive of a convergence between these sets of so-called values.[18] He recognises that the tension between European universalism and normative Islam is real from a metaphysical perspective. However, he also points to a broad alignment in substance. Islamic perceptions of human rights are not appreciably different from those discerned in Judaism and Christianity. The perceived disconnect therefore between European constitutionality and principles of Islam is not borne out by the reality. Issues such as the Muslim headscarf or the religious slaughter of animals are undoubtedly indicative of a difference in practice, but it may well be that the idea that Islam itself is hostile or oppositional to European constitutionalism, or some facets thereof, lacks any meaningful evidential foundation. It also might well be contended that European constitutionalism shares far more than one might first imagine with Islam: human rights and the rule of law being fundamental to both.

The matters addressed in this volume are not simply about an emerging fissure between Islam and European Constitutionalism; there is also a recurring concern about the existence of conflict between what Konstantinos Tsitselikis identifies as 'Old and New Islam', as well as between competing outlooks of Muslims today. Tsitselikis identifies Old Islam as 'a complex and dynamic field of applied law and politics'. He also introduces a regional dynamic into the equation, speaking of Western Europe, which has been accommodating immigrant Islam for more than a century; Eastern Europe, where Islam is present in small self-contained communities; and the post-Ottoman area, where Islam has a historical legacy and an abiding presence. Commentators generalise at their peril.

III. Securing Peaceful Coexistence, Especially for the Vulnerable

We live in febrile times. The memory is still fresh of the horrific attempt on the life of Sir Salman Rushdie, author of *The Satanic Verses* (1988), stabbed in a brutal knife attack at the Chautauqua Institute in New York State in August 2022. His work of fiction was alleged to contain blasphemous content that prompted the Iranian leader Ayatollah Khomeini to issue a fatwa in 1989 calling for the writer's death. His attacker claimed to have read only a few pages of Rushdie's novel, but still believed himself to be acting in the defence of Islamic faith. High-profile examples such as these tend to set the agenda for commentators, particularly on social media. They serve to dial up the rhetoric. But they are exceptional and certainly not representative of the broadly harmonious existence of Muslim communities in

[18] The comprehensive study by Professor Norman Doe of the substantive laws of each of the Abrahamic faiths powerfully suggests that the perceived dichotomy between Christian and Muslim approaches to human rights is without substance: see N Doe, *Comparative Religious Law: Judaism, Christianity, Islam* (Cambridge, Cambridge University Press, 2018).

many parts of Europe. Religious pluralism is beginning to permeate the political leadership of Europe, but the movement is glacial.

To some extent, the United Kingdom is ahead of the curve. To have a devout Hindu as prime minister is an encouraging optic in a country with two Christian state churches.[19] But for years Muslims have held prominent positions in political and public life, including several current or former cabinet members and the Mayor of London, Sadiq Khan.[20] Undeniably, Muslims are disproportionately present in deprived inner cities, but they are also to be found in growing numbers in traditionally middle-class areas working in traditionally middle-class occupations such as in business, manufacturing, law and education. They are active and effective in local and national government. The picture of a targeted and oppressed underclass, which the studies of Denmark and Austria reveal, is not one generally recognised in the United Kingdom.[21]

That said, Samia Bano's chapter reveals some hard truths about the experience of Muslim women in Europe. Her chapter revolves around the perennial question concerning the relationship (and possible clash) between equality and difference in the framework of their legal treatment and, more specifically, in the context of Sharia courts and other religious (Muslim, Jewish, and Catholic) tribunals in Britain, as alternative dispute resolution mechanisms in the field of family law. In this context, she tries to shed light on questions such as whether it is even possible to have gender equality in Sharia councils and religious tribunals or whether they are bound to promote patriarchy.

Minority ethnic groups are undoubtedly shaped by processes of migration and settlement, and the impact of national law. In many instances, Muslim women are disadvantaged by their treatment in Muslim religious tribunals and not afforded the constitutional rights of due process and equality before the law, which are the hallmarks of liberal European democracies.[22] For this the blame may lie with the systems of Islamic law, which are allowed to operate as a means of alternative dispute resolution. The perennial question of the extent to which subsidiary legal systems should be assimilated into state law, or at least recognised by it,

[19] The (Anglican) Church of England and the (Presbyterian) Church of Scotland.

[20] For example, Priti Patel, Suella Braverman, Nadhim Zahawi and Kwasi Kwarteng, as well as Baroness Warsi, Lord Ahmed of Wimbledon and Baroness Uddin in the House of Lords. Rehman Chishti, a member of the House of Commons, was formerly the Prime Minister's Special Envoy for Freedom of Religion. The general election of 2019 saw the highest ever number of Muslims elected to the Westminster Parliament, a total of 19 MPs on all sides of the political spectrum.

[21] See chs 10 and 12 of this volume, respectively.

[22] Similarly in Greece, as shown by L Papadopoulou, 'Trapped in history: Greek Muslim Women under the Sacred Islamic Law' in *Annuaire International des Droits de l'homme* (AIDH), Vol V, Religions et droits de l'homme (Athens/Bruxelles, Ant N Sakkoulas/Bruylant, 2010) 397–418; D McGoldrick, 'The compatibility of an Islamic/Sharia law system or sharia rules with the European Convention on Human Rights' in R Griffith-Jones, *Islam and English Law: Rights, Responsibilities and the Place of Sharia* (Cambridge, Cambridge University Press, 2013).

lies at the fulcrum of European constitutionalism and the autonomy of religious communities.[23]

After all, despite Berger's allegation that 'Sharia councils' have the right to exist, partly as a matter of freedom of religion, but also as a matter of personal freedom (autonomy) to regulate one's life in accordance with one's own wishes and convictions, it is very possible, as Venizelos notes, that similar religious courts established by Christian denominations or Jewish communities would not have been accepted by the same legal orders. At least in the case of Greece and the United Kingdom, this is definitely the case. This is an uncomfortable pinch point, where a state's liberal values of female emancipation and equality have the potential to bring governments and predominantly male Muslim leaders into conflict.

There are resonances of Bano's concerns in Enrica Martinelli's chapter devoted to the treatment of children. Martinelli examines the delicate balance between the educational needs of minors and the respect that should be afforded to the spiritual or religious orientation of parents. Undoubtedly, there is a parental right to choice, but that right is subject to the overriding principle of promoting the best interests of the child. Some believers, such as Jehovah's Witnesses, would prefer their child to die rather than have a blood transfusion, notwithstanding that, objectively assessed, that would not be in the child's best interests.

When it comes to education, migrant children are no less entitled to be educated than established citizens, but it must be fostered in an institution attuned to religious pluralism and sensitive to the particular values and aspirations of minority religions. The indiscriminate promotion of an overtly Christian or secular worldview could have damaging consequences for Muslim pupils, but also for their classmates. Children are not born intolerant: intolerance is acquired in the formative years, inherited from their parents and absorbed from among their peers. Social integration is an essential tool in promoting tolerance and civic harmony, and in combatting anti-Muslim sentiments. However, difficult questions still remain, for example, when girls are not allowed, due to their parents' religious beliefs (which the girls do not necessarily share), to take part in physical education classes, mixed swimming classes, etc. This issue is closely related to the wider discussion on how to teach religion or about religion, and how exemptions from religious and other classes should be regulated. Different commentators would answer these questions in different ways, and even the case law of the ECtHR on the subject is controversial.[24] This issue is not confined to Muslim pupils, but also affects other religious minorities, including atheists and agnostics, when religious studies generally promote the doctrine of the prevailing or state religion.

[23] See generally Griffith-Jones (ibid).

[24] See Pin's criticism (in ch 6 of this volume) of *SAS v France* App no 43835/11 (Grand Chamber, 1 July 2014) and *Osmanoglu and Kocabas v Switzerland* App no 29086/12 (Third Section, 10 January 2017); see also the critique exercised even by a former Judge of the Court, Vincent De Gaetano (in ch 11).

In this context, Martinelli's argument that an intercultural approach is optimal for the best interests of the children is convincing. Such intercultural strategies, the author underlines, 'avoid separating individuals into autonomous and impermeable cultural worlds'; instead, they promote debate and dialogue in order to address and solve conflicts and foster a mutual transformation in order to make coexistence possible.

IV. Islamophobia as Muslimophobia

Intolerance is the breeding ground for hatred. The micro-aggressions of the school or the tribunal are one end of a scale; at the other end lies Islamophobia, a topic which many try to avoid, fearing that the mere recognition of its existence might foster unrest and disharmony. Several contributors to this volume address the matter head-on and without apology. In her chapter, Merilin Kiviorg identifies how law, and European constitutionalism in particular, is ill-equipped to deal with the problem of Islamophobia. Kiviorg's focus is on how the United Nations human rights treaty monitoring bodies have assessed compliance by EU governments with their positive obligations under international human rights law. Her findings make depressing reading on two fronts: first, the prevalence and extent of negative social attitudes towards Islam; and second, the level of recorded non-compliance with treaty obligations. This is the case even if one considers that Islamophobia usually translates or is transformed into 'Muslimophobia'.[25] Here lies the biggest problem and the challenge ahead: regarding and treating Muslims both as equal citizens and also as equally 'European'. This means surmounting the majority's prejudices and deeply rooted aversion as well as combatting hatred against a religiously defined element of the community. More hope can be derived from Agustin Motilla's chapter, which identifies the tensions existing when state policies of control and surveillance press against the autonomy and self-governance of Muslim communities. Where and how the line is to be drawn will always be contentious, but the pointers here are well-informed and helpful.

The macro-aggressions discussed by Lina Papadopoulou concerns hate speech directed towards Muslims and blasphemy against Islam. Both are properly regarded as Islamophobic in their tone and content, but, argues Papadopoulou, each can and should be treated differently under the national laws of Member States and constitutional principles common to the EU and the European Convention on Human Rights. She distinguishes between hate speech (which is likely to incite hate, discrimination and physical harm against believers of whatever faith) that should undoubtedly be criminalised and properly prosecuted and defamatory comments (including blasphemy) about beliefs generally (which should not be an

[25] For this link, see Tsitselikis in ch 5 of this volume, with further reference to S Akgönül, 'Islamophobia, Muslimophobia: From Words to Acts' (2018) 9 *Yearbook of Muslims in Europe* 1.

offence irrespective of the identity of the targeted community). More significantly, she asserts that free expression of political sentiments concerning the compatibility of Islam or any other faith, religion or political belief with liberal democracy and the European way of life is an indispensable element of freedom of speech in a liberal democratic society. Not only is this a clear and incontrovertible expression of European constitutionalism, it tellingly encapsulates the intent and purpose of this volume, which is to give free voice to scholarship that both challenges and supports the complex inter-relationship between concepts of a Europe imbued with Christian inheritance and traditions, of a constitutionalism of democratic principle undergirded by a regime of human rights, and the pluralism and social cohesiveness derived from the accommodation of minority religions. Messner's observation that applying the principle of equal treatment to religious denominations could also subject Christian religions to the same constraints imposed on Islam is telling in reference to restrictions of hate speech against believers of other religions, non-believers or other groups, such as the LGBT community. The range of strongly held and sometimes contradictory opinions on this delicate issue, which are carefully expressed in the following chapters, is both indicative of its complexity and testimony to the power and value of freedom of expression in civil society and the academy.

Opinion yields to statistical analysis in the chapter by Anastasia Litina and Konstantinos Papastathis. Their chapter is enhanced with tables that merit detailed scrutiny and dissemination. Many will find the correlation between church attendance and anti-Muslim sentiment surprising and disturbing. Whilst it is never easy to extrapolate substantive conclusions of general application from raw data, their chapter reveals that self-identifying religious populations of EU countries are no different from the citizenry as a whole in respect of their suspicion of, and hostility towards, Muslims. Clearly there is a great deal that needs to be done in educating the public and disabusing some of their widely held extreme views.

For Andrea Pin, the distinction is not one of geography but of mindset. His chapter contrasts the activism of populists, whether in positions of political leadership or prominent in civil society, and supporters of what is conventionally styled liberal democracy. The picture of Europe which he paints is less homogeneous than the normative setting envisioned by Venizelos and Messner, and closer to Berger's pragmatist picture. He points to extremist leaders, such as Prime Minister Orbán of Hungary, and laws passed in countries such as France, Belgium and the Netherlands. In his assessment, Islamic minorities 'seldom receive civic respect or judicial protection' and some countries have created, intentionally or otherwise, a hostile environment towards Muslims. The constitutional acquis which arguably supplants a Christian-based settlement with postmodern liberalism, whilst superficially attractive at a high level of abstraction, disguises the lived reality for many Muslims, namely an oppressed underclass. Pin regards Islamic communities as suffering from the double impact of populists who promote an ideal of an outmoded Christian Europe, and liberals who lean towards a state secularism in which ostensibly neutral policies result in disproportionate harm to minority religions in general, and Islamic communities in particular. Pin calls for a complete reset of the type of European constitutionalism that other contributors in this volume seek to defend. Indeed, constitutional regimes require citizens and foreign residents alike to have faith in the democratic liberal regime, including secularism and a rights-based agenda that often conflicts with the Islamic faith and, as Pin argues, with other religious faiths that demand holistic allegiance from their adherents. One could even say that human rights have nowadays replaced theology and, as such, that liberal democracy tends to become a new God-free religion, a kind of secular religion that leaves limited space in the private domain for the faithful.[26] Pin's arguments presuppose one more element, which is not necessarily shared by other commentators in this book (such as Mirza), or elsewhere: that there is an inherent and irresolvable tension, if not an irreconcilable antithesis, between the human rights regimes of constitutional democracies and the Islamic faith. If this is right, which as has been observed, may not hold true for all Muslims (or even for most European Muslims), the dilemma is not doctrinal, but a political and historical choice framed in the wider geopolitical context.

There are also global issues to consider. Francis Messner draws attention to the links, financial and otherwise, which Islamic communities have with countries outside the EU. His chapter is complemented by that of Zoila Combalia, which looks at the foreign funding of Islam and the legitimacy of efforts by state governments and European institutions to restrict or control finance from overseas being used (or misused) in the promotion of radical Islam. The need for such a task to be undertaken with respect for non-discrimination, and without fostering suspicion of Islamic communities, is carefully navigated by the author who also identifies guidelines for best practice.

Messner's separate and extended argument is that Muslims within one European country have allegiances to a variety of sometimes conflicting countries of origin and descent. The result is a mixed and confusing patchwork of conflicting loyalties and identities. This fragmentation prevents the emergence of a single or dominant doctrinal discourse. He argues for better organisation amongst Muslim communities to render more straightforward discourse with the state and the cooperation and collaboration that the French, and other governments, have established with traditional majority Christian churches. Whilst one can see the attraction of a concordatarian model, such as is enjoyed by the Holy See and certain largely catholic countries, from the point of view of the state it runs contrary to the autonomy of religious organisations to direct their own affairs, as secured by the associational elements of Article 9 of the European Convention on Human Rights. However attractive it may be for national governments or European institutions, they cannot require minority religions to form themselves organisationally into a model not of their choosing. In response to this objection, which Messner acknowledges, his

[26] M Ignatieff, *Human Rights as Politics and Idolatry* (Princeton University Press, Princeton, 2001) 52.

argument that 'total indifference on the part of the state could be contrary to the general interest by facilitating breaches of public order and religious peace' should be examined more carefully and discussed more comprehensively.

Niels Valdemar Vinding shows how general legal clauses, such as public order and morality, can undermine religious liberty, especially for Muslim minorities. He further argues that the 'public order' limitation clause is usually applied based on the argued or perceived anti-democratic sentiments of Muslims in Europe and connected with the issue of securitisation. Such vague legal concepts often exercise a limiting effect on minorities' rights as they imbed in the legislation and jurisprudence the majoritarian vision of freedom and choice. Such a conceptualisation undermines the transformative dynamic of human rights as assets in the hands of minorities. Hence, they should be rarely used but always with exceptional care. A more nuanced resolution is probably called for. European liberalism, if it is to be respected, must be oriented towards the individual and their needs within the wider human rights framework. It should be flexible enough to accommodate individual needs, without replacing secular with divine law.

Messner's plea for Muslim communities to reorganise themselves to better engage with the state seems to be the opposite of what Ioannis Papadopoulos addresses in his chapter, which focusses on the need for the state to make adjustments in order to accommodate Islamic practices. However, if the capability of the liberal state to accommodate individual claims within its general human rights framework is taken seriously, both these stances can be reconciled. Much of Papadopoulos's argumentation is rooted in the jurisprudence of the Supreme Court of the United States. He points to a traditional reluctance in Europe to grant exemptions to generally applicable laws, whereas these are more readily conceded in the United States as a means of avoiding confrontations between religion and the state. He detects a growing reluctance amongst American lawmakers and judges to grant or sanction such accommodations, which were originally a benign means of protecting vulnerable religious minorities in a pluralist democracy. It may be that the concept of reasonable accommodation is beginning to be weaponised, expanding the generality of freedom of religion into demands for special treatment. Clearly some middle ground needs to be found whereby governments and religious organisations can each make measurable adjustments to satisfy the genuine needs of minorities. This would be emblematic of the cooperative model of church and state whereby the two collaborate to maximise the freedom of religious organisations and minimise the need for regulation and governmental intervention.

These two approaches are addressed in microcosm in Wolfgang Wieshaider's chapter concerning religious slaughter. His detailed critique of the activity of the Court of Justice of the EU, and particularly the opinions of various Advocates General, strongly suggest that EU Directives are being interpreted so as to sanction the prohibition of religious slaughter, violating principles of freedom of religion and equal treatment. Some of the decisions identified by Wieshaider indicate that many judges are tone deaf to doctrinal and spiritual sensibilities, and overtly hostile to the bona fide religious practices of religious minorities. Arguably the author does not go far enough: the soft Islamophobia of the judiciary, conventionally the guardians of European constitutionality, should be called out for what it is.

V. Conclusion

For some, European constitutionalism is constructed out of a Christian heritage, with the acquisition of a less godly but more liberal and democratic construct of human rights, civil liberties, due process and the rule of law; for others, the Christian bias remains and is discriminatory against minority religions, especially Islam. The latter (and its fundamentalist version in particular) is portrayed as antithetical to those constructs. But the evidence for this is yet to be fully evaluated. What is clear, however, is that behind the general normative framework, government policies can disfavour the settlement and integration of Muslim immigrants: but are these policies confected in consequence of a widespread suspicion of Islam, or is there some ingrained civic hostility, which is causative of their creation? The evidence is unclear, but the arguments are well made.

This volume is a springboard for debate and discussion, not a panacea for the unease or discomfort, which undoubtedly exist. For this reason, it consciously lacks a concluding chapter. The contributors boldly engage with issues that are both topical and controversial. There is no single right answer, and the direction of travel is far from clear. Nevertheless, the time is ripe for informed dialogue and a respectful consideration of opposing views. But the current situation is unlikely to change until the conversation moves from the 'them and us' (coming from both sides, as demonstrated by Al-Nuaimi and Tsitselikis) to the 'we'. Until social and religious integration cease merely to be aspirational and becomes a lived reality across all sections of society, the conversation cannot proceed much further. With confidence, restraint and courtesy, the means can be found to respect Islam and to advance religious liberty within the constitutionalism of Europe in the twenty-first century.

A thread that runs through this entire volume is history: the history of European constitutionalism; the 2,000-year history of Christian devotion and practice; and the history of the Islamic faith. We are informed by our history; we are moulded by our history; we are products of our history. Ali Rashid Al-Nuaimi warns that history can become a prison, locking the mind into a single, superior narrative. He observes that many Muslims have mixed up history and religion, and, in consequence, their history has become part of their religion, suggesting that some Muslims have transformed history into a vast prison. It is doubtful that this is a characteristic of Muslims alone. Other people, including Christian majorities, often exhibit the same weakness based either on religious or ideological–political beliefs. That is why it is imperative to remember that while we cannot escape our past, we must not become trapped in it or by it. Past rivalries, the trauma of European colonialism, and the oppression and discrimination of the past should remain there and not be transported into the present. Being open to the future and receptive to the otherness of all those living in Europe is a precondition for harmonious coexistence in a regime of equal liberty and dignity for everyone, everywhere.

PART I

Constitutional Challenges

2

Religious Freedom for Muslims: A Challenge to the Historical Foundations and Resilience of European Constitutionalism

EVANGELOS VENIZELOS

I. Introduction

In this chapter, I start from the position that religion is integral to the foundations of European/Western constitutionalism, but that a 'constitutional morality' different from the Christian one gradually took shape, highlighting the inseparable relationship between Western constitutionalism, the Enlightenment and modernity. This relationship continues to the present era of postmodernity. The question of whether the components of Western constitutionalism, especially democracy, the rule of law and human rights, have a universal character, or to be precise, whether they have a claim to universal acceptance and application, has been put into sharp focus recently, following the start of the war in Ukraine. The manner in which UN Member States position themselves against these components of European constitutionalism constitutes a test of the 'universality' of Western liberal democracy.

In particular, in terms of the relationship between European constitutionalism and Islam, it is necessary to distinguish between 'Islamic constitutionalism' and Islam's place in the field of European constitutionalism. The key question is whether in the name of Muslim religious freedom, the guarantees that European constitutionalism offers for the protection of every person, including Muslims, can be bent. The answers to similar questions are particularly challenging, and, for this reason, we must accept that the complexity and fragility of European societies is finally a political, and therefore, legislative issue. The role of the judge is always particularly critical, but the judiciary's function is subsequent to that of the legislator. Judges operate in the framework of judicial review of the law and the consideration of that law's compatibility with the European Convention on Human Rights (ECHR) and European Union (EU) law.

This chapter assumes the position that the religious freedom and equality of Muslims is fully guaranteed within the European constitutional area which comprises the national constitutions of the Council of Europe Member States (which includes all EU Member States) as well as the ECHR and EU law (in particular the Charter of Fundamental Rights). However, the challenges that European constitutionalism has to face in relation to Islam do not overturn the historical, value-based, and legal settlement that has been shaped in Europe from the Peace of Augsburg and the Treaty of Westphalia to the most recent case law of the European Court of Human Rights (ECtHR). These waves of European constitutionalism have all had religious freedom and equality as one of their main pillars.

II. Religion and the Foundations of European Constitutionalism

Religion, more specifically Christianity as a theological doctrine, and the church, especially the Western church, are historically at the foundation of European constitutionalism. Ecclesiastical institutions and canon law have had a decisive influence on fundamental concepts of public law such as sovereignty or representation and institutions such as parliament.[1] Christian Europe, through the conflicts (mainly religious wars) between Roman Catholics and Protestants, gave birth to the concept of the 'Westphalian state' in the seventeenth century.[2] The Westphalian state is sovereign, it has a religious (Christian, albeit linked to a specific denomination) identity, that of its ruler (*cuius regio, eius religio*), but gradually, in the centuries that followed, it accepted the distinction between state and civil society and religious freedom, which is of particular importance to followers of other Christian denominations and other religions.

The evolution of British constitutional institutions cannot be separated from the circumstances that led to the break with the papal authority of the Roman

[1] JJ Coughlin, 'Canon Law and the Human Person' (2003) 19 *Journal of Law & Religion* 1; A Podlech, 'La représentation: une histoire du concept' (2014) *Trivium*, available at journals.openedition.org/trivium/4781; B Basdevant-Gaudemet, 'Quand les constitutionnalistes puisent à l'histoire du droit canonique' (2019) *Revue du droit public* 399; T Pouthier, 'Droit canonique médiéval et droits fondamentaux modernes: une comparaison historique' Mélanges en l'honneur du Professeur Patrice Rolland (2022) 35 Editions universitaires de Dijon, available at hal.archives-ouvertes.fr/hal-03601856/document.

[2] D Philpott, 'Religious Freedom and the Undoing of the Westphalian State' (2004) 25 *Michigan Journal of International* Law 981; B Straumann, 'The Peace of Westphalia as a Secular Constitution' (2008) 15 *Constellations* 173; GA Christenson, 'Liberty of the Exercise of Religion in the Peace of Westphalia' (2012) 21 *Transnational Law & Contemporary Problems* 721. Regarding the influence that the concept of the Westphalian state still exerts to this day, see also: L Zucca, 'A Secular Globe? The Place of Freedom of Religion in the Westphalian World Order' (2015), available at ssrn.com/abstract=2520030.

Catholic Church and the formation of the Church of England as a version of Protestantism.[3]

The two great revolutions of the eighteenth century, the American and French, established the constitutional phenomenon and set the historical matrix of Western constitutionalism. Those revolutions resulted in constitutions which formed state institutions in opposition to religious ones. The French Constitution's principle of *laïcité* goes beyond the mere religious neutrality of the state and adopts the characteristics of a political religion that strove to dissociate itself from both the Roman Catholic Church and a vision of the national sovereign state that goes back to the historical presuppositions of Westphalia.[4] The American Establishment Clause is the basic constitutional, political and social precondition for the formation of a new nation on the foundations of a constitutional ideology and new patriotism that ensures religious pluralism and the coexistence of different religious (at the time it was written, mainly Christian) and ethnic groups in civil society.[5]

III. The Gradual Formation of a 'Constitutional Morality' Different from the Christian One

The Western state, as it transformed from a Westphalian state to a constitutional one, particularly after the pivotal historical impact of the two great revolutions, developed a new constitutional conception of politics, power, economy, family and private life. That new conception provided answers to questions on which the Christian view was, previously, dominant. This led to the gradual establishment of a 'constitutional morality' for personal, sexual and family relations, reproduction, and a whole range of other critical issues, which ultimately were based not on natural law, but positive law, since at the 'constitutional morality's' foundation was the formal constitution and, following that, international law on the protection of human rights (the EU legal order was added much later).[6] 'Constitutional morality' strove to impose itself gradually across the whole reach of religion.

[3] FW Buckler, 'The Establishment of the Church of England: Its Constitutional and Legal Significance' (1941) 10 *Church History* 299.

[4] H Pena-Ruiz, 'Laïcité: principes et enjeux actuels' (2004) 2 *Cités* 63.

[5] JC Jeffries Jr and JE Ryan, 'A Political History of the Establishment Clause' (2001) 100 *Michigan Law Review* 279; R McCrea, 'Rights as a Basis for the Religious Neutrality of the State: Lessons from Europe for American Defenders of Non-Establishment' (2016) 14 *International Journal of Constitutional Law* 1009; M Storslee, 'Religious Accommodation, the Establishment Clause, and Third-Party Harm' (2019) 86 *University of Chicago Law Review* 871. Regarding European issues, see JHH Weiler, 'Freedom of Religion and Freedom from Religion: The European Model' (2013) 65 *Maine Law Review* 759.

[6] P Babie, 'Religion and Constitutionalism: Oscillations Along a Continuum' (2015) 39 *Journal of Religious History* 123.

When the term 'constitutional morality' is used here, this does not denote constitutional ethics (ie to the ethics that must govern the functioning of constitutional institutions and the organisational part of the constitution as a whole) but rather the overall way in which the legal order, having the constitution as a fundamental rule of reference and control, regulates issues that belong to the sphere of personal and family life, sexual relations, reproduction, and all the related issues religions and religious organisations usually deal with.

The comparatively recent acceptance of divorce in Italy exemplifies the resistance to the imposition of this constitutional morality in a European country and founding member of both the Council of Europe and the European Union.[7] Today, the international debate, starting in the United States and its recent Supreme Court case law, is dominated by issues related to abortion.[8] It also has been affected by the COVID-19 pandemic which has given rise to many legal and bioethical debates, most prominently over the issue of vaccination, with religious communities exercising a strong influence on public opinion in many countries (most notably in the US).[9] Evidently, the primacy of scientific rationality and state competence is not always obvious even today.

The value of the human person is considered a fundamental Christian contribution to the formation of constitutionalism.[10] However, the history of Western constitutionalism shows that the free development of personality, the protection of private life, pluralism and liberalism as well as the freedoms of economic activity, intellectual pursuit, thought, speech, research and art has steadily occupied the field of religious speech and ethics. Every person as an individual and member of society exercises their constitutional rights and, in the clear majority of cases, does not sacrifice them in order to privilege their status as a member of a religious community. Religion in Western countries, whether it operates exclusively in the field of civil society or occupies a place in the public sphere (depending on the system of state–church relations that belongs to each country), loses its moral hegemony which it now shares with constitutional discourse as a discourse on democracy, the rule of law and human rights.

[7] Divorce became legal in Italy on 1 December 1970.

[8] *Dobbs v Jackson Women's Health Organization* 597 US (2022).

[9] A Madera (ed), *The Crisis of Religious Freedom in the Age of COVID-19 Pandemic* (Basel, MDPI, 2021); G Baldwin, 'The Coronavirus Pandemic and Religious Freedom: Judicial Decisions in the United States and United Kingdom' (2022) 26 *Judicial Review* 297; A González-Varas, 'Religious Freedom in Pandemic Times in Europe: A Perspective After One Year' (Canopy Forum, 5 May 2021), available at www.canopyforum.org/2021/05/05/religious-freedom-in-pandemic-times-in-europe-a-perspective-after-one-year; MJ Broyde, 'SCOTUS: Religious freedom during a pandemic' (Emory Law, 26 July 2021), available at www.law.emory.edu/news-and-events/releases/2021/07/broyde-scotus-religious-freedom-in-a-pandemic.html; G Androutsopoulos, 'The Right of Religious Freedom in Light of the Coronavirus Pandemic: The Greek Case' (2021) 10 *Laws* 1; ML Movsesian, 'Law, Religion, and the COVID-19 Crisis' (2022) 37 *Journal of Law and Religion* 9.

[10] S Müller, 'Concepts and Dimensions of Human Dignity in the Christian Tradition' (Brill, 2 July 2020), available at brill.com/view/journals/jrat/6/1/article-p22_3.xml?language=en.

That said, the role of religion is still important. In almost all Western constitutional states, the shaping of historical memory, as well as cultural and national identity, is linked with religion. Many aspects of the arts, institutions, the legal order and the 'self-evident' in any Western constitutional society cannot be understood without reference to religion, in particular to Judeo-Christian beliefs, as well as the ancient Greek and Roman foundations of Western civilisation.[11]

Today's European/Western constitutional state has historical and value-based foundations linked to Christianity through a church and religion, though the state has long since transcended its Christian identity. This is in large part due to the relationship between Christianity, the Enlightenment, modernity and, now, postmodernity.[12] Christianity fed the Enlightenment before it clashed with it as it proclaims not only the 'incarnation of God' but also the 'theosis of man'. The transition is gradually taking place from religious theology to political theology as a version of political philosophy and the formation of the Western/rational/constitutional man is becoming the basis of the national constitutional order as well as the international and EU legal orders, but also as a subject of history.[13]

The experience of 'real socialism' and its collapse confirms the strengthening of this institutional and value-based conception of Western constitutionalism. The great debate in recent years over the crisis of liberal democracy, due to the rise of so-called illiberal democracies and the violation of the value-based rule of law by EU Member States, has not been about religious freedom and church–state relations, but rather about separation of powers, press and academic freedoms, the independence of the judiciary and media pluralism.

IV. The War in Ukraine and the Test of the 'Universality' of Western Liberal Democracy

Since February 2022, following the Russian military invasion of Ukraine, the Western–Russia conflict has dominated the headlines, leading to a focus on the future of the West–China relationship. Thus, the conflict between Western democracies and authoritarian regimes has come to the fore. Russia promotes its Orthodox Christian identity, which it shares with Ukraine, while China does not shape its state ideology from a religious perspective, instead drawing on notions

[11] J Lang, 'Preface' in R Debray, *L'Enseignement du fait religieux dans l'école laïque. Rapport au ministre de l'Éducation nationale* (Paris, Odile Jacob, 2002) 23.

[12] SJ Barnett, *The Enlightenment and Religion: The Myths of Modernity* (Manchester, Manchester University Press, 2003); R Péter, 'The Enlightenment(s) and Christianity/ies: Foe(s) or Fellow(s)?' in T Porció (ed), *The Study of Religion at Szeged* (Szeged, JATEPress, 2010) 75; J de Azevedo e Dias Duarte, 'Enlightenment and Religion: Rupture or Continuity?' (2020) 13 *História de Historiografia* 83.

[13] G Hammill and J Reinhard Lupton (eds), *Political Theology and Early Modernity* (Chicago, University of Chicago Press, 2012).

from Marxism, Confucianism and meritocracy.[14] Still, there are current, pertinent, examples of the relationship between national and religious identity.

Russia's questioning of Ukraine's statehood, sovereignty and territorial integrity was accompanied by calling into doubt its national language, identity and history, and even the autocephaly of the Orthodox Church of Ukraine (OCU) granted by the Ecumenical Patriarchate (as opposed to the Ukrainian Orthodox Church (UOC), which is an entity of the Moscow Patriarchate).[15] The UOC tried to show that by breaking all administrative and spiritual ties with the Moscow Patriarchate because of its attitude towards the Russian military invasion of Ukraine. The paradox is that if the severance of relations between the UOC and the Moscow Patriarchate is real, the UOC no longer seems to have a status in the canonical order of Orthodox churches.

Western constitutional institutions and their associated guarantees and values have been transplanted outside the West, especially during the twentieth century, to regions and countries with non-Judeo-Christian origins, traditions and experiences. This growing universality of democracy, human rights and the rule of law is a clear ideological and political victory for the West.[16] However, this universality is neither a given nor is it self-evident.

The debate on the relationship between the West (in this case Western constitutionalism) and Islam often starts with the post-colonial period in Africa and Asia and swiftly reaches the current hot-spots of crisis linked to ongoing, internal security issues in the West. These perceived terrorist threats are made in the name of Islamic fundamentalism, especially after the 11 September 2001 attack. As a result, the ongoing humanitarian crisis of refugee and migratory flows into Europe from Islamic countries are seen by some European political parties as both a challenge to national identity and internal security.

The debate on the relationship between the West and Islam is not usually traced back to the period of the Arab presence on the Iberian Peninsula and the relations between the Byzantine Empire and the Muslim populations on its borders. It is not usually traced back to Greece breaking away from the Ottoman Empire

[14] DA Bell, *The China Model: Political Meritocracy and the Limits of Democracy* (Princeton, Princeton University Press, 2015); DA Bell, 'China's political meritocracy versus Western democracy' *The Economist* (12 July 2018), available at www.economist.com/open-future/2018/06/12/chinas-political-meritocracy-versus-western-democracy; A Wooldridge, 'Meritocracy, Not Democracy, Is the Golden Ticket to Growth' *Bloomberg* (16 May 2021), available at www.bloomberg.com/opinion/articles/2021-05-16/china-knows-that-meritocracy-is-the-key-to-boosting-economic-growth#xj4y7vzkg.

[15] C Hovorun, 'War and autocephaly in Ukraine' (2020) 7 *Kyiv-Mohyla Humanities Journal* 1; HJ Coleman, 'Orthodoxy and Autocephaly in Ukraine: Editor's Introduction' (2020) 62 *Canadian Slavonic Papers* 421.

[16] N Pillay, 'Are Human Rights Universal?' (2009) 45 *UN Chronicle* 4; A Kumar Sen, 'Democracy as a Universal Value' (1999) 10 *Journal of Democracy* 3; Geneva Academy, 'Universality in the Human Rights Council: Challenges and Achievements' (2016), available at www.geneva-academy.ch/joomlatools-files/docman-files/Universality%20in%20the%20Human%20Rights%20Council%20-%20Challenge%20and%20Achievements.pdf.

and the Sultan after the 1821 Revolution. However, immediately after the Greek Revolution broke out, the rebels set the adoption of a constitution as a symbol of state sovereignty and national independence, but, more importantly, also as a symbol of the integration of revolutionary Greece into the West (according to the geopolitical perception of the time).[17] The criterion for the formation of the Greek nation, and therefore for the acquisition of Greek citizenship, was any denomination of Christianity: the antithesis of Islam. This original relationship between the new, independent Greece and Christianity (specifically Orthodox Christianity) is still reflected in its Constitution, especially with regard to constitutional regulation of relations between the Greek state and the Ecumenical Patriarchate, based in Turkey.[18] Today there are still lingering problems with regard to the religious neutrality of the state, religious freedom and equality resolved through the ECHR and the case law of the ECtHR.[19]

V. The Distinction between 'Islamic Constitutionalism' and Islam's Place in European Constitutionalism

An interesting and dynamic constitutionalism as an emblem of national sovereignty and independence developed in the twilight of the colonial phenomenon during the twentieth century, in many states belonging historically, religiously,

[17] T Sakaranaho, *Religious Freedom, Multiculturalism, Islam*, Muslim Minorities 6 (Leiden, Brill, 2006) 195–224; C Joppke, 'Pluralism vs. Pluralism: Islam and Christianity in the European Court of Human Rights' in JL Cohen and C Laborde, *Religion, Secularism, and Constitutional Democracy* (New York, Columbia University Press, 2016) 89; M Chehab, 'Philhellenism and Constitutionalism: The First Greek Constitutions' in M Vöhler, S Alekou and M Pechlivanos (eds), *Concepts and Functions of Philhellenism*, Trends in Classics-Pathways of Reception 7 (Berlin, De Gruyter, 2021); N Alivizatos, 'Assemblies and Constitutions' in PM Kitromilides and C Tsoukalas (eds), *The Greek Revolution A Critical Dictionary* (Cambridge, Belknap Press, 2021).

[18] CA Frazee, *The Orthodox Church of Greece from the Revolution of 1821 to 1852* (London, Cambridge University Press, 1969).

[19] The jurisprudence of the ECtHR on matters of religious freedom as a result of individual application against Greece is very rich. For the key decisions of the last 30 years, see *Kokkinakis v Greece* App no 14307/88 (ECtHR, 25 May 1993); *Valsamis v Greece* App no 21787/93 (ECtHR, 18 December 1996); *Efstratiou v Greece* App no 24095/94 (ECtHR, 18 December 1996); *Manoussakis and Others v Greece* App no 18748/91 (ECtHR, 26 September 1996); *Canea Catholic Church v Greece* App no 25528/94 (ECtHR, 16 December 1997); *Larissis and Others v Greece* App no 23372/94 (ECtHR, 24 February 1998); *Serif v Greece* App no 38178/97 (ECtHR, 14 December 1999); *Thlimmenos v Greece* App no 34369 (ECtHR, 6 April 2000); *Agga v Greece* App no 50776/99 & 52912/99 (no 2, ECtHR, 17 October 2002); *Agga v Greece* App no 32186/02 (no 3, ECtHR, 13 July 2006); *Agga v Greece* App no 33331/02 (no 4, ECtHR, 13 July 2006); *Vergos v Greece* App no 65501/01 (ECtHR, 24 June 2004); *Alexandridis v Greece* App no 19516/06 (ECtHR, 21 February 2008); *Dimitras and Others v Greece* App no 42837/06 (ECtHR, 3 June 2010); *Dimitras and Others v Greece* App no 34207/08 & 6365/09 (no 2, ECtHR, 3 November 2011; *Dimitras and Others v Greece* App no 44077/09, 15369/10 and 41345/10 (no 3, ECtHR, 8 January 2013); *Papavasilakis v Greece* App no 66899/14 (ECtHR, 15 September 2016); *Papageorgiou and Others v Greece* App no 4762/18 and 6140/18 (ECtHR, 31 October 2019); *Stavropoulos and Others v Greece* App no 52484/18 (ECtHR, 25 June 2020).

culturally, geographically and geopolitically to the Muslim world. This 'Islamic constitutionalism', sometimes virtually and sometimes in reality, contains elements of democracy and the rule of law, while proclaiming the protection of human rights.[20] These Islamic constitutionalist states participate in the Human Rights Council through their UN membership and are bound by both the basic international texts for the protection of human rights and by the relevant rules of *jus cogens*.

The remaining question is which criteria to use in order to assess the democratic institutions, guarantees of the rule of law, and the level of protection of human rights in these Islamic constitutionalist states. This could be assessed under Western criteria, through using an institutional orientalism with the West as an institutional and cultural model or by criteria that are still demanding and essential, but which take into account the institutional equality of the UN Member States and their ethnic, religious, social and economic characteristics. This issue also concerns all non-Western states culturally, institutionally, economically and strategically aligned with a Euro–Atlantic axis. The BRICS group, which is differentiated from the dominant Western perception of international politics and the international economy, is not dominated by Islamic states.

The Parliamentary Assembly of the Council of Europe (PACE) stated that the cosignature of the Cairo Declaration by high contracting parties of the Council of Europe is incompatible with their obligations under the ECHR calling on Albania, Azerbaijan and Turkey (members of both the Council of Europe and the Organisation of Islamic Cooperation (OIC)) to consider withdrawing from the Cairo Declaration on Human Rights in Islam (5 August 1990).[21] PACE also called on Greece to intensify its attention to the application of Sharia law to the Muslim

[20] See generally N Hosen, 'In Search of Islamic Constitutionalism' (2004) 21 *American Journal of Islamic and Society* 1; R Bahlul, 'Islamic Perspectives on Constitutionalism' (Jura Gentium, 2005), available at www.juragentium.org/topics/islam/law/en/bahlul.etm; N Feldman, 'Islamic Constitutionalism in Context: A Typology and a Warning' (2010) 7 *University of St Thomas Law Journal* 436; L Ali Khan and HM Ramadan, *Contemporary Ijtihad: Limits and Controversies* (Edinburgh, Edinburgh University Press, 2011); R Grote and TJ Röder, *Constitutionalism in Islamic Countries: Between Upheaval and Continuity* (Oxford, Oxford University Press, 2012); M Gouda, 'Islamic Constitutionalism and Rule of Law: A Constitutional Economics Perspective' (2013) 24 *Constitutional Political Economy* 57; M Zain Awan, 'Islamic Constitutionalism and the Challenges Facing the Muslim World' (Central European University, 3 December, 2018), available at www.etd.ceu.edu/2019/awan_muhammad-zain.pdf; AY al-Hibri, 'Islamic Constitutionalism and the Concept of Democracy' (1992) 24 *Case Western Reserve Journal International Law*; P Longo, *Theory and Practice in Islamic Constitutionalism: From Classical Fiqh to Modern Systems* (Piscataway, Gorgias Press, 2019); AF March, 'The Theoretical Framework of Modern Islamic Constitutionalism' in S Mancini (ed), *Constitutions and Religion* (Cheltenham, Edward Elgar Publishing, 2020) 59; A Ahmed An-Na'im, 'Islam, Sharia and comparative constitutionalism' in S Mancini (ed), *Constitutions and Religion* (Cheltenham, Edward Elgar Publishing 2020) 172; B Öney, 'The Ideological Dimensionality in the Middle Eastern and North African Constitutions: A New Era in the Evolution of Islamic Constitutionalism' (2021) 19 *Political Studies Review* 209.

[21] Sharia, the Cairo Declaration and the European Convention on Human Rights (2019) Council of Europe Resolution 2253; K Robinson, 'Understanding Sharia: The Intersection of Islam and the Law' (Council on Foreign Relations, 17 December 2021), available at www.cfr.org/backgrounder/understanding-sharia-intersection-islam-and-law.

minority in Thrace region (in conjunction with the obligation to comply with the relevant ECtHR decisions, which will be addressed later). Additionally, PACE called on the UK to show necessary caution with regard to the application of Sharia law in England and Wales (not linking its application to the obligation to protect minority rights under international law) to avoid a violation of the ECHR. The Council of Europe, with the ECHR as its main tool, reflects the common denominator in European constitutionalism. The Council of Europe is a key guardian of European values, focused on human rights, the rule of law and its relationship with so-called Islamic constitutionalism on the one hand, and the application of Sharia law within its Member States on the other.

The first aspect – that of the relations between Islamic constitutionalism and Western constitutionalism is simpler and more straightforward because it concerns states, with few exceptions, outside the Western sphere. The second aspect is more complex: the Council of Europe exercises strict surveillance on its high contracting parties that are members of the OIC and co-signatories of the Cairo Declaration through all the control mechanisms at its disposal, notably the ECHR. However, Council of Europe Member States which are not also members of the OIC also raise issues related to Sharia in the Council of Europe and before the ECtHR. In many EU Member States the issue of Sharia is addressed before the Court of Justice of the European Union (CJEU) through the lens of Muslim religious freedom as protected by the ECHR and the European Union's Charter of Fundamental Rights.[22] In many EU Member States and therefore before the CJEU, issues are raised about religious freedom, as protected by the ECHR and the EU's Charter of Fundamental Rights, with Muslims being the subject of the relevant right. The crucial question therefore concerns the context in which the religious freedom of Muslims living in European liberal democracies is placed.

VI. Can Fundamental Guarantees of European Constitutionalism be Bent on the Grounds of Religious Freedom?

The basic question is whether, for reasons of respect for religious freedom and sometimes minority rights, fundamental normative and interpretative concepts and institutional guarantees of modern European constitutionalism (such as

[22] E Fokas, 'Islam at the European Court of Human Rights' (2010) 10 *Nordic Journal of Law and Social Research* 121; W Cole Durham, R Torfs, and DM Kirkham, *Islam, Europe and Emerging Legal Issues* (Milton Park, Routledge, 2012); M Adrian, *Religious Freedom at Risk. The EU, French Schools, and Why the Veil was Banned*, Muslims in Global Socities 7 (New York, Springer, 2016); J Witte Jr and A Pin, 'Faith in Strasbourg and Luxembourg? The Fresh Rise of Religious Freedom Litigation in the Pan-European Courts' (2021) 70 *Emory Law Journal* 587; T Rashid, 'Islam and the Dilemmas of Religious Freedom' (London School of Economics, 2 September 2019), available at blogs.lse.ac.uk/religionglobalsociety/2019/09/islam-and-the-dilemmas-of-religious-freedom.

religious neutrality of the state, guarantees of human dignity and gender equality) can be bent. The main question is divided into two specific questions. First, whether the fundamental rights of non-Muslims can be bent for the sake of religious freedom and equality of Muslims in Western legal orders. Second, whether the rights of Muslims, as people subject to the legal order of a European state, the ECHR or legal order of the EU, can be curtailed in order to effect collective enjoyment of religious freedom of the religious community to which that citizen belongs.

The fact that the exercise of Muslims' religious freedom within European liberal democracies poses interpretative challenges to national constitutions, the ECHR, or EU law in general, does not, in itself, constitute a weakening of the guarantees of European constitutionalism. Similar interpretative challenges continue to be posed by the exercise of religious freedom by minority Christian communities or believers of other religions.

Greece, for instance, has in recent decades been referred to the ECtHR for infringement of religious freedom.[23] Greek case law was heavily influenced by an ECtHR judgment concerning Italy, which addressed the issue of the Christian symbol of the cross or other religious icons in courtrooms.[24] The Greek Council of State subsequently ruled, based on the ECtHR's decision in the Italian case, that religious freedom and equality, the religious neutrality of the state, and the right to a fair trial are not affected by the posting of a religious image in its courtroom.[25]

The Greek courts and eventually the Supreme Court of Civil and Criminal Justice (*Areios Pagos*) accepted that Sharia law can be compulsorily applied to members of the Muslim minority of Thrace, especially to women who claim their inheritance rights. The ECtHR later found the Greek legislative provision as interpreted and applied by the Supreme Court, violated Article 14 of the ECHR and Article 1 of the (First) Additional Protocol.[26] The relevant law was subsequently amended but, albeit on a voluntary basis, Sharia law is still applied to members of the Muslim minority in Thrace and the decisions of the *mufti* (religious leader and judge of the minority) are enforced as state court decisions, unless the state court finds a contradiction with public order, which is constituted by the national, international and EU legal order.

However, were the Greek Orthodox Church to ask for the ecclesiastical courts to hear the family and inheritance cases of its faithful, with the guarantee that the decisions of those courts could then be reviewed by a state court for any contradiction to public order, its request would not have been accepted.

[23] See above n 19.

[24] *Lautsi and Others v Italy* App no 30814/06 (ECtHR, 18 March 2011).

[25] Greek Council of State (Supreme Administrative Court) 130/2018, 71/2019.

[26] *Molla Sali v Greece* (19 December 2018); J Pirjola, 'Freedom of Religion in Multi-Faith Europe: Protecting Universal or Western Sensibilities?' (2011) 29 *Nordic Journal of Human Rights* 38; CM Cerna, '*Molla Sali v. Greece* (ECtHR)' (2019) *58 International Legal Materials* 280; E Fokas, 'On Aims, Means, and Unintended Consequences: The Case of Molla Sali' (2021) 12 *Religions* 859.

The position of Greek jurisprudence brought under the control of the ECtHR is that Sharia is not linked in Greek law to religious freedom per se, but rather to the protection of the Muslim minority under international law, while, for example, a Greek Orthodox minority in Turkey would have no such rights. Furthermore, small religious groups cannot practically demand, with any chance of success, on a voluntary basis something similar to Sharia and the *mufti* in Thrace.

A Western legal order may be concerned with the clothing worn by women in public who profess the Islamic faith just as it is concerned with the Christian cross as part of the clothing of workers or students who consider that a declaration of their religious identity constitutes an element of their religious freedom, even when the context is not religious. However, the tendency of jurisprudence to respect pluralism when it comes to religious freedom and to reconcile conflicting sensibilities does not apply to matters which are at the core of European constitutional culture. For example, the Western legal order considers, without interpretative hesitation, a clitoridectomy to be an illegal act even if religious grounds may be cited for its justification while nevertheless accepting the circumcision of boys for religious reasons (which is proclaimed by both the Jewish and Muslim religions).

Although there are still problems, inefficiencies and contradictions, the grid of criteria on the basis of which the European legal culture (which, is identical to the current mature and multilayered European constitutionalism and might be called augmented constitution)[27] deals with religious freedom, has been shaped by a long, difficult, and often contradictory historical process lasting at least five centuries.

At the heart of this process are a series of relationships: Christianity and modernity; the state and Christian churches; the conflict between Papal authority and Protestantism; the particular course of Orthodoxy (especially in the Balkans); the historical and cultural memory of Byzantium and the particular course of the Orthodox churches in the Balkans; the continuing presence of Jews in Europe and the Holocaust; the experiences of two World Wars; and the Cold War.

Indeed, there are still outstanding issues in European constitutionalism concerning the religious freedom, irrespective of the increase in the number of Muslims living in EU Member States and in the contracting parties of the Council of Europe. However, matters have largely stabilised, and a high degree of legal certainty has been achieved. A single European constitutional space and a European constitutional *acquis* have been established. The relevant issues are resolved based on the religious neutrality of the state, religious freedom and equality, the primacy of the status of citizenship, and the status of a subject of human rights over the status of a believer.[28]

[27] E Venizelos, 'From the Relativization of the Constitution to the "Augmented Constitution"' (2020) 32 *European Review of Public Law* 973.

[28] J Witte Jr and A Pin, 'Faith in Strasbourg and Luxembourg? The Fresh Rise of Religious Freedom Litigation in the Pan-European Courts' (2021) 70 *Emory Law Journal* 587. For a Muslim perspective, see Rim-Sarah Alouane, 'Islam, Muslims, and Religious Freedom In Europe: A Test Of Faith'

To once more raise issues based on religious imperatives, sensibilities or practices with regard to Islam or any other religion or philosophical belief that were for the most part settled both at the level of national constitutions as well as at EU and international level would constitute a serious value-based and normative regression in the context of the single European constitutional space that communicates with the wider Western constitutional space.

It is clear that in this single European constitutional area, where democracy, the rule of law and human rights apply equally, everyone, including Muslims, has the right to judicial protection and a fair trial, the right to appeal to independent courts, and the right to use effective legal remedies. These procedural rights must be exercised fully and intensively when the interested parties consider that their religious freedom and equality have been violated. The courts, and ultimately the ECtHR and the CJEU, must provide concrete, convincing and credible solutions that strengthen the European rule of law. These solutions must not contain any element of Islamophobia or prejudice, should not reproduce negative stereotypes, and should respect the principles of equality and proportionality. That said, these solutions must also ensure the resilience of the historical value and normative content of European liberal democracy, the acceptance of which makes it inclusive and self-protective.

Islam, as a religion of European citizens and of persons subject to the European legal orders, and ultimately to the ECHR, manifestly has an institutional status equal to that of any religious or philosophical belief, while the status of all religious and philosophical beliefs is determined legally (ie by states and international organisations within the jurisdiction of each legal order).

However, the religious freedom of non-Muslims cannot be curtailed to permit the exercise Muslims' religious freedom: the legal order must equally guarantee religious freedom for all through respect for the religious neutrality of the state, even when, for organisational reasons, the religious affiliation of the vast majority, or even significant parts of the population, is considered.

VII. The Crucial Role of the Judge

With regard to their ethnic and religious dimension, European societies are already extremely complex in terms of their stratification and have ever-widening inequalities of risk and insecurity. The pursuit of social cohesion and inclusiveness is of vital importance for all citizens at a national and European level, but these

(Atlantic Council, 10 September 2018), available at www.atlanticcouncil.org/wp-content/uploads/2018/09/10_Islam_Muslims_Religious_Freedom_-_Alouane_-_Islam_and_Human_Rights_Report.pdf.

objectives can only be achieved through respect for the values and institutional *acquis* of European constitutionalism. All persons who are Muslims and fall under the jurisdiction of the legal order of the European liberal democracies must see, in practice, the importance of adhering to the values and institutional *acquis* of European constitutionalism.

European constitutionalism offers the normative and interpretative tools that allow this integration to be done in an effective and sophisticated way through the consolidation of the sense of being Muslim within the European constitutional space with respect to their freedom, equality and respect for their right to legal certainty and security.

European judicial systems, national supreme and constitutional courts, the ECtHR and the CJEU are called upon to bear a large part of the burden of this interpretative and normative challenge. The greatest burden, however, lies with the European societies themselves. The religious freedom of Muslims within the European constitutional space is one of the many tests that European liberal democracy as a basic version of Western liberal democracy must face.

Liberal democracy is broad and inclusive but cannot be politically and socially naive or unrealistic. The ECHR, though brief as a text, provides in Article 9 for the possibility of imposing restrictions on the manifestation of religious affiliation or beliefs, but only when they 'are prescribed by law and are necessary in a democratic society in the interests of public safety, for the protection of public order, health or morals, or for the protection of the rights and freedoms of others.'[29] This Article is similar to provisions on the rules of interpretation in the European Union's Charter of Fundamental Rights, and the national constitutions seek to safeguard the balances embedded from history, the value-based matrix, and the normative stock of European constitutionalism.

The rich case law of the ECtHR on Article 9 and Article 2 of the First Protocol (concerning which the judgments in applications against Greece are central) has elaborated in great depth the provisions of the Convention and highlighted their normative content within the methods of interpretation that the Court follows (especially with the application of evolutive interpretation).[30] Additionally, Article 17 of the ECHR prohibits the misuse of the protective provisions of the Treaty when it comes to circumventing the guarantees it offers in order to undermine European liberal democracy.[31]

[29] J Murdoch, 'Protecting the Right to Freedom of Thought, Conscience and Religion Under the European Convention on Human Rights' (Council of Europe Human Rights Handbooks, 2012) 35, available at rm.coe.int/16806f14e0.

[30] G Letsas, *A Theory of Interpretation of the European Convention on Human Rights* (Oxford, Oxford University Press, 2007) 74.

[31] 'Guide on Article 17 of the European Convention on Human Rights' (Council of Europe, 30 April 2022) 37, available at www.echr.coe.int/Documents/Guide_Art_17_ENG.pdf.

VIII. Conclusion

The religious freedom and equality of Muslims is fully guaranteed within the European constitutional area. However, the settlement of Muslims within European constitutionalism does not overturn the historical, value-based and legal settlement that has been shaped in Europe. This arrangement brings out the religious neutrality of the state and a 'constitutional morality' which takes precedence in value, and above all in law, over any religious faith or system of philosophical beliefs. This *acquis* is not about a Christian Europe but a Europe of liberal democracy, the rule of law and human rights. It concerns European values which, irrespective of their origins, have now become a European constitutional *acquis* within which the religious aspect operates. This movement, whether it takes place in the field of the personal and family life or in the public sphere, and concerns the relations between the state and religious groups, is governed by legal rules, which protect fundamental rights and the survival of liberal democracy.

3

When History Cripples the Future for Muslims in Europe: The Struggle between Two Notions of Constitutionalism

ALI RASHID AL-NUAIMI

I. The Challenge of History

History is the study of records of the past. As previous events, activities, discoveries and memories are collected and passed to successive generations, they become the subject of understanding how civilisations, nations, societies and groups have lived in the world. When Herodotus of ancient Greece (484–425 BCE) considered what happened in the Greco–Persian wars, he literally made history – a systematic, thorough study of the past explaining the cause and effect of events. For the medieval Muslim North African scholar Ibn Khalidun (1332–1406 CE), history was not merely the documentation of past events, but included analysis, comparison, and the falsification of information and records in order to establish an objective and true chain of events, by examining elements such as natural environment, geography, religions, social customs and political systems. Both these historians believed that human history is a subject of inquiry and reflection on the past, not the present. The question of how to read history is a longstanding and controversial issue. Answering this question requires compromise between those who claim a monopoly on history, those who allege they belong to history, and those who make history the basis for interpreting the present and anticipating the future. Nevertheless, history belongs to all of us, and we all have an equal right to read, understand and interpret it. The collective memories and common ownership of human history suggest reading and transmitting history is an open process for each nation and people both in the present and for the future.

Yet, how should we read history? And how will future generations read and interpret our own stories, events and actions? This is crucial not merely for obtaining an objective understanding of the past, but also to determine the trajectory of the future. If we want to understand history, we must look at our present reality because our current reality will be the history of the future. Are the events of our reality recorded from an objective and fair perspective? Or does each faction write and record its own narrative of existing reality according to its viewpoint, biases, interests and orientation, depending on the groups and parties to which it belongs?

A perplexing modern crisis in Muslim societies is how history, especially their own history, has been understood, transmitted and acted upon. The rise of nation-states has pulled modern Muslim societies away from the Islamic empire of the past; and the expansion of globalisation has encouraged Muslims to migrate across the world, especially towards the West, seeking a better life and career opportunities. Diverse and dispersed Muslim populations encounter the question of how to understand Islamic history in a new context. While a meta-narrative of Islamic history is still subject to debate and disagreement, some versions of Islamic history have been specifically chosen to be taught and circulated in new immigrant communities. Many modern Muslims, especially in European diaspora communities, have brought their history back to life, restored its heritage and resurrected it from its grave. During this process, they were induced to choose a certain version of events and considered this version to be definitive and monolithic. They chose one aspect of history and applied it throughout time without realising that each period had different attitudes and schools of thought, and that each era had as much diversity as our present society.

II. Freedom and Emancipation from the Prison of History

History can become a prison as it locks one's mind into a single narrative and 'superiority complex', believing one's history is only about grand achievements and enduring contributions while ignoring setbacks and shortcomings. Contrary to many narratives by certain Islamic groups, Muslims are not the only people who have a rich history that is a source of considerable pride, admiration and praise – a history that they honour, uphold and adhere to in all its particulars. Anyone blinded by a single vision of historical narrative choses to be locked in an ideological cage.

A key distinction between Muslims and other groups is that many Muslims have mixed up history and religion, and, in consequence, their history has become part of their religion. When Muslims read history, they are no longer able to differentiate between that which was influenced by human societies and that which constitutes a religious constant, between an act of man and an act of Almighty Allah, between what was revealed to the Prophet Muhammad and what people understood and implemented from these revelations. A group of Muslims has, using a narrow approach, transformed their history into a vast prison. They have declared a monopoly on the past, besieged the present and thereby suffocated the future. Their approach has spread through many Muslim communities and held many hostage to historical practices, through the reproduction of a doctrinal system that produces obsolete and outdated doctrines historically valid only for a certain time, in a certain place, for certain people. As such circumstances no longer exist in the present, there are no great similarities or connections between that historical reality and today. Nor do we connect to the historical reality through the continuation of certain practices that had a purpose only in a particular set of historical circumstances. Some have tried to import those practices from history, as in the case of ISIS (also called Daesh), which has attracted many Muslim youths, male and female, to become involved in its terrorist activities.

We are unable to move towards the future or enable our societies to obtain a suitable position in the world if we fail to understand that history is ultimately a set of human experiences constrained by specific contexts that have occurred and are now ended. At the same time, the *Glorious Qur'an* teaches how to deal with these historical experiences: one must benefit from the lessons learned. Moreover, one must take advantage of what they know of historical outcomes by distinguishing those inputs that led to successful results from those ill-founded and corrupted innovations that led to failure. In other words, people need to break free from the heavy burden of history. By doing so, history is put in its proper place and dealt with it in a way that allows people to make the most of it.

III. Controversies with History and Heritage

A delusional vision has dominated the attitudes and directions of some contemporary thinkers in the Islamic world, especially those working within political parties that use religion to attain political goals. These parties believe history and heritage comprise one solid bloc that is perfect, ideal and always successful – a source of pride for all. Furthermore, they believe that if we want to move forward and advance, we have to revive history and follow it by applying its models and means and commit ourselves to repeat it.

That superficial vision, based more on emotion than real understanding, is used by some to achieve their own political aims. The religious ceremonial clothes advocated to be worn by many Muslims leaders and activists in Europe are particularly useful in helping these groups gain popular legitimacy. But their vision is, in fact, unrealistic and ahistorical, considering that the historical periods of Muslim society to which it originates were marked by diversity and pluralism, making it impossible to classify all components of this time period in any one narrow way.

For example, the historian and geographer Al Masudi (895–957 CE), nicknamed Herodotus of the Arabs, who authored the book *Meadows of Gold and Mines of Gems* (*Muruj adh-dhahab wa ma'adin al-Jawahir*) lived during the same time period as Abul-Faraj al-Isfahani, who wrote *The Book of Songs* (*Kitab al-Aghani*). Both lived during the tenth century in the Hijri calendar, and both wrote history from their own perspectives. Al Masudi wrote a political and social history, explaining the greatness of the state and society. Al-Isfahani, on the other hand, wrote about the history of female singers, pre-Islamic brigand-poets and members of the lower class in society, who lived Bohemian lifestyles, verging on moral breakdown. An individual who limits his reading to Al Masudi will see a great, rising and developed society, while one who restricts his reading to Al-Isfahani will think that the same period of history shows a deteriorating and disintegrated society with many indicators of moral decay.

If one studies the history and heritage of the Abbasid State, one finds evidence of groups and individuals building a civilisation, establishing the House of Wisdom (also known as the Grand Library of Baghdad or *Dar al-Hikmah*), protecting the state's borders, saving the Emperor of China, and restoring his power. At the same time other groups engaged in 'destructive behaviour' like bombarding the Holy Kaaba with catapults, stealing the Black Stone (*Al-Hajaru al-Aswad*) and doing away with the *qibla*, or the direction that Muslims must face when performing their prayers (*salāh*). Accordingly, an observer sees multiple versions of history and different, sometimes contradictory, formulations of heritage. Unfortunately, those who dominate the contemporary consciousness of Muslims have imposed one version of history, which they have chosen. They thereby transformed history and heritage into a prison, a closed circle from which Muslim communities cannot escape. Muslims must liberate themselves from the burdens of that history in order to move ahead towards the future.

IV. Historical Differences and Modern Muslims

Islam by its nature is a religion open to independent reasoning (*ijtihad*), with a multiplicity of diverse ideas and interpretations. From the outset, Muslims have understood certain matters differently, and each group had its own understandings. For every understanding and interpretation there developed a different stream of thought. Over time, these streams evolved into schools of thought, and then into prominent schools of Islamic jurisprudence and doctrine. Religious denominations, sects, schools of thought and movements thus emerged. At times, they coexisted, and at other times, they struggled against and fought one another. Eventually, they shifted into a stage of intellectual regression, stagnation and jurisprudential inflexibility. Rigid doctrines and closed ideas were formed, with adherents claiming that their ideology was in alignment with the true Islam and everything outside their ideas was false.

This interpretation of Muslim heritage and its associated burdens has been placed onto the shoulders of people in the present, with personal, factional and political interests mixed in. The diversity in Muslim heritage was used to gain political interests for certain states, groups, factions and sects. Contemporary Muslims, especially those living in European societies, find themselves trapped in disagreements and conflicts unrelated to them, lacking in understanding about the history or essence of these movements and unaware of the reasons behind the disagreements and conflicts that currently dominate the narrative. Furthermore, some Muslims find themselves obliged to pay for these differences and conflicts, which are irrelevant and unrelated to them and of which they had never been a part. Yet by tradition or due to membership in a particular group, they feel compelled to take side. One should carefully examine these historical disagreements and differences between groups and understand that they have nothing to do with them. People can only look ahead, interact with the present and prepare for the future by overcoming these differences rather than focusing on them. Everyone must cooperate and work together on the things they have in common. They must accept all Muslims the way they are and not think about changing them, while recognising the reality of pluralism within the Muslim community as a human axiom and indisputable social fact.

V. Religious Fundamentals, Historical Variables and the Relativity of Heritage

Popular confusion as to how to distinguish between religious fundamentals, historical variables and the relativity of heritage may be the main reason for the religious chaos experienced by Muslim youth today. This relativity of heritage has turned into a religion itself, although this heritage simply comprises the historical conceptions of values and constants of religion and the ways in which these concepts and constants have been applied. Because of this confusion, we can no longer distinguish between what is fixed and what is variable, what is certain and what is uncertain, and what is absolute and what is relative.

History and heritage vary based on time, place and social conditions, whereas the principles of Islam remain constant. This distinction is the first step in the liberation from the prison of history and heritage, and through making such a clear distinction, one can turn both history and heritage into starting points, rather than a vicious circle of intellectual stagnation. Younger generations need a culture marked by self-confidence and opening up to the world rather than a culture of intimidation, fear and closed doors.

Islam is a universal religion for all contexts, inclusive for every place and time, and its system of major legal objectives, and the comprehensive jurisprudence rules allow, with all flexibility, the creation of an integrated system of jurisprudence. This system prevents Muslims from isolating themselves from the homeland and being alien; instead it makes them good and free citizens integrated in their homeland without compromising their religion, law or values. There is insistence on isolating Muslims in the name of the jurisprudence of minorities, while in the jurisprudence of citizenship there is exclusion from everything that causes embarrassment or distress for a Muslim, regardless of their country of residence.

VI. Muslim Communities in Europe before and after Politicisation

The 2017 feature film *Victoria and Abdul*, based on the earlier book by Shrabani Basu, *Victoria & Abdul: The True Story of the Queen's Closest Confidant* (2010), gives us a clear picture of the perception of Muslims when they began to emigrate to European countries, and how they acted and interacted with the communities there. Set in the nineteenth century, the story is based on the relationship between an Indian Muslim, Abdul, and the Queen of England, Victoria. Abdul came to Europe as a servant, travelling to a new land where Muslims could live peacefully and positively alongside their surrounding communities. When we look at the major waves of immigration to Europe, we find two distinct waves: pre-World War II and post-War. The pre-War wave was mainly economically motivated and occurred when different groups from the Indian subcontinent, the Arab world and Southeast Asia emigrated to Europe and North America. These communities were very active in integration and indigenisation and interacted positively with their receiving communities. In contrast, the post-War wave signalled a new kind of immigrant from the Muslim world characterised by two main factors. The first factor was that most emigrants were students who travelled at the cost of their respective countries to study abroad and were planning to return to the Muslim world after their studies, but ultimately chose to settle in their new land. It is important to understand that most of these students were already members of Islamic or political groups in their home countries.

The second factor is that some emigrants were political refugees fleeing their home countries because they were persecuted by the nationalist and socialist regimes that took power after the liberation of those respective countries from the colonial powers. This wave was dominated by the idea of political Islam because, at that time, their home countries were dominated by socialist and nationalist regimes, more secular than Islamic. Many of these young migrants were political dreamers who went to the West to help their own political parties or Islamic groups achieve their goals and retake control of their home countries. Historically speaking, these groups were much more highly educated, intelligent and politically active than the previous wave.

Over the course of time, the first wave of Muslim immigrants to Europe and North America faded and effectively disappeared into their adopted countries' national cultures while the second wave overwhelmed the Muslim communities in Europe and North America and controlled the majority of cultural associations and organisations as well as Islamic centres and mosques. There are more than six million Muslims in France (eight per cent of the country's population) as a result of recent migration. Islam spreads among intellectuals and thinkers as well as workers, who follow the philosophy and spirit of seeking inner transformation. However, this also can cause self-alienation and marginalisation, which results in many problems including terrorist attacks in different parts of the country. Consequently, this leads Muslim communities to face different kinds of social isolation. It has triggered Islamophobia, which has reached a peak across Europe in recent years. The good news is an ongoing revival of moderate and integrative Islamic groups are helping, albeit slowly, to bring back faith and acceptability for Muslims in French society, which is totally opposed to radicalisation and extremism. For instance, the famous French rapper, Abdel Malik, powerfully demonstrated that Islam can build individuals, sharpen their artistic skills, block negative thoughts, and enhance love for one's country.

The Muslim population of present-day Britain comprises, among others, south Asians, Africans, Arabs, Balkans, Central Asians, and a small percentage of white converts. Some of these groups argue that national values differ from religious norms, while others believe that citizenship and faith can coexist in Muslims who reside in Britain. Both groups legitimise their interpretation with the help of the *Quran* and the *Hadith*, the primary sources in Islam, but no one is refereeing that debate.

Muslim immigrants arrived in Britain in large numbers in the 1960s and 1970s, and almost all were believers of Sunni Islam. However, the radical ideas of the self-claimed 'orthodox Muslims' started gaining traction in the 1980s with an organised push from Pan-Islamic movements, namely JIMAS (*Jamiyat Ihya Minhaj al-Sunnah*). JIMAS was solely focused on promoting and spreading Safaism ('pure Islam') in Britain. Their promoters called Safaism 'the society for the revival of the prophetic ways'. In the early 1990s, a group of Muslim groups came out openly promoting the ideology through mosques like the Green Lane Mosque in Birmingham, the Salafi Institute in Birmingham, the Ibn Taymiyyah Mosque in Brixton, and the Islamic Centre of Luton. Their vision was also promoted through individuals, mostly western converts, and groups such as *Jamaat e-Islami*, *Ahl e-Quran*, *Ahle-Hadith* and *Tabligh-i-Jamaat*.

Many radical movements like *Hizb ut-Tahrir* are influenced by political Islamic groups. They believe God called on all Muslims to fight against infidels and reject the western values of democracy, liberalism and secularism. These movements perceive that these western values are incompatible with Islamic values and Islamic law. This is one reason why the largest contingent of youth who joined the Islamic State in Syria were from Britain.

This second wave began to shape the modern history of Islam in Europe and North America and succeeded in politicising the Muslim community there, changing their culture and attempting to create a new one which would be heavily dominated by foreign concerns and problems. Its dominant figures were constantly working to help other countries in preference to their newly adopted home countries. These Islamic groups managed to politicise the Muslim communities in Europe and North America, which would forever dominate the direction of those communities, and in turn, lead to the challenges of Islamic extremism we witness today.

VII. Muslim Organisations in Europe, which Encourage Isolation Instead of Integration

The politicised religious–historical narrative was one of the most important reasons many Muslim societies fail to realise the central place of citizenship in confronting social, cultural, political and economic challenges and problems faced by Muslims in non-Muslim majority countries. More than two decades ago, a jurisprudential trend known as 'the jurisprudence of minorities' emerged, which attempted to address and provide solutions to the issues and problems facing those Muslim communities. It considered that Muslims in those societies were a minority separate from the mainstream, and accordingly *fatwas* were issued that in effect caused the isolation of Muslims, failing to integrate them into their countries and communities. Because the second wave of Muslim immigrants to Europe and North America were highly educated, they discovered that to build strong communities they needed to establish organisations, associations and centres to institutionalise the Muslims who lived and worked there. Community leaders encouraged communities to start their own Islamic schools as opposed to working on introducing Islamic studies into public school curricula. In turn, it became impossible to cultivate a citizen who is also a Muslim: it had to be one or the other. Slowly, these same leaders would encourage community members to avoid political involvement in their adopted home and isolate themselves economically, even avoiding buying houses and taking mortgages, to be completely isolated from the greater non-Muslim society.

Adapting a discourse that recalls colonial traumas to deepen the rifts between Muslim communities and their newly acquired states, Muslims in Europe and North America left their homelands because they were tired of their own countries and the corruption, war and economic situation endemic in those countries. But they did not enter their new homes with the intention of fitting in to a new culture and society while still cherishing their Muslim identity. Though they were naturalised citizens of these new countries, they adopted an Islamic discourse that created an attitude of 'us versus them'. This discourse focused heavily on the historical traumas suffered within their 'homelands' during the colonial era, emphasising only the negative and connecting those experiences with the contemporary society in their adopted countries. There was a sense of bitterness, as if these immigrants wanted the society, which had welcomed them, to provide recompense for the historical wrongs of their forefathers. This discourse encouraged and pushed young Muslims to hate their surrounding society and the state because the state was perceived as having been brutal to their forefathers, stealing their property and leaving them impoverished. This discourse was widely spread in Europe more than North America, which had no colonial history with Muslim societies; in France, the United Kingdom and Spain especially, it continues to have a very negative impact on younger generations.

This attitude made Muslims in these European societies always look with a romanticism to their former home, a sense of longing to return to a homeland despite the fact they belonged to a society which had welcomed and supported them. This desire for revenge for the wrongs of colonial times grew like a disease, spreading through the younger generation of immigrants, especially in Europe. When ISIS emerged in Iraq and Syria, it offered the prospect of a hero, an aspirational fighter for justice, to right these wrongs. On the streets of Europe, we witnessed, and continue to witness, lone wolf attacks on innocent people totally unconnected with these criminals, who view any non-Muslim as an enemy who should pay the price for the sins of their forefathers.

It is very common in Muslim communities in both Europe and North America to find Friday sermons discussing issues relating to the Middle East. In these sermons, the preachers bring remote issues into discussion with Muslim communities who know nothing about them and lack the context or insight to understand them in their full complexity. Issues relating to Kashmir, Palestine and Afghanistan as well as local political issues in Egypt, Sudan or Iraq are the main issues discussed by Muslim communities in the West, keeping them constantly detached from their current societies and burdened with problems, conflicts and disasters happening thousands of miles away. Through the subconscious programming by these Islamic preachers, Muslims become remote parties to distant unknown grievances. This has been the approach for half a century and, in turn, Muslim communities have failed to become responsive to the issues of their own society around them because they are busy discussing problems happening far away. Engrossed by these issues, they take sides and disregard anyone who does not align with this global battle.

What is missing is any discussion within communities of the issues that affect their children and their futures as well as the issues that have direct and negative implications for their own lives. There is a systematic denial of the realities facing these communities and through this stigma, these issues remain taboo. There is no discussion of drugs, unemployment, homelessness and poverty, all issues which affect these communities; but which they say they are issues of the 'outside society', separating themselves from them as if they are unique to the non-Muslims. This furthers the sense of 'us versus them', the feeling that this society has issues which do not belong to Muslims, and only reinforces a feeling of detachment from the very society in which these communities live. Accordingly, Muslim youth from Europe left their own society, into which many of them were born, and went to join ISIS in Syria or Iraq to build a 'utopia' which had never existed.

Nowadays a new generation is starting to change this culture and become involved in interfaith initiatives and social service, but this is just the beginning. It needs encouragement, more involvement and a changing of the mentality of the leadership in these countries to have the courage to lead these communities towards greater involvement in their respective societies. There must be more work done that represents Islamic values and which introduces Muslims as part of the solution to their own societies.

VIII. History of Inter-Religious Coexistence and Responsibilities of European Countries

Muslim communities in contemporary Europe have grown rapidly since the end of World War II due to immigration and multicultural policies. While some challenges and uncertainty remain, most Muslim citizens have settled down and started the integration processes in their countries. It is time to explore and theorise patterns and examples of interaction and integration for European Muslims from their survival to flourishing, in the hope of providing inspiration for Muslims in other parts of the world. It can be beneficial to study and share the wisdom, strategies and approaches of Muslims in preserving their Islamic tradition and Muslim identity while living in multicultural and multi-religious societies. To indigenise Muslim communities in European states, Muslims must be treated as full citizens and not as immigrants, refugees or second-class citizens. This process entails intellectual, legal, political, economic and social endeavours to understand and reintroduce sound Muslim historical perspectives and help Muslims integrate and indigenise in European countries. The earlier history of Islam in Europe such as in the Balkans and Spain has provided examples and lessons for Muslim immigrants arriving in Europe. New Muslim immigrants, primarily from the Americas, Africa, West Asia and South Asia, will prove crucial to providing a comprehensive revisionist study of the conditions in Europe.

One of the major contributions that European history awaits is fresh thinking on the place of Muslim integration in the context of religious diversity, and the story of tolerance/cohabitation accompanying it. Europe, since the inception of monotheism, has been treated as a battlefield delineated along sectarian borderlines. While the emphasis on violent conflict between 'different' sects of monolithic faiths became the paradigm for the study of Europe's history, at its centrepiece is the idea that tolerance, inter-religious coexistence and indigenisation were not short-lived anomalies in an otherwise long history of violent relations. With new methods, a different kind of story can prevail, one that expands beyond entrenched normative approaches that made anti-Jewish discourses the necessary evil to conquer throughout European history, while Islamophobia remains. At the heart of any constructive revisionism is fresh thinking about Europe's history of religious tolerance, considering the persistence of especially sensationalist analyses of Europe's current state of inter-religious relations and the dire predictions of some for Europe's long-term viability due to diversity of communities calling Europe home. The history of coexistence and new experiments of integration can present good examples, both historical, ethnographic and sociological, of enduring complexities of relations between Europe's indigenous Muslims, Christians and Jews.

Depending on place and time, Europe's Muslims (most often consisting of native people converting to Islam) prove to have the most complicated relationship with both Jewish and Christian communities. Looking at Europe's history, spanning medieval, early modern and modern periods, the integration process must reflect the variety of relations between Muslims, Jews and Christians. Exploring the sometimes difficult relations that local communities have had with both Muslim and Christian migrant workers and the complex history of Europe's experience with Muslim integration provides useful insight into how we might shape a future world in which human diversity is celebrated as an asset, and is not seen as the fuel for political fires as has been the case in the past, exploited by both Muslim and non-Muslim political opportunists.

For example, believers in the Balkans traditionally followed a tolerant and mystical form of Islam, unlike radical or 'modern' versions of it. A large percentage of Muslims there still follow the Hanafi-Sufi Islam traditions, particularly in Kosovo and North Macedonia. Most Roma ethnic groups in Bosnia and southern Serbia are Muslims, and most of them belong to one or other moderate Islamic sect. The Islamic cultures of Muslim communities in the Balkans have largely been shaped by the legacy of integration and indigenisation of Muslims from the pre-Ottoman period until recently. Regardless of their ethnicities, Islam is deeply embedded in the cultures of Muslim communities in Europe in arts, culture, architecture and social norms.

Today, Muslim institutions and organisations, under the constitutional framework of European government, must again nurture future generations and shape the culture for Muslims to follow the ways that activate the principle of citizenship in their countries. This can be done by preparing educational curricula, religious discourses and Islamic culture based on the correct understanding of history and proper evaluation of tradition so that Muslims today are aware of the problems of the homeland where they hold citizenship, and of their causes and nature in order to interact with others, and together formulate the new citizenship. This is only achieved by a kind of self-transcendence to determine the dimensions of future citizenship in a sound understanding of history, faith and national belonging. Among its most important dimensions for Muslims is respect for others, recognition of the existence of different religions and cultures, realisation of freedoms, and non-violent participation in political, economic and social affairs, so that citizenship is a melting pot of all affiliations. Hence, Muslims, whether native or immigrants, must fulfil the legal obligations in those countries where they live, without deceit or treachery to those countries or violating their laws.

IX. Conclusion

History has presented good models and warned us to avoid negative experience. It is time for the governments and citizens of European countries to break away from the old historical prison and to open new horizons of peace and prosperity. While most European constitutions can eventually grant citizenship to immigrants, including Muslims, they must substantiate such citizenship with multiculturalism and inter-religious coexistence in order to integrate the newcomers, not alienate them. Muslims, for their part, must initiate or continue their process of indigenisation to strive for a tolerant society to live in.

4

European Values and Islam

MAURITS S BERGER

I. Introduction

'Islam in Europe' is a notion that is as easily used as it is convoluted. One element, 'Islam', has been evaluated from a security as well as theological perspective, and in political as well as sociological terms. The other element, 'Europe', is geographically undefined and can stand for a cultural identity as well as human rights values. Usually, however, the discussion on the relation between 'Islam' and 'Europe' focuses on a comparison of Islamic and European values. This kind of argumentation is faulty for two reasons. First, the intention of this debate is to assess the values held by Muslims in Europe but concentrates on the values of Islam itself because it is presumed that the values of European Muslims are identical with the values of Islam. However, believers and their beliefs are not necessarily the same. For example, Islam, like other faiths, shows a weak theological and historical track record on issues like gender equality or democracy, but its believers may very well uphold these values.[1] The comparison of values would therefore benefit more from the question 'what values do the believers have?', than 'what are the values of Islam?'. The discussion, in other words, should be about Muslims in Europe themselves rather than Islam.

The second reason why the comparison of Islamic and European values is often nonsensical is because European values are presumed to be clear, while they mostly are not. Usually, European values are equated with human rights, but what do these rights have to do with social matters like the shaking of hands or the clothes that people wear? Still, these are the issues causing enormous controversies that are played out in discussions on European values. In such instances, European values seemingly are not human rights themselves but values to be protected by those human rights. What, then, are these values? That is the subject of this chapter. As a

[1] For instance, in recent decades a discourse of 'Islamic feminism' has developed in the Muslim world, see, eg, M Badran, 'Between Secular and Islamic Feminism/s: Reflections on the Middle East and Beyond' (2005) 1 *Journal of Middle East Women's Studies* 6; Z Mir-Hosseini, 'Muslim Women's Quest for Equality: Between Islamic Law and Feminism' (2006) 32 *Critical Inquiry* 629.

tool of analysis for this question, I have proposed to view the notion of European values as consisting of two kinds: political-legal values and religious-cultural values.[2] Political-legal values stand for values that are the outcomes of political and legal deliberations. These values are fundamental freedoms (religion, expression, political action, etc) and notions like democracy, solidarity, and tolerance. These values are enshrined in constitutions, codes and treaties, and although still subject to continuous debate, their conceptual existence seems carved in granite.

Religious-cultural values relate to the customs and sense of identity of any given society. These are not legalised or otherwise registered because they are assumed to be shared by everyone. They constitute a subcurrent in the social fabric that can be loosely described as 'the way we do things around here'. The vagueness and inconspicuousness of religious-cultural values should not be underestimated: at times they can carry more weight than political-legal values.

Granted, the distinction between these two sets of values may seem arbitrary. Lawyers and political scientists will be the first to point at the ways political-legal values are influenced by religious and cultural values,[3] just like notions of multiculturalism have found their way into legal debates[4] and long-standing cultural traditions of state–religion relations have found their way into national legislation and political mores. But the purpose of this distinction between the two sets of values is not as a tool of accuracy, but as a tool of analysis.

This chapter will discuss five typical issues of conflict in this debate on European and Islamic values. It will be demonstrated that the confrontations between these two sets of values are mostly conflicts within the domain of European religious-cultural values and much less within the domain of political-legal values. When analysing these cases, it will become apparent how religious-cultural values interact with, or even override, political-legal values.

II. European and Islamic values: Five Cases

A. The Case of Secularism

The first issue of conflict between Islamic and European values is that of secularism, also known as the separation of religion and state, and sometimes as the

[2] MS Berger, 'Understanding Sharia in the West' (2018) 6 *Journal of Law, Religion and State* 236, 256–59.

[3] For religious values see, eg, HJ Berman, *Law and Revolution II: The Impact of Protestant Reformations on the Western Legal Tradition* (Cambridge, Harvard University Press, 2003); D Flatto and B Porat (eds), *Law as Religion, Religion as Law* (Cambridge, Cambridge University Press, 2022). For cultural values see, eg, R Provost (ed), *Cultures in the Domains of Law* (Cambridge, Cambridge University Press, 2017); AC Saguy and S Forrest, 'Culture and Law: Beyond a Paradigm of Cause and Effect' (2008) 619 *The Annals of the American Academy of Political and Social Science* 149.

[4] eg, MC Foblets and AD Renteln (eds), *Multicultural Jurisprudence: Comparative Perspectives on the Cultural Defense* (London, Bloomsbury Publishing, 2009); I Ruggiu, *Culture and the Judiciary: The Anthropologist Judge* (Milton Park, Taylor & Francis, 2020).

separation of church and state.[5] It is commonly assumed that this notion is fundamental to Europe but unknown to Islam. Both assumptions contain inaccuracies and ambiguities.

Let us start with Europe, where the separation of religion and state is commonly considered a clearly defined value, but, in reality, there is no uniform notion of what that value entails.[6] For instance, some countries, like the United Kingdom and Sweden, have established state churches. Other countries, like the Netherlands and Germany, only maintain state religious neutrality while countries such as France actively enforce the absence of religion in public spaces belonging to the state. Further, countries like Belgium and Bosnia recognise certain religious communities and pay the salaries of their clergy and maintenance fees of their houses of worship, while other countries make those fundings entirely the responsibility of the religious communities themselves.

We find the same ambiguities in Islam. Islam has little conceptualisation of the notion of 'the state', let alone the ways in which that state relates to religion.[7] This is not just typical of Islam, but of most religions. Christians may refer to the principle 'render to Caesar the things that are Caesar's, and to God the things that are God's',[8] but the Catholic Church has historically shown little affinity with that instruction. Throughout history, most states have deemed it necessary to align themselves with a religion, but not necessarily with that religion's teachings. So, also, has history witnessed various forms of involvement of the clergy with the state. In the case of Islam, for example, the Islamic clergy has a long tradition of maintaining independence from the state.[9] In other words, it is of little use to scrutinise the theological teachings of a religion to determine its relation to the state; one also needs to look at the actions of the state as well as of the believers of a religion and how those believers have aligned their religion with their state citizenship. In the case of Islam, we see, for instance, that most Muslim majority states during the 1950s and 1960s had little affinity with religion and tried to keep the clergy at bay, while from the 1980s onwards the relation between clergy and state has become more intimate in many of those same states.[10]

If we turn our attention to Islam in Europe and look at the believers rather than their beliefs, the following observation can be made: it appears that most Muslims

[5] These are two different but overlapping notions. For the purpose of this chapter, 'religion and state' is intended to mean the state's relation to both religion as such, and to religious institutions.

[6] The following examples are taken from G Robbers (ed), *State and Church in the European Union* (Baden-Baden, Nomos, 2005) and S Ferrari and S Pastorelli, 'Religion in the European Public Spaces: A Legal Overview' in S Ferrari (ed), *Religion in Public Spaces: A European Perspective* (Milton Park, Routledge, 2012).

[7] W Halaq, *The Impossible State* (New York, Columbia University Press, 2014).

[8] *St Mark's Gospel*, 12:17.

[9] See, eg, IM Lapidus, 'The Separation of State and Religion in the Development of Early Islamic Society' (1975) 6 *International Journal of Middle East Studies* 363; KS Vikør, *Between God and the Sultan: A History of Islamic Law* (Oxford, Oxford University Press, 2006) 185.

[10] The literature on this phenomenon of 'political Islam' is extensive. Two outstanding studies are N Ayyubi, *Political Islam* (Milton Park, Routledge, 1993) and P Mandaville, *Global Political Islam* (Milton Park, Routledge, 2007).

in Europe embrace the notion of 'separation of religion and state'.[11] The reason for this is that such separation guarantees a degree of freedom of religion, which is exactly what Muslims in Europe aspire to have. The separation of religion and state is clearly interpreted by these Muslims as a political-legal value. But if this is the case, why is the European Muslims' relation with religion and state so often questioned?

It seems that we are dealing with a mix-up between the notions of secularism and secularisation. Where the former stands for ways of separating relations between state and religion,[12] the latter stands for individuals' self-separation between themselves and their religion.[13] In Europe, more than in other parts of the world, religiosity has been diminishing rapidly.[14] In this process, the disappearance or, at best, privatisation of religion has become the dominant norm in Europe.[15] This is not a political-legal norm, however, but a religious-cultural one: the privatisation or absence of religion is not dictated by law but is what a majority population lives by. However, the two phenomena of separating relations between state and religion, on the one hand, and the self-separation between persons and their religion, on the other, have come to mean approximately the same thing: secularisation has become equated with secularism.[16] In doing so, the 'state', as referred to in the separation of state and religion, is not only meant to be the government, but also society. Consequently, the fact that most Muslims in Europe favour separation of state and religion (secularism) but many of them ostentatiously show their religiousness through action and dress is understood by both non-religious and not-so-religious Europeans to be contrary to the secularisation that has become the standard norm of 'how we do things here'.

The processes of secularism and secularisation have evolved, in some circles of society, into the notion of 'Judaeo-Christian civilisation'. For instance, at the finalising stage of the 'constitution' of the European Union in 2004, it was suggested

[11] European Union Agency for Fundamental Rights, 'Second European Union Minorities and Discrimination Survey (EU-MIDIS II): Muslims – Selected findings' (EFRA, 2017); Gallup, 'Special Report: Muslims in Europe' (Gallup, 2007).

[12] See N Hashemi, 'The Multiple Histories of Secularism: Muslim Societies in Comparison' (2010) 36 *Philosophy & Social Criticism* 326.

[13] P Berger, 'Secularization and de-secularization' in L Woodhead (ed), *Religions in the Modern World: Traditions and Transformations* (Milton Park, Routledge, 2002) 336. It must be noted that the 'secularisation theory', which is hotly debated in academic circles, deals with the causes of secularisation, not the phenomenon of secularisation itself.

[14] PEW, 'Being Christian in Western Europe' (PEW Research Centre, 2018); S Bullivent, 'Europe's Young Adults and Religion Findings from the European Social Survey' (2014–16) (Benedict XVI Centre for Religion and Society, 2018).

[15] J Casanova, *Public Religions in the Modern World* (Chicago, University of Chicago Press, 1994). It must be emphasised that this norm no longer appears to reflect reality anymore since religiousness in Europe is said to be re-emerging. See eg, C Calhoun, M Juergensmeyer and J van Antwerpen (eds), *Rethinking secularism* (Oxford, Oxford University Press, 2011).

[16] According to Charles Taylor, this development is the result of what he terms the 'Age of Mobilization'. See C Taylor, *A Secular Age* (Cambridge, Harvard University Press, 2007) 423–72.

that this term should be inserted into the preamble, but at the last moment it was decided against.[17] An interesting aspect of this concept of Judaeo-Christian civilisation is that it is devoid of religiousness: it has become an identity marker of Europeanness, with references to culture and history rather than religious doctrine.[18] The concept of Judaeo-Christian civilisation can be considered a continuation of the 'grand narrative' of Christian civilisation that was dominant in the nineteenth and early twentieth century.[19] And just like that grand narrative, the narrative of a Judaeo-Christian civilisation distinguishes between 'us' and 'them', not on the basis of political-legal values, but on cultural-religious values.[20]

B. The Case of the Headscarf

During the 1990s, the headscarf took centre stage in the debates about Islam in Europe. One reason was because it was the main visible manifestation of Islamic religiousness which was considered by many Europeans to be against secularism as well as secularisation. But the headscarf symbolised more than mere religiousness, as is illustrated by two prominent rulings by the European Court of Human Rights (ECtHR) which later served as leading precedents for numerous cases in national courts. Both cases concerned the question of whether a ban on the headscarf constituted a violation of the freedom of religion. In the first case, a teacher at a primary school was fired after she started wearing the headscarf.[21] In the second, a student at a state university was not allowed entry because of her headscarf.[22]

In both cases the Court ruled that the ban was justified because the headscarf was considered harmful to third parties as well as to general values. It is enlightening to quote the relevant arguments of the Court in these two cases (the italics are mine):

> [I]t cannot be denied outright that the wearing of a headscarf might have some kind of *proselytising effect*, seeing that it appears to be imposed on women by a precept which is laid down in the Koran and which, as the Federal Court noted, is hard to square with the principle of *gender equality*. It therefore appears difficult to reconcile the wearing of an Islamic headscarf with the message of *tolerance*, *respect for others* and, above all,

[17] The Treaty establishing a Constitution for Europe was signed in 2004 ([2004] OJ C310/1); M Heyward, 'What Constitutes Europe?: Religion, Law and Ideology in the Draft Constitution for the European Union' (2005) *Hanse Law Review*; I Bărbulescu and G Andreescu, 'References to God and the Christian Tradition in the Treaty Establishing a Constitution for Europe: An Examination of the Background (2009) 24 *Journal for the Study of Religions and Ideologies* 207.

[18] E Nathan and A Topolski, *Is there a Judaeo-Christian Tradition*? (Berlin, De Gruyter, 2016).

[19] MA Perkins, *Christendom and European Identity, The Legacy of a Grand Narrative Since 1789* (Berlin, De Gruyter, 2004).

[20] See also G Marranci, 'Multiculturalism, Islam and the clash of civilisations theory: rethinking Islamophobia' (2004) 5 *Culture and Religion* 105.

[21] *Dahlab v Switzerland*, App no 42393/98 (ECtHR, 15 February 2011).

[22] *Leyla Shahin v Turkey*, App no 44774/98 (ECtHR, 10 November 2005).

> *equality and non-discrimination* that all teachers in a democratic society must convey to their pupils.[23]
>
> [I]t is the principle of *secularism*, …, which is the paramount consideration underlying the ban on the wearing of religious symbols in universities. In such a context, where the values of *pluralism, respect for the rights of others* and, in particular, *equality before the law of men and women* are being taught and applied in practice, it is understandable that the relevant authorities should wish to preserve the secular nature of the institution concerned and so consider it *contrary to such values to allow religious attire*, including, as in the present case, the Islamic headscarf, to be worn.[24]

Perhaps the most noticeable feature of these rulings is the assumptions made by the Court about how the headscarf relates to European values. In *Dahlab*, the wearing of the headscarf is, without any explanation, associated with intolerance and disrespect for others. In *Sahin*, the headscarf is considered contrary to secularism, which the Court (without explanation and with a surprising breadth of interpretation) associates with pluralism, respect for the rights of others, and gender equality. The Court received criticism in academic circles for this reasoning,[25] but these rulings set a course of jurisprudence that would greatly impact future debates on the headscarf.

Another striking feature of this jurisprudence is that it seemed to only apply to the headscarf. The Court did rule differently in two similar cases regarding the Christian symbol of the crucifix. In the first case, where a British Airways air hostess protested against her employer's demand to remove her necklace with a crucifix, the Court ruled in favour of the air hostess noting that 'a discreet cross could not have detracted much from her corporate appearance and there was no evidence that allowing the wearing of religious dress on previous occasions had detracted from British Airway's brand or corporate image.'[26] No arguments such as the 'risk of proselytisation' or violation of 'secularism' were used.

In the other case, where parents in Italy protested against a state school brandishing crucifixes in the classroom, the Court ruled in favour of Italy's argument that this was a custom 'resulting of Italy's historical development, a fact which gave it not only a religious connotation but also an identity-linked one.'[27] Not only did the Court agree with the notion that the crucifix was part of Italy's national identity, but it also approved of Italy's argument that the crucifix, 'beyond its religious meaning, … symbolised the principles and values which formed the foundation of democracy and western civilisation, and that its presence in classrooms was

[23] *Dahlab* (n 21).

[24] *Leyla Shahin* (n 22).

[25] See eg, C Evans, 'The "Islamic scarf" in the European Court of Human Rights' (2006) 7 *Melbourne Journal of International Law*; M Adrian, 'The principled slope: religious freedom and the European Court of Human Rights' (2017) 45 *Religion, State & Society* 174.

[26] *Eweida and Others v the United Kingdom*, App nos 48420/10, 59842/10, 51671/10 and 36516/10) (ECHR, 15 January 2013).

[27] *Lautsi and Others v Italy*, App No 30814/06 (ECHR, 18 March 2011) at 67.

justifiable on that account.'[28] And while the Court considered the headscarf to constitute a form of religious indoctrination, it emphatically dismissed that argument in the case of the crucifix in the school and chose not to discuss it in the case of the crucifix worn by the air hostess.[29]

C. The Case of the Burqa

While it would seem consistent to discuss the ban on the full-face veil (or burqa) together with the headscarf, there is an important difference from an analytical perspective: while the impediments to the headscarf were issued by a court of law, burqa bans were promulgated by national legislatures. In the latter case, parliaments hold a considerable political say in the matter. The first three European countries to introduce a burqa ban were Belgium, the Netherlands and France. In all three instances there is a similar pattern: the national State Councils strongly advised against such a ban based on legal arguments and the bans were passed by a parliament with distinctly cultural and religious motives.

In these three countries, the State Councils act as the legal conscience of the state by closely reviewing each draft law before it is passed back into the legislative process. In Belgium, it was decided by Parliament not to submit the draft law to the State Council, while both the Dutch and French State Councils had the same arguments against such a ban.[30] The first argument was that considerations of security were not adequate to justify a burqa ban because there was already sufficient legislation in place to achieve that particular goal. The second argument was that individual citizens enjoy 'personal autonomy', that is the fundamental right to decide for oneself how to live one's life. The State Councils argued that since there was no evidence that the burqa was forced upon the few women who were wearing it, there was no justification in banning the burqa.

These political-legal arguments were overruled by the ample religious-cultural arguments put forward by the parliaments:[31] the burqa was considered a violation of human dignity, gender equality, women's empowerment and 'Western values'.

[28] ibid.

[29] *Lautsi* (n 27) at 73–74.

[30] (France) Conseil d'Etat, 'Etude relative aux possibilités juridiques d'interdiction du port du voile intégral' (25 March 2010); (Netherlands) Raad van State, zaaknummer W03.07.0219/II, 21 September 2007.

[31] (France) 'Proposition de loi visant à fixer le champ des interdictions de dissimuler son visage liées aux exigences des services publics, à la prévention des atteintes à l'ordre public' (no 2544, 20 May 2010); (Belgium) 'Propositions de Loi, visant à interdire le port de tout vêtement cachant totalement ou de manière principale le visage, interdisant de porter dans les lieux et espaces publics des tenues vestimentaires marquant le visage, sur l'exercice de la liberté d'aller et venir sur la voie publique' (DOC 53 0219/004, 18 April 2011); (Netherlands) 'Voorstel van de leden Wilders en Fritsma tot wijziging van het Wetboek van Strafrecht in verband met een verbod op het dragen van gezichtsbedekkende sluier's of nikaabs op een openbare plaats (verbod op de gezichtsbedekkende sluier)' (Kamerstukken II 2006/07, 31 108, nr 1-3).

The burqa was further said to be contrary to Islam itself and to pose an impediment to integration. Keeping in mind that legislation of the prohibiting kind is commonly subject to strict scrutiny of a political-legal nature, it is significant that most arguments seemed to respond to the gut feeling 'that is not how we do things around here!'.

The Dutch burqa ban stumbled over a change of government and was eventually promulgated in a lighter version in 2020. The Belgian and French burqa bans became effective in July 2011, and were later followed by similar bans in Denmark, Norway, Austria, Germany, Spain, Italy, Bulgaria, Kosovo and Bosnia-Hercegovina. So far, only the French burqa ban has been challenged before the ECtHR.[32] The Court meticulously went through all France's arguments supporting its burqa ban. The argument of public safety was rejected as an insufficient justification because, just like the French and Dutch State Councils' argument against the ban, the Court considered this goal sufficiently covered by legislation already in place. France's other legal argument was protection of rights and freedoms of third parties and was described by France as 'respect for a minimum number of values that apply in an open democratic society'. France argued that three values were relevant here: gender equality, human dignity and 'living together' (*vivre ensemble*). The Court rejected the first two values as justifiable reasons for a burqa ban arguing that there is no indication that the Muslim women concerned 'seek to express a form of contempt against those they encounter or otherwise to offend against the dignity of others'.[33] However, the Court accepted the value of 'living together' as a ground for the burqa ban. It shared France's view that 'the face plays an important role in social interaction' and that it is understandable that persons in public spaces do not wish to be confronted with 'practices or behaviour' that hinder such social interaction. After all, this social interaction, according to the Court, is 'by established consensus an inseparable part of social life' in France.[34]

The burqa ban is an intriguing example of the way political-legal and religious-cultural values interact. The burqa is a practice that unquestionably does not suit the majority culture of European societies. But, at the same time, European political-legal values demand a high degree of toleration for deviant behaviour. In this case, however, the legislature took the contrary stance, and prescribed by law what is or is not religiously and culturally appropriate.

D. The Case of Sharia

In 2003, the ECtHR stated in *Refah v Turkey* that 'Sharia clearly deviates from the values of the [European] Convention [on Human Rights]'.[35] This statement has

[32] See *SAS v Frankrijk*, App no 43835/11 (EHRM, 1 July 2014).
[33] ibid at 120.
[34] ibid at 121.
[35] *Refah v Turkey*, App nos 41340/98, 41342/98, 41343/98 and 41344/98 (EHRM, 13 February 2003).

since then often been quoted in political and legal debates. It was referred to in a motion submitted (but not followed up) in the European Parliament in 2019[36] and again in a resolution passed in the Parliamentary Assembly of the Council of Europe.[37]

However, from a legal perspective, it was strange that the Court did not define what it meant by 'Sharia', and the Court has been criticised for that.[38] This lack of explanation is not only surprising, but has also created confusion. It is surprising because a key characteristic of legal language is the intention to create clarity of terminology. In court rulings, especially in higher courts, matters of law are spelled out and interpreted down to the most minute detail. In *Refah*, however, not only did the Court introduce a term that is alien to European legal vocabulary, but it also failed to clarify what it meant by it. That was careless, because 'Sharia' is not a code or book of law, but rather an umbrella term with a myriad of meanings, ranging from the harsh and intolerant control of people (like the Taliban or ISIL) to a scholarly method of extracting rules from sacred texts containing rules concerning crime and punishment as well as instructions for prayer, fasting and burying the dead.[39]

In *Refah*, members of a political party had made remarks about Islam and Sharia that were perceived as a threat to national security. While these members did not specify what they meant exactly with their desire for 'Sharia', their remarks were truly frightening. One Refah MP said in a 1996 television interview that 'Sharia was the solution for the country' while another Refah MP said in 1997 that 'if someone attacks me, I will strike back. I will fight to the end to introduce Sharia.' Another Refah member said, 'the system has to change. We have waited, and we will wait a little longer … And let the Muslims keep alive the anger, revenge, and hatred they feel in their hearts.' Other members also spoke of 'jihad' and the possibility of using violence to seize power.[40]

Surely, these remarks can be considered sufficiently threatening to justify a ban of the party. The Turkish state thought so, and the Court considered that decision justified. But the Court continued, uninvited and unprompted by the lawyer's

[36] European Parliament, Motion for a European Parliament resolution on political Islam in the European Union (B-9-2019-0227, 9 December 2019): 'C. whereas the objective of these associations and groups is the application of Sharia law, namely a legal system which is incompatible with the founding principles of the EU, in particular with the principles of human dignity, freedom, democracy, equality and human rights.'

[37] Parliamentary Assembly of the Council of Europe, Resolution 2253 (2019), Sharia, the Cairo Declaration and the European Convention on Human Rights: '5. The Assembly is also greatly concerned about the fact that Sharia law – including provisions which are in clear contradiction with the Convention – is applied, either officially or unofficially, in several Council of Europe member States, or parts thereof.'

[38] eg, K Boyle, 'Human Rights, Religion and Democracy: The Refah Party Case' (2004) 1 *Essex Human Rights Review*; D Schilling, 'European Islamophobia and Turkey – Refah Partisi (The Welfare Party) v. Turkey' (2004) 26 *Loyola of Los Angeles International & Comparative Law Review*.

[39] See, eg, W Hallaq, *Sharia* (Cambridge, Cambridge University Press, 2012) and KS Vikør, *Between God and the Sultan* (London, C Hurst & Co Publishers, 2005).

[40] *Refah* (n 35) at 31–40.

submissions, to pass judgment on the notion of 'Sharia' itself. In doing so it created confusion about Islam in Europe. All the rules of Islam, ranging from the manner of burial or prayer to contracts and homicide, are called 'Sharia'. While some extremist Muslims have given intolerant and violent interpretations to some of these rules, most devout Muslims live in accordance with the rules that pertain to religious rituals. It was probably not the intention of the Court to consider those rules as violations of the Convention, but this was effectively what the Court did in denouncing 'Sharia' in its entirety as contrary to European values, essentially denouncing all the rules of Islam and therefore, Islam itself.

What seemed to have happened here in this case is that the judges were guided more by their perceptions of Sharia than by their legal professionalism. European perceptions of Islam in general, and Sharia in particular, are notoriously negative. Some of that negative association may be justified, but much of it is the result of centuries-old perceptions embedded in the European collective memory.[41]

E. The Case of Sharia Courts

Related to the issue of Sharia is the situation regarding the so-called Sharia 'courts' or 'councils'. Here an uncritical use of terminology has created confusion about what is actually happening.

Let us first clarify the terminology used here. A 'court' is the term for a judicial institution whose rulings are recognised by the state and that can be enforced by state authorities. In most instances, these courts apply state law, but that is not always the case. In some instances, the state recognises court rulings based on laws other than state law. This used to be the case with Catholic personal status law in countries like Italy and Spain, and Greek Orthodox personal status law in Greece. Nowadays, the only surviving non-state law recognised by a European state is Islamic personal status law in the Greek province of Western Thrace:[42] specialised courts apply Islamic personal status law to Muslims who opt for it and these institutions can be considered the only 'Sharia courts' in Europe.

While no other religious courts exist in Europe, there are plenty of religious tribunals or councils. Most of them used to be state-recognised courts that lost that authority and now only function for believers who want to make use of them. Hence, there are still many Catholic, Jewish, Orthodox Christian and various Protestant tribunals in Europe, each with their own judges, procedures and

[41] MS Berger, *A Short History of Islam in Europe* (Leiden, Leiden University Press, 2004); D Norman, *Islam and the West: The Making of an Image* (Edinburgh, Edinburgh University Press, 1960); JV Tolan, *Saracens: Islam in the Medieval European Imagination* (New York, Columbia University Press, 2002).

[42] MS Berger, *The Last Shari'a Court in Europe* (The Hague, Eleven Publishers, 2021); Y Sezgin, 'Muslim Family Laws in Israel and Greece: Can Non-Muslim Courts Bring About Legal Change in Shari'a?' (2018) 25 *Islamic Law & Society* 235.

laws.[43] This is where Sharia councils come in; they are tribunals set up by learned people who act as arbiters in cases of marriage and divorce, to which they apply rules of Islam. At the time of this writing, these councils only exist in the United Kingdom,[44] and they have been extensively studied and vehemently criticised.[45] That criticism mostly centres around the argument that the assumption of voluntary use of these councils by the Muslim communities is not correct because they are mostly used by women who feel it is their only option to get out of unwanted Islamic marriages.[46] This criticism is not specific to Islamic councils because it applies to most religious tribunals (in particular to Jewish councils where the husband's refusal to use his exclusive right of divorce can cause his wife to remain trapped in her marriage).[47]

From a political-legal perspective, the religious tribunals (including Sharia councils) have the right to exist, partly as a matter of freedom of religion, but also as a matter of personal autonomy so that people can regulate their lives in accordance with their own wishes and convictions regardless of how strange or objectionable that may seem to others. From a religious-cultural perspective, one could argue that Christian and Jewish courts and councils have always existed and can therefore be considered part of the Judaeo-Christian cultural heritage. That begs the question why it causes such indignation when Muslims want to do the same. A likely answer is that secularised Europeans have little, if any, knowledge of the other religious tribunals that have existed for so long in their societies.

III. Conclusion

The examples discussed above, when seen through the prism of political-legal and religious-cultural values, provide us with several insights regarding Islam in Europe. First, there appears to be a distinct bias against Islam. This is evident in the argumentations used in the rulings of the European Court of Human Rights

[43] MJ Broyde, *Sharia Tribunals, Rabbinical Courts, and Christian Panels: Religious Arbitration in America and the West* (Oxford, Oxford University Press, 2017); N Doe, 'The Legal Position of Religious Organizations' in N Doe, *Law and Religion in Europe: A Comparative Introduction* (Oxford, Oxford University Press, 2011).

[44] D Torrance, 'Sharia law courts in the UK, House of Commons Library' (Number CDP-2019-0102, 2019).

[45] eg, S Bano, 'An Exploratory Study of Shariah Councils in England with respect to Family Law' (Reading, 2012); J Brechin, 'A Study of the Use of Sharia Law in Religious Arbitration in the United Kingdom and the Concerns that this Raises for Human Rights' (2013) 15 *Ecclesiastical Law Journal* 293; A Shachar, *Multicultural Jurisdictions: cultural differences and women's rights* (Cambridge, Cambridge University Press, 2011). See also ch 8 of this volume.

[46] eg, M. Siddiqui et al, 'The Independent Review into the Application of Sharia Law in England and Wales' (UK Parliament, 2018).

[47] MJ Broyde, *Marriage, Divorce, and the Abandoned Wife in Jewish Law: A Conceptual Understanding of the* Agunah *Problems in America* (KTAV Publishing House Inc, 2001); J Wexler, 'Gotta Get a Get: Maryland and Florida Should Adopt Get Statutes' (2009) 17 *Journal of Law and Policy*.

regarding the Sharia and the use of religious symbols, as well as the justification used by several European legislatures in banning the burqa. Calling the wearing of the headscarf an act of intolerance without providing an explanation of what exactly constitutes this intolerance implies that the judges were guided by preconceived notions rather than by legal rationalism. A similar attitude can be detected in the legal discussions regarding Sharia and the burqa. There, subconscious notions of Islam ingrained in the European religious-cultural memory appear to have overridden the political-legal standards Europeans had set for themselves.

This bias leads us to a second observation: the use of double standards. Christian symbols like crucifixes are given a different evaluation than headscarves, just as Sharia tribunals are judged much more harshly than religious tribunals of other faiths. It is evident that the mechanism of 'us versus them' is active here, whereby the 'us' stands for Europeans belonging to an imaginary Judaeo-Christian civilisation, while the 'them' denotes Muslims of alien origin. This is confirmed by various discrimination monitors and surveys conducted in the past few decades.

These two mechanisms lead to the third observation that there is a development in Europe wherein religious-cultural values are given precedent over political-legal values when it comes to issues of Islam. This happens in two ways. One way is to interpret political-legal values in religious-cultural terms, as happened when the crucifix was described as a marker of Italy's national identity and a symbol of democracy, or when the headscarf was called a symbol of intolerance contrary to gender equality. The other way is to legalise religious-cultural values, meaning that the values in question are transferred from the religious-cultural domain to the political-legal domain. This was done by the legal ban of the burqa and by the attempt to include 'Judaeo-Christian values' in the European constitution.

The question is whether this is a bad thing. Why not give preference to the religious-cultural values cherished by the majority? The problem is that some of the fundamental political-legal values are put in place precisely to prevent that: the rights of minorities should not be overruled by those of the majority. One of these political-legal values – toleration – demands that the majority must endure actions and behaviour they might consider absurd or even unacceptable. According to certain Judaeo-Christian rules and practices, women have an inferior status to men, but what if it is their own choice to live in accordance to those rules? The burqa may be offensive to some, but is this not also the case with facial tattoos or certain extravagant modes of dress? The ECtHR deemed it one of the foundations of the European democratic order that all opinions must be permitted, even if they 'shock, offend, and disturb'.[48] In the case of certain modes of Muslim dress or behaviour, which some find shocking, offensive and disturbing, should people not display a similar tolerance?

If, on the other hand, such behaviour can indeed be considered intolerant, we face Karl Popper's tolerance paradox: by tolerating the intolerant, we risk losing

[48] *Handyside v UK*, App no 5493/72 (ECHR, 7 December 1976).

the very institutions that stand for an open and tolerant society.[49] To prevent that from happening, one must fight the intolerant with intolerance, but in doing so, also risk dismantling the foundations of today's Europe. Toleration, therefore, is the key to the balancing act between political-legal and religious-cultural values. But that key demands a keen scrutiny in defining what is meant by political-legal values, and why.

[49] K Popper, *The Open Society and its Enemies* (first edn 1945, Abingdon, Taylor & Francis, 2011).

5

Old and New Islam in Europe: A Methodological Approach

KONSTANTINOS TSITSELIKIS

I. Introduction[1]

Studying Islam in the European context is a complex task and requires a multifaceted and multi-disciplinary approach. Over the last few decades, Islamic studies have taken on a new prominence in academic circles in response to a greater demand for that research. Governments have increasingly requested research on the Islamic world to inform foreign policy and regulate relations with domestic Muslim communities. At the same time, legislators and the judiciary lack the knowledge to comprehend new aspects of ethno-religious alterity that seem not to be akin to 'Europeaness'. Sometimes, these discrepancies can be connected to increased security policies after the rise of Islamic fundamentalism following the 11 September attacks. Often, European governments approach Muslims (either their own citizens or migrants) as an irregular phenomenon needing special policies and law.

Policymakers, lawmakers and public opinion often feel awkward, if not hostile, towards Islam. Old perceptions about 'what Europe is' conflict with developing ideas about what 'Europe will be' in numerous areas. A rise in extreme right-wing discourse and practices have been fostered by these assumptions. Studying European Islam is a fascinating field of research, revealing aspects of both multiple 'Europes' and 'Islams'.[2] Islam in Europe brings out a wide spectrum of cultural, ethnic and political stances across Europe, from East to West.[3] Many of these

[1] This chapter is based on K Tsitselikis, 'European Islams and Muslim Europes. Some Thoughts about Studying Europe's Contemporary Islam' (2013) 5 *Yearbook of Muslims in Europe* 1.

[2] On the notion of a 'multifaceted Europe' or 'multiple Europe(s)' see, eg, B Strath (ed), *Europe and the Other and Europe as the Other* (Brussels, Peter Lang, 2000) and R Hudson 'One Europe or Many? Reflections on Becoming European' (2000) 25 *Transactions of the Institute of British Geographers* 409.

[3] See B Maréshal, 'Introduction' in B Maréshal, S Allievi, F Dasseto and J Nielsen (eds), *Muslims in the enlarged Europe* (Leiden, Brill, 2003); X Bougarel, 'Balkan Muslims and Islam in Europe' (2007) 4 *Südost Europa* 355; K Górak-Sosnowska, 'Muslims in Europe: Different Communities, one Discourse? Adding the Central and Eastern European Perspective' in K Górak-Sosnowska (ed), *Muslims in Poland*

stances remain outside the sphere of public debate. Islamic studies, public debate and law often see the world as if it is composed of separate social echelons, perpetuating the notion of imaginary places, such as 'Christendom', 'the Islamic World', 'the First World', 'the Third World' and even 'Europe' itself. These notions are misrepresented as separate socio-cultural entities, rather than as integral parts of the human world. Whatever the content or approach of the relevant literature, it seems that developing global methodological and comparative approaches would be useful to understand the similar or different backgrounds that tend to homogenise or divide these multiple and multifaceted 'Europes' and 'Islams'.

For some, it is difficult not to consider Muslims as a collective subject merely because of their religion. The majority European ideology often views this as a negative or incompatible trait. This chapter will attempt to deal with a multidimensional approach to Islam in Europe in two ways: (1) through the geographical areas that represent different structural characteristics; and (2) through a system of variables, such as democracy, human rights, minority status or citizenship.

II. Different Islam(s) in Different Europe(s): Legal, Political and Historical Legacies as a Background

Attempting to define or to quantify 'Islam' and 'Muslims' is not an easy task, as European Muslims are spread across 46 countries of the European continent and within the 26 European Union (EU) Member States.[4] In most cases, Muslims constitute a small minority (between one and 10 per cent, in countries like Ireland, Poland, the United Kingdom (UK), France, Germany and Greece). In some non-EU states Muslims may be a large minority (between 20 to 45 per cent of Bosnia-Herzegovina and North Macedonia) or even a majority of the population (in Albania, Azerbaijan, Kosovo and Turkey/Northern Cyprus).

Though containing important contradictions and differences, Europe constitutes a common canvas of coexistence for 46 countries and countless societies. On this canvas one can discern three distinct areas where Islam is placed, acting and counter-reacting through different ways or patterns and legacies:

> *Area A – The West*, which has been accommodating Muslim immigrants for about a century, forms a new indigenous Islam along with incoming immigrant Muslims. With a sizable population and significant presence in all aspects of life, Western European Islam is an important component of today's Europe.

and Eastern Europe. Widening the European perspective (Warsawa, University of Warsaw, Faculty of Oriental Studies, 2011).

[4] See N Jeldoft, 'On defining Muslims' (2009) 1 *Yearbook of Muslims in Europe* 9; K Öktem, 'Counting Muslims: Censuses, Categories, Policies and the Construction of Islam in Europe' (2014) 6 *Yearbook of Muslims in Europe* 1.

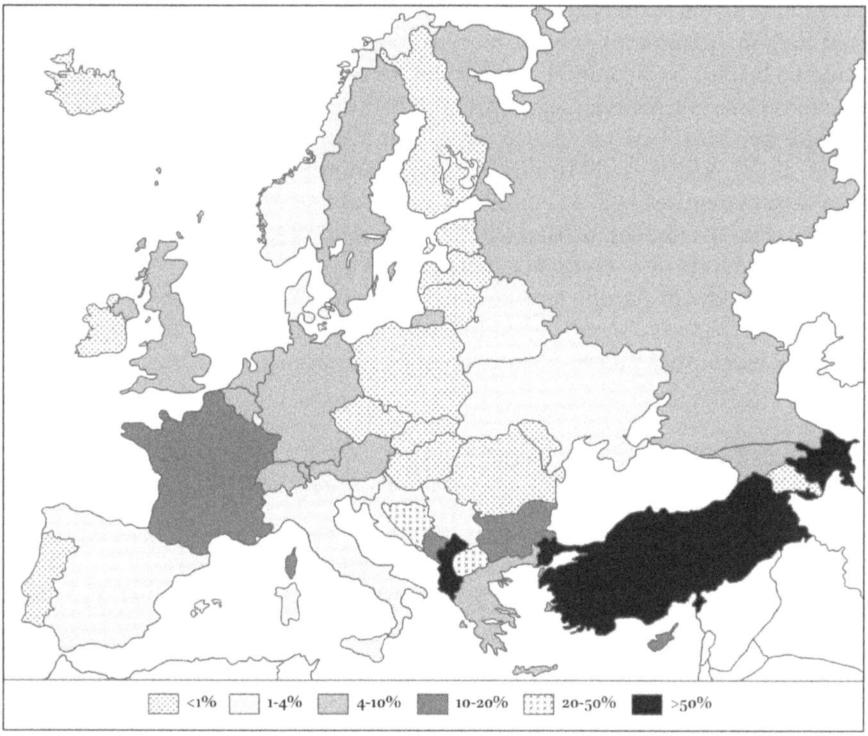

Map 5.1 Islam in Europe[5]

Area B – The East, where Islam is present in the form of small communities. Except for Azerbaijan and the Muslim populations on the periphery of Russia, historical and immigrant Islam currently seems to play a minor role in any political, economic and societal transformations. Considering this, it could be asserted that, here, Islam lacks particular significance in central politics.

Area C – The post-Ottoman area, where Islam is characterised by a history that, to a certain extent, still plays a crucial role in today's societies. Its national affinities and well-established ideological connotations are of key importance for both majorities and minorities in these countries. Muslim majorities in Turkey, Kosovo, Albania, and Muslim Bosnia shape the Muslim profile in the broader area.

These three 'areas' can be seen also as shaping more or less unified sub-regions in Europe with common legacies that influence policies and societies. There are no

[5] Tsitselikis (n 1) 12.

clear-cut boundaries between these three areas, and thus they should be considered as soft boundaries subject to convergence. This proposed categorisation could be helpful for a comprehensive appraisal and contextualisation of European Islam considering regional legacies that left their mark on political, ideological or legal domains. One could also argue that West-East/South-East represents a major divide. Russia could be discussed in relation to the post-colonial area, and the Balkan countries with a communist past could be discussed in relation to the Eastern area. Lastly, the division in the proposed categories could render more visible the trends of convergence between 'old' and 'new' Islam.[6] However, state policies and law in Europe tend to draw a harsh border line between 'Old' and 'New' Islam that sets a significant differentiating factor between the two categories, although recent societal experiences suggest convergence rather than division.

A. Post-Colonial: The West

EU Member States: Austria, Belgium, Denmark, France, Finland, Germany, Ireland, Italy, Luxemburg, Malta, the Netherlands, Portugal, Spain, Sweden

Non-EU states: Iceland, Norway, Switzerland, the UK

Post-colonialism shaped an economic environment that facilitated migration from former colonies to former colonial empires. In this context, Muslims settled before decolonisation as early as the nineteenth century in Western Europe (in the UK, France, the German and Austrian Empires). Today, many Muslims of Western Europe are descendants of these early migrants and are residents and citizens of the respective states. Intermarriage and conversion, along with the transmission of Islam over generations, created multiple Muslim communities with variable connections to both Islam and the national ideologies from their ancestor's state of origin. In their different ways, these Muslims are interconnected to colonial subjugation and anti-colonial or counter-colonial narratives. Anti-colonial narratives analyse the identity politics that are the social and cultural perspectives of the 'subaltern' colonial subjects, dealing with parts of Muslim society. The way Islam is perceived within the post-colonial identity determines the 'Us and Them' binary social relation, as a power relation, between the West and the non-West, often imagining non-Western Europe through a 'local' orientalism.[7] The post-colonial era has witnessed tremendous transformations in Europe and European Islam is among the societal material that has been part and parcel of this transformation.

[6] I use the term 'Old Islam' as a reference to Muslim communities with a long presence in Europe, whose members are citizens of the respective state. 'New Islam' would comprise Muslim immigrants. As second- or third-generation immigrants acquire citizenship of their state of residence, there is a gradual tendency towards convergence between the two categories. Converts could be seen as part of 'New Islam' as individuals or of 'Old Islam' if they adhere to a historical community.

[7] See J Sharp, *Geographies of Postcolonialism* (London, SAGE, 2008) 109–31.

Muslim immigration since 2001 has been connected to new reflexes based on notions such as 'security' or 'national interest' and a new position of Islam has been formed first in the West, and then in the East.

Islam has been displaced from the margins to the centre and from the post-colonial past to the European present as it follows various historical trajectories and creates new interpenetrations between different cultural codes, values, and practices.[8] These interconnected histories of Muslims and Europe raise the issue of what post-colonial Europe means for Europe. The dichotomy of European–non-European is shaped through collective memory and today's experiences determined through the mirror of the postcolonial politics of the West.

On the other hand, as Peter Frank puts it in the literature on Western Europe's Muslims,

> the question of whether Muslim beliefs and practices are transforming (or not) in a historically new environment and, one hastens to add, in a new global setting, has become a central issue in the course of the last decade or so. In an often highly politicised environment where transformation continues to be measured by the criteria of compatibility with supposedly European values, interest in this question has notably stimulated an ongoing debate about the structure of religious life inside Europe's Muslim populations.[9]

Scandinavian countries could be seen as forming a subgroup of the West, since they were not colonial powers and did not experience a wave of 'Old Muslim' immigration. Except for Finland, Scandinavian countries are not home to traditional Islam. However, as highly developed democracies and stable economies, they have been gradually attracting considerable numbers of Muslim immigrants and refugees since the early 1970s. Finland, once under Russian/Soviet influence, has a historical Muslim minority (the Tatars) which could be placed together with the countries of the 'East'. However, the Muslim immigration of the last two decades makes Finland a country with strong similarities to countries of Western Europe.

B. Post-Communist/Socialist: The East

EU Member States: Czech Republic, Estonia, Hungary, Latvia, Lithuania, Poland, Slovakia

Non-EU states: Armenia, Azerbaijan, Belarus, Georgia, Moldova, Russia, Ukraine

Many of the countries in Central and Eastern Europe once belonged to the territory of the Russian and Austrian Empires and, until 1990, had communist regimes.

[8] See N Göle, 'Decentering Europe, Recentering Islam' (2012) 43 *New Literary History* 665.

[9] P Frank, 'Individualisation and Religious Authority in Western European Islam' (2006) 17 *Islam and Christian–Muslim Relations* 17, 105. This article provides a broad survey of the current literature and presents some of the key scholarly contributions aims to explore convergences and divergences with respect to the questions of individualisation and religious authority.

These countries could be grouped as belonging to a post-communist area that experienced parallel transition patterns towards democratic pluralism. They share a common legacy in relation to the position of Islam which contributed to the shaping of national ideology, law and policies. The Balkan countries also shared this transitional experience (except for Greece) while also sharing a common past as part of the Ottoman Empire. This common Ottoman legacy left strong ideological and political influences on the way that Islam is perceived, as either a minority or majority religion. Consequently, these countries will be treated as 'post-Ottoman'.

In the late 1980s, Islam had the second largest number of believers in the Soviet Union with 45 million Muslims. At that time, Soviet law forbade religious activity outside the approximately 500 mosques and Islamic schools by means of tight government control. As immigration to the Soviet Union was rare, no migrant Islam was present during this period with the sole exception of Muslims who migrated from the Soviet Socialist Republics of Central Asia to Soviet Russia. In other East European socialist countries, very small and dispersed communities of Muslims resulted from this kind of immigration, inter-marriage, or student mobility (such as to East Berlin and Prague).[10]

Russia has similarities to the (post-)colonial West with regards to the mobility of Muslims from the periphery to the metropolis. However, Russia inherited from its colonial and Soviet past a territorial continuity that comprises important Muslim populations. Today, as a federal state with seven federal republics, each with ethnic local Muslim majorities or strong minorities (comprising also unresolved conflicts related to the Muslim ethnicity in Chechnya and Daghestan), Russia constitutes a rather complex case to study.

A subgroup of this area comprises countries also with historical Muslim minorities under legal protection. These fall under the category of 'traditional religious community' (mostly Tatars) such as in Poland, Belarus, Lithuania and Ukraine, albeit representing a rather small percentage of the total population. In contrast, Azerbaijan is the only country of this area with a majority Muslim population. In Azerbaijan, Shi'a Islam is considered as part of the national identity and Sunni Islam represents a minority.

After 1991, all these countries except for Belarus became representative democracies, gradually joining the Council of Europe, and some the EU. In all former socialist countries, secularism or institutional neutrality towards religion seems to be coupled with state control of Muslim organisations; both these features are a legacy borrowed from the pre-1990s regimes. In most of these countries, there were strong claims from all religious communities to restore the status quo ante. In this context, Muslim communities were, to a certain extent, granted collective rights to property (over *waqf* real estates) and religious leadership (right to

[10] See E Račius, *Islam in Post-communist Eastern Europe: Between Churchification and Securitization* (Leiden, Brill, 2020); E Račius, *Muslims in Eastern Europe* (Edinburgh, Edinburgh University Press, 2018).

select the *Mufti*).[11] In addition to traditional Islam, EU Member States (Poland, Hungary, Czech Republic, Slovakia, Estonia, Lithuania and Latvia) started attracting immigrant Muslims after the early 2000s. As a result, they are experiencing similar trends to those in Western Europe. However, it seems rather unlikely that these countries will achieve similar levels of immigration the ones in the West in the near or even distant future.[12]

What makes Eastern Europe different (in general terms both post-communist and post-Ottoman) when compared to the West is the economic factor as determinant for the settlement of New Islam. The division between East and West is illustrative in the internal division between East and West Germany: in the *länder* of the former East Germany, immigrant Islam represented less than one per cent of the local population whereas in what was West Germany Muslims represented three to 10 per cent of the population.

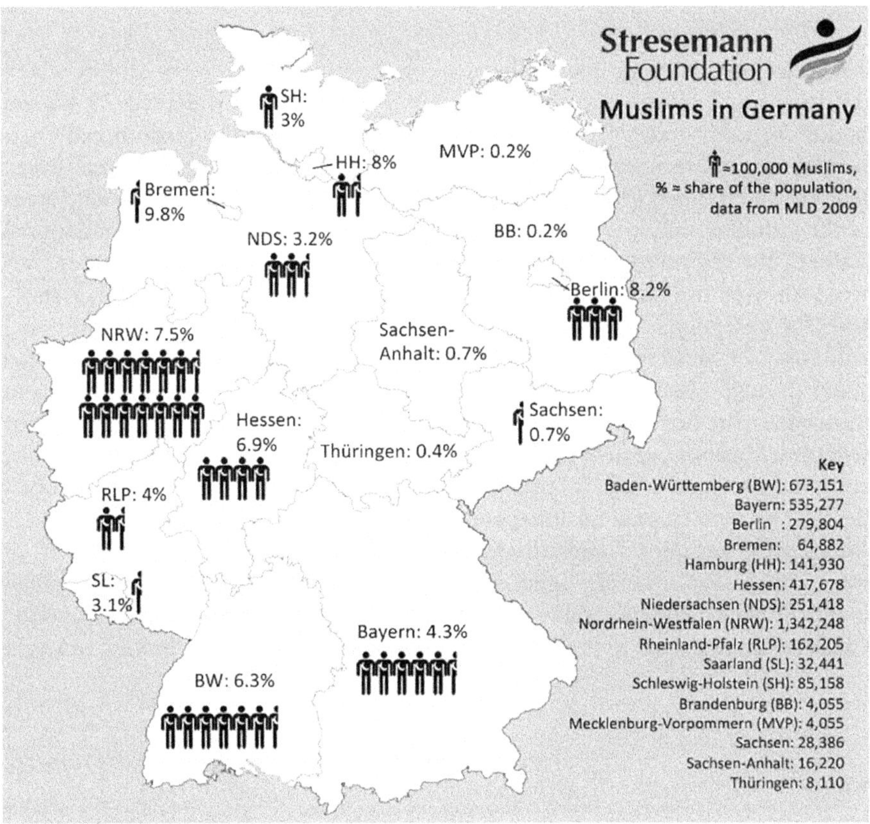

Map 5.2 Muslims in Germany

[11] See A Nalborczyk and B Pawel, 'Relations between Islam and the State in Poland: the Legal Position of Polish Muslims' (2011) 22 *Islam and Christian-Muslim Relations* 343.

[12] See Górak-Sosnowska (n 3) 18.

One additional point concerns Western perceptions of the traditional Islam of the East. Locally important Muslim populations, such as in Russia and the Caucasus, are perceived in the eyes of the 'West' as not essentially 'European' (indeed, in the eyes of certain researchers even Russia does not belong to European civilisation).[13] The further East in the European context Islam is, the less Europe perceives it as a part of Europe, a stance with clear hegemonic resonance. The presence of a strong historical Islam in Eastern Russia and the Caucasus is precisely the geographical point where the borders of 'Europe' become blurred.

C. Post-Ottoman: The South-East

EU Member States: Bulgaria, Croatia, Cyprus, Greece, Romania, Slovenia

Non-EU states: Albania, Bosnia-Herzegovina, Kosovo, Montenegro, North Macedonia, Serbia, Turkey

The term 'post-Ottoman' means the areas once part of the Ottoman Empire where the legal and political accommodation of ethno-religious difference is known under the term *millet*.[14] The legacy of *millet* determined the institutional position of religious minorities within the Christian states of the Balkans and Turkey that were established gradually from the early nineteenth century to the detriment of the Ottoman Empire (which collapsed in 1923). The consolidation of national states by the beginning of the twentieth century found Muslim communities scattered all over the Balkans forming minorities within Christian national states with the exceptions of Albania, Kosovo and Bosnia. This legacy of institutional autonomy for Muslims and non-Muslims was kept within post-Ottoman Christian states through Muslim communities, which acquired special protection status as minorities. The perception of non-Muslims in the old Ottoman Empire had been reversed; Muslims began to enjoy equality and minority rights but potentially they could be governed under a 'special status'. Christians saw these Muslim minorities as a price to be paid for independence. In that context, Muslim communities were legally recognised and attributed special status, whereas 'New Islam' is, in most cases, institutionally ignored. As Todorova remarks, 'ironically, Balkan nationalism, which irrevocably destroyed the imagined community of Orthodox Christianity, managed to preserve a frozen, unchangeable and stultifying uniform

[13] See S Huntington, 'The Clash of Civilisations and the remaking of world's order' (1993) 72 *Foreign Affairs* 22.

[14] The Ottoman authorities granted ethno-religious communities a certain institutional autonomy from the 15th to the 20th century. Greek-Orthodox, Armenians and Jews were the 'minority' communities falling under this special status under the hegemonic position of Islam. On the *millet* system, see K Barkey, *Empire of Difference. The Ottomans in Comparative Perspective* (Cambridge, Cambridge University Press, 2008) 13, 152. Barkey illustrates how 'difference and separation was a value pursued by the Ottoman state and the communities themselves' and how the Ottomans instituted boundaries of different degrees of permeability, while organising communities across such classificatory systems.

Muslim community, and consistently dealt with it in terms of *millet*.'[15] According to the mainstream national discourse of the Christian nation states of the Balkans, the Muslim presence still constitutes an 'alien element' to the area. However, Balkan Muslims have deep-rooted feelings of representing Islam and feel entitled to historical rights and political powers over the land.[16]

The structural formation of these Islamic communities was able to embed national ideas where appropriate, quite often acquiring Turkish nationalism or (as in Bosnia) to develop a distinct nationalism. Albania constitutes the only case where national identity was not based on religious affiliation. In Turkey, national identity is built on Islam, despite the legal–theoretical establishment of secularism. Greece is the only case that has not experienced a socialist/communist regime and thus its *millet*-like legal status remained unchanged. Cyprus has a unique position on this spectrum, since, after the division of the island in 1974, Greek Cypriots and Turkish Cypriots separated based on ethno-religious affiliation. Moreover, as the only post-colonial state in Europe, Cyprus retains a flow of emigration towards the West (specifically the UK). This pattern is not unknown throughout the Balkans, especially Turkey, from where a significant Muslim emigration has settled in the West, representing a transposition of 'Old Islam' from the post-Ottoman area into the West as a form of 'New Islam'.

* * *

There are no clear-cut boundaries between the three areas as various trends of convergence are developed. The overlapping features and similarities are not rare and is subject to change. Eventually, over time, differences that are visible today will no longer be in the future. The sharp divide between 'Old' and 'New' Islam seems to be fading out as Muslim immigrants settle in the East and the Balkans. New patterns of behaviour, policies and societal transformations are formed as 'Old' and 'New' Muslims are converging and 'New' Islam (in the West) tends to become 'Old'. Converts are also part of this trend. At some point, a new classification and contextualisation would be needed to understand new patterns of accommodation of Muslim communities within Europe.

Although each group of countries relies on today's law and policies, European Muslims do have internal divisions, as with any part of society, which are susceptible to change with new and multiple affiliations. This dichotomy between stability and mobility could be considered along the following lines.

[15] M Todorova, 'The Ottoman legacy in the Balkans' in *Imperial Legacy: The Ottoman Imprint and on the Balkans and the Middle East* (New York, Columbia University Press, 1996) 68.

[16] For an overview see A Popovic, *L'Islam balkanique* (Berlin, Osteuropa-Institut an der Freien Universität, 1986); X Bougarel and N Clayer (eds), *Le nouvel Islam balkanique. Les musulmans, acteurs du post-communisme 1990–2000* (Paris, Maisonneuve & Larose, 2001).

III. A System of Variables to be Considered

To locate degrees of variability that could determine the relation between Islam and Europe, certain questions should be addressed. Do Muslims have identical characteristics in the countries of 'origin' with those on the European continent? What makes Islam a *brand*[17] and under which modalities? Which factors render Islam a flexible/inflexible religion or a permeable/impermeable culture and what are the gradations and characteristics of resistance to societal contacts between Muslims and non-Muslims? How does religion affect society and what is the role of Islam in this discussion? How do states treat and accommodate Muslim communities, and how do the latter set up organisational structures? In which ways do communities voice their claims for rights or for a better position? Do international relations and foreign interference affect Islam in European societies? How does loyalty to both state and Islam affect the position of Muslim communities, their image and self-perception? Does citizenship play a role in the position of Muslims in Europe? To discuss these questions, one would need to consider, on a comparative basis a series of variables such as:

- state institutional organisation/legal tradition;
- international politics/international legal commitments;
- Muslim community organisation/leadership/membership;
- degree of religiosity (Muslims/non-Muslims);
- integration/exclusion;
- 'Old Islam' (traditional or historical)/'New Islam' (immigrants/converts);
- Islam as a minority/majority;
- citizenship;
- transnationalism/nationalism;
- security for people/security for the state;
- religious and cultural uniformity/pluralism;
- class position (access to socio-economic rights); and
- past/present/future.

It is helpful to consider five of these variables which highlight the differentiated law and policies forming the European canvas on which European Islam(s) are placed.

[17] With reference to the presentation by S Allievi, 'Islam as a brand' at the conference organised by the University of Copenhagen, Helsingør, 20–23 May 2013.

A. Majority/Minority and Historical Minority/Immigrant Community

Traditional minorities[18] have the prerogative to share a common political, legal and symbolic area with the national majority where they can socialise through common citizenship. First-generation immigrants most likely do not, while their children and grandchildren will most probably do so. In the European legal tradition, as formed within the Council of Europe,[19] minorities and migrants are two distinct groups subject to different categories of norms. However, the cultural, political and socio-economic changes taking place in Europe due to long-term migration may affect this legal dichotomy. Only in a few European countries do Old and New Islam coexist (Greece, Bulgaria, Romania, Finland, Poland and Russia). Only since the early 1990s, in most cases, has Eastern Europe experienced immigrant Islam. As mentioned above, in the West, old Muslim immigration tends to become 'Old Islam'[20] through acquiring citizenship in a quite different ideological and cultural sphere.[21] Policies and law are unable to define, in many cases, the boundaries between a historical minority and an immigrant community (staying in the host country over two or more generations through gaining citizenship would attribute minority characteristics to groups which formerly would be called 'immigrant'). More than 'Old Islam', which was related to the notion of 'minority', 'New Islam' in Europe has brought up the question of 'multiculturalism'. With the increasing mobility of capital and labour, new economic and political challenges have produced new policies, theories and practices. Traditional cultural otherness and recent immigration represent, in effect, two sides of the same challenge: to redefine European citizenship and accommodate internal ethnic and religious divides. Does the 'common cultural heritage' as set out by European self-perception encompass Islam as a religion, or as a culture, including Muslims' ethnicities and languages? Would Islam be a part of the European future, or would the difference mark out religion as a potential area of conflict?

Muslim immigrants and minority Muslims often share a distinction from other groups in society in terms of origin, language, culture and religion. The convergence of the two under a unified legal framework would entail reconsidering religious and linguistic specificities, instead focusing on social participation

[18] The term is used in both numerical and power relation terms.

[19] See the Framework Convention on National Minorities and the Charter of Minority or Lesser Used Languages.

[20] Research also suggests that the offspring of Yemenis who settled in Liverpool after 1869, thus creating 'Old Islam', became 'New Islam' when later migration merged the two groups (see www.liverpoolarabiccentre.org.uk).

[21] F Dasseto, S Ferrari and B Marechal, 'Islam in the European Union: What's at stake in the future', 23 June 2007, European Parliament, available at www.euromedalex.org/sites/default/files/Islam_in_Europe.pdf.

factors. Thus, immigrant Islam and historical Islam would have to be seen under the scope of equal social inclusion. Both groups may or may not preserve their own culture and religion, having to make a strategic choice between 'assimilation' and 'integration'. The comparison of two categories of 'minoritised' Islam, as converging political paradigms, would redefine the notion of 'minoritisation' and its ideological justification and play down the cultural and the ethno-religious difference.

B. State–Religion Affairs

The position of religious communities within the legal order is set according to different institutional modalities that go from strict neutrality (France) to hegemony of religion (Ireland and Greece). The distinct political, ideological and juridical legacies of predominantly Christian countries often shape, in different ways, the institutional position of Muslim minority communities. In this variable framework, each European government attempts to regulate its local version of Islam in different ways, for different reasons. In some countries, like the UK, there is no official institution, but ethnic and religious-based visibility is guaranteed within the sphere of civil society. Others attempt to balance a top-down approach, where the state requests the establishment of a representative body by the Muslim communities, like in Italy. In Greece, institutional visibility is guaranteed to only 'Old Islam' (according to the Treaty of Lausanne of 1923), whereas Russia imposes a strict government-controlled Islam community system. In other cases (like France, Belgium and Spain) Muslims are free to choose, by election or appointment, their own representatives. However, the institutions and representation procedures are set by law and the government retains the right to co-opt additional members.

Also, an additional factor should be considered: states conduct administrative and organisational changes in accordance with their political agenda and within the frame of binding international treaties. When domestic law does not implement these obligations properly, minority-state relations as well as those between 'host' state and kinstate[22] are affected. Dealing with Muslim communities often becomes a foreign policy issue.[23] In such cases, Turkey or Saudi Arabia act or even are invited as kinstates.[24] Patterns of political involvement through religion differ among post-Ottoman and post-colonial spheres. In the post-communist sphere, there are no kinstate of historical Muslim minorities, and those of immigrant Islam seem to be (to date, at least) reluctant to assume such a role. In the West, and

[22] Kinstate is considered to be the 'homeland' for its 'kin-minority', so the minority with which there are ties of national, religious or linguistic kinship.

[23] See B Bruce, 'Transnational Islams, National Angst: The Politics of Muslim Diasporas in Europe' (2020) 11 *Yearbook of Muslims in Europe* 12.

[24] K Tsitselikis, *Old and New Islam in Greece: From Historical Minorities to Immigrant Newcomers* (Leiden, Martinus Nijhoff, 2012) 170–75.

to a certain extent in the East, *neo-radicalism* exerts a strong influence and politicises Islam. In the East and South-East, *neo-sufi* movements, such as the one led by Fethullah Gülen (until 2013) also play an important role in reshaping Islam.[25]

C. Human Rights

The increasing importance of human rights includes safeguarding freedom of religion, legal mechanisms for protection, and supervision. Human rights bodies constitute institutions that could accommodate claims for 'common' rights or to resolve disputes interrelated to the preservation of the community. Thus, strategic litigation before national or international bodies (such as the European Court of Human Rights or the supervising organs of the Framework Convention for the Protection of National Minorities) by members of Muslim minorities, whether they be historical or migrant, could instigate new legal status and alteration of socio-economic position. The right to be recognised as a religious or ethnic group and most of all the right to equal participation in the socio-economic sphere are important topics for research. Research on economic rights and their interrelation to class position and mobility of Muslims, in a comparative perspective of vertical and horizontal relations within the Muslim community and within broader society could also reveal hitherto less explored aspects of European Islam.

In recent decades, Western Europe has experienced the emergence of new national or local 'Islams', whereas in post-communism and post-Ottoman regions, local 'Islams' long ago formed their own distinct socio-cultural and ethnic profile. Accommodating these particularities became a concern for policymakers and lawmakers through the principle of non-discrimination. When Islam is perceived as a cultural/security threat, domestic tensions are stirred,[26] fuelling xenophobia and nationalist or ultra-right political discourses. Islamophobia is linked to 'Muslimophobia', and words become weaponised against individuals, minority groups, and Islam as a religion.[27] Under such circumstances, human rights need to provide sufficient means of legal protection and mechanisms capable of defusing tensions.

D. Ideology and Ethnicity

National or religious ideologies, shaping minority and majority identities, form communities beyond borders. Muslim communities are subject to a complex

[25] See AR Solberg, 'The Role of Turkish Islamic Networks in the Western Balkans' (2007) 55 *Südost Europa* 429.

[26] See Bruce (n 23).

[27] For a detailed discussion see S Akgonul, 'Islamophobia, Muslimophobia: From Words to Acts' (2018) 9 *Yearbook of Muslims in Europe* 2.

ethnicisation process stemming from the national origins of the community or the national identity fostered by the state. Contemporary globalisation has entailed a series of socio-economic, political, legal and symbolic changes for states. Hybrid identities, which accommodate both state-national ideology and Islam, break the formal types of Islam and contribute to socio-cultural pluralism. However, monolithic interpretations of religion, either stemming from majorities or minorities, could hamper the integration process. Some cultural and normative aspects of Islam which reinforce self-referential schemes putting forward community values may at times lead to social exclusion based on ethnic identities.[28] Conversely, there are cases of Muslims who opt for membership of the majority's identity, culture or religion. Hence, transnationalism, or the trend towards a change in ethnicity over generations, counters those trends towards religious fundamentalism and radicalises the role of Islam as a strong and visible entity in Europe.[29] Converts and reverts act as a bridge or a buffer between Muslims and non-Muslims as a symbolic and pragmatic border area. Orientations in Islam among Muslims, such as the *salafisation* of individuals or communities and the *sunnification* of Bektashis and Alevis, illustrate how these borders are continuously shifting.

E. Civic and Legal Citizenship

Muslims in Europe are divided into those who are citizens of a European state and those who are not. Possessing citizenship in the state of one's residence unquestionably constitutes a fundamental factor for social integration, while not being a citizen may become a potential factor for social marginalisation. Thus, acquisition or loss of citizenship, dual citizenship or statelessness take on major importance when it comes to social inclusion. The choice by the state to permit or to prevent dual (or multiple) citizenship is essentially political in nature, regulated by law and conditioned by historical factors that reflect the state's view of its national character. This choice affects the position of 'old' and 'new minorities', Muslims included. In this context, *ius sanguinis* and *ius soli* offer European legislators a series of options embedding ideological stances. The divide based on citizenship is not static and affects the institutional visibility of individuals and communities.

IV. Conclusion

Europe is made up of old and new evolving cultural, ethnic, religious and societal realities. Scientific research on Islam in Europe seeks to comprehend the different

[28] Having 'Muslim descent' does not mean the individual is a practising Muslim.

[29] See R Grillo, 'Islam and Transnationalism' (2004) 30 *Journal of Ethnic and Migration Studies* 861; I Merdjanova, *Rediscovering the Umma. Muslims in the Balkans between Nationalism and Transnationalism* (New York, Oxford University Press, 2013) 55.

legacies and the patchwork of dynamic and changing legal, political and socio-economic features which determine the status of persons and groups by virtue of their nationality or religion. If 'Old' and 'New Islam' indicate two distinct standpoints, one cannot ignore the process of convergence between the two that is ongoing in many cases. One of the major challenges for scientific research is to approach the trend holistically and discuss the features of assimilation, coexistence and integration.

Political and institutional legacies affect the differing political and societal importance of Islam in the West and in the East/South-East Europe. This dichotomy is reflected in the literature on Islam: in the West, it focuses on immigration, whereas in the East/South-East, it focuses on history and ethnicity. Moreover, hegemonic scientific narratives from the West have been overwhelmingly exported to and reproduced by the East.

Law and policies on state–religion, civic citizenship, human rights and ethnicity, among other issues, which are related to Muslims in all European states, need to find the means to understand the different overlapping realities of coexisting worlds as multiple and variable sides of a European society in constant flux (either through the lens of the EU integration programme, or through broader Europe), marked by inner contradictions, constraints and limitations.

The subject of Islam in Europe must confront all the aforementioned questions (as well as others not discussed here) through interdisciplinary approaches and synergies. Rapid transformation patterns that characterised Europe in past decades through new political ideologies, nationalisms and economic neoliberalism further complicate the picture and require more rigorous classification and analysis. In this changing context, religion, on the one hand, becomes an ambivalent marker for ethnicity and national belonging, while on the other, it constitutes for many communities a factor of solidarity, with cultural, social and political connotations within the context of each European state. This makes 'European Islams' and 'Muslim Europes' a key challenge for law and politics.

6

Constitutionalism, Populism and Islam in Europe

ANDREA PIN

I. Introduction

The legal treatment of Islam in Europe is complex and evolving. Social and political developments across the continent in the last few decades have harmed the condition of Muslims, compromising their integration into civil society.[1] Since the early 2000s, multiple Islamist attacks on European soil, which left many dead or badly wounded, have damaged the reputation of Islam, making it a matter of public concern and not just a demographic phenomenon.[2] Europe has meanwhile become the primary recruiting ground for jihadists in Syria, Iraq and Libya.[3] The inflow of Muslim refugees and migrants fleeing wars and political crises, famine, or other dire conditions, has caused concern among Europeans. Many European Union (EU) citizens and governments have insisted that EU institutions intervene to stop this influx and criticised the EU's open internal borders, which curtail the national ability to control the flow of migrants and refugees.[4] The growth of the Muslim population in Europe is challenging its overwhelmingly Christian heritage, and the dichotomy between the secular and the religious spheres that has hitherto dominated the European cultural framework.

If the Muslim presence in Europe has become a matter of controversy, in a time of political and legal polarisation, the topic of Islamic integration has tapped into an equally heated legal debate: the resilience of constitutionalism vis-à-vis the challenges of populism. It is widely believed that populism threatens the protection of religious minorities and the inclusion of Islam in the European social sphere.

[1] M Saral 'Muslims Between Discrimination and Protection at the Legislative, Executive and Judicial Levels in Western Countries' in M Saral and SO Bahcecik (eds), *State, Religion and Muslims: Between Discrimination and Protection at the Legislative, Executive and Judicial Levels* (Leiden, Brill, 2020) 1.

[2] A Rettman, 'Blasphemy and Jihad: Macron Launches EU Debate' *EU Observer* (12 January 2022).

[3] VE Parsi, *Titanic, Naufragio o Cambio di Rotta per l'Ordine Liberale* (Bologna, il Mulino, 2022) 142.

[4] P Khanna, *Move* (New York, Simon & Schuster, 2021) 124–25.

In actuality, the legal and political treatment of Islam in Europe reveals that both constitutionalism and populism can be detrimental to Muslim religious needs and interest. Distrust and even resistance to Muslim minorities is a phenomenon that cuts across most of the ideological spectrum and confirms the impression that 'while Europe has generally been welcoming toward Slavic and Balkan peoples, it has had much more difficulty absorbing Arabs, Africans, and Muslims in general.'[5] This chapter identifies the main features of constitutionalism and populism in Europe and distils how each treats Islam. It focuses first on populism, generally considered the more controversial, and then explores the political culture of liberal constitutionalism and its agenda at the national as well as supranational level.

II. Populism in Europe

The rise of populist forces has engulfed the global political and legal debate, particularly since the late 2010s. Europe is no exception, with several of its Member States experiencing the growth of such movements. The precise causes and contours of this phenomenon are a matter of contention, as varying definitions of populism and its legal significance abound, often in conflict.[6] Indisputably, most populist narratives are hostile towards integrating Islam within the European public and social sphere, or doubtful as to its efficacy.[7] Anti-Islamist sentiments are not the product of populism. On the contrary, populists have found fertile ground in pre-existing opposition to new religious minorities, most especially Muslim immigrants. Despite internal variations, a sizable political and constitutional rhetoric that depicts Muslims as outsiders has built up over recent years. Political stunts, such as parading pigs in places where mosques were under construction have been a cheap and crass means of discouraging integration and the enjoyment of religious freedom by Muslims. But more impactful initiatives aimed at opposing Muslim immigration and the public presence of Islam have surfaced more than once.[8] In the early 2000s, when populist sentiments were emerging, some Austrian regions made the integration of newcomers more difficult by implementing naturalisation tests that emphasised the cultural component of Austrian identity.[9] More significantly, the majority of the Swiss population voted, in a 2009 referendum, to impose a nationwide constitutional ban on *minarets*, altering the fundamental

[5] ibid.

[6] The populist phenomenon and its origins, especially against the background of supra-nationalism in Europe, were explored in A Pin, 'The Supranational Drivers of Populist Backlash: The Role of Courts' (2019) 20 *German Law Journal* 225.

[7] A Arato and JL Cohen, *Populism and Civil Society. The Challenge to Constitutional Democracy* (Oxford, Oxford University Press, 2021) 46.

[8] SO Bahcecik, 'State, Religion and Muslims Between Discrimination and Protection at the Legislative, Executive and Judicial Levels: An Overview' in Saral and Bahcecik (n 1) 599.

[9] D Nusche, C Shewbridge and CL Rasmussen, *Oecd Reviews of Migrant Education – Austria* (2009) 7.

equilibrium of the Constitution itself, which devolves church and state relations to the Cantons.[10]

Populism in Europe has emboldened pre-existing anti-Islamic sentiments and provided them with a broader cultural framework. Critics of European Islam have found within the march of populism stronger theoretical foundations, and a more comprehensive political alternative. Anti-Muslim forces have thus joined populist platforms, helping to give it shape. The rise of populism has even affected the legal and constitutional framework of some European countries, Hungary and Poland being the most notable examples. These two countries have attracted widespread criticism, especially after they embarked on a series of reforms that reinforced the national political leadership, disempowered the judiciary, and threatened the EU's internal cohesion. The Hungarian leader, Viktor Orbán, promotes a form of 'illiberal constitutionalism' that focuses more on general needs than individual rights. In Poland, the Constitutional Court has denied the supremacy of EU law over domestic legislation.

Populist agenda have also come into prominence beyond Central and Eastern Europe.[11] The global financial crisis of the late 2000s undoubtedly boosted the rise of similar political movements, especially in Southern Europe,[12] and the agendas of such movements have expanded to challenge other core components of liberal constitutionalism. The lack of confidence in supranational organisations, the instability of the Mediterranean region following the Arab Spring, and the influx of immigrants in countries that had traditionally experienced emigration rather than migration, have mobilised such political forces, bringing them closer to the populists in Central and Eastern Europe, with whom they have developed alliances.[13] Populist forces have thus prompted changes in the national political culture of several countries by bringing more political parties within their nationalistic and anti-immigration rhetoric. Accordingly, a wide array of movements across Europe now support the disempowerment of the judiciary, the strengthening of the executive, and strong identification between the people and their political leaders. These movements frequently leverage pre-existing narratives of identity politics, bringing the concept of nation back to the centre stage after decades in which the ideals of supra-nationalism have monopolised legal and constitutional arrangements.[14] Eurosceptics and supporters of more state-centred political agenda have found in populism a bastion for their beliefs and a tool capable of thwarting the process of European integration and weakening pan-continental institutions.[15]

[10] Constitution of Switzerland, Art 72.

[11] M Avbelj and JL Cernic, *The Impact of European Institutions on the Rule of Law and Democracy: Slovenia and Beyond* (Oxford, Hart, 2020).

[12] *Facing the New Far Right in Southern Europe* (Brussels, Coppetiers, 2021) 218.

[13] ibid, 219.

[14] T Drinoczi and A Bien-Kacala, *Illiberal Constitutionalism in Poland and Hungary* (New York, Routledge, 2022) 132.

[15] On the anti-European sentiment that spread across the EU, especially after the 2008 economic crisis and the austerity measures that the EU put in place along with other global financial institutions,

In the belief that supra-national institutions would have the effect of blending and diluting national identities, populist regimes and platforms have revived a language based on tradition and legacy. Their agenda have often claimed to redeem the Christian heritage, making it one of the core elements of their identity. The preamble to Hungary's Constitution declares that 'King Saint Stephen built the Hungarian State on solid ground and made [the] country a part of Christian Europe one thousand years ago.'[16] In seeming defiance of widespread received wisdom that Christians and Christianity were among the engines of European integration in the aftermath of World War II,[17] the preamble even acknowledges 'the role of Christianity in preserving nationhood'.[18] Such ideological leanings have found support among Christian believers and institutions. Orthodox Churches have voiced their distrust of, and even hostility towards, 'liberal individual human rights' and modern life altogether.[19] The Holy Synod of the Orthodox Church openly criticised the EU Charter of Fundamental Rights.[20] Further, Catholics have become sympathetic to populist forces, mostly as a reaction to the EU's, new, rights-based agenda and its denial of Christian roots during the process that was intended to have given birth to a Constitution of Europe in the early 2000s.[21] Populist politicians in Western Europe have exploited the concern about the future of Christian traditions in Europe, as exemplified by events on 18 May 2019, when the leader of the Italian League Party, Matteo Salvini, rallied his supporters in Milan's central square in front of the Cathedral, holding a rosary and a Bible in his hands.

That said, European populists have not always identified with overtly Christian symbolism and rhetoric. For instance, the French National Front has displayed similar levels of anti-European sentiment, attachment to national values, and a rejection of globalisation, but deployed language in more secular terms. Probably in an attempt to gain credit within the strongly secularised French society, the Front has progressively emphasised its belief in the French ideal of *laicité*, with which it has replaced its earlier reliance on the Christian heritage of Europe and France.[22] What has united several populist forces, however, is the belief in the need to retrieve and re-establish a sense of traditional identity that would exclude, discourage, or set an extremely high threshold for, the integration of Muslims has united several populist forces. Populists tend to focus their discourse in European,

see MA Wilkinson, *Authoritarian Liberalism and the Transformation of Modern Europe* (Oxford, Oxford University Press, 2021) 263–65.

[16] Constitution of Hungary, Preamble.

[17] JHH Weiler, *Un'Europa cristiana* (Milan, Rizzoli, 2003).

[18] Constitution of Hungary, Preamble.

[19] K Stoeckl, *The Russian Orthodox Church and Human Rights* (Oxford, Routledge, 2014) 8–9.

[20] ibid, 12–13.

[21] A Pin and L Vanoni, 'Catholicism, Liberalism, and Populism' (2021) 46 *Brigham Young University Law Review* 1301, 1304–05.

[22] D Almeida, 'Exclusionary Secularism: the Front National and the Reinvention of *Laïcité*' (2017) 25 *Modern & Contemporary France* 249, 249.

Western or national rhetoric, adopting identity politics as a bastion against the integration of Islam.[23]

III. Liberalism in Europe

Within more liberal states, difficulties in accommodating Islam have surfaced time and again. Countries that used to be confident and well advanced in integration and multicultural accommodation, such as the United Kingdom (UK), have lately given 'increased attention' to 'Islamic practice', which has proved hard to treat on an equal footing with other religious minorities.[24] Such attention has translated into opposition, and even hostility. In 2008, when Rowan Williams, then the Archbishop of Canterbury, suggested accommodating some aspects of Islamic law to meet the religious needs of Muslims in Britain, his proposal was met with widespread criticism.[25] Compared to the reactions to William's argument in favour of accommodating Islam in the UK, the resistance to the integration of Muslims in other European countries, and at the pan-continental level, has been much stronger and morphed into specific institutional approaches and policies. France and the Netherlands probably showcased political hostility to Islam at the highest level when largely anti-Islamic, anti-Turkey and anti-immigration sentiments persuaded their citizens to cast their votes against a European Constitution in national referenda that was held in 2005. After several months of deliberation, the majority of the citizens of France and the Netherlands, both countries with a recognised liberal pedigree, hijacked the EU constitutional process mainly out of fear that the document could later pave the way for Turkey (now self-identifying as Türkiye) joining the EU.

There are even more instances, however, in which countries embracing liberalism or republicanism have repeatedly and openly targeted Muslim practices. France and Belgium are probably the best-known examples, since they prohibited the use of religious clothing in schools and public places, a measure that was largely aimed at banning the Muslim headscarf for women. France even made the fight against the Muslim veil one of its key political imperatives: the ban was presented as a drastic solution for a matter of grave concern, although the number of women to whom such a measure applied was in the region of 2,000 (a minuscule proportion of the population).[26] Attempts to limit the visibility of Islam within

[23] This is also the case of the French National Front, see A Easat-Daas, 'France: State, Religion and Muslims: Between Discrimination and Protection at the Legislative, Executive and Judicial Levels' in Saral and Bahcecik (n 1) 204.

[24] C McCrudden, *Litigating Religion* (Oxford, Oxford University Press, 2018) 39.

[25] ibid. 41. See also R Griffith-Jones (ed), *Islam and English Law: Rights, Responsibilities and the Place of Sharia* (Cambridge, Cambridge University Press, 2013) ch 1.

[26] SH Cleveland, 'Banning the Full-Face Veil: Freedom of Religion and Non-Discrimination in the Human Rights Committee and the European Court of Human Rights' (2021) 34 *Harvard Human Rights Journal* 228.

the public sphere, especially in public schools, have further escalated in France, as rules have gradually extended the scope of such prohibitions, up to the point of banning 'long black skirts' because they 'appear[ed] too ostentatious and symbolic of Islam'.[27] France's Council of State upheld the decision to deny citizenship to a Muslim woman because she refused to shake hands with the public official awarding her French citizenship, notwithstanding that the ceremony did not require handshaking[28] (a judicial approach that has found resonance in Germany and Switzerland).[29]

The Belgian–French approach is not an outlier in Europe. The Netherlands has also promoted and enforced a morally selective approach to integration, affecting individuals who usually subscribe to conservative values, including Muslims. The Dutch policies on citizenship have lately favoured an extreme version of liberalism, requiring applicants for naturalisation to do much more than merely abide by the law. Applicants are expected to express their personal and moral approval, not simply their acceptance, of same-sex partnerships: a requirement that clearly affects their freedom of conscience.[30] In their volume on the rise and the perils of populism in Slovenia, Matej Avbelj and Jerner Letnar Cernic have argued that populists nurture a specific private and public morality, tending to spread the perception that:

> What is at stake is not the entire demos, a people, but only the part of it that is culturally homogerus and morally sound: the right people. … This distinguishes neatly between the morally impeccable, our people, and all the others, who in the populists' own judgment do not live up to those unilaterally imposed moral expectations.[31]

Dutch citizenship policies seem to be plagued with the same perception, although the Netherlands is considered to be on the liberal side of the political spectrum.

The status of religious freedom for Muslim minorities in several states of Europe seems to be increasingly precarious. As Liav Orgad persuasively demonstrates, some countries with a sizable Muslim population have recently overturned more flexible jurisprudence.[32] In 1993, the Federal Supreme Court of Switzerland had exempted female Muslim students from mixed-gender swimming lessons.[33] But in 2012 it made a U-turn, rejecting this approach.[34] The German Federal Administrative Court accorded an exemption from physical education classes

[27] Easat-Daas (n 23) 216.

[28] *Conseil d'Etat* (11 April 2018) 412462.

[29] More examples are found in L Orgad, 'Forced to Be Free: The Limits of European Tolerance' (2021) 34 *Harvard Human Rights Journal* 1, 3–10.

[30] S Mancini, 'L'Olanda dalla "tragedia multiculturale" alla deriva identitaria' in G Cerrina Feroni and V Federico (eds), *Strumenti, Percorsi e Strategie dell'Integrazione nelle Società Multiculturali* (Naples, Edizioni Scientifiche Italiane, 2018) 478–79.

[31] M Avbelj and JL Cernic, *The Impact of European Institutions on the Rule of Law and Democracy. Slovenia and Beyond* (Oxford, Hart, 2020) 242.

[32] Orgad (n 29) 11.

[33] *Bundesgericht* (18 June 1993) 119.

[34] *Bundesgericht* (7 March 2012).

that included swimming in 1993,[35] but refused the same request in 2013.[36] Pan-European institutions have approved these policies. Indeed, the Council of Europe and the EU have been increasingly suspicious of Islam and deferential to Muslim-hostile national policies. The Council of Europe has long recognised religious freedom among its core concerns. When the European Commission of Human Rights was subsumed into the Strasbourg court in 1998, it offered applicants an important forum to seek redress for domestic violations of human rights, including religious freedom. The EU's core business was largely confined to economic issues for decades. Only in the early twenty-first century, after the proclamation of the Charter of Fundamental Rights (2000), did the EU adopt a more rights-focused agenda. The EU further strengthened its protection of fundamental freedoms, including freedom of religion, when in 2007 it entrenched in its Treaty the obligation to respect the European Convention of Human Rights.

Neither the European Court of Human Rights (ECtHR) nor the EU has developed a universal model of the relationship between religions and the state. Such a task is beyond their powers, as it would interfere with the multi-various national models that exist among Member States. The ECtHR has thus addressed issues pertaining to religious freedom for decades within an impressively diverse spectrum of church and state relationships, ranging from French *laicité* and Greek confessionalism to English religious establishment. The EU has explicitly committed not to implement policies which interfere with national church and state relationship models.[37]

Despite the variety of national models and its own limited power, the ECtHR has promulged the conception that the Convention adheres to a model of 'state neutrality', an expression meant to convey the importance that Member States place on the protection of religious pluralism.[38] The ECtHR itself, however, has displayed a limited concern for religious pluralism, especially in cases concerning Islam. Multiple applications challenging prohibitions of wearing headscarves and other Muslim garments in public places were lost at the ECtHR, which found that such provisions were within the state's margin of appreciation. The way the Court carved out such a margin is unpersuasive, especially if one considers the ban on Muslim veils. The Court afforded France a wide margin of appreciation, after stating that it had not been able to identify any general trend in Europe on that issue that would make France an outlier. In fact, the Court did not identify any state pattern on the ban of veils simply because the overwhelming majority of countries had not enacted any rules on the subject. As a result, the Court

[35] *Bundeswerwaltungsgericht* (25 August 1993).

[36] *Bundeswerwaltungsgericht* (8 November 2016).

[37] A Pin and J Witte, 'Meet the New Boss of Religious Freedom: The New Cases of the Court of Justice of the European Union' (2021) 55 *Texas Journal of International Law* 223, 230.

[38] On the concept of 'neutrality' and its use to protect religious pluralism within the European Court of Human Rights' caselaw, see A Pin, 'Does Europe Need Neutrality? The Old Continent in Search of Identity' (2014) 3 *Brigham Young University Law Review* 605, 613.

paradoxically read the lack of a ban in several European states in favour of the state that had introduced such a prohibition.[39] The Court did not always resort to using the margin of appreciation to legitimise limitations on religious freedom for Muslims. Sometimes it explicitly endorsed controversial domestic policy arguments, such as the duty that citizens 'socialise' with each other. Although no article of the Convention mentions the obligation to 'socialise', the Court adopted this obligation to reinforce the legitimacy of the French prohibition on wearing veils in public places,[40] as well as to justify a Swiss school's denial of an exemption to Muslim girls from mixed swimming lessons.[41]

When the Court of Justice of the European Union (CJEU) started confronting religious freedom issues, it drew heavily on the jurisprudence of the ECtHR in a way that was largely detrimental to Muslims. The most well-known examples concern Muslim employees wishing to wear the religious headscarf in the workplace. Despite the EU Charter's concern for religious freedom, the EU Court ruled against the employees, finding that a firm can prohibit the use of religious garments in order to protect its own image of neutrality.[42] Religious freedom for Muslims has also yielded to animal rights in the CJEU. In a long strand of cases, notwithstanding EU provisions that protect religious slaughter, Belgian bans on Jewish and Muslim slaughter practices have survived the Court's scrutiny.[43] As a result, in part of Belgium it has become unlawful for both Muslims and Jews to slaughter animals according to their millennia-old religious dietary rules.

Although the CJEU has started dealing with religious freedom recently,[44] its approach is much more capacious and capable of affecting the lives of Muslims in Europe in the medium and long term to a much greater extent than the ECtHR. The ECtHR has mostly condoned state limitations on religious freedom and crafted a legal framework (consisting of the concept of neutrality and the duty to socialise) to justify its deferential approach toward domestic policies. However, the CJEU has actively prioritised corporate image and animal welfare over individual and collective religious needs. Since EU law prevails over national laws, and the Court's rulings are directly enforceable in domestic courts,[45] the CJEU's case law on religious freedom for Muslims is likely to have a significant effect on domestic policies. For instance, the Court's concept of neutrality is capable of

[39] Cleveland (n 26) 224–25.

[40] *SAS v France*, App no 43845/11 (2014) (Grand Chamber).

[41] *Osmanoglu and Kocabas v Switzerland*, App no 29086/12, decided 10 January 2017 (Third Section).

[42] *Achbita v G4S Secure Solutions*, C-157/15, 14 March 2017; *IX v WABE and MH Mueller Handels GmbH v MJ*, C-804/18 and C-341/19, 15 July 2021.

[43] *Liga van Moskeeën en Islamitische Organisaties Provincie Antwerpen VZW and Others*, C-426/16, 29 May 2018; *Œuvre d'assistance aux bêtes d'abattoirs (OABA) v Ministre de l'Agriculture et de l'Alimentation*, C-497/17, 26 February 2019; *Centraal Israëlitisch Consistorie van België et al v Vlaamse Regering*, C-336/19, 17 December 2020.

[44] See M Hill, 'Freedom of Religion: Strasbourg and Luxembourg Compared' in C Durham and D Thayer (eds), *Religion and Equality: Law in Conflict* (Abingdon, Routledge, 2016) 25–34.

[45] ibid.

shielding economic enterprises desirous of banning headscarves and other religious symbols not just from individual complaints, but also from state policies designed to protect Muslims' rights. All in all, a significant number of institutions and legal orders in Europe seem to have subscribed to an idea of human rights as a secular religion – 'a creed … a metaphysics', as Michael Ignatieff called them in his 1999–2000 Tanner Lectures.[46] Such a practice seems to fail Islamic minorities, who seldom receive civic respect or judicial protection. The combination of national and supra-national policies and judicial rulings that formally align with the values of liberalism but actually embody an aggressive version of secularism, seems to have created a hostile environment for Muslims. Religious groups, which are perceived as exotic or not well-rooted in European societies, find it very hard to have their needs heard, understood and met to the maximum extent.

IV. Conclusion

Ronan McCrea defined the EU's approach to religion as 'based on two pillars: the predominantly Christian religious heritage of its Member States; and the strong secular and humanist tradition that limits the political and legal influence of religion and requires some degree of separation between religion and state.'[47] McCrea's statement also defines the ambivalence in Europe to Islamic claims and needs. Populist forces often emphasise their Christian component to resist Muslims' requests, while liberal supporters pursue the same objective by arguing that religious diversity should find its proper place in a purely secular environment.

Populism has been a matter of concern in Europe since the early 2010s. Its anti-immigration and anti-globalisation stance, ambivalence toward rights, and national identity-based narratives have certainly worsened the position of Muslims in Europe and made their integration more difficult. Curiously, liberal forces that promote constitutionalism in Europe, at both the national and supranational level, have also been somewhat reluctant to provide Muslims with strong religious freedom protections. The explanation for this phenomenon is that the populists' attachment to European religious heritage treats Islam as an exotic demographic presence, rather like an uninvited guest. On the other hand, the type of European liberalism that has espoused secularism often fails to understand the extent to which ostensibly neutral policies end up harming the religious freedom of minorities. Some strands of liberalism even take the position of opposing Islamic education and Muslim lifestyle altogether as they understand contemporary liberalism to be a thick and demanding public philosophy, rather than a basic common framework. And, given the size of Muslim communities now living in

[46] M Ignatieff, *Human Rights as Politics and Idolatry* (Princeton, Princeton University Press, 2001) 52.

[47] R McCrea, 'Religion in the Constitutional Order of the European Union' in S Mancini (ed), *Constitutions and Religion* (Cheltenham, Edward Elgar, 2020) 307.

countries that have the reputation of being particularly attached to modern and postmodern freedoms, such as France, Belgium and the Netherlands, the impact of these countries' policies on Islam is broader and more comprehensive than what occurs in Poland or Hungary, which host much smaller numbers of Muslims.

The paradoxical result of the clash between populist forces that exploit prevailing religious traditions and liberals who are antagonistic to religion is troubling – and not just for European Muslims. The social ramifications of the hostility toward Muslims from both populists and liberals are potentially very harmful for anyone, particularly in light of the grip of violent extremism within certain Islamic groups in Europe. Terrorists such as ISIS and their supporters have developed a strategy that leverages the socio-cultural rifts between Muslims and non-Muslims in Europe. They are confident that their terrorist activities will problematise Islam as a threat to Europe and widen the gap of mistrust between Muslims and non-Muslims. This process will further isolate Muslim believers from the rest of the society, pushing them to embrace, or at least sympathise with, extremism. Paradoxically, the populists sceptical about the possibility of integrating Muslims and the supporters of liberalism in Europe who aim to integrate Muslims into a forcibly neutral public sphere both play into the hands of these extremists.

The time seems to be ripe for a thorough reconsideration of constitutionalism in Europe both at the state level and at the supra-national level. Europe is in need of a framework that neither replaces national models and traditions with a one-size-fits-all secularism and church–state separation, nor overlooks religious minorities willing to contribute to public life. Such a reconsideration will be helpful to Muslims as well as to other Europeans who seek to preserve peace and avoid the development of self-isolated communities wherein extremism can flourish.

For Islam to be integrated in Europe, Europeans as well as Muslims must be persuaded that they both belong here. As Rowan Williams once emphasised, 'to understand *belonging* in our society today is to try to come to terms with a very broad range of identities, motives, visions.'[48] The issue is what type of constitutionalism is the more likely to foster such an approach.

[48] R Williams, 'The Archbishop of Canterbury's speech at the launch of Inter Faith Week' (21 November 2011), available at www.rowanwilliams.archbishopofcanterbury.org.

PART II

Religious Freedom and Other Human Rights

7

Respecting Human Rights by Reconciling the Rights of Muslim Communities and State Policies

FRANCIS MESSNER

I. The Current Context

Muslim populations in European states do not form a homogeneous group that shares the same religious ideas and cultural traditions.[1] On the contrary, they are divided into different (sometimes doctrinally antinomic) streams, which are, more often than not, also dependent on foreign states. Muslims of Turkish origin are thus composed of individuals affiliated with the Turkish-Islamic Union for Religious Affairs (DITIB), (which is both an administrative part of the Turkish state and a religious authority), Millî Görüş (referred to as the Turkish Muslim brothers) and Alevis, a denomination close to Shiism. Similarly, in France, while North African Islam is the majority denomination of Islam, Turkish Islam prevails in Eastern France, while in the *département* of Reunion Island, Islam of Indian origin predominates.[2] Accordingly, Muslim populations can be greater in number or, conversely, tiny and even almost non-existent. In this sense, the example cited of Islam as a community of believers united in the *Ummah* remains an objective still to be achieved.

Problems relating to the organisation and status of the Muslim faith that are now constantly being raised and dealt with by European states have been generated by this fragmentation and fostered by various religious prelates and political powers abroad. These problems have arisen due to the lack of, and difficulty in

[1] For sociological and legal data on Islam see the EUREL database at www.eurel.info; for France, see P Portier and JP Willaime, *La religion dans la France contemporaine: Entre sécularisation et recomposition* (Paris, Armand Colin, 2021).

[2] M Arkoun, *Histoire de l'islam et des musulmans en France* (Paris, Albin Michel, 2006) 1220; H Amod, 'Les statuts des imams à l'île de la Réunion' in F Messner (ed), *Le statut des ministres du culte musulman en France: Etudes comparatives et proposition de charte nationale* (Strasbourg, Presses universitaries de Strasbourg, 2021) 153–64.

setting up, centralised representation as well as the difficulty of creating rules to detail the various elements of any proposed organisation's structure and operation. As a result, the training, recruitment and status of leaders and ministers of the Muslim faith constitute a major hurdle in most countries with prominent Muslim communities.[3]

The argument as to the 'specificity' of the Muslim faith has often been put forward to justify this chaotic situation. Under this argument, Islam's 'own character', the way it sees itself, and its right to freedom of organisation, all constitute obstacles to its integration within the ecclesiastical law. Under that view, public authorities would be harming Islam by making it fit into a single and centralised framework, while drawing on religious policies that are now outdated, such as Regalism, Gallicanism, nineteenth-century Josephism, or even post-colonial responses. In France, some socio-political actors believe that there is no reason to engage in discussions on organising the Muslim faith and integrating it into the French system of legal status of religious bodies because the system does not actually exist, as religion is an exclusively private matter within French *laïcité*.

Yet the 'specificity' argument of the Muslim faith is undermined both by Islamic doctrine and the legal statutes and administrative practices in force in European and non-European states where Islam is the majority religion. Indeed, if the founding texts of the Muslim religion do not impose an organisational model (which is also the case for the founding texts of Christianity and Judaism), they also do not oppose the structured organisation of Muslim communities. Moreover, many non-European countries where Islam is the state religion, or a recognised form of religion, have organised Islam in an authoritarian manner within their administrative structure. As a result, the status of ministers of religion is, in most cases, determined by Muslim states, while it is actually ignored in *fiqh* jurisprudence.[4] Even Saudi Arabia, which is opposed to the codification of Islamic law, has conferred a status on imams. Finally, some European states (notably Austria, Belgium and Spain)[5] have taken up, with varying degrees of success, the challenge of integrating Islam into the first levels of their statutes or system of faiths.

The relative disorganisation of the Muslim communities in Europe can be explained by various factors. Islam does not benefit from the same anteriority and, consequently, expertise in ecclesiastical law as historically European religions, which have, over the centuries and decades, fit into the mould they have negotiated with public authorities. These historically European religions also benefit from

[3] See Messner (ibid); F Messner (ed), 'Quel statut pour les ministres du culte ?' (2019) 8 *Revue du droit des religions*.

[4] See A Moussa Ramadan, 'Les conditions de l'imamat dans la prière rituelle: La position des juristes musulmans' in Messner (n 2) 19–46; S Diamil Niane, 'Les statuts des imams au Sénégal' in Messner (n 2) 233–48.

[5] See G Robbers (ed), *State and Church in the European Union* (Baden-Baden, Nomos, 2019); M Ventura (ed), *The Legal Status of Old and New Religious Minorities in the European Union* (Granada, Comares, 2021); R Potz and W Wieshaider (eds), *Islam and the European Union* (Leuven, Peeters Publishers, 2005).

the support of a solid network of legal experts. In addition, some Muslim leaders have wanted to distance themselves from the national system of faiths in order to assert their religious differences and refuse what they felt to be the westernisation or 'churchification' of Islam. Above all, European Islam is made up of communities of national origin (notably Algerian, Moroccan, Turkish and Pakistani) for which consular representations continue to play a predominant role by strongly influencing how these communities function.[6] Only the Muslim Brothers has institutionally distanced itself from foreign states and somewhat adeptly favours the cross-disciplinarity of Sunni schools of law.

This situation is unsatisfactory both for Muslim communities and public authorities in Europe. The institutional fragmentation of Islam does not facilitate the emergence of doctrinal discourse accepted as legitimate and capable of imposing itself on the various communities that are faced by the multiplication of fundamentalist and radical discourse disseminated by individuals and marginal communities, generally through social networks. This lack of a liberal counter-discourse adapted to the European context is reinforced by public servant imams dispatched on secondment by Algeria, Turkey and, to a lesser extent, Morocco. These religious officials do not always master the language of the host country and have limited knowledge of its socio-religious context. Their impact on young Muslims is therefore weak and causes them to seek answers elsewhere. This situation does not favour the integration of Muslim populations and, on the contrary, provokes reactions of incomprehension, particularly among populations of states where assimilation was until recently the rule.

This lack of organisation is also disadvantaging Muslim communities, slowing down their ability to act. As a result, in France, the representative body of the Muslim faith, the French Council of the Muslim Faith (*Conseil français du Culte musulman*/CFCM), as well as the regional councils of the Muslim faith (*Conseils régionaux du culte musulman*/CRCM), are, unlike the Christian and Jewish faiths, underpinned by common law on associations in accordance with Article 1 of the statutes of the CFCM, drawn up with public authority approval. Such structuring prevents creation of any union of religious associations representing the Muslim religious community at the national level.[7] Such lack of organisation has financial consequences. Associations formed under the Law of 1901 that represent the Muslim faith do not benefit from tax advantages attached to the special status of religious associations. The lack of a clear separation between cultural and religious activities is also an obstacle to effective management of the various religious, cultural and educational activities. Lastly, organising and representing the Muslim faith takes place outside the legal system of religious bodies established to facilitate

[6] S Akgönül, *Religions de Turquie, religions des Turcs: nouveaux acteurs dans l'Europe élargie* (Paris, L'Harmattan, 2005).

[7] Any such union would need to be made up exclusively of religious associations, as is the case with the Israelite Consistory of France, the Synod of the United Protestant Church of France and the Episcopal Conference of France.

relations, cooperation or dialogue between the French state and religions, and above all to integrate religions into society.[8]

II. Recommended Solutions

Policy on religion in European states concerned by a significant rise in Islamist radicalism, lack of organisation of Muslim communities and interventionism of foreign states is characterised by the desire to integrate Islam into the legal status of religious bodies, encourage adherence to common values, and facilitate recruitment and training of religious leaders in Europe.

A. Religions Committing to Respect Fundamental Rights

For many years, the doctrine of majority religions in Europe has nurtured the foundation for common values. Today, European states make their support for Islam and, more broadly, all religious communities conditional on a commitment to respect fundamental rights. This reversal is the norm in all states today, even if its application differs according to individual procedures. As a result, the agreements signed on 26 January 2015 between the State of the Grand Duchy of Luxembourg and religious communities established in Luxembourg, stipulate in their preambles that the religious communities benefiting from the agreements guarantee 'respect for constitutional rights and freedoms, public order and democratic values, the promotion of human rights and equal treatment, as well as equality between men and women.'[9] Breaking these commitments will result in the termination of public subsidies. Luxembourg, which has ruled out the idea of negotiating a concordat and favoured the signing of public law agreements with the archbishop, treats all the religions covered by the agreement equally in this respect, whereas other states continue to make a distinction between the various religious groups.

Along the same lines, the 2013 agreement signed between the City-State of Hamburg and Muslim communities stipulates that both partners identify with a foundation of common values resulting from the German Basic Law, which notably includes human dignity, respect for fundamental rights, tolerance towards other forms of religion and philosophical thought, and respect for democratic principles within life in society. What is more, both partners jointly commit to combating all forms of discrimination based on origin, gender, sexual orientation,

[8] R Puza and N Doe (eds), *Religion and Law in Dialogue: Convenantal and Non-convenantal Cooperation between State and Religion in Europe* (Leuven, Peeters Publishers, 2006).

[9] F Messner, 'La réforme des cultes au Grand-Duché du Luxembourg en 2015' (2016) 3 *Revue du droit des religions* 185; Robbers (n 5) 353–62.

religion and political convictions.[10] Such demands have not yet been formulated in the conventions and agreements signed between other German federal states and the Catholic and regional Protestant churches.

Similarly, Article 2 of the Austrian Islam Law 2015 states that Muslim religious societies, their local communities and their individual members have a duty to respect the laws. Doctrine and rules specific to Islam cannot be a substitute for Austrian law.[11] The Austrian Government was less strict with the Catholic Church in the early twentieth century. The Concordat of 5 June 1933 states in Article 1 that '[the Republic of Austria] recognises the right of the Catholic Church to enact laws, decrees and regulations within the scope of its powers; it will not prevent or complicate exercising this right.'

Lastly, in France, the 2021 law[12] reinforcing respect for the principles of the French Republic has introduced an *a priori* system of recognition of religious associations and made granting public subsidies to associations (including associations with a religious purpose that have not been recognised as religious associations) subject to a commitment to the Republic.[13]

Generally speaking, a Muslim federation that refuses to sign the Charter of Principles for French Islam[14] drafted by the CFCM with the support of the public authorities will end up marginalised. The CFCM's eight-page charter includes a commitment to respect human and civil rights – liberty, equality and fraternity, *laïcité*, public order and the laws of the Republic – while also promoting reason and free will. The Charter also calls for changing one's religion not to be criminalised, promoting equality between men and women, rejecting all discrimination based on gender and sexual orientation, combating all forms of instrumentalisation of Islam for political purposes, and respecting the secular neutrality of public services. Federations that have not signed the charter are no longer considered representative of French Islam and are no longer invited to the Islamic dialogue bodies created by the Ministry of the Interior. In addition, they are at risk of being barred from receiving any public funding.[15]

[10] Agreement between the City State of Hamburg and the Muslim Communities 20/5038, Art 2.

[11] See R Potz, 'State and Church in Austria' in Robbers (n 5) 435–60; F Messner, 'La loi de 2015 sur l'Islam en Autriche' (2016) 2 *Revue du droit des religions* 177.

[12] Loi n° 2021-1109 du 24 août 2021, *JO*, 25 août 2021.

[13] Art 12, loi du 24 août 2021, the associations concerned are committed, first, 'To respect the principles of liberty, equality, fraternity and dignity of the human person, as well as the symbols of the Republic within the meaning of Article 2 of the Constitution. Second, not to call into question the secular character of the Republic; third, to abstain from any action prejudicial to public order.' See CC, 13 août 2021, n° 823 DC, *JO*, n° 197 du 25 août 2021. The symbols of the Republic include, according to the decision of the Constitutional Council in 2021, the national emblem, the national anthem, and the motto of the Republic. Similarly, according to the Constitutional Council, 'by actions prejudicial to public order' is meant actions likely to cause serious disturbances to peace and public security.

[14] www.aa.com.tr/uploads/userFiles/a0375fc1-552e-4508-bc69-6dc1b8417822/Charte-des-principes-17.01.2021-1-.pdf.

[15] See F Messner, 'Le financement des paroisses et des mosquées en droit local alsacien-mosellan. L'affaire de la construction de la mosquée Eyyub Sultan de Strasbourg' (2021) *Revue du droit local* 7.

In this context of respect for state law, the question of the application of Sharia law is, with few exceptions, theoretical. In most European states, forms of normative regulation of religions are not legal orders generating law recognised by the state or binding on the state. When the judge is confronted with an element relating to the internal law of religions, this element is qualified as a religious matter. The religious matter in this case characterises a social or individual, yet non-legal, reality. The state intervenes in a religious conflict which it is called to decide upon according to its own principles and legal rules. Judges do not take on board a confessional normative order which they do not recognise.

B. Consolidating National Funding for Faiths, Putting an End to Secondment of Imams and Promoting Training of Imams in European States

Foreign states are keen to maintain control over their nationals who have settled in Europe. These individuals become potential pressure groups within European states and are likely to support or generate opposition to the political regime of their country of origin or, on the contrary, to bolster its power. This foreign state influence is most often achieved through economic dependence, which can take two forms: either sending imams who are public servants in the state of origin or paying an annual endowment to certain mosques (which are sometimes owned by the funding foreign state).[16] These external interventions, which were initially accepted as a lesser evil, are now perceived by European states as mechanisms that facilitate communitarianism, undermining integration policies and adherence to commonly shared values. Policies implemented by governments in the relevant states to counter such initiatives focus on the same objective, but their implementation varies according to the particularities of the laws governing national religions. For example, Austria requires members of Muslim religious societies incorporated under public law to self-fund all religious and worshipping needs. One of the aims of this provision is to end the secondment of imams who are public servants of the Turkish Directorate of Religious Affairs (*Dyanet*). Austrian Imams, therefore, need to be trained and recruited within Austria.[17] For the legislator, financial support from a foreign state creates a dependence, which does not guarantee the lasting existence of a religious society incorporated under public law. In the Austrian example, the emphasis is on training Muslim religious leaders, which is delivered by the state university thanks to the creation of a faculty of Muslim theology at

Also see R Potz and W Wieshaider (eds), *Juridictions religieuses et l'Etat – Religious Adjudication and the State* (Granada, Comares, 2015).

[16] The municipal council of Angers opposed the acquisition of a mosque by the kingdom of Morocco; see www.lefigaro.fr/actualite-france/angers-s-oppose-a-la-cession-d-une-mosquee-au-maroc-20201027.

[17] See Potz (n 11).

the University of Vienna.[18] 'Religious leader' is meant to include not just imams, but also teachers of Muslim religion in state schools. Similarly, in Germany, five faculties of Muslim theology (Tübingen, Münster, Osnabrück, Frankfurt am Main and Giessen) were created in state universities following a recommendation by the German Science and Humanities Council (*Wissenschaftsrat*) in 2010.[19] This Council believes that creating faculties of Muslim theology in state universities will guarantee the quality of teaching and research within this discipline, enable debate with other forms of thought and ideology, and provide the conceptual basis for inter-religious dialogue as a guarantee of religious peace. The Council also believes that imams should be trained in Germany.

Belgium recognised the Muslim faith in 1974 and later paid the imams of this religion due to difficulties related to the emergence of its representation. But this integration of Islam into the system of recognised religions in Belgium, which was not accompanied by any ban on foreign funding, has not prevented Turkey from continuing to appoint imams for secondment, while all imam positions paid for by Belgium are not filled. Creating a faculty of Muslim theology remains an objective in Belgium. As a result, the Faculty of Theology and Religious Studies of the Catholic University of Leuven has complemented its master's degree in religious studies with an option in 'Muslim theology', which is closer to human and social sciences of religions than theology. Attempts to create a Muslim theological faculty in Leuven have not yet succeeded, despite the creation of an institute to promote training on Islam in Wallonia.[20]

In France, the President of the Republic has announced the end of secondment of imams for 2024.[21] Agreements with Algeria, Turkey and Morocco will not be renewed and *laïcité* has not prevented the search for a solution to training imams on national territory. Initially, the Government recommended training on the integration of Muslim ministers via a university diploma based on knowledge of French institutions, French religious history, *laïcité* and the laws of the Republic, and legal status of religious bodies. This solution, aimed at educating seconded imams, has made it possible to avoid awkward discussions on the theological training of ministers of the Muslim faith, the implementation of which is deemed by the administration to be contrary to *laïcité*. A 2017 decree has made this diploma mandatory for chaplains paid for by the state.[22] The diploma requirement

[18] See W Wieshaider, 'Les enjeux de l'ancrage de la théologie musulmane dans une université publique en Autriche' in F Messner (ed), *L'enseignement universitaire de la théologie musulmane. Perspectives comparatives* (Paris, Cerf, 2018) 113–20.

[19] www.wissenschaftsrat.de/download/archiv/9678-10.pdf?__blob=publicationFile&v=1.

[20] JF Husson, 'Le statut des imams en Belgique' in Messner (n 2) 165–84; and Husson, 'Attentes des pouvoirs publics en matière de formation des cadres musulmans. Le cas Belge' in Messner (n 18) 149–62, For the training of religious leaders, especially Muslims, in European states, see F Messner (ed), 'La formation des cadres religieux en Europe' (Granada, Comares, 2015).

[21] www.elysee.fr/emmanuel-macron/2020/10/02/la-republique-en-actes-discours-du-president-de-la- republique-sur-le-theme-de-la-lutte-contre-les-separatismes.

[22] F Messner and PH Prélot, 'Un diplôme pour l'aumônerie des services publics' (2017) 4 *Revue du droit des religions* 181.

initially envisaged for Muslim chaplains has been extended, for reasons of non-discrimination, to paid chaplains of all relevant religious denominations.

The creation of civil and civic training has not solved the question of theological training and, more broadly, training in the human and social sciences of Islam. The 2015 Messner report on the training of Muslim religious leaders advocated for the establishment of centres of excellence in the human and social sciences of Islam within certain universities to bring together the best French specialists in this field 'while developing networks associating research lecturers and researchers from universities abroad'.[23] Similarly, the report on the training of imams and Muslim religious leaders by Catherine Mayeur-Jaouen, Mathilde Philip-Gay and Rachid Benzine (submitted to the Ministers of Education and the Interior in 2016) advocates the creation of centres of excellence in Islamology, Muslim worlds and religious matters.[24] Both reports recommended the creation of courses split between public universities and private training institutes for imams.[25] These split courses would give access to learning non-theological disciplines in the field of humanities and social sciences. The decision to put an end to secondment of imams has led to a recent acceleration in the creation of non-denominational institutes of Islamology capable of training Muslim religious leaders. In Strasbourg, for instance, a regional institute of Islamology, constituted as an inter-faculty department, will offer a bachelor's and master's degree in Islamology, a master's degree in inter-religious studies, and a university diploma in civil and civic education, as well as diplomas adapted to the career paths of Muslim religious leaders and the implementation of research programmes on Islam. The Great Mosque of Strasbourg and the training school for Muslim chaplains in Strasbourg have already committed themselves to enrolling their current or future managers in one of these diploma courses, thereby assuming the responsibility of complementing the courses delivered by the public university with their own courses in denominational theology. This solution enables these students to benefit from a status and acquire a state diploma at the end of their course while preparing for the duties of being an imam or teacher of religion.

C. Organisation and Representation of the Muslim Faith

The fragmentation of Muslim communities into federations and nationalities and the influence of foreign states do not facilitate unified organisation of the Muslim

[23] F Messner, 'Rapport sur la formation des cadres religieux musulmans' (Paris, Ministère de l'intérieur, Ministère de l'Éducation nationale, de l'Enseignement supérieur et de la Recherche, 2014) 27.

[24] 'Mission de réflexion sur la formation des imams et des cadres religieux musulmans', Report, available at www.letudiant.fr.

[25] By dual course, we mean a system of training for ministers of the Muslim faith, certified by a central organisation of the Muslim faith, including a course in the humanities and social sciences of Islam provided by public universities and a course supported by private establishments of Muslim theology belonging to religious communities.

faith. This organisation has two key elements: the creation of clearly identified representation; and integration of this religion into the legal status of religious bodies. Both elements are linked.

Thus, in France, organisation and representation of the Muslim faith occurs outside the system of religions established by legal texts,[26] whereas the purpose of this system is to facilitate relations between the French state and religions, and to integrate religions into society.[27] Avoiding resorting to religious association status in representing the Muslim faith stems from a desire to distinguish the respective areas of competence of the CFCM/CRCM and the federations. The CFCM would be entrusted with tasks of an essentially administrative nature, while the CRCM would be entrusted with supervisory activities related to spirituality, doctrine and theology. The CFCM, which represents the Muslim communities and several member federations that have not signed the Charter of Principles for French Islam and have therefore become *persona non grata* in their dealings with public authorities, is currently in a state of collapse. In future, public authorities will essentially cooperate or engage in dialogue with local or *département* councils for the Muslim faith in line with government policy on religion. These partners will constitute representation at national level in a form yet to be determined. In practice, the Government is setting out the rules of the game and choosing its partners according to their acceptance of those rules. It is difficult, in this case, to speak of strict separation.

Moreover, the Law Reinforcing Respect of Republican Principles (2021) tends to organise the Muslim communities within the framework of religious associations. If public authorities cannot force local Muslim communities to organise themselves within the framework of the Law of 1905 (religious associations), they have the possibility of making them more attractive and thus diverting these communities away from associations formed under common law (Law of 1901). These associations, most often mixing the cultural and the religious, will henceforth be subject to the same financial checks and obligations as religious associations for their religious activities, without benefiting from the same tax advantages. Associations under the Law of 1901 which are in charge of the exercise of worship will accumulate all the disadvantages without being able to access advantages granted to religious associations. The religious nature of an association, which allows it to benefit from tax advantages, must now be established by the state representative in the *département* at the time of its creation and no longer *a posteriori* as part of a procedure for accepting a donation or a legacy.

Under the German law concerning religions, a religious community must have one main objective – to meet the religious needs of its members – and it must provide lasting guarantees and be run by an authority which has the legitimacy

[26] Loi du 9 décembre 1905.

[27] F Messner, 'Zur schwierigen Organisation muslimischer Gemeinschaften im französischen Recht' in Von der Decken and A Günzel (eds), *Staat – Religion – Recht: Festchrift fur Gerhard Robbers zum 70* (Baden-Baden, Nomos, 2020) 439–56.

to interpret and define dogma.[28] However, the federal states concerned consider that these conditions are not being met in their entirety by Muslim communities. Some federal states have added a further condition to the law: respect for German law. This condition must then be written into the statutes of the public law entity and authorities representing it must have an attitude that does not contradict this commitment. The absence of a clearly identified representation of the Muslim religion and the difficulty for the *Länder* to establish Muslim communities as public law corporations have not prevented them from creating faculties of Muslim theology with the support of the German state and from implementing Muslim religious education in state schools. In some cases, this lack of representation is circumvented, and original mechanisms are found to respond to urgent situations.

III. Conclusion

A recurring theme in this book is the extent to which the treatment of Muslims by national governments constitutes a violation of their human rights. At first sight, an evaluation of European religious policies would suggest the contrary: that the approach adopted by European states is to force Muslim communities to share and accept the guarantees laid down in human rights with an emphasis on non-discrimination, gender equality and freedom of religion (which includes the right to change one's religion). The values commonly shared in Europe are now underpinned by human rights, not religious principles. While this insistence on respect for human rights is not yet systematic for historical Christian religions, they may be collateral victims of these new policies on religion. The application of the principle of equal treatment between religious denominations sometimes subjects them to constraints recently imposed on the Muslim religion.

This adherence to human rights is considered the condition *sine qua non* for constructing a European Islam, which filters down into each nation under the headings of French, Belgian, Austrian etc. Islam. In this sense, policies on religion pursued by European states affected by the presence of a significant Muslim community resemble one another in regard to their means of effectively achieving this affiliation. In any case, it is important to establish legitimate representation at national level, facilitate the financial autonomy of Muslim communities, and train leaders of this religion (in particular, imams in European countries) in line with the academic criteria in effect in public or public/private universities. These three elements have the same objective of integrating the Muslim communities into European society and its foundation of values by loosening or erasing the bonds of dependence tying it to foreign states.

[28] K Hartung, 'Gesetz zur Regelung der Verleihung von Körperschaftsrechten an Religions- und Weltanschauungsgemeinschaften (Körperschaftsstatusgesetz)' (2015) 60 *Zeitschrift für evangelisches Kirchenrecht* 165.

The principles of neutrality of the state and autonomy of religious denominations could certainly be invoked to justify state non-intervention or non-interference in this area. However, total indifference on the part of the state could be contrary to the general interest by facilitating breaches of public order and religious peace. Indeed, the institutional fragmentation of a religion with significant social influence in a multitude of communities is facilitating production and circulation of communitarian and radical discourse in the absence of a contextualised religious discourse perceived as legitimate by the Muslim community. In other words, counter-discourses are having a hard time gaining the upper hand when faced with fundamentalist religious ideas. The lack of structure in Islam is also leading to the emergence of self-proclaimed imams without training, verified by the central religious authorities, who deliver discourses out of step with social reality. This splintering into multiple religious communities can be without consequence for society and therefore ignored by the state when it involves micro-minorities with no influence. Things are different, however, when it facilitates deviation of religious discourse and interference by a foreign power on national territory and gives rise to violence.

Integrating the Muslim faith by organising it within the favourable framework of legal status of religious bodies logically entails a trade-off in line with the principle of *do ut des*. Such organisation is a possibility that does not impede freedom of choice for Muslim groups. They can organise themselves freely within the framework of common law, without any particular supervision, when they do not wish to benefit from privileged treatment.

8

Equality and Difference: Muslim Religious Practice, Religious Tribunals and Muslim Women

SAMIA BANO

I. Introduction

Historically, Muslim women's religious experience and practice has been measured by ideas of self-identity and belonging, attendance at places of worship, frequency of prayer, study of religious texts, and adherence to religious doctrines. Much of this scholarship focuses not only upon issues concerning the rise and/or decline of Islamic religiosity and religious practice, but also the growing influence of secularism and secularisation upon religion and its consequences on emerging Muslim identities in Europe. One important contribution lies in debates on equality and difference. To what extent is this frame useful to better understand notions of inequality and disadvantage in the context of religious tribunals? Feminist scholarship draws upon feminist critiques of power to highlight the differential positions of power within social, familial and legal life. Historically, feminist scholars have focused on the patriarchal nature of religion and the limits religious practice and belief impose upon women, thereby limiting female autonomy, choice and women's rights in both the public and private spheres.[1]

The right to religious freedom and expression also underpins discussions on human rights, citizenship and equality in liberal democracies throughout western Europe. Further, the impact of secularisation upon women's religiosity raises questions of personal autonomy, choice and consent while belonging to religious communities. Debates over the legal limits of state intervention into the private lives of individuals, and the extent to which liberal principles of equality, non-discrimination and individual autonomy are manifested in law also raise important questions regarding religious freedom and belief in the context of civic society.

[1] G Stopler, 'The Liberal Bind: The Conflict between Women's Rights and Patriarchal Religion, Liberal State' (2005) 31 *Social Theory and Practice* 191.

These discussions have interacted with feminist commentary to enable critical exploration of the ways, and the extent to which, religious practice and belief may limit women's lives, in both the public and private spheres. Feminist scholars have also documented and explored the tensions inherent in much Western political theory regarding the normative values that underpin the liberal state and the difficulties associated with the social and legal regulation of minority and majority communities.[2] This literature conceptualises our understanding of equality, difference and rights, while seeking to provide a clearer framework regarding the relationship between individuals' diverse systems of belief, religious activity and the state, and debates on equality and difference.

This chapter analyses some of the complexities in contemporary debates on equality and difference through applying them to some of the debates on European Muslim women's experience of religious laws and religious tribunals to better understand how this relationship takes shape and to consider whether it produces specific outcomes for European Muslim women. Is there a conflict between traditional and/or orthodox religious belief systems and thought with secular values of equality and difference in western liberal democracies? To what extent is there a clash between 'secular' values of human rights, in particular women's equality and autonomy, and religious ideas, norms and values? This chapter uses a case study of British Muslim women and their experience of religious tribunals to consider the ways in which concepts such as equality and difference may operate and clash within and between state law and minority religious groups.

II. Muslim Law in Europe

The presence of diverse Muslim communities in Europe has raised questions over the extent to which norms and values based on religious belief and identity practised by Muslims are deemed antithetical to the values and aspirations of western liberal democracies. Indeed, the emergence of transnational and trans-local communities and its consequences for liberal legality has recently received extensive and sophisticated scholarly attention. From this body of literature, one is better placed to understand the underlying socio, economic and political factors that carry this process along and how possible conflicts and interactions take shape. One sees how identities, allegiances and relationships are built and forged, and their impact on local institutions, agencies and populations.[3] One can learn the ways in which social actors, networks and communities expand and emerge,

[2] A Phillips, *Multiculturalism without Culture* (Princeton, Princeton University Press, 2007).

[3] I Barbero, 'Migrant Struggles and Legal Pluralism: claiming citizenship across multiple scales' (2013) 45 *Journal of Legal Pluralism and Unofficial Law* 357.

which raises fundamental questions about what is understood as the self, community, religion, and the role of the law in the formation of religious identity.

In Europe, the legal dimension plays a significant role as, in its positive form, it delineates the boundaries of the public/private spheres (and those deemed insiders and outsiders) and where conflicts between the legal and non-legal take shape. In this way Benda-Beckmann and Griffiths describe law 'as a powerful form of cultural expression that operates as a potential source for social, economic or political power, constraining and enabling social practices, with both intended and unintended consequences.'[4] The mobility of law as a process of transnational laws, and translocal relations as a series of interacting local and national laws which intermesh and conflict, can create new visions of law and legal relations in western societies and the rest of the world. As regards Western Europe, the focus has been on the 'mass migrations from the South, particularly to Europe, but also to other parts of the global North.'[5] There is now a body of scholarship which analyses the ways in which migration has resulted in structural adjustments in various legal systems and, in particular, the ways in which European legal systems have had to grapple with a renewed assertion of religious identities and wider debates on equality and difference. The role of the state in both promoting and limiting the recognition of such practices has also been subject to criticism.

Scholars focus on the possible differences generated by majority and minority Muslim communities and how such differences may generate different claims, rights and responsibilities. Discussion has largely focused on the different types of integration models recognised by legal systems to reflect the plural and culturally diverse nature of societies. European societies are grouped as being modelled on four key types – assimilation, overlap, segregation and acculturation – and each legal system reflects this difference. Yet transnational migration also illustrates recent examples where Muslims share common concerns, for example, the banning of Islamic headscarves across Europe, the role of Islamic scholars in Europe and the Muslim world and, in particular, the role of the internet where Islamic scholars issue edicts and fatwas.[6] The place of Islam in Europe therefore continues to be subject to extensive social and political commentary with a more recent focus on the rising numbers of Muslims in Europe. The visible presence of Muslims in public is deemed as problematic leading to political initiatives to limit this presence.

[4] K Benda-Beckmann and A Griffiths, *Mobile People, Mobile Law: Expanding Legal Relations in a Contracting World*, (Farnham, Ashgate, 2005) 51.

[5] P Shah and W. Menski (eds), *Migration, Diaspora and Legal Systems in Europe*, (London, Routledge, 2006).

[6] S Ali, 'Cyberspace as emerging Muslim discursive space? Online Fatawa on women and gender relations and its impact on Muslim family law norms' (2010) 24 *International Journal of Law, Policy and the Family* 338.

III. Equality and Difference and Feminist Critiques

Throughout history, the circumscribed values that underpin Western conceptions of law and justice have strongly influenced how law is perceived and understood by contemporary feminist political and legal theorists. In describing how the law deals with questions of justice, political philosophers analyse the fragmented nature of legality and the relations between normative orders and individual rights.[7] Law is an important potential source of power and the pursuit of justice in response to the challenges presented by diverse cultural and religious communities reveals contradictory practices. The *effects* of a plural and multicultural society upon the development of English law have been extensively documented over the past 20 years by anthropologists, sociologists and, increasingly, legal scholars.[8] The debate over the nature of this interaction is often characterised as a clash of a given set of values, identities, interest claims by state law and the demands of minority religious communities. This, in turn, gives rise to central and difficult questions regarding the appropriate level and type of legal accommodation to be afforded.

Contemporary liberal thinkers, shaping the terms of liberal values in Western societies and the postcolonial world, have advanced a rather conservative agenda. Significantly, they have done so through liberal rights discourse rather than in opposition to it.[9] For many of these thinkers, the focus on religious women serves as a yardstick to consider the conflict between the rights of religious communities and the rights afforded by the liberal state. As Shireen Razack points out, women's bodies have long been the ground on which national difference is constructed.[10] When the Muslim woman's body is constituted as simply a marker of a community's place in modernity and an indicator of who belongs to national community, the pervasiveness of violence against women in the West is eclipsed. Saving Muslim women from the excesses of their society marks Western women as 'emancipated'.

In theorising these issues, it is important to begin with the recognition that religious women belong to many diverse communities and their lived experiences must therefore be understood as complex, strategic and, at times, contradictory.[11] Rosemary Hunter critiques the concept of equality as one that may be a useful frame of analysis upon which to base equality claims, but in practice ultimately fails to explain women's oppression and continued disadvantage.[12] The question

[7] R Dworkin, *Law's Empire* (London, Fontana, 1986).

[8] M Malik, *Minority Legal Systems in the UK: Multiculturalism, Minorities and the Law* (British Academy Policy Papers, 2012).

[9] R Kapur, *Erotic Justice: Law and the New Politics of Postcolonialism: Postcolonial Feminism Law Sexuality* (London, Glass House Press, 2005).

[10] S Razack, *Casting Out: The Eviction of Muslims from Western Law and Politics* (Toronto, University of Toronto Press, 2008) 86.

[11] N Ali, VS Kalra and S Sayyid (eds), *A Postcolonial People: South Asians in Britain* (London, Hurst, 2006).

[12] R Hunter, 'Alternatives to equality' in R Hunter (ed), *Rethinking Equality Projects in Law: Feminist Challenges*, Onati International Series in Law & Society (Oxford, Hart Publishing, 2008) 81–101.

of equality and difference has been addressed most closely in relation to women, religious practice and personal systems of family law.

Over the past three decades, feminist theorists have grappled with the question of how to reconcile Western interpretations of sexual equality and the autonomy of women's agency with cultural and religious difference.[13] Debates have largely focused on a clash of values scenario, within which liberal notions of equality, free will and choice have been deemed 'progressively modern' and open to all, while the continued traditional religious adherence of women belonging to minority communities has been presented as illiberal, backward and a barrier to the enhancement of women's rights. In these debates, the law and juridical liberalism (for example, anti-discrimination legislation) serve as the starting point to enhance the rights of all women. Feminist scholars have long critiqued the position of women within religious ideology and practice as conceptualised within church–state and intra-community relations. Under the project of gaining equality, feminist scholars had historically charted the ways religious doctrine served to entrench the inferior legal status of women in Western societies. Male religious leaders' control of women, denial of women's rights to freedom, choice and autonomy, and their role in defining acceptable patterns of female behaviour, underpin many of these feminist critiques.

In France, debates over the role and place of religious life in public spheres has, over the past decade, manifested itself in relation to French Muslim communities. The French state's position on secularism (*laïcité*), as one demonstrating a neutral public civic space, has been challenged on several grounds through religious practice, dress and religious personal life. In his work, El-Yousfi, traces both the formal and informal nature of religious practice within Muslim communities and the ways the French state embraces forms of governmentality of religious groups through state funding.[14] Religious identity then becomes synonymous with state funding and managing religious practice. Selby traces the historical context of the French secular model and how the nations separation of religion and politics renders Muslim religious dress (hijabs) problematic.[15]

One of the key points of contention between rights to equality and difference are enshrined in secular human rights principles and law. In contrast, religious doctrine often fails to promote these rights or actively undermines them. This has generated conflict between the notions of secularism and the religious, a conflict described as both permanent and intractable. Feminist literature explores the relationship between feminism, multiculturalism and religion in the lives of religiously diverse women living in both majority and minority communities.[16] More

[13] The concept of agency is often understood in relation to concepts of the individual, the person and the self; discussion of these questions falls outside the scope of this paper.

[14] A El-Yousfi, 'Muslims and Mosques in France: navigating the cultural/religious dichotomy through God's witnessing and the holism of Islam' (2021) 49 *Religion, State and Society* 297.

[15] JA Selby and L Beaman, 'Reposing the 'Muslim Question' (2015) 4 *Critical Research on Religion* 8.

[16] A Sundari and A Gill, 'Coercion, Consent and the Forced Marriage Debate in the UK' (2009) 17 *Feminist Legal Studies* 165.

specifically, the focus has been on the relationship between religion, women's issues, gender roles and culture. Feminism has been at the fore of attempts to understand the experience of religious women's lives in a complex and nuanced way.

Feminist writing provides many avenues for conceptualising multiple identities and multiple forms of inequality.[17] Feminist political theorists, such as Nancy Fraser and Iris Young, approach the question by considering a matrix of factors (both social and structural) which position women in particular contexts. Fraser links social relations to distinct economic and cultural societal structures and to related forms of redress, recognition and redistribution.[18] She approaches oppression as a process whereby social collectivities operate along a spectrum from injustices of distribution to recognition. For Fraser, therefore, the issue of multiple identity raises several key questions such as:

> Which identity claims are rooted in the defense of social relations of inequality and domination? And which are rooted in a challenge to such relations? … Which differences … should a democratic society seek to foster, and which, on the contrary should it aim to abolish?[19]

Meanwhile, Young provides five criteria of oppression: exploitation; marginalisation; powerlessness; cultural imperialism; and violence.[20] While her analysis can be applied to various groups (such as the elderly, or gays and lesbians), she draws upon the social constituency of 'women' to reflect upon the different dimensions of oppression they may experience on account of their gender. For both theorists, it is apparent that claims of cultural and religious difference (part of a pluralist model of power that affords minority groups limited yet significant autonomy) can be recognised only if they do not involve the oppression and subordination of women.

For many feminist legal scholars, the focus has also been squarely on the question of equality and subordination in the context of the ways in which legal regulations construct, and respond to, intersecting orders of inequality. This approach ultimately draws upon the work of legal feminists and others, who maintain that the law tends to reflect masculine values; many of the values around which the law is built, including its assumption of an individualistic 'reasonable' person, are those used and valued by men. Scholars such as Patricia Collins and Kimberley Crenshaw use the concept of intersecting identities (in this context race, class and gender) to illustrate how the law and legal relations fail to grasp the complexities of black women's lives.[21] For example, juridical liberalism expressed

[17] D Cooper, *Challenging Diversity, Rethinking Equality* (Cambridge, Cambridge University Press, 2004).

[18] N Fraser, *Scales of Justice: Reimaging Political Space in a Globalizing World* (New York, Columbia University Press, 2009).

[19] M Fraser, *Unruly Discourses: Power, Discourse and Gender in Contemporary Social Theory* (Cambridge, Polity Press, 1989).

[20] I Young, *Justice and the Politics of Difference* (Princeton, Princeton University Press, 1990).

[21] P Collins, 'Learning from the outsider within: The sociological significance of Black feminist thought' (1986) 33 *Social Problems* 14; K Crenshaw, 'Demarginalizing the Intersection of Race and Sex: A Black Feminist Critique of Antidiscrimination Doctrine' (1989) 1 *University of Chicago Forum* 139.

via legislation, such as anti-discrimination legislation, remains inadequate in understanding the position of minority ethnic women who may be situated in multiple social locations. As such, these laws simply fail to effectively redress the claims of discrimination.

Post-colonial feminist legal scholarship has identified and critiqued the hierarchical positions of power that many Western feminists occupy in equality debates. For example, Gayatri Spivak has challenged the representations of non-Western women made by both liberal inclusionists and structural bias approaches to women's human rights.[22] As Sally Engle-Merry points out, there is an urgent need to attend to cultural and religious differences and to see similar types of oppression in both majority and minority communities.[23] In addition to questioning First World feminist understandings of culture and religion, such critics also challenge structural bias, with its focus on culture, as the principal site of women's oppression. This scholarship produces a critique of power relations in the public and private spheres to demonstrate how power operates both unevenly and strategically to disempower the weak and marginalised within communities. The intersection of feminism with post-colonial analyses develops new forms of methodologies to produce 'new ways of seeing' and post-colonial knowledge. More specifically, it centres the experience of women by drawing upon political critique and analyses grounded in personal narratives.

Feminist interpretations of autonomy encourage women to make personal choices that include the autonomy of being and the right to go against what is considered the norm. This raises a number of important questions relating to how we understand autonomy, choice and agency, and whether, ultimately, autonomy and equality can ever be reconciled.

IV. European Muslim Women, Religious Practice and Sharia Councils

Family law pluralism within European Muslim communities have focused primarily upon debates on Islam law, the position of Muslim women, and what should be the limits of accommodation of religious practices within western liberal societies. These debates have raged within the United Kingdom, France, Sweden and Germany. Fadel explains:

> Given the general anxiety surrounding Islamic law in Western democracies, the fact that fear of Islamic law should be a substantial stumbling block to increasing legal pluralism in the domain of family law is ironic given the pluralistic nature of Islamic

[22] G. Spivak, 'Can the subaltern speak?' in N Nelson and L Grossberg (eds), *Marxism and the Interpretation of Culture* (Chicago, Illinois University Press, 1988).

[23] S Engle-Merry, *The New Legal Realism, Studying Law* Globally (Cambridge, Cambridge University Press, 2016).

> law's regulation of the family. At the same time, legal recognition of family law pluralism is not without genuine risks. The rules of Islamic family law, as well as the rules and traditions of other subcommunities within a liberal polity, are not substantively equivalent to the generally applicable rules of civil law.[24]

In her work, Mulki Al-Sharmani traces divorce practices among Somali Muslim migrants in Helsinki. In an in-depth four-year qualitative study she demonstrates the ways in which family ties and relationships are navigated among national contexts and the ways in which gender operates as a marker of difference and power creating new forms of religious discourse demonstrating that 'gender and religion are interconnected and experienced in fluid, dynamic and layered ways'.[25]

Applying this analysis to the use of religious tribunals, one can see ways in which power relations embedded within religious tribunals affect the experience of Muslim women. The rule-making capacity of such bodies may be relational and specific to local contingencies but is also dependent upon certain shared cultural and religious attributes that designate identity and the boundaries of such alternative dispute resolution mechanisms to the authority of the religious scholar(s). In the case of Sharia councils, important questions remain in relation to what kinds of structures are created and what types of communication take place between the sources of authority, religious scholars and primary users, most often Muslim women. Furthermore, in what ways do principles of justice, rights and gender equality differ from liberal values and how do such bodies operate as decision-making processes? What is the institutional design and the constitutive elements in the operation of justice? And does this system of dispute resolution recognise its own contingencies? In other words, is it even possible to have gender equality in Sharia councils and religious tribunals?

V. Muslim Divorce and Sharia Councils in Britain

We have now a large body of scholarship charting the development and settlement of British Muslim communities and their interactions with state law. The process of migration, the settlement of communities and the emergence of community state relations is well known and extensively documented.[26] Less known, however, are the intricate and complex ways in which communities form and construct informal family law processes and the role of those systems of dispute resolution in matters of Muslim divorce. Nevertheless, over the past three decades we have

[24] MH Fadel, 'Political Liberalism, Islamic Family Law and Family Law Pluralism' in JA Nichols, *Marriage and Divorce in a Multicultural Context* (Cambridge, Cambridge University Press, 2012) 614.

[25] M Al-Sharmani, Divorce among Transnational Finnish Somalis: Gender, Religion and Agency (2017) *7 Religion and Gender* 70.

[26] T Modood, 'Accommodating religions: Multiculturalism's new fault line' (2013) 34 *Critical Social Policy* 121.

witnessed the resurgence of family law debates focusing on the question of religious and cultural difference and the question of whether minority groups should be afforded a different family law regime considering specific cultural and religious norms. This underpins debates on the role of religion in society, the limits of secularism, and the extent to which the state should intervene in the private space of our family and personal relations to protect 'minorities within minorities' against injustice, unfairness and abuse.

In her ethnographic research, Kaveri Qureshi identifies an increase in marital breakdown in Muslim communities to unpick the context upon which Muslim divorce takes shape.[27] Interestingly, she demonstrates the embeddedness of British Muslims in extended family relations but also points out Muslim divorce does not deviate in all respects from wider marital breakdown in Britain. So what is the relationship between Muslim divorce and Sharia councils?

The history of Sharia councils has now been widely documented in Britain and can be traced to a diverse set of social, political and religious developments in civil society as part of the emergence of a British Muslim identity forged as part of multicultural practices.[28] The question of how such bodies should be classified and understood (for example as groups, associations, institutions or alternative dispute resolution mechanisms) often rests upon the way they operate and the nature of their relationship to multicultural practices and internal rules of process, institution, reliance on a hierarchal relationship, the structures and processes of decision-making, and methods of enforcement. Sharia councils operate as unofficial legal bodies specialising in Muslim family law and providing advice and assistance to Muslim communities on these matters. They are neither unified nor represent a single school of thought but instead are made up of various bodies representing the different schools of thought in Islam. Many Sharia councils are closely affiliated to mosques and this reflects developments in Islamic religious practice in Britain. In essence, a Sharia council has four key functions: issuing Muslim divorce certificates; fostering reconciliation; mediating between parties; and producing expert opinion reports on matters of Muslim family law and custom to the Muslim community, solicitors and the courts. The research report 'Social Cohesion and Civil Law: Marriage, Divorce and Religious Courts in England and Wales' looked specifically at the relationship between religion, divorce and access of law.[29] The study focused on the work of three tribunals – the Birmingham Sharia Council, the London Beth Din of the United Synagogue, and the National Tribunal for Wales of the Roman Catholic Church – and found both diversity and commonalities between these three mechanisms of dispute resolution because each sought

[27] K Qureshi, *Marital Breakdown among British Asians* (London, Palgrave, 2016).

[28] S Bano, Shariah Councils and Muslim Women: Transcending the Boundaries of Community and Law (Basingstoke, Palgrave Macmillan, 2012).

[29] G Douglas, C Doe, S Gilliat-Ray, R Sandberg and A Khan, *Social Cohesion and Civil Law: Marriage, Divorce and Religious Courts* (Cardiff, Cardiff University, 2011).

to avoid conflict with state law in matters of family law. Therefore, interaction with state law is often avoided raising important questions of justice and equality before the law.

Another example of Muslim family law is the Muslim Arbitration Tribunal (MAT), set up in June 2007, which aims to settle disputes in accordance with religious Sharia law. The authority of this tribunal rests with the Arbitration Act 1996 which permits civil matters to be resolved in accordance with Muslim law within the ambit of state law. For many, this process of resolving disputes may provide the ideal forum that allows arbitrating parties to resolve disputes according to English law while fulfilling any obligations under Islamic law. The advantages of arbitration, it is argued, allow the parties to achieve some level of autonomy in the decision-making process. This, coupled with the informal setting, lower costs, flexibility and time-efficiency means that, for some, it may prove a more attractive alternative to the adversarial courts system in England and Wales. However there remain real concerns over whether this process can restrict women's equality, and over issues of fairness and justice in family law. The establishment of the MAT has been controversial for a number of reasons. First, it has been claimed that Sharia courts have been allowed through the back door; second, that MATs directly challenge the superiority of the English legal system; and third, that they undermine the principles upon which English family law are based. As Blackett explains:

> [I]t is important to point out that the Muslim Arbitration Tribunal does not resemble or operate as a court but is an arbitration tribunal that must have the consent of the parties to rule on an issue. MAT has no power of enforcement but decisions can be enforced by the English county or high courts. This process therefore means that the decisions made by these arbitration bodies have to be in line with principles of English law or judges will not enforce them under sovereign rule.[30]

In 2011, the Arbitration and Mediation Services (Equality) Bill, a private members bill, was introduced by Baroness Cox in the House of Lords. This Bill was reintroduced in October 2015 and, at that point, generated considerable media attention as it aimed to make clear the limits of arbitration and amend the Arbitration Act to ensure its compliance with the Equality Act 2010 while seeking to outlaw discrimination on the grounds of sex. Clause 7 of the Bill proposes an amendment to the section of the Courts and Legal Services Act 1990 and criminalises 'falsely claiming legal jurisdiction' to prevent the ousting of jurisdiction in matters of family and criminal law. Although the Bill does not specifically mention Islamic law, it was widely believed to target Muslim communities and attempt to limit the powers of organisations such as MAT and Shariah councils. But for many scholars, it also raised the question of the extent to which state law should intervene in religious councils and tribunals. It has been criticised for promoting the idea that the practice of Muslim family law is not only based upon unfair and unequal principles,

[30] R Blackett, 'The Status of Religious "Courts" in English Law' 11 *Decisions, Decisions: Dispute Resolution & International Arbitration Newsletter* (December 2009).

but specifically targets and discriminates against Muslim women as primary users of Muslim dispute resolution bodies. Furthermore, the formalist top-down state interventionist approach as epitomised by the Bill in seeking to limit the powers of religious bodies, has also been criticised as being predicated on fixed and homogenous notions of Islam and Islamic legal practice which fails to recognise the dynamism and pluralism within the communities themselves. As Eekelaar argues:

> It is a mistake to think of Shari'a as a monolithic system, impervious to change. In fact the bodies apply it in different ways, and it is subject to internal arguments and contestation. Might it be better to allow it to develop within its communities and responding to its internal critiques and influenced by the culture around it? Alongside this, its adherents could be encouraged to make more use of the civil law, including a greater readiness to enter legally recognised marriages without thereby severing their relationship with their religious norms.[31]

The legal response to religious divorce has been interesting. The Divorce (Religious Marriages) Act 2002 made it a legal requirement that no decree of divorce can be made absolute without a declaration that both parties have taken steps to ensure the dissolution of a religious marriage. The provisions have been used successfully by the Jewish community, but as Gohir and Akhtar-Sheikh point out:

> [T]his process can also apply to Muslims if an order is granted by the Lord Chancellor to include the Muslim community as 'other prescribed' usages under the act. Thus, where the couple have entered into a both civil and Islamic marriage, the courts can ensure that the husband grants the Islamic divorce by withholding the decree absolute.[32]

At present, British Muslims instead seek to use Sharia councils to dissolve religious marriages on the basis that Islam provides Muslim women with the option to divorce. The *AI v MT* case also raised important questions as to whether religious arbitration was now recognised as a process of dispute resolution in English family law.[33] In effect the court endorsed the outcome of the Beth Din dispute resolution process where the parties, observant Orthodox Jews had come to an agreement that did not usurp English family law principles on children, fairness and equality.

VI. The Experience of British Muslim Women

So, what are the experiences of Muslim women using religious mechanisms of dispute resolution in matters of divorce? Do religious tribunals promote patriarchy and gender inequality? At present, there are several significant pieces of research which provide important insights into how Sharia councils in Britain govern as

[31] J Eekelaar, 'Law and Community Practices' in J Eekelaar and M Maclean (eds) *Managing Family Justice in Diverse Societies* (Oxford, Hart Publishing, 2013).

[32] S Gohir and N Akhtar-Sheikh, 'British Muslim Women and Barriers to Obtaining a Religious Divorce' in S Bano (ed), *Gender and Justice in Family Law Disputes, Women, Mediation and Religious Arbitration* (Massachusetts, Brandeis Press, 2017).

[33] *AI v MT* (2013) EWHC 100 (Fam).

alternative dispute resolution mechanisms in the field of family law. In my work, *Shariah Councils and Muslim Women: Transcending the Boundaries of Community and Law*, I draw three key conclusions from undertaking extensive empirical research with five shariah councils and interviews with 25 British Muslim women.[34] First, the claim that seeing culture and forms of religious practice as a mode of legitimising claims to power and authority dramatically shifts the way the debate on liberalism and universalism versus relativism is understood. In other words, the view that Muslims increasingly seek the freedom to live under Sharia is not only problematic, but fails to capture the complexity of British Muslim identity as fragmented, porous and hybrid. Second, anthropological scholarship points to the importance of locating gender and gender relations as key sites to the debate; thus, the ways in which Muslim women engage with Sharia councils in Britain illustrates how processes and concepts of Sharia law are mobilised, adopted and transformed. Underlying this process are power relations that define the nature of the interaction, define meaning of Sharia within Sharia councils, and construct possibilities of change and action. Third, an essentialised understanding of Muslim religious practice does not reflect the experience of British Muslim women. A more dynamic understanding of British Muslim identity is required which does not label the needs of Muslims to accommodate Sharia as fixed but understands this process as temporal, with shifts from cultural to religious practice and vice versa. Elham Manea argues that limited recognition of legal pluralism and multiculturalism has led to the recognition of culture and religion as homogeneous ignores individual voices and arguments at the expense of collective arguments.[35] In particular, her empirical research with Sharia councils and female Muslim users of those bodies found examples of practices such as forced marriage, underage marriage, condoning domestic violence, criminal sanctions and inequities in inheritance.

Gohir and Aktar-Sheikh draw upon case files from the national organisation Muslim Women's Network (MWUK) to illustrate the problems Muslim women experience in their use of Sharia councils.[36] One of the key findings from this research is that the lack of a valid marriage propels Muslim women to use Sharia councils. The focus on reconciliation and mediation remains of significant concern. They found:

> [N]o evidence to suggest that Sharia council members, mediators and caseworkers have had any adequate training in mediation, arbitration, or even general counselling. They, therefore, have neither the skills nor the knowledge to deal with family and divorce matters, whether from an Islamic or UK perspective. It is also of concern the

[34] S Bano, 'Feminist Methodologies, Legal Pluralism and Muslim Family Law in Britain' in R Scarciglia and W Menski (eds), *Normative Pluralism and Religious Diversity: Challenges and Methodological Approaches* (Padova, Kluwer Press, 2018).

[35] E Manea, *Women and Shari'a Law: The Impact of Legal Pluralism in the UK* (London/New York, IB Tauris, 2016).

[36] Gohir and Akhtar-Sheikh (n 32).

> panelists can interchangeably acts as mediators with no separation of role or procedure. The lack of training, lack of transparency, and lack of accountability and discriminatory processes make it essential that the issues surrounding certain Sharia councils be addressed as soon as possible.

In her research, Perveen argues that Sharia councils provide an important service for Muslim women and that the state should neither ban nor ignore them and instead assist them in providing an essential service 'while remaining faithful to normative Islam'.[37]

The question of choice, consent, agency capabilities and autonomy has long remained both an important and a vexed question for feminist scholars from multiple traditions. These debates are underpinned by important questions of moral self and viable choices all taking place relationally under various contexts of identity and belonging. Feminist scholarship informs us that agency cannot be exercised without choice and that the relationship between choice and agency is a complex one. This relationship between agency and choice becomes even more complicated within wider debates of identity, belonging and citizenship for women living within minority Muslim communities. For many feminists, autonomy and choice remain difficult and elusive concepts to define, each overlapping but also pointing to points of departure and how individual meanings and interpretations challenge the very foundations upon which they may be understood. Furthermore, the acquiesce of choice is an important aspect of understanding how choice may operate.[38]

For many scholars, the question of personal autonomy and choice underpins debates on the recognition of religious councils and tribunals in Britain. The debates fall largely within two spectrums of scholarly work. The first can be described broadly as orientalist discourses which accord Muslim women little if any agency and personal choice as members of Muslim families and communities. The second points to the fact that all debates on equality and free choice are circumscribed by 'difference' along multiple and complex factors including context, place and time with notions of belonging, identity and being. The extent to which free choice is therefore expressed can simply be one based on personal and strategic decision-making in the face of conflicting and competing demands. Thus, the language of choice, commitment and faith, as described by religious scholars, fits in neatly with the discourse of belonging to a wider Muslim community (*Umma*) and the importance attached to the development and formation of a local Muslim community-identity.

[37] R Parveen, 'Do Sharia Councils Meet the Needs of Muslim Women?' in S Bano (ed), *Gender and Justice in Family Law Disputes, Women, Mediation and Religious Arbitration* (Massachusetts, Brandeis Press, 2017).

[38] R Hunter and S Cowan (eds), *Choice and Consent: Feminist Engagements with Law and Subjectivity* (London, Routledge, 2007).

VII. Conclusion

This chapter outlined some of the key debates and issues relating to the experience of European Muslim women and religious practice with a focus on the use of British Muslim religious tribunals. At the heart of these debates lie questions of equality and difference and the role of state law in accommodating religious tribunals as alternative mechanisms of dispute resolution. The complex feminist debate as to whether women from religious communities exercise agency in their practice of religious laws must also be contextualised in relation to cultural and religious difference and the limitations of formal substantive equality laws that may fail to capture lived experience, but still provides important protections and access to justice to women across European Muslim communities.

9

From Foreigners to Citizens: Freedom of Religion, Education and Policies for Social Integration of Muslim Minors

ENRICA MARTINELLI

I. The Role of Religion in Postmodern Society

An analysis of the policies of social integration can be tackled many ways, but they must all include a serious reflection on the role that religion and its various features play in today's multicultural society. In contemporary society, religion is more diversified and has a much more important role than it had in the recent past. The most important difference is found in the increased public visibility of religious variability which has emerged with overwhelming intrusiveness in post-modern society from the private and personal sphere in which it was confined in the modern age.

Today, religion not only influences but often determines what collective actions are taken. It conditions the political options of the national and international institutions which are called upon to manage issues of transnational importance, such as peace between peoples and the protection of human rights including justice, health and education. Those who had announced 'the death of God' predicting the irreversible social irrelevance of religion[1] have found themselves on the wrong side of history. With the crumbling of national borders, and in the face of the consequent and progressive loss of identity, we are witnessing a renewed need for religiosity and the advent of what has been called the revenge of the God.[2]

[1] For some exemplary works, see, eg, S Acquaviva, *L'eclissi del sacro nella società industriale* (Milan, Edizioni di Comunità, 1961); JT Altizer and W Hamilton, *Radical Theology and the Death of God* (Indianapolis, The Bobbs-Merrill Company Inc, 1966); AT Robinson, *Honest to God* (London, SCM Press, 1963).

[2] Well described, amongst many, by G Kepel, *The Revenge of God: The Resurgence of Islam, Christianity and Judaism in the Modern World* (Cambridge, Polity Press, 1993); SP Huntington, *The Clash of Civilizations and the Remaking of World Order* (New York, Simon & Schuster, 2011).

In the West, the geography of religion has profoundly changed. Today's confessional pluralism is the outcome of two different factors: the now systemic migratory flows and the freedom of the individual to seek a personal spiritual dimension, for which modern laws provide robust protection. In a time of globalisation, which seems to be the precursor of a transnational community with global aspirations, we see the emergence of a paradoxical incapacity to harmonise the symbolic values of different peoples with their immense heritages, the traditions and religious cultural principles which have been preserved and handed down over time. The existence of different confessional affiliations – certainly one of the most significant aspects of a pluralistic society – combined with widespread religious illiteracy,[3] have exacerbated and brought to the fore fanaticism, fundamentalism and integralism, or, in other words, pathological forms of religious militancy that have awoken the interest and concern of scholars and educators, who are aware that what is at stake is the social sustainability of religious pluralism which has been growing spontaneously on untilled ground.

Today, there is much talk of ensuring equality in schools, cultivating participation in the political and cultural life of society, and creating a feeling of shared citizenship. These issues are the real challenges in the formation of a multi-ethnic and multicultural society.[4] But there can be no real inclusion or true integration of community life without the key prerequisite of religious literacy within society. Religious literacy fosters knowledge of the other from within oneself and alleviates the anxiety inevitably generated when one does not recognise themself in the other.

Even from this brief premise, one can see how policies aimed at the social inclusion of children of Islamic faith must be closely linked to the idea of religious freedom through an intertwining of cultural and educational choice. The values of religious cultures, expressed in multiple confessional affiliations, have become the new heritage of a global society and their transmission, especially to younger generations, is a task which the secular and democratic state cannot leave to chance if it wants a peaceful and fruitful process of integration in places where multi-ethnic and multicultural coexistence is facultative. This is especially true in schools.

In the process of shaping new citizens, the school has a prominent role and the interweaving dynamics therein are witness to the extreme complexity and particularly delicate nature of the religious affiliations, each with their own set of rules and regulations to observe in the classroom, as in life. Of course, schools must cooperate with the family in the education of their children and the best way to do so would be by establishing a special relationship, a synergy between the parents and the school, aimed at guaranteeing an education which respects the family's

[3] A Melloni (ed), *Rapporto sull'analfabetismo religioso in Italia* (Bologna, il Mulino, 2014). This work is a useful tool to contextualise the theme of the absence of the religious in educational processes and offers an organic reflection on what is ignored by the school system and on the historical-theological as well as the historical–political reasons for these omissions and gaps.

[4] For an interesting reflection on this topic, see M Santerini, *Da stranieri a cittadini. Educazione interculturale e mondo globale* (Milan, Mondadori Università, 2017).

religious affiliation or spiritual leanings, while still guaranteeing the religious freedom of the child respecting their right to choose.

II. Children's Self-Determination and Parents' Educational Choices

The life of a child is one of constant evolution and profound change, which eventually leads to a permanent adult identity. It is not easy to define the level and scope of those freedoms in the sphere of existential choice, which the law can recognise, in questions such as whether a child enjoys the fundamental freedom of religion, conscience, thought, expression and association. These questions were given a positive answer in the UN Convention on the Rights of the Child in 1989.[5]

The necessary alignment of domestic laws with supranational and international sources allows that, though children are persons in need of protection and special care and attention, they are active holders of the rights of individual personality and fundamental freedoms. Therefore, being a child does not mean enjoying reduced rights but, rather, having full recognition of the dignity which belongs to every human, at every stage of their life. Obviously, such rights must also be guaranteed to the child in the context of their family's social set-up, where the notion of a legal relationship can be characterised as an abstractly non-conflictual relationship, as it is structurally aimed at connection and collaboration between the various subjective legal situations that make it up.[6] Clearly, the family unit is the primary social formation in which the child forges and expresses their personality.

The assertion of parental responsibility[7] is therefore based on the goal that children grow and mature in an environment which is attentive to their needs without the parents subjecting them to pressure or coercion in the choices to be made.

[5] For the protection of the fundamental freedoms of children in educational communities see T Hammarberg, *A school for children with rights. The significance of the United Nations Convention on the Rights of the Child for modern education policy*, Innocenti Lectures no 2, Florence, Unicef International Child Development Center (1998).

[6] About 'the parental role and the limits of state intervention, and/or their abstention concerning the exercise of constitutional rights on behalf of children', see L Papadopoulou, 'Children and Religious Freedom: An Enquiry into Children's Capability of Being Holders of Rights and the Nature of Religious Freedom in the Western World' in P Lødrup and E Modvar (eds), *Family life and human rights: Papers presented at the 11th World Conference of the International Society of Family Law* (Oslo, Gyldendal Akademisk, 2004) 536.

[7] The notion of 'parental responsibility' as used in the UK's Children Act 1989 was introduced by international conventions (the New York Convention of 1989 on the rights of the child, the Strasbourg Convention of 1996 on the exercise of children's rights, as well as EC regulation no 2201/2003) and, subsequently, adopted by the national civil codes of the EU countries, in accordance with the fundamental principle by virtue of which the powers and duties of which parents are invested in respect of children are attributed to them by law exclusively for the purpose of pursuing the best interests of the minor. For an examination of the legal situation relating to 'parental responsibility' in European countries, see G De Cristofaro, 'Dalla potestà alla responsabilità genitoriale: profili problematici di una innovazione discutibile' (2014) *Le nuove leggi civili commentate* 782, 786.

The family, conceived as an open social formation where communication must be fostered and where each member can offer their own critical and responsible contribution, thus becomes an ideal space for freedom and autonomy.

The instrument to be applied in order to achieve the sometimes-necessary harmonisation of the parents' educative discretion and the child's requirements for self-determination is the pre-eminent interest of the child itself in a healthy and balanced upbringing.[8] Regarding the exercise of the right to a harmonious development of personality, the regulation of the child's activity cannot be separated from the level of their discernment in making choices, following what can be called a 'modular model', because it is made up of many distinct abilities and directly relates to the specific area where it arises.

With respect to the characteristics and complexity of the particular existential situation to be faced, the judicial system will have to determine, in each case, the actual fitness of each child to participate directly in the identification of their best interest, as the level of discernment reached is inversely proportional to the effect of the power of care managed by the parents. A child is in constant evolution but remains a child until, for the sake of legal expediency, their 18th birthday. There must be a concrete assessment of the child's critical capacity and ability to make sound decisions, which allows them to be aware of and responsible for their own existential choices in harmony (or sometimes in disharmony) with the parents' rights and duties to support and guide their child and, in some cases, to make the choice themselves.

Thus comes the delicate issue of potential conflict between the educative discretion of parents and the exercise of the freedoms of a child endowed with discernment and a decision-making ability. In fact, it is difficult to find any domestic legislation on self-determination and its existential aspects that allows the effective protection of the freedoms and fundamental rights of children when confronted by the choices or impositions of parents. The functional dimension of the right and duty of parents to educate and be responsible for the upbringing of their offspring can produce particularly problematic results if placed in dialectical relation with the constitutional protection of the fundamental freedom of thought, conscience and religion of the children. When important ideological choices are involved, there are always difficulties in identifying a fair balance between the right of self-determination of child and the right of parents to raise them by giving them an education anchored to the family's shared ethical, religious, and spiritual principles.

Today, the educational challenge is more complex than in the past when the process focused on bringing up a child to become a member of a mostly monocultural and monoreligious society. Nowadays, the goal must be set to forge fellow citizens who are not only aware of the values of coexistence between diverse people but also open to these values.

[8] That the interest of the minor must be considered paramount is established by Art 3 of the New York Convention of 1989 on the rights of the child, the European Convention of 25 January 1996 on the exercise of children's rights, and Art 24 of the Charter of Fundamental Rights of the European Union.

Any discussion on the religious freedom of children within the parental relationship in a multicultural society is also further complicated by the plurality of family models. What is recognised by national laws as a right to freedom is often seen, from the point of view of religious confessions, as a specific duty that parents are required to fulfil (as is the case of the Muslim family).

III. The Muslim Family

When we speak of the Muslim family, of the Muslim universe, we do not mean a monolithic cultural and religious block, but an immense dynamic real-life situation. Muslim immigrants are not an undifferentiated mass coming from a single social and cultural fabric.[9] However, it can be said that in general terms the roles of the mother and father are different in the conception of the traditional Islamic family. The mother has the biological bond with the child and introduces the child into the cultural sphere through a variety of means including deeds and customs, prohibitions and taboos, and popular traditions and stories, until the moment when what is allowed and what is forbidden are specified.

The father exercises wide-ranging parental authority over the offspring, a prerogative that entails the duty of maintenance, education, conduct, decency, control of their assets and marriage choice for both males and females. The admission of the child into the religious sphere also takes place through the father, and the child's upbringing has the goal of transferring the child from the universe of the mother to that of the father, and in so, becoming 'socially' Muslim.

In general, Muslim immigrant communities who come originally from a traditional rural environment are subject to a twofold process of acculturation. First, they encounter modernity, to be understood as an anthropological, sociological and cultural journey within their own context, and, second, and more difficult, is their 'transplantation' into a migratory situation which is, more often than not, completely different. Especially, Muslim children find themselves having to face a series of crucial moments in their cultural journey during their adaptation to the new environment, particularly in entering a different model of education in a language system that they have yet to learn. There are further difficulties for those who have been reunited with one or both of their previously emigrated parents when emotional ties have to be repaired, having been destabilised due to the separation. Instead, for children arriving as babies or born in the West, the major difficulty is with traditional identity, having to understand the codes and norms of their original culture, which they sporadically come up against even though they partly live this reality through their upbringing in the rules and ideas imparted on them by their parents.

[9] For an examination of family dynamics in the light of Islamic ethical-juridical norms in Great Britain, but with extensive references to European countries, see R Grillo, *Muslim Families, Politics and the Law. A Legal Industry in Multicultural Britain* (London, Routledge, 2017); R Aluffi Beck-Pecoz, 'Relazioni familiari nella società islamica' (2002) *Il matrimonio tra cattolici ed islamici* 159.

Muslim migrant children can find themselves at the centre of dissonant expectations such as the need to integrate into the host society while at the same time preserving the values and cultural references of their origin, especially in a family that fears losing its roots. To avoid the risk of suffering from the stress of 'transculturation', a good relationship is necessary with both the culture of origin and the religion to which they belong, as these relationships are decisive factors in the process of developing one's own identity, so as to not feel like 'foreigners' both in their country of residence and country of origin.[10]

In the dense intertwining of educative rights and duties, Muslim parents – fathers in particular – have the prerogative of transmitting to their children a spiritual education based on their own heritage of culture, traditions and customs, together with their personal faith. However, in bringing up a child, the interest of the child is pre-eminent in its various and complex forms. Therefore, while religious education is a value that national legal systems protect, it must be reconciled with other values.[11] To mention a significant example, authoritarian and coercive systems are banned because the health and psycho-physical integrity of children are pre-eminent when compared to the religious freedom of their parents. Clearly, bringing a child up within a faith will have a greater impact in early childhood when the child has not yet developed the mental faculties to consciously question its ideas. It is more difficult when the parents find themselves in front of an adolescent with self-determination and they have a duty to respect their choices, whether positive or negative, in the religious or spiritual field.

The exercise of religious freedom can thus be understood as a specific aspect of the best interests of the child, who can engage in conduct which expresses their spiritual orientation even before the age of 18.

When the options of the children are expressed in harmony with the religious ideas given by the parents, the highest degree of cohesion of the family structure is generated. The opposite is also true when there is incompatibility between the religious positions held by parents and their underage children. There, a complex situation arises because the entire existence of the person is shaped and permeated by religious sentiment with its eschatological aspects and the irrepressible vocation to provide answers to the ultimate questions of man, relating to earthly life and the afterlife.

In a monist society, 'religious values are one of the major parts of national identity and of social cohesion. In a pluralist society, however, religious values … come to be a factor of fragmentation, division, and conflict'[12] as they are often the only element of identity of the immigrant community in the foreign land. Religious values are then defended at all costs, even if they are in open conflict with human

[10] See M Nabeel Musharraf and F Bushra Nabeel, 'Schooling Options for Muslim Children Living in Muslim-Minority Countries – A Thematic Literature Review' (2015) 3 *International Journal of Social Science and Humanities Research* 29.

[11] See, in particular, the Declaration on the Elimination of All Forms of Intolerance and Discrimination Based on Religion or Belief (UN General Assembly, 25 November 1981), Art 5, para 5.

[12] G Dalla Torre, 'Valori e principi non negoziabili' (2013) 1 *Studi cattolici* 84.

dignity and the fundamental principles of the host state.[13] It can, therefore, become difficult to guarantee the freedoms of thought, conscience and religion of the child within families that do not normally allow equal rights and duties to their members, nor consider minors – and often women – to be completely subordinate to the authority of the father-husband.[14] In the cases described, the best interests of the child coincide with the protection of the minors' conscious freedom to differentiate themself from the teachings imparted by the family and, in the cases where the conscious will of the child is lacking, are found in the protection that must be guaranteed to the child when part of an educational programme not in line with the rules derived from the democratic, pluralistic, egalitarian and individual-based principles on which European legal systems are founded.[15]

IV. The School as a Place of Education for Inter-Religious Coexistence

The school as a public institution is intrinsically connected to the notion of the multicultural society, and has, in fact, become a yardstick for public authorities in ensuring an effective assertion of constitutional principles, especially pluralism and the protection of fundamental freedoms. Respect for these values requires state and non-state schools to be free from conditioning and bias, and allow children with an immigrant background to assert their personality at every stage of their education and autonomously express their own inner dimensions. This educational challenge takes place entirely within the nexus of religious pluralism and the public space because the school embraces the religious pluralism of its pupils, which helps to instil in them the virtue of social cohesion, overcoming the fear of 'the other' and creating a space in which to meet and re-acknowledge each other.

It is necessary in educational contexts to develop the specific skills essential to understand cultures, recognise and critique folkloristic and stereotypical

[13] See S Ferrari, 'Comportamenti "eterodossi" e libertà religiosa. I movimenti religiosi marginali nell'esperienza giuridica più recente' (1991) 114 *Il Foro Italiano* 271, 271–85; A Fuccillo, *Giustizia e Religione vol II: Matrimonio, famiglia e minori tra identità religiosa e rilevanza civile* (Turin, Giappichelli, 2011) 70.

[14] Parents who impose fideistic principles and the dogmatic patrimony of the irreligious affiliation to children who have self-determined away from the family's beliefs often obtain nothing but 'coerced assent' which, in the outward observance of religious precepts, harms the existential dimension and the fundamental rights of the adolescent.

[15] In this regard, it is significant that the protection of this particular declination of the child's best interests was fully accepted in the proposal of the very recent draft law on religious freedom, presented by the Astrid study group. See R Mazzola, 'La proposta di legge in materia di libertà religiosa nei lavori del gruppo di studio Astrid. Le scelte operate nel campo della libertà religiosa individuale' (2017) 20 *Stato, Chiese e pluralismo confessionale* 1, 4. The full recognition of the dignity of minors, their existential dimension, and their conscience arrives in the draft law as a 'self-determining precept' forming the personality of children, in light of their 'religious and philosophical convictions' (Art 6, para 2) and the choices that, starting from the age of 14, they can make in matters of 'religion or belief' (Art 6, para 3). In this regard, see A Zaccaria, S Domianello, A Ferrari, P Floris and R Mazzola (eds), *La legge che non c'è. Proposta per una legge sulla libertà religiosa in Italia* (Bologna, Il Mulino, 2019) 123.

approaches, and find points of contact that make a peaceful coexistence possible in inclusive educational environments, so allowing the growth of both mutual trust and an awareness of a common responsibility for the future.

The first task that the school is required to take on is that which is 'strictly cognitive aimed at providing an accumulation of knowledge not only of its nation's own history and culture and its religious traditions but also that of other religious cultures, especially those recently arrived in the actual social context.'[16] This objective is far from obvious. A pluralistic society cannot define itself as democratic and secular by freedom to believe alone; it must also guarantee the right of the people to be informed. In this regard, I recall the four key principles on which to base the educational systems as identified by the 'UNESCO Report of the International Commission on Education for the 21st century', which are: 1) learning to know; 2) learning to do; 3) learning to be; and 4) learning to live together.[17]

More precisely, the issues concerning religion at school testify to the complexity of the issues at stake and confirm, above all, the need for religion to be part of the educational curriculum of young people. The European educational communities must make the effort to provide a foundation to the history of religion, as a fundamental tool of education for global citizenship and as an antidote to fear, discrimination, and fundamentalist and integralist tendencies. Despite the multiculturalism of today's schools, a branch of knowledge that deals with religion is almost universally lacking. As a result, one of the problems most felt in schools is not knowing how to exercise religious freedom and where the limits of its expression are. This knowledge gap must be bridged in a society with such a complicated spiritual dissymmetry.

In theory, the law satisfactorily guarantees the personal and collective freedom of religion to children of Islamic faith. However, in practice, civil society, namely through the educational institutions, makes scarce provision for the tools necessary to satisfy the best interests of the children to learn both secular and scientific religious facts which would foster peaceful coexistence and common citizenship. There are manifold examples in support of this statement but a quick read-through of many of the school textbooks used today in Europe is enough to get an emblematic picture of the repetition of stereotypes, distortions and plainly wrong information that have been offered –and continue to be offered – to students for generations. It comes naturally to ask what the image of Islam and Muslims is that western schools impart through the various textbooks.

There have been many discussions on this issue recently in the Muslim world, Europe and America, with different approaches and no completely consistent conclusions. In 2011, the German institute Georg Eckert For International Textbook Research conducted a survey on the school textbooks used in Austria, France,

[16] See V Turchi, 'Educazione alla convivenza e pluralismo religioso. Modelli a confronto. Spunti metodologici' in E Camassa (ed), *Democrazia e religioni. Libertà religiosa diversità e convivenza nell' Europa del XXI secolo, Atti del Convegno Nazionale ADEC, Trento, 22–23 ottobre 2015* (Napoles, Editoriale Scientifica, 2016) 372.

[17] See J Delors, *Learning: the treasure within Report to UNESCO of the International Commission on education for the twenty-first century* (UNESCO, 1996).

Germany, Great Britain and Spain, concluding that they all reveal a 'cultural racism' towards Islam as they tend to transmit and reinforce stereotypes and prejudices towards the Muslim religion and culture.[18] The results of the survey showed that, in general, Islam is viewed as a monolithic, backward, unchanging and anti-feminist religious system with no discourse on its pluralism in different planes whether they are historical, juridical, ideological, political, national or cultural as well as religious, and that there was also no mention of any processes of modernisation.

Furthermore, the textbooks often contained distorted analyses of the Islamic creed, fuelled by stereotypes that encourage Islamophobia, and mediocre pseudo-intercultural solutions apparently aimed at respecting sensitivities and promoting processes of inclusion.[19] A possible solution would include overcoming the essentially synchronous method used in most textbooks, since this method does not take into account the historical evolution that has taken place since the founding of Islam, and hardly mentions any development towards modernisation, with the result that the representation of the Muslim world is placed on the same archaeological plane as that of the ancient Greeks and Romans and is, therefore, devoid of any evolution to the modern day.[20]

Alongside these critical issues, the fact that the teachings of some subjects, such as history, philosophy and the sciences, includes contents that can cast doubt on dogmas of faith or cultural heritage arouses a logical concern among Muslims (and also other religious confessions). In the same way, the religious freedom of Muslim children is hindered by the obligation to practise physical education wearing clothing that is not in keeping with the dictates of their faith or by the educational institution not providing Muslim girls the use of a single-sex gym, in violation of the precept of separation between the sexes in Islam.[21]

Another important issue is the running of school dining halls and the close relationship between food and religious pluralism. This particular aspect of the exercise of freedom of religion translates, in this case, as the right of every Muslim student to eat at school together with their schoolmates, sharing the moment of conviviality,[22] in compliance with food restrictions.[23] A further issue is the wearing of clothing which shows adherence to a certain belief. For example, the wearing

[18] 'No Chance of Belonging? Islam and Modern Europe Remain Segregated in European Text books' press release (Georg Ekhert Institute, 11 October 2013), available at gei.de/en/gei-aktuell/details/no-chance-of-belonging-islam-and-modern-europe-remain-segregated-in-european-textbooks.

[19] See Amnesty International, 'Europe: Choice and prejudice: discrimination against Muslim in Europe' (2012).

[20] See G Vercellin, *Istituzioni del mondo musulmano* (Turin, Einaudi, 2002).

[21] V Fronzoni, 'The School Education of Muslim Children in Europe: A review of Comparative Perspectives' (2020) 1 *Al-·Ulūm Journal of Islamic Studies* 1.

[22] It is also necessary to keep in mind the needs of students of the Islamic faith who, from puberty on, are required to fast completely from dawn to dusk during the Ramadam period. See L Musselli and CB Ceffa, *Libertà religiosa, obiezione di coscienza e giurisprudenza costituzionale* (Turin, Giappichelli, 2014).

[23] The Foundation 'Benvenuti in Italia' conducted research in the schools of some large European cities to determine the level of organisation required to meet the dietary needs of children and young people belonging to different religious communities in the area. This research was conducted in Italy in the cities of Turin, Milan and Rome. The results can be found at benvenutiinitalia.it/fondazione.

of the veil: some Muslim girls are required by their parents to use it upon reaching puberty, while for others it is a free choice of faith that must also be protected.

V. Multiple Identities and Integration Processes

Generally, the European position on integration policies – considering the necessary distinctions from country to country – has seen an overall change in the international political climate towards the migratory phenomenon. Forms of mixophobia (fear of mingling) and defensive closing-up have re-emerged from various quarters, putting forward assimilation as the only form of social inclusion. As assimilation literally means to be made similar, this is to be understood as a reductive version of integration, centred on the need of the indigenous society to maintain the social order and feel safe rather than on the expectations of equal inclusion of minorities and on the enhancement of different cultural identities. In reality, the variables in structure, individuals, relational aspects and context influence the integration processes that map out very different starting conditions, trajectories and outcomes.

Although the migratory story and those factors relating to family background (such as socio-economic status, the educational level of parents and inter-relational dynamics) heavily influence educational outcomes and the processes of integration, other significant factors are also in play. Particularly important is the experience of moving and settling into new housing and schools where the social and ethnic make-up of the school and what other opportunities are on offer locally are relevant, with particular attention focused on the sociality and inter-ethnic relational climate both at school and beyond the classroom.

The dominant experience of Muslim children and adolescents today is of having been born in Europe, having arrived at a very young age, or having been partially schooled in the country of origin but now permanently residing in European countries with their families, thus investing their own existential and educational projects in the European continent. In other words, their experience is not of fleeing an emergency situation into Europe. This means letting go of the widely held assumption of migration as a surprising and temporary phenomenon, and implementing a policy of structural intervention that can bring an effective integration apparatus and practice to the system within a project of interculturality.[24]

This implies a primary investment of resources in tools aimed at developing the services, knowledge and professional skills necessary to build intercultural schooling. These interventions do not concern only Muslim children but the school community as a whole, including teachers, educational practices, families and other institutional actors in the area who are responsible for care and education.

[24] For more information on intercultural education, see A Cucinello and S Pasta (eds), *Studenti musulmani a scuola. Pluralismo, religioni e intercultura* (Rome, Carocci Editore, 2021).

VI. Intercultural Education as a Tool for Social Inclusion

The intercultural education project, which finds its first experimentation in the reality of school, does not represent an option to choose, concede or, even worse, capitulate. It is the paradigm, whether in a political, ethical, juridical or educational sense, which is most appropriate to the changes imposed on European countries by world events. School is brought into play because it is the training ground for civil coexistence, the laboratory of citizenship, the workshop of legality and, after the family, the most important environment for engendering both relational and emotional literacy.

In other words, educational communities are called upon to enrich, from early childhood through a 'pedagogy of consensus', the contents of the right to religious freedom of the children and their family, in acknowledgement of the non-negotiability of human dignity and the beneficial transformation of the multicultural and multi-religious society into an intercultural and inter-religious society.[25] The approach to interculture is thus open to diversity while still rooted in identity and aimed at individuals with equal rights but different customs, habits, traditions and religion. The main feature of intercultural education is to foster mutual change. One does not assimilate the other by forcing a denial of their origins, just as one does not accept the other when they defend customs that harm human integrity.

The intercultural approach seems to offer a valid response in the perspective of effective social inclusion at a global level, since the subject of interculture is the 'cultural community', which can be defined as an integrated social system that is transnational by nature, as in the case of the Muslim community.[26] Intercultural strategies avoid separating individuals into autonomous and impermeable cultural worlds. Instead, they foster debate, dialogue and mutual transformation, to make coexistence possible and deal with the resulting conflicts.

In the global world, interculturalism, understood as the ability to understand and appreciate differences, as a process of common growth in which the wealth of the other is acknowledged, in which each gives up something in the name of affirming shared values, is not only important but it is an essential instrument of social cohesion, inspired by a truly participatory and inclusive vision of citizenship.

[25] On intercultural dialogue, see, R Grillo, *Interculturalism and the Politics of Dialogue* (Lewes, B and RG Books of Lewes, 2018). On interculture as an educational response, see L Bekemans, *Educational challenges and perspective in multiculturalism vs interculturalism: citizenship education for intercultural realities* in M Barret (ed), *Interculturalism and multiculturalism. Similarities and differences* (Council of Europe Publishing, 2013) 169ff.

[26] A Perotti, 'L'Europe et la diversité. Enseigner la diversité culturelle' (1998) 17 *Revue Internationale d'Éducation* 33, 43.

10

Regulating Islam: Limitations on Freedom of Religion in Denmark

NIELS VALDEMAR VINDING

I. Introduction: The Rise of a Trend in the Danish Regulation of Islam

A recent trend has emerged in the Danish regulation of religion that is testing the limits of the ways in which the Constitution regulates Islam and Islamic faith communities, which politically may be found to be extreme, radicalising, or 'against Danish values'. A majority political will in Parliament and governments have sought to limit the freedom of religion of these Islamic communities by exploring the 'Limitation Clause' in Article 67 of the Danish Constitution, which declares that 'nothing at variance with good morals or public order shall be taught or done', and reinterpreting the Non-Discrimination Clause in Article 70.

While for some years such political sentiment has been identifiable in far-right political and public opinion, the call to legally limit Muslims' freedom of religion gained mainstream prominence in Danish politics and grew into a common legal ambition in the months and years after the three-part television documentary, *Mosques Behind the Veil*, first broadcast in March 2016. The documentary provided important insight into the teaching and preaching taking place in particular mosques. However, all hopes of critical understanding and nuance in the documentary were sacrificed for the dual goal of demonstrating the prevalent extremism and fuelling political debate. The documentary was similar to BBC One Panorama's *Secrets of Britain's Sharia Councils* (2013) and the Dutch SBS6's *Undercover in Nederland*.[1] It employed the same controversial journalistic techniques and dubious undercover informants with hidden cameras driving the main narrative. While factual insight into the nature of the problems in Danish

[1] NV Vinding, 'The Question of Sharīʿa in Denmark' (3 August 2016) Sharia Source at Harvard Law School, available at shariasourceblog.wordpress.com/2016/08/03/264.

mosques and Islamic communities is worth investigating, the documentary sparked a political outcry and gave a strong impetus to a remarkable legislative agenda, effectively seeking to limit freedom of religion.

Amongst the most significant reactions to the documentary, the then Minister for Immigration and Integration, Inger Støjberg, said, before the first episode had aired, that she 'would prefer that we raze Grimhøj-Mosque to the ground' and that she would go to the 'very limits of the Constitution' to stop the imams.[2] This sentiment was echoed days later by the then Prime Minister, Lars Løkke Rasmussen, who invited all parliamentary parties to a round of legislative negotiations to combat anti-democratic sentiment. He, too, was ready to challenge the Constitution: 'We do not give up on the first-and-best limitation argument the Constitution sets,' he declared, quickly adding that Denmark is bound by the rule of law and international conventions.[3] The prime minister's sentiment was shared by the leader of the Social Democratic opposition, Mette Frederiksen, who said that, 'In many ways, we have a strong Constitution, but I see that it is challenged when you use our freedoms to work against Denmark, our open democratic society, and minority groups.'[4] The right-wing Danish People's Party called for action and challenged the prime minister to 'set aside international conventions' and adhere solely to the Danish Constitution.[5] The Conservative Party concurred, and while it did not seek to change the wording of the Constitution, it wanted to challenge constitutional interpretation. According to its spokesman, Naser Khader, Denmark 'should not tinker with the Constitution, but challenge it in relation to the part that deals with preaching against public order and morality.'[6]

Less than four months after the first episode had aired, on 31 May 2016, the then Minister for Culture and Ecclesiastical Affairs, Bertel Haarder, presented the results of the negotiations in an Agreement Paper (popularly dubbed 'the imam package') which outlined seven legislative and administrative initiatives to curb the activities of religious preachers who sought to undermine Danish laws, freedoms and values, and support parallel views of the law.[7] An in-principle agreement was reached by the Liberal Party minority government, the Social

[2] M Sommer, 'Støjberg: Jeg så helst, at vi jævnede Grimhøjmoskeen med jorden' (29 February 2016), available at www.dr.dk/nyheder/indland/stoejberg-jeg-saa-helst-vi-jaevnede-grimhoejmoskeen-med-jorden. All translations, here and below, are by the author of the chapter.

[3] A Ritzau, 'Løkke vil udfordre grundloven i kamp mod radikale imamer' (15 March 2016), available at www.avisen.dk/loekke-vil-udfordre-grundloven-i-kamp-mod-radikale-i_376233.aspx.

[4] ibid.

[5] J Hvass, 'DF til Løkke: Ignorer konventionsforpligtelser' (18 March 2016), available at www.jyllands-posten.dk/politik/ECE8523785/df-til-loekke-ignorer-konventionsforpligtelser.

[6] A Ritzau, 'K: Grundloven skal udfordres i kamp mod omstridte imamer' (22 March 2016), available at www.sn.dk/danmark/k-grundloven-skal-udfordres-i-kamp-mod-omstridte-imamer.

[7] 'Aftale mellem regeringen og Socialdemokraterne, Dansk Folkeparti og Det Konservative Folkeparti om initiativer rettet mod religiøse forkyndere, som søger at undergrave danske love og værdier og understøtte parallelle retsopfattelser' (31 May 2016), Kirkeministeriet, dok nr 65672/16.

Democrats, the Danish People's Party and the Conservatives, which collectively represented a substantial majority in Parliament. The Agreement Paper states its purpose: to present new initiatives on three themes, namely, withdrawing public recognition from a number of religious communities, limiting the entry of so-called 'hate preachers' and establishing sanctions to be imposed on individuals and communities deemed 'contrary to Danish basic values and democratic principles'. The Agreement Paper declares that:

> The parties to the agreement are resolved that there must continuously be a great deal of leeway in the freedom of thought. None of the parties wants to be the thought police. There must be room for different religious communities in Denmark. *However*, we want to set a limit for authorities on religious doctrinal teaching that exhibits behaviour that undermines Danish laws and values and supports parallel legal views. (Author's italics)[8]

Since 2016, following the Agreement Paper, more than a dozen laws, amendments and executive orders have come into force that have not only addressed immigration, asylum seekers and foreigners in Denmark, but have also had a considerable impact on Islam and Muslims in the country, as well as on other religious communities.[9] I have previously analysed this trend in the Danish volume of *Annotated Legal Documents on Islam in Europe* and found the existence of a move towards delegitimising and disabling public religion beyond the Church of Denmark, both in general and particularly regarding Islam and Islamic communities. The legislature's political will to go as far as possible constitutionally to limit religious freedom has led to a particular and possibly dangerous interpretation of Islamic and Islamist iterations as being subversive to democracy, against gender equality, or arguing for parallel legal orders. In the individual amendments and bills, it is clear the drafting jurists have changed existing constitutional interpretations and sought to limit freedom of religion (Article 69) and freedom from discrimination (Article 70).

This chapter will present, analyse and discuss this recent trend of limiting freedom of religion for all by framing and interpreting Islam and Muslims as being contrary to 'public order and morality' and 'to Danish basic values and democratic principles'. This chapter will not discuss the new Danish constitutional arguments in full detail but rather take them as a starting point for discussing the human rights questions they raise about the justifiable limitations of freedom of religion by state institutions. This chapter will give examples from other ongoing European discussions on limitations of Muslim religious freedom. However, the focus is particularly on the human rights jurisprudence and recommendations of former UN Special Rapporteur on freedom of religion or belief, Heiner Bielefeldt.

[8] ibid.

[9] For these sections of the Agreement Paper and its impact on legislation, see NV Vinding, *Annotated Legal Documents on Islam in Europe: Denmark* (Leiden, Brill, 2020).

II. Justifiable Limitation of Freedom of Religion in the International Standards

The starting point for exploring the justifiable limitation of freedom of religion begins with the many international standards that exist, such as the International Covenant on Civil and Political Rights (ICCPR), Article 18(3); the Convention on the Rights of the Child, Article 14(3); the International Convention on the Protection of the Rights of All Migrant Workers and Members of Their Families, Article 12(3); the 1981 Declaration of the UN General Assembly, Article 1(3); the Commission on Human Rights resolution 2005/40, para 12; the Human Rights Council resolution 6/37, para 14; and, of course, the European Convention on Human Rights (ECHR), Article 9(2). These all share the same overall basic language:

> Freedom to manifest one's religion or beliefs shall be subject only to such limitations as are prescribed by law and are necessary in a democratic society in the interests of public safety, for the protection of public order, health or morals, or for the protection of the rights and freedoms of others.[10]

The UN Human Rights Committee has set out its own understanding of this limitation language in its General Comment no 22, para 8, on the interpretation of ICCPR, Article 18(3) – 'Limitations imposed must be established by law and must not be applied in a manner that would vitiate the rights guaranteed in Article 18' – and further:

> The Committee observes that paragraph 3 of Article 18 is to be strictly interpreted … Limitations may be applied only for those purposes for which they were prescribed and must be directly related and proportionate to the specific need on which they are predicated. Restrictions may not be imposed for discriminatory purposes or applied in a discriminatory manner. The Committee observes that the concept of morals derives from many social, philosophical and religious traditions; consequently, limitations on the freedom to manifest a religion or belief for the purpose of protecting morals must be based on principles not deriving exclusively from a single tradition.

In the 2016 *Freedom of Religion or Belief: An International Law Commentary*, these references represent the starting point for Heiner Bielefeldt, Nazila Ghanea and Michael Wiener in setting out their legal thinking on the limitation of freedom of religion and belief. The book deals with the criteria set out for drawing limitations to freedom of religion or granting clauses (as Jeremy Gunn labels them in his work).[11] They begin with a warning about limiting human rights and freedom of

[10] See more on this in H Bielefeldt, N Ghanea and M Wiener, *Freedom of Religion or belief: An International Law Commentary* (Oxford, Oxford University Press, 2016) 550ff. See also, S Ferrari, M Hill, A Jamal and R Bottoni (eds), *Routledge Handbook of Freedom of Religion or Belief* (Milton Park, Routledge, 2021).

[11] TJ Gunn, 'Permissible Limitations on the Freedom of Religion or Belief' in J Witte and MC Green (eds), *Religion and Human Rights: An Introduction* (Oxford, Oxford University Press, 2012) 254–68.

religion that is particularly relevant to the developments in Denmark, especially regarding the Islamic challenge as a 'highly politicised issue', risking that the enjoyment of rights might become subject to the discrimination or arbitrary whims of state agencies. As they put it:

> Human rights are not unlimited. This is a truism and therefore dangerous since reference to the undeniable reality that some limits inevitably exist can easily serve as a pretext for unduly curtailing the scope of human rights or even relativizing their binding force altogether. The seemingly 'technical' question of where to draw limitations and how to justify them can therefore become a highly politicized issue. Dealing with this issue adequately requires caution, precision, and diligence.[12]

The freedoms guaranteed by ICCPR, Article 18 and ECHR, Article 9 concern both internal and external freedom. However, whereas internal freedom is understood to be unconditional, the exercise, expression or manifestation of external freedom is relative and may be limited.[13] Following this, Bielefeldt, Ghanea and Wiener give a legal exposition of the language of ICCPR, Article 18(3)/ECHR, Article 9(2), highlighting the three sets of conditions that must be met for restrictions to be permissible, ie they must: (a) be prescribed by law; (b) be necessary; and (c) protect public safety, public order, health or morals, or the rights and freedoms of others.

In the individual acts of legislation 'prescribed by law' is understood to be 'provided for by national law that should apply to all' and means that limitations should 'not be discriminatory in intent or application'. Included in the thinking of Bielefeldt, Ghanea and Wiener (as well as Gunn) are the general criteria of legislative quality, which stress that one should 'be able to foresee that an action is a violation of the law'.[14] This may be problematic for the many headscarf cases in Europe, including Denmark, where a 'masking ban' is curtailed by a case-by-case 'assessment of whether the cover serves a qualifying purpose'.[15]

Similarly, the question of necessity can be difficult to argue. Bielefeldt, Ghanea and Wiener highlight the fact that 'necessary' means 'based on justifying grounds', 'responding to pressing public or social needs' and 'with a legitimate aim … proportionate to that aim'.[16] Necessity and proportionality are closely linked and point to the idea that limitations of freedom of religion should be understood in relation to the harm that states seek to avoid. In *Leyla Şahin v Turkey*,

[12] Bielefeldt et al (n 10).

[13] Bielefeldt et al (n 10) 553; also JF Renucci, *Article 9 of the European Convention of Human Rights: Freedom of Thought, Conscience and Religion*, Human Rights Files, No 20 (Strasbourg, Council of Europe Publishing, 2005) 10.

[14] Bielefeldt et al (n 10) 555 (referencing Gunn (n 11) 260).

[15] 'Forslag til lov om ændring af straffeloven' (6 February 2018), available at www.justitsministeriet.dk/sites/default/files/media/Pressemeddelelser/pdf/2018/lovforslag_tildaekningsforbud.pdf.

[16] Bielefeldt et al (n 10) 555.

the European Court of Human Rights (ECtHR) raised the question of necessity and noted that 'in a democratic society, the state was entitled to place restrictions on the wearing of the Islamic headscarf if it was incompatible with the pursued aim of protecting the rights and freedoms of others, public order and public safety.'[17] The argument there was that state bodies (and others) 'may regulate the manifestation of the rites and symbols of a religion' and that the headscarf is a 'powerful external symbol'.[18] As for the Danish legislative trend, the question of necessity and proportionality is discussed in reference to limiting freedom of religion and freedom of expression for preachers who might be engaged in hate speech, but not for politicians, opinion makers and other comparable persons in positions of trust.

Of the third set of conditions, 'public order' and 'morals' are particularly relevant to the Danish debate as these two are literally expressed in Article 67 of the Constitution. Bielefeldt, Ghanea and Wiener follow the Siracusa principles in defining public order as 'the sum of rules which ensure the functioning of society or the set of fundamental principles on which society is founded.'[19] 'Morals' are much more difficult to define and vary across time, place and culture. 'Morals' (*sædelighed* in Danish, the equivalent of *Sittlichkeit* in German) are understood to be an ethical order that expresses fundamental values of the community. Bielefeldt, Ghanea and Wiener cite the UN Human Rights Committee, which

> observes that the concept of morals derives from many social, philosophical and religious traditions; consequently, limitations on the freedom to manifest a religion or belief for the purpose of protecting morals must be based on principles not deriving exclusively from a single tradition.

As such, states may call on public morals as a limitation argument only if it can 'demonstrate that the limitation in question is essential to the maintenance of respect for fundamental values of the community.'[20]

There remains, of course, a certain margin of appreciation for states. With reference to *Leyla Şahin*, Ranucci notes that a margin of appreciation is particularly appropriate when it comes to the regulation of religion 'since rules on the subject vary from one country to another depending on national traditions and there is no uniform European conception of the requirements of "the protection of the rights of others" and of "public order".' Such a margin of appreciation is particularly relevant to the Danish examples because with it also comes room for interpretation and reinterpretation.

[17] *Case of Leyla Şahin v Turkey* App No 44774/98, 10 November 2005; Renucci (n 13) 53–54.
[18] Renucci (n 13) 53–54.
[19] Bielefeldt et al (n 10) 556.
[20] ibid, citing 'Siracusa Principles on the Limitation and Derogation Provisions in the International Covenant on Civil and Political Rights' UN Doc E/CN.4/1985/4, Annex (1985).

III. Justifiable Limitations of Freedom of Religion in the Danish Constitution

Many ongoing discussions and interpretations of Islam point to the need to expressly limit the exercise of religious freedom for Muslims in Europe. One recent example is Emanuel Macron's new French paradigm that establishes 'Enlightenment Islam' (*un Islam des Lumières*, or *Islam Républicain*) against 'Separatist Islam' in a move to limit international influences on Muslim communities in Europe.[21] Such a limitation is not just financial and political; it is material and physical. The influences of the Diyanet or the Moroccan organisations and their operations in Europe are, of course, the most significant example of what the French paradigm seeks to limit, but the logic is furthered by cases of Islamist terrorism and the influence of ISIS and goes as far as framing the international migration crises in terms of a domestic Muslim issue.

The growing anti-Sharia sentiments are another example, as when the Parliamentary Assembly of the Council of Europe resolved in January 2019 that it was 'greatly concerned about the fact that Sharia law … is applied, either officially or unofficially'.[22] Although criticised by scholars and practitioners as a 'counter-productive reductionist tirade against Sharia',[23] these and similar fears of Sharia as parallel legal orders which are 'incompatible', 'theocratic' and 'totalitarian' exist widely in legal and political institutions across Europe.[24]

With the 2016 Danish Agreement Paper and the subsequent trend in legislation, Denmark has placed itself at the heart of these discussions and at the forefront of developments. After the initial reactions in March 2016, the Standing Parliamentary Committee on Aliens and Immigration requested from the Legislative Secretary of Parliament a legal brief with a concise description of Articles 67, 69, and 70 of the Danish Constitution, with a 'special focus on the legislative power's ability to limit religious freedom'.[25] This request, by itself, demonstrated the committee's explicit legislative intent to limit religious freedom. The brief was made ready for the committee on 6 April 2016.

Of the three constitutional articles, the legal brief from the Legislative Secretary of Parliament focused mostly on Article 67, which states 'members of the public are entitled to associate in communities to worship God according to their convictions, but nothing may be taught or done that contravenes decency ['morality'] or public order'.[26] From this, it follows that the legislature is precluded

[21] N Käsehage, 'No Country for Muslims? The Invention of an Islam Républicain in France and Its Impact on French Muslims' (2021) 13 *Religions* 38.

[22] UN Resolution 2253, 2019, sec 4.

[23] R Sandberg and F Cramer, 'The Council of Europe and Sharia: An Unsatisfactory Resolution?' (2019) 21 *Ecclesiastical Law Journal* 203, 208.

[24] N Doe, *Comparative Religious Law: Judaism, Christianity, Islam* (Cambridge, Cambridge University Press, 2018), 1–3.

[25] 'Lovsekretariatets Notat om Grundlovens §§67, 69 og 70' (Folketinget, 6 April 2016).

[26] My Constitutional Act, 2012, 38.

from restricting or prohibiting the worship of God by citizens in connection with religious communities, as long as there are no actions or teaching contrary to morality or public order. This limitation is directed at actions and doctrine, and the Legislative Secretary of Parliament highlighted the fact that, for example, counselling that is contrary to morality or public order is not protected against intervention by the state. Of great importance is the fact that legislation may not be directed at a particular or singular religion or religious group, but Parliament may implement new general legislation or clarify existing legislation that addresses other considerations and interests, which may in turn limit freedom of religion and belief. The Legislative Secretary of Parliament has stressed that actions and teachings by religious groups that '[violate] religiously neutral Danish legislation will probably also be contrary to morality or public order', adding that freedom of religion does not make religious groups 'exempt from generally complying with Danish legislation'. This thinking was confirmed and made explicit in the drafting of the Act on Religious Communities outside the Church of Denmark in 2018, which clarified what was to be understood by 'teaching or actions that contravene morality, public order or other weighty considerations for society or the rights of others'. The drafting comments said that the Act 'basically means that the religious community's teachings and activities must comply with applicable legislation'.[27] The Legislative Secretary of Parliament has acknowledged that legislative power has a wide discretion in relation to determining the limits of morality or public order, but that the legal literature emphasises requirements for proportionality between the purpose of a restriction on religious freedom and consideration of the religious practices.[28]

Whereas Article 67 positively articulates the freedom to associate and to worship, Article 70 negatively defines the guarantee whereby 'nobody may be deprived of access to the full enjoyment of civil and political rights or evade the fulfilment of any general civic duty on the grounds of his or her profession of faith'.[29] The particular wording of Article 70 of the Constitution means that no one may be deprived of the full enjoyment of civic or political rights by reason of 'one's creed', using the singular possessive pronoun. In most legal thinking, and in Denmark's ratification of international standards and conventions, this has been understood to be a general non-discrimination clause.

The legal brief from the Legislative Secretary of Parliament represents a baseline of legal thinking that has changed with the recent trend, and with it a struggle can be seen to be unfolding between political will and the legal imagination. The vocal statements on Islam mentioned previously show that such wide discretion would be applied and tested in future legislation and that morality and public order change over time.

[27] Lov om trossamfund uden for folkekirken (LOV nr 1533 af 19/12/2017), lovforslag som fremsat.
[28] ibid.
[29] My Constitutional Act, 2012, 39.

The challenge, then, was firstly to legislate so as to fulfil the condition of 'prescribed by law', then to argue necessity, and then to demonstrate that public order and morality (as an ethical order that expresses fundamental values of the community) were indeed being threatened, in a generally applicable, and non-discriminatory way. The ambition and intention in doing so was clearly driven by a particular occasion of demonstrated, or perhaps perceived, Islamic radicalism and extremism. This is a tall order for the drafting jurists in the ministries, who would apply a fair amount of legislative imagination and reinterpretation of freedom of religion and non-discrimination.

IV. Criminalising Hate Speech, Particularly of Preachers[30]

As part of the May 2016 Agreement Paper, the Government, the Social Democrats, the Danish People's Party and the Conservative People's Party proposed initiatives aimed at religious preachers who seek to undermine Danish laws and values and support parallel judgments. They argued that:

> The agreement means that in the future it must be punishable explicitly to support terror, killings, rape, acts of violence, incest, paedophilia, false imprisonment, coercion and polygamy as part of religious education. This applies regardless of whether the statements are made in private or in public. The agreement also means that both the activities of religious preachers and those of others acting as part of religious education must be covered by the criminalization.[31]

Therefore, a particular scenario was explicitly criminalised by a bill amending the Danish Criminal Code. The political ambition of the Agreement Paper found its legal form in the regulation making it illegal to 'expressly approve certain criminal acts as part of religious education', with an added list of such criminal acts, by reference to articles in the Criminal Code. The wording is peculiar, as incitement to hatred or violence, for example, is already a criminal offence, whereas much of the Danish political establishment has been championing freedom of speech as an absolute right. This amendment falls right between these two positions, yet the most significant criticism concerns the fact that it merely regulates the religious aspects of condoning criminal acts, not the political or public condoning of criminal acts.

In the draft and preparatory remarks for the bill, the drafting jurists at the Ministry of Justice argued that there have been examples of publishers of religious material in Denmark seeking to undermine Danish laws and values and support parallel beliefs. This religious material includes statements containing support for,

[30] This section of the chapter closely follows, but also expands upon Vinding (n 9) 114–20.
[31] Agreement Paper, 5.

for example, the stoning of women or corporal punishment of children, but the remarks did not cite concrete examples or case law to support them.

The Criminal Code already contains several provisions that criminalise statements in various forms. One is Article 266(b) on the dissemination of threats and racism, while Articles 267 and 270 are on defamatory and derogatory statements. In addition, the Criminal Code also makes it possible to punish a person who, by encouragement, advice or deed, has abetted a criminal offence. However, a prerequisite for penalising someone for complicity, for example by encouraging the deed, is that a specific criminal offence has been committed and that the intention of the person in question has, to a certain extent, been manifested. Finally, the Criminal Code, in addition to the general rule on participation, contains explicit prohibitions on encouraging or recruiting people to commit offences. Examples of these are the article on public incitement to crime, Article 114(c) on recruitment for terrorism and Article 114(e) on promoting a terrorist organisation. It is thus legal under current law to express support for, or approve, for example, the stoning of women or corporal punishment of children, provided that the person in question does not thereby publicly encourage crime.

However, the bill that resulted from the May 2016 Agreement Paper and the new Article 136, section 3, applies expressly to religious education. The bill is understood to be a tightening of the criminal law regarding religious preachers who, according to the logic of the bill, are seen to have special authority over their congregations (especially children in situations where they might be impressionable). Religious preachers, and others who provide religious education, speak from a general point of view, with particular insight and authority in relation to people who must be considered particularly vulnerable to their influence, when they seek to and participate in a community of religious action. Therefore, the legislative logic is that it is particularly problematic if these individuals, through their behaviour, counteract and undermine Danish values by condoning certain criminal offences.

In the draft of and preparatory remarks for the bill, the Ministry's drafting jurists follow the political mandate and state the purpose of the amendment, which is to:

> [C]ounteract behaviours that undermine Danish laws and values and support parallel legal beliefs by criminalizing the explicit denial of the existence of certain criminal acts as part of religious instruction. The bill thus safeguards public order and can therefore be implemented within the framework of Article 67 of the Constitution.[32]

The bill goes on to list examples of cases it is intended to cover, all of which are listed without reference to concrete examples or case law; rather, they look like the product of the Ministry's legal imagination.[33] The examples include the following

[32] 3.2.1, 7, Forslag til Lov om ændring af straffeloven (Kriminalisering af udtrykkelig billigelse af visse strafbare handlinger som led i religiøs oplæring), som fremsat 5. oktober 2016, available at www.retsinformation.dk/eli/ft/201612L00018.

[33] ibid, 14.

cases: that of a religious preacher or other person who, as part of religious training in a 'sunday school', says that it is acceptable for him to beat his children as part of their upbringing; the case of a religious preacher who writes an editorial in a religious magazine circulated among his congregation that argues it is only natural, and thus acceptable, to have more than one wife; the case of a religious preacher who states, during a sermon or a confidential conversation with a person who has sought religious guidance, that it is acceptable to force intercourse on his wife; and, the case of a religious preacher who makes hateful posts in a religious Facebook group primarily aimed at followers of another particular religion. The references contain various pictures of stoning or decapitation, accompanied by supporting quotations from religious texts on the same subject. The final example discusses a religious preacher who writes in an editorial that, according to religious writings, women should be stoned for adultery and that he agrees with this and subsequently confirms this as part of religious education. While all of these appear applicable to all religions, references to beating children, polygamy, marital rape, stoning, decapitation and interreligious hate make much of it seem like a thinly veiled reference to what the legislature associates with Islam.

This bill met with remarkable criticism. The first criticisms were from the Danish Institute for Human Rights, which holds the express mandate to promote and protect human rights and equal treatment in Denmark. In criticising the bill, the Institute underlined that its potential reach and wide application across religious communities required a better assessment of the proportionality of the criminalisation and questioned whether enough had been done to protect the two fundamental freedoms of speech and religion. Further, the Institute found that the bill increased the risk of justice becoming arbitrary in targeting religious preachers and that the evidence supporting its enactment was very weak. Finally, the Institute found that the limitations on religion and speech were discriminatory and that the arguments for holding that such discrimination was 'factual and proportionate' were not strong enough.[34]

The Danish Bar and Law Society Council was also critical of the bill and recommended not presenting it to Parliament. It noted that the bill criminalised speech in private and that such a legislative limitation of liberties was 'remarkable' compared to other limitations. It noted that it would make even a priest in confession criminally liable. It found that the 'estimates' and political arguments were not 'weighty enough reasons' and that such limitations to freedom of speech and religion required 'significant documentation in arguing that this measure is both proportionate and necessary in a democracy'. By highlighting this, the Council precisely pointed to the fact that the bill was politically motivated and had little evidence or case law to support it.

[34] Dansk Institut for Menneskerettigheder, 'Høring over udkast til lovforslag om ændring af straffeloven' (2016) dok nr 16/02064-4, available at www.menneskeret.dk/sites/menneskeret.dk/files/08_august_16/hoeringssvar_til_udkast_til_lovforslag_om_aendring_af_straffel_pdf.

Justitia, an independent legal think tank headed by Jacob Mchangama, called the bill 'superficial and inadequate' and said that it risked violating the legal quality criteria of the ECHR and that justice risked becoming 'unpredictable' and 'arbitrary'.[35] Mchangama further highlighted the problem the Ministry of Justice caused by not putting forward any ECtHR precedent or a single court case that would support such a bill and recommended the bill should not come before the Parliament.

Retspolitisk Forening (the Judicial Policy Association) was perhaps most vociferous in its criticism of the basis and proportionality of, and need for, the bill. In addition to most of the points of criticism discussed, which it also put forward, *Retspolitisk Forening* argued:

> [It is] doubtful whether the Ministry's considerations are sound. It must be assumed that the interpretation of the Qur'an, which appears in the television broadcast mentioned above [the Mosques documentary], has been used for several years. Therefore, if evidence could have been obtained that such preaching was contrary to the law of morality or public order, intervention should have taken place long ago, if in fact it was deemed necessary [in accordance with the ECHR's Article 9(2)]. And such necessity has at least to be probable. Now this bill is predicated upon the sole basis of a single piece of evidence, which would then constitute necessity [in ECHR, Article 9(2)]. It remains the opinion of *Retspolitisk Forening* that it is greatly exaggerated to claim that the content of the said TV broadcast constitutes a threat to or a violation of morality or public order.[36]

The most far-reaching change in legal thinking in the bill was pointed out by Professor Lisbet Christoffersen, who challenged the argument of the legislature that the provision forbids discrimination against an individual on the basis of 'his' religion but still allows for general discrimination among religions, as long as it is equitable, proportionate, and warranted. Christoffersen criticised this argument and argued that relative discrimination was compared to other groups, such as politicians, media pundits and others with equally extreme viewpoints who are not limited in their exercise.[37] Usually, and in the light of international law and human rights law, Article 67 is understood to imply that only law may limit freedom of religion, but the new legal thinking of the bill significantly widens the degree of discretion that may be allowed in disadvantaging religion comparably.[38]

[35] J Mchangama, 'Analyse: Lovudkast om kriminalisering af religiøse ytringer er uklart og problematisk i forhold til menneskerettighedskonventionen' (2016), available at www.justitia-int.org/analyse-lovudkast-om-kriminalisering-af-religiose-ytringer-er-uklart-og-problematisk-i-forhold-til-menneskerettighedskonventionen.

[36] *Retspolitisk Forening*, 'Høringssvar ad Forslag til Lov om ændring af straffeloven (Kriminalisering af udtrykkelig billigelse af visse strafbare handlinger som led i religiøs oplæring)', available at www.retspolitik.dk/wp-content/uploads/2014/01/H%C3%B8ringssvar-ad-Forslag-til-Lov-om-%C3%A6ndring-af-straffeloven-religi%C3%B8s-opl%C3%A6ring-.docx.

[37] L Christoffersen, 'Religionsretlig lovgivning 2014–2019: Introduktion til bidrag og temaer i kirkeretsantologi 2019' in A Christoffersen, A Jørgensen and A Andersen (eds), *Religionsretlig lovgivning. Kirkeretsantologi 2019: Trossamfundslov. Blasfemibestemmelse* (Frederiksberg, Eksistensen Akademisk, 2019) 17.

[38] ibid, 22–23.

In arguing for the bill in response to the hearing process, the drafting jurists at the Ministry of Justice restated the legal basis for the bill and argued against amending or changing it. They argued that while freedom of religion is protected in Article 67 of the Constitution, this freedom is limited by the fact that nothing is taught or done that is contrary to morality or public order. In being limited, this freedom is subject to the restriction that, in the exercise of worship, nothing must be done or taught that is contrary to morality or public order. Thus, the Ministry argued that 'it is assumed that the legislative power is left with a wide discretion to determine the boundaries arising from considerations of morality or public order'.

In response to the criticisms of the amendment bill, with particular reference to Article 70, the Ministry wrote:

> [A]s it is thus assumed that Article 70 of the Constitution only prohibits discrimination on the *basis of a particular creed*, and since the bill must apply for anyone who expressly endorses certain criminal acts as part of religious education, the bill does not raise, in the view of the Ministry of Justice, questions in relation to section 70 of the Constitution.

Further, it argued that:

> [A]ccording to the case law of the European Court of Human Rights, the provision that persons in comparable situations as a starting point must be treated equally and discrimination is justified only if it has a legitimate purpose and at the same time is in a reasonable relationship with that purpose. The Ministry of Justice finds that the bill, which is limited to applying only explicit approval of certain criminal offences in the context of religious education, does not discriminate against comparable groups.

Ultimately, according to the Ministry's arguments, in limiting religious freedom, it is left to legislators to 'assess', using their 'wide discretion', what 'morality' and 'public order' mean, despite the lack of documentation and evidence that it is proportionate and necessary to do so. It further persists in limiting both religious freedom and freedom of speech despite there being little factual evidence, no case law, a poor assessment of proportionality and a lack of weighty and important reasons to support the effect of such limitation. Despite all this, the amendment to the Criminal Code became law on 13 December 2016.

V. Bielefeldt and his Criticism of the Danish State of Religion[39]

In terms of the interpretations of the exercise of religious freedom, the recent legislation that has passed through the Danish Parliament demonstrates a want of

[39] For a fuller discussion of Bielefeldt's report, see NV Vinding, 'Discrimination of Muslims in Denmark' in *State, Religion and Muslims* (Leiden, Brill, 2020) 144–96. For a European comparison, see, M Saral and SO Bahçecik (eds), *State, Religion and Muslims: Between Discrimination and Protection at the Legislative, Executive and Judicial Levels* (Leiden, Brill, 2020).

'empirical validity of the underlying ascriptions' and 'proportionality of restrictive legislation', as Bielefeldt, Ghanea and Wiener had warned.[40]

A relevant event in the narrative of the recent legislative trend is the visit made to Denmark between 13 and 22 March 2016 by Dr Bielefeldt as a special rapporteur. While his report from 28 December 2016 is general and touches upon significant aspects of freedom of religion and belief in Denmark, Dr Bielefeldt looked particularly at the special challenges faced by Muslims and the issues of potential discrimination against Muslims in Denmark.[41]

In his report, Dr Bielefeldt recognised the challenge to freedom of religion and belief, with respect to Muslims and warned against the foreboding limitations:

> In order to remain in line with European and international conventions that Denmark has ratified – in particular Article 9 of the Convention for the Protection of Human Rights and Fundamental Freedoms and Article 18 of the International Covenant on Civil and Political Rights – Article 67 of the Constitution requires a broad interpretation of the scope of protection and a cautious interpretation of the limitation clause.[42]

Dr Bielefeldt further criticised the unqualified understandings that held all Muslims accountable for the actions of an extreme few:

> Conditioning the free and peaceful existence of freedom of religion by Muslims, which includes the right to construct and maintain places of worship, on the behaviour of an extremist minority within Islam (whose words might as well merit criminal prosecution as incitement to hatred or violence, but do not represent the views of the majority of Muslims) is unacceptable.[43]

Most critically, however, Dr Bielefeldt emphasised the hard-line and overzealous political and legislative responses to religious extremism as the most explicit threat to freedom of religion and belief in Denmark. While extremism warrants a clear political response, the harsh rhetoric targets all Muslims.

While the move to reinterpret and significantly tighten the judicial view of the limitation clause in Article 67 of the Constitution on the freedom of religion and belief came after his visit, Dr Bielefeldt nevertheless warned against it. In unequivocal terms, Dr Bielefeldt stressed that such a legislative move would be out of line with the internationally prevailing understanding of freedom of religion and belief by giving legislators free and uncontrolled means of eliminating basic human rights and, therefore, was not at all justifiable. In addition, such an interpretation to limit freedom of religion and belief would also threaten 'to strip Muslim communities from their achieved status position in Denmark or to develop new tools for controlling religions, particularly Islam'.[44]

[40] Bielefeldt et al (n 10) 145.

[41] H Bielefeldt, 'Report of the Special Rapporteur on freedom of religion and belief on his mission to Denmark' (A/HRC/34/50/Add.1) (28 December 2016), available at documents-dds-ny.un.org/doc/UNDOC/GEN/G16/442/36/PDF/G1644236.pdf.

[42] ibid, 4.

[43] ibid, 9.

[44] ibid, 10.

VI. Conclusion

Given the many ongoing struggles regarding the regulation of Islam in Europe, there is good reason to consider the recent legislative developments and trends in Denmark, which have pushed against the existing jurisprudence and interpretations on limiting freedom of religion and belief. The political will to regulate Islam, specifically, and religion, generally, to the very limits of the Constitution came in the wake of a deep undercover documentary, which caused a spike of moral panic.[45] It seems clear from the context, occasion and motivations explicitly stated by politicians and legislative jurists that the changes are in danger of being indirectly discriminatory. The particular measure against religious preachers explicitly condoning extremism effectively produces religious preachers who are more dangerous than others in positions of trust.

The use and applicability of *ordre publique* (public order) limitation clauses seems principally based on the 'argued' or 'perceived' anti-democratic sentiments of Muslims in Europe. This is often discussed in terms of securitisation, although politicians are struggling with framing the legislation. While it must be argued that it is the business of public authorities to work for equality, democracy, rights and freedoms, against subversive institutions and their negative impact on social cohesion and public order, it must equally be stressed (as many of the critical voices do) that such efforts must be within the framework of good governance and the rule of law and must live up to the criteria of the quality of law. Much of the actual legislation has been criticised and some of it does not meet international standards, or fails to live up to the criteria of proportionality or necessity. Bielefeldt, Ghanea and Wiener's warning that the handling of this issue 'requires caution, precision and diligence' seems warranted. The irony is not lost. The Danish Government, in its zeal and moral panic and against explicit advice not to, is limiting freedom of religion and widening the discretion for discrimination in the name of requiring religious groups to work for equality, democracy, rights and freedoms.

[45] KS Mirza, *Æresrelaterede forbrydelser* (Copenhagen, Jurist-og Økonomforbundets Forlag, 2018).

PART III

Supranational and Comparative Approaches

11

Islamic Headgear: The Case Law of the European Court of Human Rights

VINCENT A DE GAETANO

I. Introduction

There is an old saying, *cucullus non facit monachum*,[1] which was often resorted to in the years following the Second Vatican Council to allay concerns about Catholic clergy discarding their *soutanes*, or religious habits, in favour of the clerical suit or indeed completely lay clothing. Why, then, does society give so much importance to outer appearance in dress in the context of religion or religious belief? Perhaps, because people need easy visible references, which their minds can process, to arrive at a conclusion about something or someone. From a purely religious or ecclesiastical point of view, dress is symbolic; a symbol of one's dedication to a way of life, of one's belonging to a religious or ecclesial community, or, at a higher level of spirituality and (particularly in the Christian tradition), of one's consecration and witness to evangelical poverty.

I am often asked: what is the position of the European Court of Human Rights (ECtHR) on the wearing of religious clothing and symbols? My answer, perhaps in a rather tongue-in-cheek fashion, is invariably couched in the words a young Thomas Aquinas is said to have replied with when questioned by his master, Albert the Great, 'it depends', to which Albertus Magnus is said to have retorted, 'Exactly'.

II. The Stance and Reasoning of the European Court of Human Rights

There is, in reality, no one, fixed or definite position taken by the ECtHR in Strasbourg on the wearing of religious clothing and symbols, be they Christian,

[1] Which means that a person should not be judged on external appearance, or more colloquially, never judge a book by its cover.

Islamic or associated with any other religious denomination. The function of the ECtHR is not to lay down hard-and-fast rules of dos and don'ts in this field of the external manifestation of one's beliefs through clothing, nor to harmonise legislation across the 46 Member States of the Council of Europe (that may be the task of some other court, however) or to impose on any state a particular legislative choice.[2] All this stems, in the main, from a combined reading of Article 1 of the European Convention of Human Rights (an article often ignored because everyone rushes on to the substantive provisions that follow) and of Article 19[3] (another procedural provision) – the Court is there only to ensure that a state signatory is, in the concrete case that comes before it, securing to the applicant a particular right or freedom in a practical and effective manner, and not merely in a theoretical or illusionary one. In coming to a conclusion that there has been, for instance, a violation of Article 9[4] of the Convention, the Court will explain *why* it has come to that conclusion, but it will not normally say what the state is to prescribe or to proscribe, in its domestic legislation (although that may be implied in the reasoning leading up to the conclusion of a violation or no violation).[5] The Court will first ask itself a number of questions: was there a law on the basis of which the alleged interference with the right espoused in Article 9 was carried out? Was this law publicly promulgated, clear, available to all and, above all, predictable in its consequences (the 'quality of law' criterion or exception)? If all the answers to the questions are in the affirmative, then comes the next examination with the application of the famous (or infamous, depending on which side of the fence one happens to be when judgment is delivered) doctrine of the 'margin of appreciation'. Was the interference with the right, apart from being prescribed by law, also necessary in a democratic society in the interests of one or more of the other values (the purported aims of the interference)

[2] Formerly 47 Member States. The Russian Federation was expelled from the Council of Europe on 16 March 2022 and ceased to be a High Contracting Party to the European Convention on Human Rights (ECHR) on 16 September 2022.

[3] ECHR, Art 1: 'The High Contracting Parties shall secure to everyone within their jurisdiction the rights and freedoms defined in Section I of this Convention.' Also see ibid at Art 19, which reads 'To ensure the observance of the engagements undertaken by the High Contracting Parties in the Convention and the Protocols thereto, there shall be set up a European Court of Human Rights, hereinafter referred to as "the Court." It shall function on a permanent basis.'

[4] Art 9(1), which reads 'Everyone has the right to freedom of thought, conscience and religion; this right includes freedom to change his religion or belief and freedom, either alone or in community with others and in public or private, to manifest his religion or belief, in worship, teaching, practice and observance.'

[5] On the contrary, in a so-called 'pilot judgment', where the purpose is to identify a structural or other systemic problem in the country concerned, which has given or may give rise to applications raising the same issue, the judgment not only identifies the problem but also indicates the type of remedial measures which the state is required to take at the domestic level. The Court may also set a time limit for these measures to be brought into effect. The 'pilot judgment' procedure is governed by Rule 61 of the Rules of Court which can be found at www.echr.coe.int/Documents/Rules_Court_ENG.pdf.

mentioned in Article 9(2)?[6] Did, for instance, the domestic courts carry out a thorough and proper examination of the case, applying, in the process, the basic teleological and other interpretative canons that the Strasbourg Court would apply? One of these crucial canons is that of the principle of proportionality: was the restriction of, or the interference with, the right in question limited to the extent 'necessary in a democratic society'? Otherwise stated, was the interference or restriction proportionate to the legitimate aim pursued? Again, a limitation to a right, or steps taken positively to protect and fulfil it, will not be proportionate, even allowing for a margin of appreciation, where the state institutions (including the domestic courts) have not balanced, or have not sufficiently balanced, the competing individual and public interests when deciding on the limitation of a right. Likewise, where the requirements to be met to avoid the interference in a particular case are so high as not to permit an effective and realistic balancing process, the ECtHR will invariably go for a violation.[7]

In matters touching upon issues of Article 9 (or sometimes other provisions of the Convention but with a religious background to the facts) people often ask: why have two apparently similar cases been decided so differently by the Court? The classic, almost iconic, example is that of *Schüth v Germany*[8] and *Obst v Germany*,[9] both decided on the same day. Both cases addressed dismissal of church employees for similar reasons of alleged sexual impropriety: the organist and choirmaster in a small Catholic parish, Mr Schüth and the Europe Director of Public Relations of the Church of Jesus Christ of Latter-day Saints (commonly called the Mormons), Mr Obst. In the first case, a violation of Article 8 was found; in the second there was no violation. The reason lies in the various steps, according to the rules and canons briefly outlined, which the Court undertakes in the consideration of every case. This is a rigorous examination process which will generally not appear in the media reports about a case, the media reports focusing invariably only on the facts and the outcome.

III. Religious Dress in Society

For someone like me, who was brought up in the 1950s and 60s with people wearing all sorts of dress associated with religion (from elaborate nuns' wimples, to the

[6] ECHR, Art 9(2), which reads 'Freedom to manifest one's religion or beliefs shall be subject only to such limitations as are prescribed by law and are necessary in a democratic society in the interests of public safety, for the protection of public order, health or morals, or for the protection of the rights and freedoms of others.'

[7] See generally D Harris, M O'Boyle, E Bates and C Buckley, *Law of the European Convention on Human Rights*, 2nd edn (Oxford, Oxford University Publishers, 2018) 10–11; B Rainey, E Wicks and C Ovey, *The European Convention on Human Rights*, 6th edn (Oxford, Oxford University Press, 2014) 450–51.

[8] *Schüth v Germany* App no 1620/03 (ECtHR, 23 October 2010).

[9] *Obst v Germany* App no 425/03 (ECtHR, 23 October 2010).

quaint collar worn by the De La Salle Brothers (which is derived from the quite lay rabat worn in France in days gone by), to the black cincture worn by Jesuits to keep their unbuttoned cassock in place) issues connected with the prohibition of wearing veils and other religious symbols sometimes seem surreal. The reality is, however, that in the last 30 years some governments have become more aggressively secular and this has triggered, even if unwittingly, more problems with the wearing of such apparel, whether in public open or public closed spaces. The events of 9/11 in 2001 of course did not help – what was just a piece of cloth worn as a positive declaration of faith suddenly became for some people a sinister public statement associated with radical forms of Islam. Certain laws in some countries, like the French law of 15 March 2004 banning the display of 'conspicuous' religious symbols from the classrooms of all French public schools, and which first brought the issue of religious dress to wider public attention in Europe, also exacerbated matters.[10]

For analytic purposes, one can identify certain factors which have had a determining effect on the outcome of cases brought to the ECtHR involving interference with the use of the Islamic veil and other headgear. These situations include: (i) an aggressively secular state versus a state which is less so; (ii) whether the veil and other headgear is worn in public or in a private place; (iii) whether the public space is an open-air public space or a closed public space (like offices or schools); and (iv) whether the interference is just temporary for security reasons or otherwise. In many cases there is a permutation and combination of one or more of these situations, and the Court often struggles to distinguish or isolate them all in any one particular case.

In relation to the last-mentioned scenario – the requirement temporarily to take off the veil or headgear for security identification or for official documents, here we have a raft of decisions, mainly involving France and Turkey, where the Commission, and later the Court, threw out as inadmissible complaints alleging a violation of Article 9. The oldest of these cases was *X v the UK*, a July 1978 Commission decision involving the Sikh turban.[11] The applicant had been fined for not wearing a crash helmet on a motorcycle and alleged before the Commission that his religion required him to wear the turban at all times, making it impossible for him to wear the helmet. In a telegraphic inadmissibility decision of just three paragraphs, the Commission held that reasons of 'health' justified the interference, although ironically it also stated that, subsequent to the filing of the application, an amendment was introduced in English law towards the end of 1976 exempting Sikhs from wearing the crash helmet.[12]

[10] See generally P Cumper and T Lewis, 'Empathy and Human Rights: The Case of Religious Dress' (2018) 18 *Human Rights Law Review* 61.

[11] *X v the UK* App no 7992/77 (ECtHR, 12 July 1978).

[12] See the Motor-Cycle Crash Helmets (Religious Exemption) Act 1976. The Sikh turban is now allowed instead of the peaked or forage cap in the military uniforms, including ceremonial uniforms, of a number of Commonwealth countries.

The two significant cases in this category dealing with Islamic headgear are *El Morsli v France*,[13] a Chamber decision of March 2008, and *Karaduman v Turkey*,[14] a Commission decision of May 1993. In *Karaduman*, a female student had completed all her studies at university but had not been issued a diploma confirming this. The diploma required a photo of the student and university rules required the student's head to be uncovered in this photograph. The student, for religious reasons, refused to have a photo taken of her without the veil. In a rather convoluted decision invoking both 'the rights and freedoms of others' and the secular nature of the university and its rules, the Commission, by a majority, threw out the application as inadmissible. In the later case of *El Morsli* the complaint under Article 9 was held to be manifestly ill-founded. There, the applicant had gone to the consulate-general of France in Morocco to request a visa. To enter the premises, she was asked to remove her veil for an identity check, which she refused to do; she was prevented from entering and was therefore unable to obtain the visa. The Court took account of the security considerations and the brief time the applicant would have been uncovered. Moreover, the Court rejected the applicant's argument that she would have been prepared to remove her veil in the presence of a woman. The Court held that the fact that the French authorities had not assigned a female officer to carry out the identification of the applicant did not exceed the state's margin of appreciation in these matters (this amorphous concept once again).

As Peter Cumper and Tom Lewis point out in an article published in the *Journal of Law and Religion*, the central consideration in the whole veil and headgear issue is the extent to which a particular state wants to implement its secular policy with regard to dress in public spaces.[15] The manifestation of religious belief through dress poses a challenge to the European Convention system because of a central paradox: while the Convention, and indeed other human rights instruments and written constitutions, expressly protect freedom of religion and of belief as a human right, modern human rights doctrine is essentially secular in nature. This is the product of a shift from a religious to a secular culture at the time of the Enlightenment in eighteenth-century Europe, and the complete jettisoning of the Christian natural law theory (which was central to the rule of law and whatever vague concepts of human rights existed from Augustine down to the Middle Ages). According to Cumper and Lewis, the concept of secularism is far from straightforward; in broad terms 'it may be seen as an attempt to separate religion and State so that the former becomes a private matter while the latter refrains from coercion in the field of belief or conscience'.[16] The state becomes a

[13] *El Morsli v France* App no 15585/06 (ECtHR, 4 March 2008).

[14] *Karaduman v. Turkey* App no 16278/90 (ECtHR, 3 May 1993).

[15] P Cumper and T Lewis, 'Taking Religion Seriously'? Human Rights and Hijab in Europe – Some Problems of Adjudication' (2008) 24 *Journal of Law and Religion* 599.

[16] ibid, referencing B Berger, 'The Limits of Belief: Freedom of Religion, Secularism and the Liberal State' (2002) 39 *Canadian Journal of Law and Society* 49.

neutral and impartial arbiter where issues of the legitimacy of religious beliefs or the ways those beliefs are expressed are concerned. There is a lot of literature that links the notion of secularism with individual autonomy, including the autonomy to express one's beliefs as one wants, and therefore the way a state acts or reacts towards claims based on individual autonomy, ostensibly in line with its duty to be neutral and impartial, is really the gauge of whether the secularism in question is a benign one (or an aggressive one, like in France and (until recently) Turkey).

IV. Voluntary Submission to Restrictions on Religious Dress

One of the reasons advanced by the Commission for rejecting the applicant's claim of a violation of Article 9 in *Karaduman* was that the applicant had voluntarily chosen to attend a secular university (there is no indication in the judgment of what other choices she really had so *præstet fides supplementum*). This, according to the Commission, implied her acquiescence and (*semble* voluntary) submission to the university rules, rules established to preserve the secular nature of the institution and, what the Commission called, 'the harmonious coexistence between students of different beliefs'. No attempt was made to see, for instance, whether these rules were necessary for such peaceful coexistence, and the Commission seems to have taken the state's view on this, as we say in Italian, *a bocca baciata* (from mouth to mouth). Nor is there any credible explanation of how or why, having gone through university wearing the veil, she could now be blocked from obtaining formal recognition of years of effort in her studies simply because of the way she was to be portrayed in the photograph. There is a sense of disproportion in this decision, which is not easy, even for me, to articulate.

V. Religious Dress as Implicit Proselytism

The issue of religious dress was again considered in *Dahlab v Switzerland*, another inadmissibility decision, but this time by the Court.[17] There, a primary school teacher who had converted to Islam was prevented from wearing her headscarf in class. There had been no complaints by the parents of the children she taught or the school administration until the intervention of a school inspector. The Court concluded that there had been an interference with the applicant's right under Article 9(1) but that the interference was justified and was within the margin of appreciation of the state. In doing so, the judges seem to have relied

[17] *Dahlab v Switzerland* App no 42393/98 (ECtHR, 15 February 2001).

on a combination of factors: the denominational neutrality of the Swiss educational system, and the 'tender' and 'impressionable' age of the pupils she taught. It was, perhaps, the more general comments about the headscarf in this case that betray a latent suspicion of the Islamic form of dress. The Court suggested that the applicant's decision to wear the headscarf in the classroom 'might have some kind of proselytising effect' on her young pupils (even though no parents ever complained) and added that it was 'difficult to reconcile the wearing of an Islamic headscarf with the message of tolerance, respect for others and, above all, equality and non-discrimination that all teachers in a democratic society must convey to their pupils'. These words suggest the Court was seeing some sort of association between the Islamic headscarf and militant forms of Islam, even though there was absolutely no evidence the applicant ever had a political or even proselytising agenda (indeed, even the Swiss Federal Court had accepted that she wished to wear this type of veil in order to obey what she considered to be a religious precept). This is similar to the case of Nadia Eweida, one of the four applicants in *Eweida and Others v the UK*, who only wanted to wear a tiny cross with her British Airways uniform as an external manifestation of her deeply held Christian belief; however, there, the ECtHR ruled in her favour.[18]

VI. The Turning Point of *Leyla Şahin v Turkey*

The November 2005 case of *Leyla Şahin v Turkey* needs little introduction not least because of the excellent analysis of the expression 'necessary in a democratic society' by Baroness Tulkens in her dissent.[19] Six months after Leyla Şahin enrolled as a medical student at Istanbul University, the vice-chancellor of the university issued a circular prohibiting the wearing of the Islamic headscarf for women (and beards for men). Şahin was refused access to the university campus, lectures and examinations, and eventually her enrolment was cancelled. Her attempts to have her ban revoked before the domestic courts failed. Before the ECtHR she invoked, inter alia, Article 9. A Chamber of the Court found that there had not been a violation of Article 9. The case then went before the Grand Chamber, and this is perhaps where the greatest damage in this clash between the freedom to manifest one's religion and secularism was done. Because before the Grand Chamber the judges were faced with something of an ultimatum based on arguments that had been building up over the years in support of the 'benefits' of secularism in some states. The Turkish Government argued (quite forcefully and, in view of previous pronouncements of the Court, quite cogently) that the headscarf ban in universities was necessary primarily to protect the constitutional values of secularism. The

[18] *Eweida and Others v the UK* Apps nos 48420/10, 59842/10, 51671/10 and 36516/10 (ECtHR, 15 January 2013).

[19] *Leyla Şahin v Turkey* App no 44774/98 (ECtHR, 10 November 2005).

Government further argued that the Turkish Constitutional Court had repeatedly stated that secularism was the guarantor of democratic values, the meeting point of liberty and equality, a check on the state according preference to a particular religion, and a safeguard which protected the individual from arbitrary interference by the state. All these were hallowed values that the Strasbourg Court had affirmed in numerous previous judgments. In effect, the Government was telling the Court: look here, if you dilute the principle of secularism in this case and do not uphold the Chamber judgment, democracy and human rights protection, for which that democracy is a pre-requisite, would be seriously eroded. And the judges – at least 16 of them – took the bait. They held that since the headscarf had taken on a 'political significance' in recent years, restrictions on the use of that piece of garment was justified by a pressing social need. But then, why only at state universities and state institutions, and not everywhere? Even though no evidence whatsoever had been adduced to show that the Islamic headscarf had provoked disorderly conduct or caused disruption to the everyday life of the university (nor any evidence that the applicant herself posed any threat to secular values) the Court accepted the state's claim that this fact-insensitive law was, in essence, necessary to protect the nation's secular values and, a fortiori, critical for the survival of Turkish democracy. As Baroness Tulkens observed in her dissenting opinion, it is not sufficient to examine an issue *in abstracto* (abstract rights and abstract duties lead to nowhere in the field of human rights), but instead, such issues must be examined *in concreto* and rigorously. She said:

> Once the majority had accepted that the ban on wearing the Islamic headscarf on university premises constituted interference with the applicant's right under Article 9 of the Convention to manifest her religion, and that the ban was prescribed by law and pursued a legitimate aim – in this case the protection of the rights and freedom of others and of public order – the main issue became whether such interference was 'necessary in a democratic society.' Owing to its nature, the Court's review must be conducted in concreto, in principle by reference to three criteria: firstly, whether the interference, which must be capable of protecting the legitimate interest that has been put at risk, was appropriate; secondly, whether the measure that has been chosen is the measure that is the least restrictive of the right or freedom concerned; and, lastly, whether the measure was proportionate, a question which entails a balancing of the competing interests.

VII. Subsequent Case Law

In the Grand Chamber case of *SAS v France*[20] – July 2014 – both Article 8[21] and Article 9 were invoked. This was, incidentally, a relinquished case, meaning that

[20] *SAS v France* App no 43835/11 (ECtHR, 1 July 2014).

[21] ECHR, Art 8(1), which reads 'Everyone has the right to respect for his private and family life, his home and his correspondence.' Also see ECHR, Art 8(2), which reads 'There shall be no interference

the Chamber relinquished jurisdiction to the Grand Chamber. The case involved the wearing of the full-face covering (the niqab and the burqa) not merely the headscarf or hijab (of which there are a number of varieties, but which all keep the face clear and fully visible). Here the issue was unusual: the niqab and burqa were banned in all open public spaces. In a Chamber judgment delivered against Turkey only four years before, the Court had concluded that the prohibition on the wearing of attire associated with a religion or a sect (in this case a black turban, black sirwal trousers and a black tunic, with a baton in hand) in public open spaces where there was no concrete threat of any disturbance, was a violation of Article 9.[22] In *SAS* the Court approached the matter differently. France could not rely on 'secularism' (not even French secularism) to ban religious symbols or the manifestation of one's religious belief in attire in public open spaces. The French Government argued the ban was necessary for reasons of public safety (one of the legitimate aims mentioned in Article 9(2)); but this argument was rejected by the Court, which held that the complete blanket ban on the niqab and burqa was not 'necessary in a democratic society' as there was no general security threat when the Law of 11 October 2010 was passed and, in any case, if in individual cases it was necessary to ascertain the identity of a person, a woman could be asked to temporarily lift the veil. The Court then went on, however, to find no violation by roping in another legitimate aim: the protection of the rights and freedoms of others. This aim, according to the Court, included respect for the notion of 'living together'. The Court, therefore, accepted that the barrier raised against others by a veil concealing the face was correctly perceived by France as breaching the right of others to live in a space of socialisation which made living together easier, and that in doing so and in imposing the ban, France had not overstepped the margin of appreciation accorded to it under the Convention. Two judges, Nußberger and Jäderblom, disagreed. In their dissenting opinion they tried to show how, in their view, concrete individual rights guaranteed by the Convention were being sacrificed to essentially abstract principles and how their colleagues, by what could be regarded as a double or triple somersault, had read too much into the 'rights and freedoms of others'.[23]

by a public authority with the exercise of this right except such as is in accordance with the law and is necessary in a democratic society in the interests of national security, public safety or the economic well-being of the country, for the prevention of disorder or crime, for the protection of health or morals, or for the protection of the rights and freedoms of others.'

[22] *Ahmet Arslan and Others v Turkey* App no 41135/98 (ECtHR, 23 February 2010).

[23] It is interesting to note in this respect that in two separate opinions, both delivered on 17 July 2018 (in *Yaker v France* and *Habbadj v France*) the United Nations Human Rights Committee came to a conclusion diametrically opposed to that of *SAS*. The Committee held that the concept of 'living together' is not a fundamental right and that France had failed to establish a connection between any fundamental rights of others and the ability to see veiled women's faces in public. The Committee concluded that the ban was not necessary to serve a legitimate interest, and thus found that it violated the applicants' right to freedom of religion. The Committee also concluded that the ban disproportionately affected the applicants as Muslim women and introduced an unjustified distinction between them and other individuals who are permitted to cover their faces under the exceptions contained in the law in question. The Committee, therefore, held that the ban violated the applicants' right to non-discrimination.

Abstract principles also featured in my dissenting opinion in the case of *Ebrahimian v France* in November 2015.[24] Ms Ebrahimian had worked for full two years, on annual contracts, as a social worker with the psychiatric department of a public hospital. She regularly wore the Islamic headscarf, the hijab, as a sign of her affiliation to her Islamic faith. At some stage, she was told not to wear it to work. She refused and was informed that her contract for the third year would not be renewed because of her insistence on wearing the veil. The argument of the French authorities and of the majority of the Chamber of the Court in Strasbourg, which incidentally included Judge Jäderblom, who this time did not find any problem in concurring with the majority of the Court that there was no violation of Article 9, proceeded on the doubtful premise that users of public services cannot be guaranteed an impartial service if the public official serving them manifests, in the slightest way, their religious affiliation (even though quite often, from the very name of the official displayed on the desk or elsewhere in the office, one can be reasonably certain of their religious affiliation).

And finally, the case of *Hamidović v Bosnia and Herzegovina* of December 2017.[25] This is the only significant recent case of which I am aware concerning the wearing of some form of headgear associated with Islam where the consequent interference by state authorities was found to be in breach of Article 9. It was a messy case at domestic level, involving issues of contempt of court and whether the domestic court's ruling on the ban of religious symbols in the courtroom was indeed backed by a specific law. The applicant, who had complied fully with a court order to appear in court as a witness, was expelled from the courtroom, convicted of contempt and slapped with a hefty fine for refusing to remove his skull cap. It is a case which shows how issues of secularism can get out of hand and endanger human rights.

VIII. Conclusion

I end this chapter by reproducing my short concurring opinion in *Hamidović*, an opinion which ends with a reference to another concurring (but longer and more erudite and scathing) opinion, namely that of my predecessor as judge elected in respect of Malta at the ECtHR, Giovanni Bonello, in the case of *Lautsi and Others v Italy*[26] of decided in March 2011:

1. This is a case which has everything to do with freedom of religious expression and very little, if anything, to do with contempt of court or keeping order in the courtroom. Unfortunately, at domestic level everything was conflated.
2. The applicant appears to have been caught in the slipstream of the decision taken under Article 242 of the Code of Criminal Procedure in respect of Mr Jašarević

[24] *Ebrahimian v France* App no 64846/11 (ECtHR, 26 November 2015).
[25] *Hamidović v Bosnia and Herzegovina* App no 57792/15 (ECtHR, 5 December 2017).
[26] *Lautsi and Others v Italy* App no 30814/06 (ECtHR, 18 March 2011).

and the other two defendants (see paragraph 6 of the judgment). It is difficult to conceive how the applicant's behaviour, in merely keeping his skullcap on as a manifestation of his deeply held religious belief, can be regarded as being either disrespectful towards the court or as engendering disorder or a lack of decorum in the courtroom. If the applicant had been a Catholic bishop, would he have been prevented from appearing in court wearing the pectoral cross? Or if he had been an Orthodox bishop, would he have been compelled to remove the black headdress? And what if he had been a Sikh? In the last-mentioned case, the removal of the headgear would have been a rather complicated, and possibly time-consuming, affair.

3. While I agree that in this case there was a violation of Article 9 of the Convention and that there is no need to examine the case under Article 14, the Court's analysis should have stopped at the examination of whether the measure in question was 'prescribed by law'. At the time of the incident in 2012 the High Judicial and Prosecutorial Council of Bosnia and Herzegovina had not yet expressed the position referred to in paragraph 14 of the judgment. Article 242 § 3 of the Code of Criminal Procedure was never intended to authorise a presiding judge to impart any order whatsoever – that would be sheer arbitrariness – but only such orders as were or might be necessary for the proper maintenance of order in the courtroom and for the proper expedition of business. Likewise, Rule 20 of the House Rules of the Judicial Institutions of Bosnia and Herzegovina (see paragraph 19) was entirely vague. While a certain sobriety and propriety in one's dress can be read into the expression 'dress code applicable to judicial institutions', that expression could not reasonably have been foreseen at the time as referring to such things as the applicant's skullcap. I am particularly disturbed at the way paragraph 33 of the judgment is worded. The applicant was, in my view, punished on the basis of a general and vague provision of law, a vagueness which no amount of circumlocution by the Constitutional Court could effectively veil. Moreover, a trial judge's inherent power to regulate the proceedings does not extend to provoking unnecessarily a situation of conflict, particularly where a fundamental human right – in this case, that of freedom of religious expression – is concerned'.

4. I likewise fail to see how the reference in paragraph 35 of the judgment to *Lautsi and Others v. Italy* ([GC], no. 30814/06, § 58, ECHR 2011 (extracts)) can be said to be relevant. The issue in the instant case is not one of 'philosophical convictions', as was the case in *Lautsi and Others*. Only in exceptional cases, such as when the principle of secularism is embedded in the constitution of a country or where there is a long historical tradition of secularism, can secularism be said to fall, in principle, within the ambit of the expression 'for the protection of the rights and freedoms of others' for the purposes of the second paragraph of Article 9. The separation of church and State is no more an excuse for an aggressive form of *laïcité* than it is for promoting secularism at the expense of freedom of religion. As Judge Bonello put it in his concurring opinion in *Lautsi and Others*: 'Freedom of religion, and freedom from religion, in substance, consist in the rights to profess freely any religion of the individual's choice, the right to freely change one's religion, the right not to embrace any religion at all, and the right to manifest one's religion by means of belief, worship, teaching and observance. Here the Convention catalogue grinds to a halt, well short of the promotion of any State secularism.

Hamidović is, in my view, symptomatic of how issues involving the external manifestation of one's beliefs can end up intertwined with issues of conscience and conscientious objection, against a backdrop of avowed secularism and often with more than a tinge of prejudice towards anything remotely resembling a confessional attitude by a state. This was strikingly demonstrated by the Chamber judgment in the *Lautsi* case, overturned by the Grand Chamber, with the governments of Armenia, Bulgaria, Cyprus, the Russian Federation, Greece, Lithuania, Malta, Monaco and the Republic of San Marino being granted leave to intervene at the level of Grand Chamber.[27] There was also a clear conflation of issues in *Eweida and Others v the UK*.[28] If one adds the concrete versus abstract analysis paradigm to the equation, it is perhaps no wonder that some of the aforementioned judgments leave one with a feeling that at the end of the day the complainant, both at domestic level and before the Strasbourg organs, was short-changed in the face of aggressive secular principles which find no proper anchorage in the European Convention on Human Rights.

[27] ibid. Eight of these governments (Armenia, Bulgaria, Cyprus, the Russian Federation, Greece, Lithuania, Malta and the Republic of San Marino) were also granted permission to collectively make oral submissions which supported the Italian position that the Chamber had gone too far.

[28] See n 16.

12

Hunting Grounds for Religious Slaughter: A Case Study from the Court of Justice of the European Union*

WOLFGANG WIESHAIDER

I. Introduction

On three occasions between 2018 and 2020 the Court of Justice of the European Union (CJEU) gave preliminary rulings on religious freedom and equal treatment with regard to the slaughter of animals for food production according to religious laws. The first ruling in chronological terms, from Belgium, dealt with the approval of temporary slaughterhouses as a response to the demand during the Muslim Feast of Sacrifice.[1] The second ruling, from France, concerned the compatibility of religious slaughter with organic production.[2] The third, another Belgian case, addressed an actual prohibition of religious slaughter.[3] The Court ruled three times against religious slaughter, although the opinions of the Advocates General had contradicted in two of the cases.[4]

II. Temporary Slaughterhouses

After the legislative power in the field of animal welfare had been transferred from the Belgian Federal Parliament to the regions in 2014, the Muslim communities

* This article is in essence the English rendering of a text of mine: (2021) 68 *Österreichisches Archiv für Recht & Religion* 244 (in German).

[1] Case C-426/16 *Liga van Moskeeën en Islamitische Organisaties Provincie Antwerpen VZW & Others v Vlaams Gewest* [2018] ECLI:EU:C:2018:335.

[2] Case C-497/17 *Œuvre d'Assistance aux Bêtes d'Abattoirs v Ministre de l'Agriculture et de l'Alimentation & Others* [2019] ECLI:EU:C:2019:137.

[3] Case C-336/19 *Centraal Israëlitisch Consistorie van België & Others, Unie Moskeeën Antwerpen VZW, Islamitisch Offerfeest Antwerpen VZW, JG, KH, Executief van de Moslims van België ua, Coördinatie Comité van Joodse Organisaties van België – Section belge du Congrès juif mondial et Congrès juif européen VZW & Others v Vlaamse Regering* [2020] ECLI:EU:C:2020:1031.

[4] Opinion of AG Nils Wahl with regard to *Liga van Moskeeën* (n 1) [2017] ECLI:EU:C:2017:926; opinion of AG Nils Wahl with regard to *Œuvre d'Assistance* (n 2) [2018] ECLI:EU:C:2018:747;

were no longer granted use of temporary slaughterhouses in Flanders to prepare for the Feast of Sacrifice.[5] This policy change was challenged by the Liga van Moskeeën en Islamitische Organisaties Provincie Antwerpen VZW and others. The Dutch-speaking court of first instance in Brussels[6] referred the question of whether Articles 4(4) and 2(k) of Regulation (EC) 1099/2009[7] infringe Article 9 of the European Convention on Human Rights (ECHR),[8] Article 10 of the Charter of Fundamental Rights of the European Union (CFREU),[9] or Article 13 of the Treaty on the Functioning of the European Union (TFEU)[10] to the CJEU for a preliminary ruling. Accordingly, religious slaughter could be performed exclusively in slaughterhouses which meet the requirements of Regulation (EC) 853/2004,[11] even if their capacity did not suffice and it appeared disproportionate to adapt temporary but controlled slaughterhouses to all the requirements of Regulation (EC) 853/2004.[12] The Advocate General and the CJEU answered in the negative, arguing that religious freedom was not restricted.[13] The Advocate General argued that the provision was 'perfectly neutral … with no connection to religious convictions'.[14] The CJEU agreed and added that the restriction to permanent slaughterhouses was a proportionate compensation for allowing religious slaughter without additional stunning according to Article 4(4) of Regulation (EC) 1099/2009.[15]

While it may rightly be asked why a provision should exclude an interference from the outset just because of its neutral wording,[16] there is a remarkable difference between the Advocate General's reasoning and that of the Court. The Advocate General examined the case assuming an interference.[17] He argued that such an interference could not be justified[18] because it did not appear inconceivable to him that

> slaughtering without stunning, carried out in proper circumstances, will be less painful for the animal than slaughtering the animal after stunning it in circumstances in which, for obvious reasons of profitability, and given the widespread industrialisation of the

opinion of AG Gerard Hogan with regard to *Centraal Israëlitisch Consistorie van België* (n 3) [2020] ECLI:EU:C:2020:695.

[5] *Liga van Moskeeën* (n 1) §§ 13–19.

[6] *Nederlandstalige rechtbank van eerste aanleg Brussel.*

[7] Regulation on the protection of animals at the time of killing, OJ L 303/2009, 1–30, as last amended by Implementing Regulation (EU) 2018/723, OJ L 122/2018, 11–13.

[8] Convention for the Protection of Human Rights and Fundamental Freedoms, CETS 005.

[9] CFREU, OJ C 202/2016, 391–407.

[10] TFEU, OJ C 202/2016, 47–390.

[11] Regulation laying down specific hygiene rules for food of animal origin, OJ L 139/2004, 55–205, as last amended by Regulation (EU) 2021/1756, OJ L 357/2021, 27–30.

[12] *Liga van Moskeeën* (n 1) §§ 23–26.

[13] ibid, § 84; opinion of AG Nils Wahl with regard thereto (n 4) § 141; also see the critical comment by M Vordermayer-Riemer, 'Rituelle Schlachtungen im Recht der Europäischen Union' (2019) 72 *Die Öffentliche Verwaltung* 693, 700.

[14] Opinion of AG Nils Wahl with regard to *Liga van Moskeeën* (n 4) § 78.

[15] *Liga van Moskeeën* (n 1) §§ 61–65.

[16] Vordermayer-Riemer (n 13) 694 f; J Witte Jr and A Pin, 'Faith in Strasbourg and Luxembourg? The Fresh Rise of Religious Freedom Litigation in the Pan-European Courts' (2021) 70 *Emory Law Journal* 587, 659.

[17] Opinion of AG Nils Wahl with regard to *Liga van Moskeeën* (n 4) §§ 90–133.

[18] ibid, §§ 95, 128, 133.

> production of food of animal origin, the stress and suffering experienced by the animal when it is killed are exacerbated.[19]

Hence, according to the Advocate General's conclusion, to limit slaughter to slaughterhouses within the meaning of Regulation (EC) 853/2004 would not be a necessary measure regarding the aim of animal welfare.[20] As for food safety, this measure would not even be a suitable one.[21]

III. Organic Food Production Label

The association Œuvre d'Assistance aux Bêtes d'Abattoirs had aimed at stopping the organic labelling of halal beef, from cattle slaughtered without additional stunning, by filing requests to the French Minister for Agriculture, the certification body Ecocert France SAS, and the controlling Institut National de l'Origine et de la Qualité.[22]

After various rejections, the case was brought before the administrative court of appeal of second instance in Versailles[23]. That court referred the question to the CJEU to determine whether Article 13 TFEU, Regulation (EC) 834/2007[24] and Implementing Regulation (EC) 889/2008[25] allowed or prohibited the labelling of meat produced through religious slaughter according to Article 4(4) of Regulation (EC) 1099/2009 with the European Organic Farming Label.[26] The CJEU concluded that Article 3 and Article 14(1)b of Regulation (EC) 834/2007 did not permit the organic labelling of such meat.[27] The judges explicitly referred to their earlier judgment concerning temporary slaughterhouses[28] and emphasised that Article 4(4) of Regulation (EC) 1099/2009, read in conjunction with the recital, authorises the slaughter of animals according to religious rules without additional prior stunning 'in order to ensure observance of the freedom of religion'.[29] However, the Court did not consider religious slaughter equivalent to the other slaughter methods from an animal welfare perspective.[30] The CJEU referred to the Advocate General's

[19] ibid, § 107.
[20] ibid, §§ 123–28.
[21] ibid, §§ 131–33.
[22] *Œuvre d'Assistance* (n 2) § 17.
[23] *Cour administrative d'appel de Versailles.*
[24] Council Regulation on organic production and labelling of organic products and repealing Regulation (EEC) 2092/91, OJ L 189/2007, 1–23, as last amended by Regulation (EU) 848/2018, OJ L 150/2018, 1–92.
[25] Regulation (EC) 889/2008 laying down detailed rules for the implementation of Regulation (EC) 834/2007, OJ L 250/2008, 1–84, as last amended by Implementing Regulation (EU) 2021/1165, OJ L 253/2021, 13–48.
[26] *Œuvre d'Assistance* (n 2) § 33.
[27] ibid, § 52.
[28] *Liga van Moskeeën* (n 1) §§ 55–57.
[29] *Œuvre d'Assistance* (n 2) § 48.
[30] ibid, §§ 49 f.

opinion only once, in relation to scientific studies on stunning.[31] However, the Court did not refute or even mention the Advocate General's other arguments, which had led the latter to a contrary result. The Advocate General had not considered the rejection of organic labelling an interference in religious freedom because it did not concern the compliance with religious rules. Nonetheless, it is indeed disadvantageous for consumers and producers of kosher or halal meat.[32] The Advocate General did not discern an explicit link between labelling and slaughter provisions,[33] adding that 'every killing is problematic from the viewpoint of animal welfare'.[34] Finally, the Advocate General came to the systematic conclusion that the organic labelling of meat products may not be denied with regard to animals that have undergone religious slaughter[35] because

> [i]t would appear to be somewhat contradictory to refer to Regulation No 1099/2009 – even though that regulation makes no reference to 'high levels of animal welfare' – to support the assertion that stunning has, in accordance with Article 4(1) of that regulation, been established as a principle, and at the same time to consider that a reference to that regulation is no longer relevant in the case of the derogation from prior stunning set out in Article 4(4) of that regulation. It follows that the general objective of respect for 'high levels of animal welfare' will still be met, whatever the slaughtering method employed. I do not think that the principle of prior stunning laid down in Regulation No 1099/2009 leads to the conclusion that the requirement of 'high animal welfare standards' necessarily means that slaughter is to take place with prior stunning.[36]

For Regulation (EC) 1099/2009 itself is the result of weighing different goals.[37] As the CJEU had pointed out elsewhere,[38] 'the protection of animal welfare is the main objective pursued by Regulation No 1099/2009 and, in particular, by Article 4(4) thereof, as is clear from the title of the regulation and recital thereof.'[39]

IV. Religious Slaughter

Departing from previous regulations,[40] the regions of Flanders and Wallonia had prescribed a special reversible form of prior stunning for religious slaughter

[31] ibid, § 47.
[32] M Lottini and M Giannino, 'Slaughtering Without Pre-Stunning and EU Law on Animal Welfare: The Particular Case of Organic Production' (2019 14 *European Food and Feed Law Review* 502, 510; opinion of AG Nils Wahl with regard to *Œuvre d'Assistance* (n 4) §§ 36–40, 99.
[33] Opinion of AG Nils Wahl with regard to *Œuvre d'Assistance* (n 4) §§ 52, 67 f.
[34] ibid, § 43.
[35] ibid, § 93.
[36] ibid, §§ 82 f.
[37] ibid, § 104.
[38] ibid, § 77.
[39] *Liga van Moskeeën* (n 1) § 63.
[40] *cf* W Wieshaider, 'Europäischer Überblick' in R Potz, B Schinkele and W Wieshaider (eds), *Schächten. Religionsfreiheit und Tierschutz* (Freistadt, Plöchl and Egling, Kovar, 2001) 166, 167 f.

in 2017 and 2018.[41] The corresponding decrees had been challenged before the Belgian Constitutional Court[42] which referred three questions to the CJEU for a preliminary ruling with regard to the Flemish decree.[43] First, whether Article 26(2)c of Regulation (EC) 1099/2009 permits Member States to authorise religious slaughter only after additional prior reversible stunning. If the first question is answered in the affirmative: whether such an interpretation infringes religious freedom as guaranteed by Article 10(1) of the CFREU or the principle of equal treatment as guaranteed by Articles 20, 21 and 22 of the CFREU, while the killing of animals during hunting, fishing, cultural and sporting events are exempted from the regulation.[44] On a side note, the Parliament of the capital region of Brussels rejected an analogous bill[45] in June 2022.[46]

The CJEU answered the first question in the affirmative and the other two in the negative. Assuming an interference in Article 10 of the CFREU,[47] the CJEU verified its potential justification on the basis of Article 52(1) of the CFREU, which states:

> Any limitation on the exercise of the rights and freedoms recognised by this Charter must be provided for by law and respect the essence of those rights and freedoms. Subject to the principle of proportionality, limitations may be made only if they are necessary and genuinely meet objectives of general interest recognised by the Union or the need to protect the rights and freedoms of others.

The first condition, the basis in law, was obviously fulfilled.[48] The second, the respect for the essence of the freedom, was satisfied, according to the CJEU, because the Flemish provision was said not to prohibit, but only restrict religious slaughter.[49]

The goal of fostering animal welfare did not pose any problem.[50] The Court accepted that the measure was suitable in regard to the scientific studies mentioned in recital 6 of Regulation (EC) 1099/2009.[51] As for the necessity test, the Court attributed a wide margin of appreciation to the Member States and, again, referred to the aforementioned scientific premises.[52] Finally, the Court accepted

[41] Amending Art 15 of the Animal Welfare Act (*loi relative à la protection et au bien-être des animaux*), MB 1986, 16382 by *Decreet houdende wijziging van de wet van 14 augustus 1986 betreffende de bescherming en het welzijn der dieren, wat de toegelaten methodes voor het slachten van dieren betreft*, BS 2017, 73318 and by *Décret modifiant les articles 3, 15 et 16 et insérant un article 45ter dans la loi du 14 août 1986 relative à la protection et au bien-être des animaux*, MB 2017, 60636, respectively; see also Art D.57(1) of *Code wallon du Bien-être des animaux*, MB 2018, 106772.

[42] *Grondwettelijk Hof, Cour constitutionnelle.*

[43] Case 53/2019 [2019] ECLI:BE:GHCC:2019:ARR.053.

[44] *Centraal Israëlitisch Consistorie van België* (n 3) § 32.

[45] See A-345/1-20/21 and A-444/1-21/22.

[46] *Brussels Parlement, Parlement bruxellois*, CRI 36 (21/22) 37.

[47] *Centraal Israëlitisch Consistorie van België* (n 3) §§ 53–55.

[48] ibid, § 60.

[49] ibid, § 61.

[50] ibid, § 62 f.

[51] ibid, § 66.

[52] ibid, §§ 47, 67.

proportionality for several reasons.[53] The non-lethal stunning method had no negative impact on bleeding and avoids pain and stress; the animals died of bleeding exclusively. Moreover, the Court found that changes in values and ideas needed to be taken into account while interpreting the CFREU. Beyond that, Article 26(4) of Regulation (EG) 1099/2009 retained the possibility of importing meat produced by slaughtering without additional prior stunning. Therefore, the Court did not consider religious freedom to be violated:

> Consequently, it must be found that the measures contained in the decree at issue in the main proceedings allow a fair balance to be struck between the importance attached to animal welfare and the freedom of Jewish and Muslim believers to manifest their religion and are, therefore, proportionate.[54]

The CJEU did not see an infringement of the equal treatment principle either. A reference to the exception of cultural and sporting events was held to be irrelevant because it was said that it lacked economic importance in comparison with the production of meat.[55] Finally, the Court found that

> if the concepts of 'hunting' and 'recreational fishing' are not to be rendered meaningless, it cannot be argued that those activities are capable of being carried out in respect of animals which have been stunned beforehand.[56]

Accordingly, this exemption was also considered justified. Regarding farmed fish, the killing of which only Article 3(1) of Regulation (EC) 1099/2009 applies to, the Court identified a necessity for further scientific and economic research.[57]

V. Assessment

Neither the arguments nor the result of this judgment are convincing; in fact, quite the reverse.[58] This impression is reinforced in a synopsis of all three aforementioned judgments. To start with, a procedural remark: pursuant to Article 23(2) of the Statute of the CJEU[59] and Article 96(1)b of its Rules of Procedure,[60] Member States can submit statements of case or written observations in the context of a reference for a preliminary ruling. Thus, it is remarkable that the legal orders of those three Member States which made use of this right prohibit religious slaughter by prescribing additional prior stunning without exception.[61] For Denmark,

[53] ibid, §§ 75–78.
[54] ibid, § 80.
[55] ibid, § 87 f.
[56] ibid, § 91.
[57] ibid, § 93.
[58] *cf* M Ruffert, 'Europarecht: Rituelle Schlachtung von Tieren' (2021) 61 *Juristische Schulung* 470, 472.
[59] Protocol on the Statute of the Court of Justice of the European Union, OJ C 80/2001, 53–66, as last amended by Regulation (EU, Euratom) 2019/629, OJ L 111, 1–3.
[60] OJ L 265/2012, 1–42, as last amended by OJ L 316/2019, 103–106.
[61] *cf* opinion of AG Gerard Hogan with regard to *Centraal Israëlitisch Consistorie van België* (n 4) § 14.

this is stipulated by sections 11–14 of the regulation on slaughter;[62] for Finland, by section 42 of the regulation on animal welfare;[63] and, for Sweden, by Chapter 5, section 1 of the Animal Welfare Act.[64]

A. The First Question

The CJEU referred to Article 27(1) of Regulation (EC) 1099/2009, but not to its Article 27(2). Nonetheless, an analysis of the latter is worthwhile. According to Article 27(2), the Commission had to report to the Parliament and the Council on systems restraining bovine animals by 8 December 2012. This report had to 'take into account … their acceptability by the religious communities'. Since Article 27(2) follows Article 26(2)c of Regulation (EC) 1099/2009, which permits Member States to adopt stricter rules than those provided by Article 4(4), Article 27(2) would lose its meaning if religious slaughter had already been prohibited under Article 26(2)(c). This wording underlines that it is the standpoint of the religious communities which should be relevant. Therefore, pursuant to a systematic interpretation, Article 26(2)(c) of Regulation (EC) 1099/2009 cannot be understood as authorising the prohibition of slaughter according to religious rules.[65]

B. The Second Question

First, it should be recalled that the religious rules in question aim at sparing the animals avoidable pain and suffering, a requirement also laid down in Article 3(1) of Regulation (EC) 1099/2009.[66] The Advocate General stressed this in the case concerning the temporary slaughterhouses.[67] There, the Court had already rightly

[62] *Bekendtgørelse om aflivning, herunder slagtning, af dyr*, Lovtidende A 1751/2020.

[63] *Eläinsuojeluasetus Djurskyddsförordning*, SDK . FörfS 396/1996, as last amended by SDK . FörfS 674/2010.

[64] *Djurskyddslag*, SFS 2018:1192, as last amended by SFS 2021:175.

[65] W Wieshaider, 'Equal Treatment, not just Religious Freedom: On the Methods of Slaughtering Animals for Human Consumption' in A Lange, K Mayerhofer, D Porat and LH Schiffman (eds), *Comprehending and Confronting Antisemitism: A Multi-Faceted Approach* (Berlin, De Gruyter, 2019) 503, 509 f.

[66] Gen 9, 1–18; *cf* IM Levinger, *Schechita im Lichte des Jahres 2000* (Bonn, Zentralrat der Juden and Jerusalem, Machon Maskil L'David, 1996) 13–16; IM Levinger, 'Die jüdische Schlachtmethode – das Schächten' in Potz, Schinkele and Wieshaider (n 40) 1, 3; H Mousa, 'Schächten im Islam' in ibid, 16, 24 f; P Lerner and AM Rabello, 'The Prohibition of Ritual Slaughtering (Kosher Shechita and Halal) and Freedom of Religion of Minorities' (2006/07) 22 *Journal of Law and Religion* 1, 3–5 and 49; N Solomon, 'Conservation' in M Berenbaum and F Skolnik (eds), *Encyclopaedia Judaica*, vol 5, 2nd edn (Detroit, Macmillan Reference and Keter, Jerusalem, 2007) 163, 165 f; L Bezoušková, 'Práva zvířat, nebo náboženská svoboda? Rituální porážky' in H Müllerová, D Černý and A Doležal (eds), *Kapitoly o právech zvířat. 'My a ony' z pohledu filosofie, etiky, biologie a práva* (Praha, Academia, 2016) 608, 610–14.

[67] Opinion of AG Nils Wahl with regard to *Liga van Moskeeën* (n 4) § 107 fn 42.

emphasised that different positions within religious communities enjoy similar protection and must not be offset against each other.[68]

Whenever a provision is meant to strike a balance between two aims, it needs to take both into account. A prohibition of religious slaughter modifies the weighting and does not meet the requirement of respecting the essence of the fundamental right as laid down by Article 52(1) of the CFREU.[69] The CJEU could only maintain its line of reasoning by supposing, unlike the Advocate General,[70] that the Flemish decree restricts but does not prohibit religious slaughter. Therefore, the Court interpreted religious rules itself[71] and incorrectly disregarded religious autonomy.[72] In contrast, as conveyed in the proceedings, the religious authorities declared that the decree conflicts with their religious precepts.[73] This supposition by the Court had a further impact on the proportionality test. Assuming that the Flemish decree was suitable, necessary and adequate to strengthen animal welfare, the applicants of the main proceedings would still not make use of this kind of slaughter, because it contradicted their religious rules.

By referring to the subsidiarity Member States enjoy with regard to Article 4(4) of Regulation (EC) 1099/2009, according to its recital 18, the CJEU does not attach importance to the wording of the latter, which reads 'a certain level of subsidiarity', in contrast, again, to the Advocate General.[74] It is this 'certain level' that emphasises the legislator's effort to protect the exercise of religion, despite the different approaches in the Member States. In the case of organic labelling, the CJEU itself had argued

> that Article 4(4) of Regulation No 1099/2009, read in the light of recital 18 thereof, permits the practice of ritual slaughter as part of which an animal may be killed without first being stunned, [...] in order to ensure observance of the freedom of religion.[75]

[68] *Liga van Moskeeën* (n 1) §§ 50 f; opinion of AG Nils Wahl with regard thereto (n 4) §§ 55–57; opinion of AG Gerard Hogan with regard to *Centraal Israëlitisch Consistorie van België* (n 4) § 47.

[69] T Kingreen in C Calliess and M Ruffert (eds), *EUV/AEUV: Das Verfassungsrecht der Europäischen Union mit Europäischer Grundrechtecharta: Kommentar*, 6th edn (München, CH Beck, 2022) Art 52 GRC; E Rumler-Korinek and E Vranes in M Holoubek and G Lienbacher (eds), *Charta der Grundrechte der Europäischen Union*, 2nd edn (Wien, Manz, 2019) Art 52 GRC, point 18; HD Jarass, *Charta der Grundrechte der EU*, 4th edn (München, CH Beck, 2021) Art 52 GRC, points 28 f.

[70] Opinion of AG Gerard Hogan with regard to *Centraal Israëlitisch Consistorie van België* (n 4) §§ 49, 64.

[71] *cf Centraal Israëlitisch Consistorie van België* (n 3) §§ 54 and 61.

[72] See the different opinion of AG Gerard Hogan with regard to *Centraal Israëlitisch Consistorie van België* (n 4) § 47; M Borowski, 'Der Grundrechtsschutz des religiösen Selbstverständnisses' in A Haratsch, N Janz, S Rademacher, S Schmahl and N Weil (eds), *Religion und Weltanschauung im säkularen Staat* (Stuttgart, Boorberg, 2001) 49; C Grabenwarter in K Korinek, M Holoubek, C Bezemek, C Fuchs, A Martin and UE Zellenberg (eds), *Österreichisches Bundesverfassungsrecht: Kommentar* (Wien, Verlag Österreich, 1999 ff, loose-leaf) Art 9 EMRK, point 19 (6th service 2003); M Morlok in H Dreier (ed), *Grundgesetz. Kommentar*, vol I, 3rd edn (Tübingen, Mohr Siebeck, 2013), Art 4 GG, point 60 with further references; P Unruh, *Religionsverfassungsrecht*, 3rd edn (Baden-Baden, Nomos, 2015) point 92; CD Classen, *Religionsrecht*, 3rd edn (Tübingen, Mohr Siebeck, 2021) points 149–59.

[73] *Centraal Israëlitisch Consistorie van België* (n 3) § 14.

[74] ibid, §§ 45–47 and 69; see also opinion of AG Gerard Hogan with regard thereto (n 4) § 71.

[75] *Œuvre d'Assistance* (n 2) § 48.

The approach of the CJEU to interpreting religious rules independently is also reflected in the adequacy test: a weighting appears different if a measure must be considered as a prohibition rather than mere restriction. The inclusion of value shifts in the field of animal welfare seems dim in view of the Court's arguments concerning equal treatment as addressed in the third question. In this respect, Matthias Ruffert rightly recalled the character of the fundamental rights protecting minority positions in particular.[76] Adequacy cannot be saved by pointing at the possibility of importation. Twenty years ago, such an argument as advanced by the ECtHR[77] had not been convincing[78] while, in contrast to Belgium, France had not prohibited religious slaughter but only restricted its exercise to one central religious body. The Advocate General did not see any impact of the importation possibility on his reasoning either.[79] Rather, he came to the conclusion that Article 26(2)(c) of Regulation (EC) 1099/2009 solely authorises enacting stricter rules within the framework of its Article 4(4), but not beyond it, as in the Flemish decree.[80]

In view of the prohibitive character of the latter, the deduction of the CJEU appears rash. Little remained of the Court's own statement expressed somewhat more than two years previously that

> the derogation authorised by Article 4(4) of Regulation No 1099/2009 does not lay down any prohibition on the practice of ritual slaughter in the European Union but, on the contrary, gives expression to the positive commitment of the EU legislature to allow the ritual slaughter of animals without prior stunning in order to ensure effective observance of the freedom of religion.[81]

C. The Third Question

Eventually, the CJEU was confronted with Regulation (EC) 1099/2009, which excepts certain events fully or predominantly from its scope of application; or, to put it more precisely with regard to the matter under examination here, from the requirement of an additional stunning prior to the killing of an animal. In this respect, the Court considered the exemption of cultural and sporting events to

[76] Ruffert (n 58) 472.

[77] Case 27417/95 *Cha'are Shalom ve Tsedek v France* [2000] ECLI:CE:ECHR:2000:0627JUD002741795.

[78] *cf* the dissenting opinion of JJ Nicolas Bratza, Marc Fischbach, Wilhelmina Thomassen, Margarita Tsatsa-Nikolovska, Tudor Panţîru, Eglis Levits and Kristaq Traja with regard to *Cha'are Shalom ve Tsedek v France* (n 77); F Wittreck, 'Religionsfreiheit als Rationalisierungsverbot. Anmerkungen aus Anlaß der Schächtentscheidung des Bundesverfassungsgerichts' (2003) 42 *Der Staat* 519, 524 f; Vordermayer-Riemer (n 13) 702; L Hehemann, 'Religious Slaughtering, a Stunning Matter: Centraal Israëlitisch Consistorie van België and Others' (2021) 6 *European Papers* 111, 117.

[79] Opinion of AG Gerard Hogan with regard to *Centraal Israëlitisch Consistorie van België* (n 4) § 79.

[80] ibid, §§ 67–75; *cf* Hehemann (n 78) 116.

[81] *Liga van Moskeeën* (n 1) § 56.

be justified because in those cases, the animals are not killed primarily in order to produce meat for human consumption. The killing of animals at such events is not regulated by any other provision of the EU, however. Therefore, it would have been more appropriate to argue exactly the opposite, since the production of meat constitutes a more pressing need than the organisation of cultural and sporting events. Whereas the Court refers to the minor economic significance in this context, it refused to consider the minor economic significance of meat from religious slaughter, as was emphasised by the applicants of the proceedings before the national court.[82]

Faced with the presence of roast venison and game stew on European menus, the CJEU seemingly needed to find a different justification for the exemption of hunting. The justification which the Court eventually presented[83] could, however, have been applied just as well to religious slaughter. For the latter would be 'meaningless', too, under the Flemish decree. It remains unanswered why this argument may be used with regard to hunting but not to religious slaughter.[84]

The Advocate General, who had already replied to the second question differently from the CJEU, did not go further into the third question.[85] In view of the Court's arguments, it would have been interesting to read the Advocate General's opinion in this context. What such a continued reasoning could have looked like, the Advocate General had proved in the case concerning the temporary slaughterhouses.[86]

Finally, the CJEU discussed farmed fish and thereby confirmed that the reasoning can go beyond the concrete questions presented for the preliminary ruling. This is of significance because the Court refused to refer at the same time to another exception, namely that concerning slaughter for domestic purposes. Pursuant to its Article 1(3)b, Regulation (EC) 1099/2009 does not apply to 'poultry, rabbits and hares slaughtered outside of a slaughterhouse by their owner for his/her private domestic consumption'.

Reduced quantities apart, the Regulation here sends a signal for treating different animal species differently. Even if recital 17 only refers to the burden of monitoring and a lack of repercussions on the competitiveness of commercial slaughterhouses, this exception applies in general. It is not obvious why the species concerned should be exposed to more pain when slaughtered pursuant to religious rules in controlled slaughterhouses than when slaughtered for domestic consumption by their owners.

[82] *Centraal Israëlitisch Consistorie van België* (n 3) §§ 20 and 88.
[83] ibid, § 91.
[84] With regard to the equal treatment priniciple see eg S Hölscheidt in J Meyer and S Hölscheidt (eds), *Charta der Grundrechte der Europäischen Union* (Baden-Baden, Nomos, 2019) points 16–28; *cf* M Rossi in Calliess and Ruffert (n 69) Art 20 GRC, point 29.
[85] *cf* opinion of AG Gerard Hogan with regard to *Centraal Israëlitisch Consistorie van België* (n 4) § 88.
[86] Opinion of AG Nils Wahl with regard to *Liga van Moskeeën* (n 4) §§ 90–133.

A further argument focuses on equal treatment with regard to Regulation (EC) 1099/2009 and starts with an exact reading of Article 2(f), pursuant to which stunning is defined as 'any intentionally induced process which causes loss of consciousness and sensibility without pain, including any process resulting in instantaneous death'. While stunning, according to this definition appears to be a method of sparing any pain, a closer look at Annex I of Regulation (EC) 1099/2009 challenges this understanding. In addition to this and beyond religious slaughter, this definition clarifies that the Regulation acknowledges two kinds of methods for bringing about an animal's death: those of killing and some of those of stunning. This fact should not be ignored when religious slaughter is characterised as slaughter without prior stunning, despite its stunning effect.[87] Only simple stunning as mentioned by Article 4(1) of Regulation (EC) 1099/2009 does not lead to the animal's death.

Chapter I of Annex I of Regulation (EC) 1099/2009 enumerates mechanical, electrical, gas and other stunning methods. According to Table 1 therein, the mechanical methods include the penetrative and the non-penetrative captive bolt device, the firearm with free projectile, maceration, cervical dislocation and a percussive blow to the head. Both captive bolt device methods are considered simple stunning, even if Table 1 explains that the penetrative device causes irreversible damage to the brain.

The electrical methods of Table 2 are head-only and head-to-body electrical stunning and the water bath, all of which are considered simple stunning methods, with the exception of a water bath with a maximum frequency of 50 Hz. Chapter II of Annex I of Regulation (EC) 1099/2009 supplements Chapter I with specific instructions for certain methods. According to its division 6.2, 'Birds shall be hung by both legs.' Division 5.2 of Annex II of Regulation (EC) 1099/2009 lays down 'that birds … will not remain hung conscious longer than one minute. However, ducks, geese and turkeys shall not remain hung conscious longer than two minutes.'[88]

The gas methods enumerated in Table 3 of Chapter I of Annex I of Regulation (EC) 1099/2009 are carbon dioxide at high concentration, in two phases, or carbon dioxide associated with inert gases, inert gases alone, and carbon monoxide, either pure or associated with other gases. Carbon dioxide at high concentration or associated with inert gases or inert gases alone are considered to be simple stunning methods for pigs and poultry under the conditions specified in Table 3.

Table 4 of Chapter I of Annex I of Regulation (EC) 1099/2009 lists only lethal injection as another method, which is not used for slaughter purposes.

[87] See Levinger, *Schechita* (n 66) 58–112.

[88] *cf* K Troeger, 'Schlachten von Tieren' in HH Sambraus and A Steiger (eds), *Das Buch vom Tierschutz* (Stuttgart, Enke, 1997) 510, 523.

Hence, it does not seem that the stunning methods are as painless as those postulated by Article 2(f) of Regulation (EC) 1099/2009.[89]

Even in Switzerland, with its tradition of prohibiting religious slaughter dating back to the nineteenth century,[90] Article 179b(4) of the Animal Welfare Ordinance[91] exempts poultry from additional stunning prior to slaughter pursuant to religious rules.

While the scientific studies of European Food Safety Authority (EFSA)[92] referred to in recital 6 of Regulation (EC) 1099/2009 do not cover religious aspects,[93] they differentiate and include references to the disadvantages of the individual stunning methods.[94] In contrast, it was noticed regarding religious slaughter that '[w]hen the cattle were restrained in a comfortable upright position, a skillful cut made with the special, long kosher knife caused less behavioural reaction than a hand waved in the face of the animal.'[95] Such findings are in line with research on slaughter methods and meat quality.[96] Therefore a prohibition of

[89] See SJ Shields and ABM Raj, 'A Critical Review of Electrical Water-Bath Stun Systems for Poultry Slaughter and Recent Developments in Alternative Technologies' (2010) 13 *Journal of Applied Animal Welfare Science* 281, 283 f, 288–90.

[90] *cf* P Krauthammer, *Das Schächtverbot in der Schweiz 1854–2000. Tierschutz, Politik und Fremdenfeindlichkeit* (Zürich, Schulthess, 2000) passim.

[91] *Tierschutzverordnung*, AS 2008 2985, as last amended by AS 2021 926.

[92] See Regulation (EC) 178/2002 laying down the general principles and requirements of food law, establishing the European Food Safety Authority and laying down procedures in matters of food safety, OJ L 31/2002, 1–24, as last amended by Regulation (EU) 2019/1381, OJ L 231, 1–28.

[93] EFSA, 'Scientific Report of the Scientific Panel for Animal Health and Welfare on a request from the Commission related to welfare aspects of animal stunning and killing methods (EFSA-Q-2003-093)' (2004) 45 *The EFSA Journal* 1, annex 17; EFSA, 'Scientific Report of the Scientific Panel on Animal Health and Welfare on a request from the Commission related to the welfare aspects of the main systems of stunning and killing applied to commercially farmed deer, goats, rabbits, ostriches, ducks, geese and quail (EFSA-Q-2005-005)' (2006) 326 *The EFSA Journal* 1, annex 13.

[94] EFSA, *2004* (n 93) annex 135: 'Catching, restraint applied by humans during shackling, and hanging inverted on shackles are distressing and painful to birds. The legs of birds are inevitably compressed during shackling and the degree of compression could be as high as 20 %, which is extremely painful. … The possibility of live birds entering scald tanks cannot be excluded. Fast throughput rates do not facilitate execution of effective backup stunning procedures.' EFSA, *2006* (n 93) annex 53; *cf* opinion of AG Nils Wahl with regard to *Liga van Moskeeën* (n 4) §§ 107–09.

[95] T. Grandin, 'Making Slaughterhouses More Humane for Cattle, Pigs, and Sheep' (2013) 1 *Annual Review of Animal Biosciences* 491, 503; *cf* Troeger (n 88) 523: *'Dabei muß anerkannt werden, daß das Schächten nach mosaischem Ritus durch Sachverständige, eigens dazu ausgebildete Personen mittels spezieller und nur für diesen rituellen Akt vorgesehener Werkzeuge vorgenommen wird ("Chalaf") und somit dem Tier möglicherweise geringere Schmerzen zugefügt werden'.*

[96] EMC Terlouw, C Arnould, B Auperin, C Berri, E Le Bihan-Duval, V Deiss, F Lefèvre, BJ Lensink and L Mounier, 'Pre-slaughter conditions, animal stress and welfare: current status and possible future research' (2008) 2 *Animal* 1501; MM Farouk, HM Al-Mazeedi, AB Sabow, AED Bekhit, KD Adeyemi, AQ Sazili and A Ghani, 'Halal and Kosher Slaughter Methods and Meat Quality: A Review' (2014) 98 *Meat Science* 505; K Nakyinsige, AQ Sazili, I Zulkifli, YM Goh, F Abu Bakar and AB Sabow, 'Influence of Gas Stunning and Halal Slaughter (No Stunning) on Rabbits' Welfare Indicators and Meat Quality' (2014) 98 *Meat Science* 701.

religious slaughter infringes the equal treatment principle unless a society starts to forego the consumption of meat in general.[97]

VI. Binding Force and Outlook

Preliminary rulings pursuant to Article 267 TFEU bind the national courts or tribunals deciding the referred case.[98] Accordingly, the Belgian Constitutional Court decided on the basis of the CJEU ruling.[99] But the Belgian court's decision followed the reasoning of the CJEU both in respect of the national weighing of religious freedom[100] and equal treatment,[101] even beyond the implications of EU law.[102] At least, it emphasised that by prescribing a stunning method, the Flemish decree does not intend to interpret religious precepts.[103]

In addition, the applicants had claimed a violation of the separation of church and state,[104] the right to work and free choice of occupation, freedom to engage in entrepreneurial activity, free movement of goods, and freedom to provide services.[105] The Constitutional Court rejected all of these claims.

Preliminary rulings do not have a further formal binding force. National courts or tribunals of last instance which interpret differently than the CJEU, are, however, obliged to bring the matter again before the CJEU, pursuant to Article 267(3) TFEU.[106]

The Advocate General introduced his opinion in the case concerning religious slaughter by pointing out that

> [t]he present reference for a preliminary ruling provides the Court with a unique opportunity to revisit and expand upon its case-law on Regulation No 1099/2009 and the

[97] *cf* M Rohe, *Der Islam – Alltagskonflikte und Lösungen. Rechtliche Perspektiven* (Freiburg, Herder, 2001) 177; Lerner and Rabello (n 66) 19 f; Bezoušková (n 66) 628 f; Wieshaider (n 65) 513.

[98] C Gaitanides in H von der Groeben, J Schwarze and A Hatje (eds), *Europäisches Unionsrecht*, vol IV, 7th edn (München, CH Beck, 2015) Art 267 AEUV, point 89; M Kotzur in R Geiger, DE Khan and M Kotzur (eds), *EUV/AEUV: Vertrag über die Europäische Union und Vertrag über die Arbeitsweise der Europäischen Union: Kommentar*, 6th edn (München, CH Beck, 2017) Art 267 AEUV, point 36; BW Wegener in Calliess and Ruffert (n 69) Art 267 AEUV, point 50.

[99] Cases 117/2021 [2021] ECLI:BE:GHCC:2021:ARR.117 and 118/2021 [2021] ECLI:BE:GHCC:2021:ARR.118.

[100] ibid, §§ B.14.1–28.

[101] ibid, §§ B.41–48.3.

[102] *cf* with regard to this aspect, S Wedemeyer, 'Neue Entwicklungen des pluralen Grundrechtsschutzes im europäischen Mehrebenensystem?– Anmerkung zum Urteil des EuGH (GK) v. 17.12.2020, Rs.C-336/19 (Centraal Israëlitisch Consistorie van België)' (2021) 56 *Europarecht* 732, 740–42.

[103] Cases 117/2021 [2021] ECLI:BE:GHCC:2021:ARR.117 and 118/2021 [2021] ECLI:BE:GHCC:2021:ARR.118, §§ B.31.3–B.31.4.

[104] ibid, §§ B.29–34.

[105] ibid, §§ B.35–40.

[106] Gaitanides (n 98) Art 267 AEUV, point 92; Kotzur (n 98) Art 267 AEUV, point 37; Wegener (n 98) Art 267 AEUV, point 52.

> reconciliation of the objective of protecting animal welfare and an individual's right under Article 10(1) of the Charter to comply with dietary rules imposed by their religion.[107]

Since the Court's reasoning is not convincing in many respects[108] and also raises further questions concerning the connection between the three rulings, the matter has been returned to its original starting point.

[107] Opinion of AG Gerard Hogan with regard to *Centraal Israëlitisch Consistorie van België* (n 4) § 9.
[108] cf JA Rovinsky, 'A Stunning Decision: How the E.C.J. Butchered Both Religious Freedom and Animal Welfare' (2021) 29 *Tulane Journal of International & Comparative Law* 273.

13

Reasonable Accommodation of Islamic Practices: Europe and America Compared

IOANNIS PAPADOPOULOS

I. Introduction

The conflict between positive law and eccentric, paradoxical, charismatic or eschatological religious practices is becoming increasingly common in advanced democracies, especially in countries or international organisations with religious pluralism such as the United States (US) or the Council of Europe. Indeed, in an era of constant expansion of the regulatory functions and interventions of the state in areas such as public education, the fight against discrimination, environmental protection, spatial planning, public health, nutrition and pharmaceutical safety, the religious commitments of numerous people (especially religious minorities) frequently conflict with public regulations.[1] This trend towards a normative clash between public policies enacted in the name of the general interest and freedom of religious exercise has been exacerbated in recent times as religion has become an integral part of a politics of division (also known as the 'cultural wars' in the US).

Both the Council of Europe Member States' national law and the European Convention on Human Rights (ECHR) have been rather reticent in recognising duties of accommodation to address the barriers to the full enjoyment of equal

[1] An impressive collection of such, sometimes harsh, conflicts in the US can be found in Part One of M Hamilton, *God vs. the Gavel: The Perils of Extreme Religious Liberty*, 2nd edn (Cambridge, Cambridge University Press, 2014). For a collection of policies, rules, and practices entailing reasonable accommodation measures in Europe see L Waddington, 'Reasonable Accommodation: Time to Extend the Duty to Accommodate beyond Disability?' (2011) 36 *Netherlands Juristen Comite voor de Mensenrechten Bulletin* 186.

rights and religious freedom.[2] In contrast, American law has generally been open to accommodation of religion vis-à-vis generally applicable laws for people who claimed exemptions from legally imposed burdens on their free exercise of religious worship.[3] Even though civic republicans (most prominently the Founding Father Thomas Jefferson)[4] were against any 'natural rights' opposing civic and societal duties (such as military service) ordained by law, the pragmatism of Americans urged them to grant accommodation as the best possible way to deflect a potential confrontation between law and religious convictions, and thus to avoid phenomena of civil disobedience or strife that would come at a great cost to social peace.[5]

The idea of constitutionally required or permissible religious exemptions from generally applicable laws was never uncontested, even in as remarkably religious and diverse a country as the US. Many scholars find it hard to reconcile this idea with the basic aim of political liberalism, that of constructing a well-ordered democratic society based on fair terms of cooperation between people with reasonable but irreconcilable disagreements concerning their conceptions of a good life.[6] For the Kantian universalist tradition that many liberals cherish, the law is the cement of civil society and cannot but be neutral and general in its applicability (universalisable), suffering no exceptions (at least as far as practically possible) if a society is to avoid preferential treatments or particularistic regimes that might fatally fragment the political community.[7] Safeguarding, to the fullest possible extent, our fundamental liberty of religious belief and practice, while also installing equality before the law and imposing fairness of treatment of all irrespective of religion, seems like a difficult equation for political liberalism and has provoked much philosophical and legal debate. The problem of accommodation must be placed in the context of this debate.

[2] K Henrard, 'Duties of reasonable accommodation on grounds of religion in the jurisprudence of the European Court of Human Rights: A tale of (baby) steps forward and missed opportunities' (2016) 14 *International Journal of Constitutional Law* 961. Nevertheless, the argument has been made that duties of reasonable accommodation are ultimately about realising equal opportunities and thus substantive equality, so as to overcome the strong European predisposition towards state neutrality vis-à-vis religion; see K Henrard, 'Duties of reasonable accommodation in relation to religion and the European Court of Human Rights: A closer look at the prohibition of discrimination, the freedom of religion and related duties of state neutrality' (2012) 5 *Erasmus Law Review* 59.

[3] PA Hamburger, 'A Constitutional Right of Religious Exemption: An Historical Perspective' (1992) 60 *George Washington Law Review* 915.

[4] See T Jefferson, 'Letter to the Danbury Baptist Association' (1 January 1802), available at founders.archives.gov/documents/Jefferson/01-36-02-0152-0006.

[5] MW McConnell, 'The Origins and Historical Understanding of Free Exercise of Religion' (1990) 103 *Harvard Law Review* 1409; *cf* I Papadopoulos, 'La désobéissance civile pour des motifs religieux en philosophie politique et en droit constitutionnel américains' (2012) 6 *Les annales de droit* 157.

[6] J Rawls, *Political Liberalism*, 2nd edn (New York, Columbia University Press, 2005).

[7] I Kant, *Critique of Practical Reason* (first published 1788, Mary Gregor tr, 2nd edn, Cambridge University Press, 2015); I Kant, *The Philosophy of Law: An Exposition of the Fundamental Principles of Jurisprudence as the Science of Right* (first published 1797, W Hastie tr, The Lawbook Exchange 2010).

II. The Philosophical Origins of Accommodation

The notion of accommodation originates from North America, especially the US and Canada. This is the reason why the European Court of Human Rights (ECtHR) refers to the United States Constitution and Title VII of the Civil Rights Act (1964) and also to the Canadian Charter of Rights and Freedoms (1982) in its relevant comparative law developments.[8] In order to understand the general attitude of American law on accommodation of religious practices, we must first understand the basic constitutional text and its underlying philosophy. The First Amendment to the US Constitution states that 'Congress shall make no law respecting an establishment of religion, or prohibiting the free exercise thereof'.[9] The most relevant theoretical model regarding the political and moral philosophy underlying the free exercise of religious worship is that of religious autonomy (or religious voluntarism), as expounded by the Founding Father James Madison in his famous pamphlet 'Memorial and Remonstrance against Religious Assessments'.[10] In this pamphlet, Madison protested against a Virginia bill that would have violated religious liberty by requiring taxpayers to support a Christian church. Madison's fundamental argument was that religion 'must be left to the conviction and conscience of every man; and it is the right of every man to exercise it as these may dictate', because it depends on 'the evidence contemplated by their own minds' and 'cannot follow the dictates of other men'. Ultimately, religion must be 'exempt from the authority of the Society at large', and 'still less can it be subject to that of the Legislative Body'. In other words, religious conviction is a natural and inalienable right of every person over which no government could have legitimate power.

This model promotes a principle of religious autonomy guaranteeing the free and voluntary (dis)connection between individuals and a specific religion, or religion in general. Heavily influenced by Madison's philosophy, the Free Exercise Clause was written to guarantee freedom of conscience, preventing any coercion regarding religious beliefs or practices. The idea of Madison can thus be expressed as a constitutional prohibition, not just of any direct restriction on the free religious conscience of individuals, but also of indirect restrictions capable of seriously encroaching on that freedom through more subtle discriminations. Even though this is not explicitly written in the 'Memorial and Remonstrance', it is conceivable that one way for the state to impinge upon the principle of religious autonomy is to bring indirect restrictions to certain minority religious practices in a way that is

[8] See, eg, *Eweida et al v the United Kingdom*, App Nos 48420/10, 59842/10, 51671/10 and 36516/10, 15 January 2013, [48]–[49]. Only US constitutional law will be analysed here because of its seniority and preponderance.

[9] The first part of the First Amendment ('Congress shall make no law respecting an establishment of religion') has come to be known as the Establishment Clause, and its second part ('or prohibiting the free exercise thereof') as the Free Exercise Clause.

[10] J Madison, 'Memorial and Remonstrance against Religious Assessments' (*c* 20 June 1785), available at founders.archives.gov/documents/Madison/01-08-02-0163.

incidental to the implementation of a neutrally formulated law of general validity. Therefore, in such cases, accommodation of said religious practices is called for as a shield against such abusive legislation.

III. The US Supreme Court Accommodation Case Law in a Nutshell

Relevant US Supreme Court case law that has accepted claims of accommodation starts with the seminal case *Sherbert v Verner*.[11] There, Adell Sherbert, a member of the Seventh Day Adventist Church, was fired from her job because she refused to work on Saturdays (the Sabbath for the Adventists). However, South Carolina's unemployment insurance fund considered that Sherbert did not have 'good cause' for turning down available work on Saturday, and therefore rejected her claim for unemployment benefits. *Sherbert* clearly was a case of unequal treatment at work since South Carolina law at the time prevented employers from demanding that their employees work on Sundays, which meant that only those who observed the Sabbath on other days could be denied unemployment benefits for their refusal to work. Nevertheless, Justice Brennan's opinion for the Court was ambiguous. He ultimately analysed the constitutional question not as one of equal protection, but rather by considering whether any 'compelling state interest … justifies the substantial infringement of [Sherbert's] First Amendment rights'.[12]

Thus, the Supreme Court applied, for the first time, the strict scrutiny standard which requires the state to prove a 'compelling state interest' (a state interest of the highest order) before a court will allow it to reject a claim for unemployment benefits filed by employees discharged because of a conflict between their employer's requests and their religious beliefs. This case clearly rejected a 'religion blindness' philosophy (the legislator's indifference to the possible impact of legislation on the freedom of worship of specific religious observers) and eventually became the precedent for the idea that religious conduct is presumptively entitled to a constitutional exemption from generally applicable laws. Thereafter, anytime a government policy was found by a judge to substantially burden a religious practice, it would be subject to the compelling state interest test, by means of which religiously motivated persons are constitutionally entitled to an *in concreto* judicial accommodation of their religion, by disregarding an *in abstracto* valid law, unless the government can demonstrate not only that a state interest of the highest order is at stake but also the means the state has chosen to pursue that interest are the least restrictive possible for the enjoyment of a Free Exercise right.

In 1972, in an impressive ruling in *Wisconsin v Yoder*, the Supreme Court ordered the state of Wisconsin to exempt members of an Amish–Christian group

[11] *Sherbert v Verner*, 374 US 398 (1963).
[12] ibid, 406.

from its compulsory school attendance law, which required all persons up to 16 years of age to attend public or private school or else their parents would be subject to a fine.[13] While the Court accepted that universal education is indeed a strong state interest, it nevertheless balanced it against the fundamental right protected by the Free Exercise Clause and the traditional interest of parents with respect to the religious upbringing of their children. In doing so, the Court rejected Wisconsin's argument that its interest in universal education would be adversely affected by granting an exemption to the Amish accommodating their religious objections by forgoing up to two additional years of compulsory education (from 14 to 16 years of age). The Court held, after considering expert testimony, that such an accommodation would not impair the physical or mental health of Amish children, result in an inability to be self-supporting or discharge the duties and responsibilities of citizenship, or in any other way materially detract from the welfare of society.

In *Thomas v Review Board*, another unemployment insurance decision, Eddie Thomas, a metallurgical worker and Jehovah's Witness, refused on religious grounds to be transferred to a department building military equipment and instead asked to be laid off.[14] After his request was denied, he quit, asserting that his religious beliefs prevented him from participating in the production of weapons, and he was subsequently denied unemployment compensation benefits under the Indiana Employment Security Act. As in *Sherbert*, the Court held that 'a person may not be compelled to choose between the exercise of a First Amendment right and participation in an otherwise available public program'.[15] A substantial burden on religion exists every time the state conditions the receipt of an important benefit upon conduct proscribed by a religious faith, or inversely where it denies such a benefit because of conduct mandated by a religious faith, thereby putting substantial pressure on an adherent either to modify his behaviour and to violate his beliefs, or to lose his employment.[16] It is interesting here that the particular belief of the petitioner might not have been mainstream in his church, since it appears other Jehovah's Witnesses had no scruples about producing tank turrets, but in Chief Justice Burger's opinion, 'Courts should not undertake to dissect religious beliefs because the believer admits that he is 'struggling' with his position or because his beliefs are not articulated with the clarity and precision that a more sophisticated person might employ'.[17] Finally, the state's professed reasons for this impingement on Thomas's religious freedom were not considered sufficient to justify the Indiana Employment Security Act as the least restrictive means of achieving a compelling state interest.

[13] *Wisconsin v Yoder*, 406 US 205 (1972).
[14] *Thomas v Review Board of the Indiana Employment Security Division*, 450 US 707 (1981).
[15] ibid, 716.
[16] ibid, 716–18.
[17] ibid, 715.

The next instalment in the string of unemployment benefits cases came in 1987 with *Hobbie v Unemployment Appeals Commission*.[18] There, Paula Hobbie, a freshly converted Seventh Day Adventist, told her employer she would no longer accept work on Saturdays, and was immediately discharged. Her claim for unemployment compensation was denied for 'misconduct connected with her work' under the applicable Florida statute. The Supreme Court once again applied the *Sherbert* compelling state interest test and found in favour of the petitioner stating that the timing of Hobbie's religious conversion was legally irrelevant and the only thing that mattered was the existence of a serious burden on her religious freedom.[19] The final act in this line of cases concerning unemployment benefits was *Frazee v Illinois Department of Employment Security*, where the petitioner was also granted the exemption he sought from the obligation to work on Sundays on the same grounds as in *Hobbie*.[20]

The technicalities of this case law can be summarised as follows. If a person refuses to obey the law by invoking religious reasons and seeks a constitutionally guaranteed exemption from this law, that person will have to preliminarily prove: a) a sincere religious belief that b) is at odds with a legislative provision or a regulation. If both criteria are satisfied, the burden of proof will then shift to the state, which will have to overcome a presumption of unconstitutionality by demonstrating both of the following: a) that the law pursues a compelling state interest and b) that an exemption from that law would substantially hinder that interest (otherwise said, that the state has used the least restrictive means for the pursuit of its compelling interest). Thus, the Supreme Court has, in a series of judgments, established a presumption in favour of the accommodation of sincere religious believers and a form of proportionality review of legislation restricting the exercise of the religious freedom of an individual or a minority.

IV. The Benefits and Shortfalls of Accommodation

That is how American law tried for 27 years to reconcile, in a particularly liberal way, individual religious claims with neutral laws of universal scope so as to prevent the possibility of strong regulatory conflicts between secular legal obligations and divine moral commands in people's lives. Through its acceptance of some claims of accommodation, the US Supreme Court has rejected a dogmatic and absolutist view of the separation of church and state. It also has evidently concluded that there is a sort of 'required accommodation' sphere, which recognises that the appearance of the *in abstracto* neutrality of the law vis-à-vis a religion might have an adverse *in concreto* impact depending on the status of

[18] *Hobbie v Unemployment Appeals Commission of Florida*, 480 US 136 (1987).
[19] ibid, 144.
[20] *Frazee v Illinois Department of Employment Security*, 489 US 829 (1989).

the person to whom the law is enforced upon. Consequently, the whole point of accommodation of religion seems to be genuine equality of treatment, which sometimes, at least, requires the granting of concessions (often in the form of exemptions) to those whose sincere religious beliefs are substantially affected by the applicable regulation. But, of course, things can become complicated since, beyond that sphere of required accommodation, there is also room for the legislator to allow for the establishment of some wider 'permissive accommodation' of religious practices, even when this is not required by the Constitution.

Nevertheless, there is a flip side to this liberal approach to religious accommodation. Several scholars have warned against the acceptance of an open-ended right to claim religious accommodations because they see such a normative state of affairs as liable to grant religiously motivated persons a 'presumptive constitutional right to disobey the laws that everyone else is required to follow'.[21] To them, the *Sherbert* compelling state interest test standard creates a constitutional entitlement for religious orthodoxy since it gives an across-the-board preferential treatment to religious commitments at the expense of other legitimate public values or purposes. An indiscriminate recognition of a constitutional right to disregard any legal rule that falls short of satisfying the compelling state interest test would wreak havoc in any organised society, where people are regularly called upon by the law to act in ways that they dislike so that society is able to function.[22] In brief, for some scholars, claims for judicially enforceable exemptions from general laws morph into 'a special interest demand'.[23]

These reservations about the very notion of accommodation raise the question whether they are merely a device to avoid or to circumvent unpleasant regulatory obligations contrary to the principle of equality before the law. If every religious believer becomes automatically entitled to exceptional treatment, the very concept of law as a universal source of obligations is undermined, opening a Pandora's box for government in devising unending customised arrangements, and divesting legal regulation of its functionality.

Despite some important beneficial effects for religious minorities, the *Sherbert* line of cases has revealed an ad hoc balancing system of adjudication lacking an intelligible and coherent normative foundation. The case law reveals a balancing method of adjudication in which judgment on the nature and weight of the burden imposed on religious exercise as well as on the gravity of the state's interests naturally invites 'indeterminacy and ad hockery'.[24] The compelling state interest test

[21] CL Eisgruber and LG Sager, *Religious Freedom and the Constitution* (Cambridge, Harvard University Press, 2007) 11; *cf* Hamilton (n 1) 1–3, 8–9, 349–51; IC Lupu, 'Reconstructing the Establishment Clause: The Case Against Discretionary Accommodation of Religion' (1991) 140 *University of Pennsylvania Law Review* 555; IC Lupu, 'The Trouble with Accommodation' (1992) 60 *George Washington Law Review* 743.

[22] That is the basic idea underlying Joseph Raz's concept of 'exclusionary reasons for action' in J Raz, *Practical Reason and Norms*, 2nd edn (Princeton, Princeton University Press, 1990) 185.

[23] D Laycock, 'Sex, Atheism, and the Free Exercise of Religion' (2011) 88 *University of Detroit Mercy Law Review* 407, 422.

[24] Eisgruber and Sager (n 21) 85.

is a judicial, not merely prudential, standard. It does not simply counsel policy-makers to accommodate as many bona fide demands as possible for religiously motivated exemptions without altering the democratic scheme of government; it actually reverses the presumption of constitutionality of legislation by requiring that policymakers 'bear the burden of proving that their refusals to make accommodations are well justified'.[25]

It is therefore not surprising that the *Sherbert* compelling state interest test experienced an increasing number of drawbacks over the years, until it was abolished by the controversial Supreme Court decision *Employment Division v Smith*.[26] Regulatory tension was mounting between the *in concreto* protection of religious freedom via the *Sherbert* standard, if necessary even by carving out areas of exemptions from the general law, and the need to reduce administrative complexity and fraud, inequality between believers of different religious beliefs and, more generally, to limit the application of special immunity from universal laws to only relatively innocuous cases in which the harm made to third parties is minor.[27] In effect, for 27 years (between 1963 and 1990), even though the Supreme Court was nominally committed to the idea that religiously motivated persons enjoy a presumptive right to accommodate their religious needs via exemptions from generally applicable laws, it 'repeatedly found excuses to avoid the consequences of this nominal commitment' from a consequentialist standpoint because in many cases the outcome would have been too radical.[28]

Thus, in *United States v Lee* (1982), the Amish community's newest request for an exemption (this time from the obligation of Amish employers to pay social security taxes because of their religious opposition to the national social security system) was rejected by the Supreme Court on the grounds that a fully uniform, and with no exemptions, enforcement of the Social Security Act is necessary for its effective administration.[29] In essence, the Government has a compelling state interest in sustaining a viable scheme of social insurance, and the only way to satisfy this interest is through the universal collection of social security contributions from all the taxable persons, since the administration would face insuperable problems in the implementation of the Act were it to examine all exemption claims. Then in *Tony and Susan Alamo Foundation v Secretary of Labor* (1985), the Supreme Court ruled that non-profit religious organisations are not exempt from the Fair Labor

[25] ibid, 86.

[26] *Employment Division v Smith*, 494 US 872 (1990). This important case will be presented and assessed in the following section.

[27] JE Ryan, Note, '*Smith* and the Religious Freedom Restoration Act: An Iconoclastic Assessment' (1992) 78 *Virginia Law Review* 1407, 1417 reports the very low success rate of accommodation claims under the compelling state interest test in the Supreme Court and the federal courts of appeal until *Employment Division v Smith* was handed down in 1990; *cf* Eisgruber and Sager (n 21) 12, 41–43, 98–100.

[28] Eisgruber and Sager (n 21) 280. P Horwitz, 'The *Hobby Lobby* Moment' (2014) 128 *Harvard Law Review* 154, 168 sees it inversely: 'The rule [the compelling state interest test] may have been weakly or inconsistently applied, but there was little doubt that it *was* the rule.'

[29] *United States v Lee*, 455 US 252 (1982).

Standards Act (the basic federal labour law imposing an obligation on employers to pay minimum wages) even though their employees did not want to receive cash salaries and instead worked in exchange for food, clothing, shelter, transportation and medical benefits.[30] Despite the argument of the Alamo Foundation that its businesses were 'infused with a religious purpose', a unanimous Court found that the specific enterprises in question were commercial in nature and competed with other commercial businesses.[31] The Court circumvented the Alamo Foundation's specific claim for exemption by holding that the challenged labour policy had not really burdened religious exercise at all.

In *Goldman v Weinberger* (1986), the Supreme Court denied the request of a Jewish military doctor to wear his yarmulke under his helmet during service on the grounds that the Free Exercise Clause applies less strictly to the military than to ordinary citizens and that military regulations need to be uniform in order to 'foster instinctive obedience, unity, commitment, and esprit de corps'.[32] Using this logic, the Court found that the First Amendment does not require the military to accommodate such practices as wearing a religious symbol since that would detract from the uniformity sought by dress regulations. This is tantamount to saying that the compelling state interest test should not apply in the military context. This line of reasoning was also followed in the prison context. In *O'Lone v Estate of Shabazz*, the Supreme Court denied the request of Muslim inmates to accommodate the prison's work programme and allow them to attend a Muslim congregational service on Fridays.[33] The Court reasoned that respect and deference for the judgement of prison administrators is a constitutional requirement, and therefore strict scrutiny does not apply when it comes to incarceration. On the contrary, a more relaxed and deferential standard of 'reasonableness' implies that when the policies challenged are reasonably related to legitimate penological interests, there is no offence to the Free Exercise Clause.[34] It is obvious (and noteworthy) that in the last two cases, traditional respect for military and penitentiary institutions played a key role.[35]

Finally, in *Lyng v Northwest Indian Cemetery Protective Association* (1988), when the US Forest Service decided to build a road through a sacred Indian burial ground on federal land and to allow for timber harvesting in the same area, the Supreme Court flatly rejected the Native Americans' claim of accommodation by holding that the compelling state interest test did not apply to government decisions about how to use its own property.[36] At that particular moment, the Court seemed to have reached a sort of tipping point regarding the *Sherbert* standard on

[30] *Tony and Susan Alamo Foundation v Secretary of Labor*, 471 US 290 (1985).
[31] ibid, 298.
[32] *Goldman v Weinberger*, 475 US 503, 507 (1986).
[33] *O'Lone v Estate of Shabazz*, 482 US 342 (1987).
[34] ibid, 350–53.
[35] It is worth noting that both opinions for the majority were delivered by the conservative Chief Justice William Rehnquist and that strong dissents were filed by the liberal Justices.
[36] *Lyng v Northwest Indian Cemetery Protective Association*, 485 US 439 (1988).

religious accommodations, as is made obvious by Justice O'Connor's opinion for the majority: 'The Free Exercise Clause is written in terms of what the government cannot do to the individual, not in terms of what the individual can exact from the government.'[37] It is true that both in the case of the Jewish military officer and the preservation of Native American sacred land, Congress moved fast to remedy these harms to religious practices by crafting a specific exemption from the military dress regulations in the former case[38] and by defunding the Forest Service road in the latter case.[39] However, as far as judicial accommodations to religion were concerned, it had become evident by the end of the 1980s that the *Sherbert* frame of mind had reached the end of the road.

V. The Backlash against Accommodation and its Aftermath

That is how the Supreme Court arrived at the reversal of 1990 in *Employment Division v Smith*.[40] There, two Native Americans from Oregon were discharged from their employment because of their sacramental ingestion of peyote (a prohibited hallucinogenic drug traditionally at the heart of the religious practices of Native Americans, in much the same way as wine and bread for Christians). When they sought unemployment benefits, they were turned down because, under Oregon law, employees discharged for work-related 'misconduct' were disqualified from receiving such benefits. The Supreme Court ruled that a person may not defy neutral laws of general applicability, even as an expression of religious belief because, according to Justice Scalia, 'To permit this would make the professed doctrines of religious belief superior to the law of the land, and in effect to permit every citizen to become a law unto himself.'[41] Consequently, generally applicable laws no longer have to meet the strict standard of *Sherbert*'s compelling state interest test when they do not directly target specific religious practices for discrimination. For the *Smith* Court, anything else would create a 'private right to ignore generally applicable laws' and would be 'a constitutional anomaly'.[42]

Smith effectively overruled *Sherbert* and opened a new era of legal egalitarianism[43] in which, according to Eisgruber and Sager, individuals, organisations, and religious practices must fairly share the burdens and limitations that

[37] ibid, 451 (quoting Justice William O Douglas's concurring opinion in *Sherbert*).

[38] 10 USC § 774.

[39] US House Committee on Appropriations, *Department of the Interior and Related Agencies Appropriations Bill*, 100th Congress, 2nd session, 1988, House of Representatives Reports 100–713, 72.

[40] *Smith* (n 26).

[41] ibid, 879 (quoting from *Reynolds v United States*, 98 US 145 (1879)).

[42] ibid, 886. Note that *Smith* made clear that despite the inglorious end of judicially ordered exemptions, the legislator remained free in principle to craft 'nondiscriminatory religious-practice exemptions' from generally applicable laws. ibid, 890.

[43] The expression is by Horwitz (n 28) 170.

result from life in every organised society. Therefore, accommodations should no longer be granted to individuals or minority religious groups if some similar accommodation has not been granted, on an equal basis, to another religious (or even secular) social group.[44] Nonetheless, too strict an egalitarianism would certainly provoke injustice to religious minorities such as Native Americans, since their sacramental use of peyote would not get the same kind of favourable treatment that the sacramental use of wine already enjoys in Oregon under 'local option dry laws' (state statutes that give counties the option to decide whether to ban the purchase and consumption of alcohol and that explicitly exempt sales of 'wines to church officials for sacramental reasons').[45] More importantly, criticism of *Smith* pointed out that a sweeping passage in Justice Scalia's opinion seemed to renounce altogether the Court's traditional role as protector of minority rights against majority oppression:[46]

> It may fairly be said that leaving accommodation to the political process will place at a relative disadvantage those religious practices that are not widely engaged in; but that unavoidable consequence of democratic government must be preferred to a system in which each conscience is a law unto itself or in which judges weigh the social importance of all laws against the centrality of all religious beliefs.[47]

Having been widely considered as diminishing the protections of the Free Exercise Clause and as effectively ending the previous liberal regime of accommodation, *Smith* was reviled, and accordingly ignited a firestorm of controversy.[48] The reaction against it managed to build an impressively diverse political coalition of liberals and religious conservatives. This coalition brought the affair to Congress and found a receptive audience among its members, having almost fully suppressed the complexities in the application of the *Sherbert* compelling state interest test.[49] Eventually, in 1993, Congress unanimously passed the Religious

[44] Eisgruber and Sager (n 21). *Smith* (n 26) 885–86 seems to think so as well, since it professed that, contrary to what happens in the field of religious freedom where it creates a constitutional anomaly, the compelling state interest test has produced genuine constitutional norms in the fields of treatment on the basis of race and of regulation of the content of speech (ie, equality of treatment and an unrestricted flow of contending speech, respectively).

[45] Oregon Revised Statutes § 471.510. Besides, federal drug law had already exempted the use of peyote in Native American religious ceremonies since 1967 (21 Code of Federal Regulations § 1307.31). It is worth noting that after *Smith*, Oregon passed a law specifically exempting the ritual use of peyote (Oregon Revised Statutes § 475.992[5], [6]).

[46] M McConnell, 'Free Exercise Revisionism and the *Smith* Decision' (1990) 57 *University of Chicago Law Review* 1109, 1129.

[47] *Smith* (n 26) 890.

[48] KL Karst, 'The First Amendment, the Politics of Religion and the Symbols of Government' (1992) 27 *Harvard Civil Rights-Civil Liberties Law Review* 503; *cf* R West, 'The Supreme Court, 1989 Term – Foreword: Taking Freedom Seriously' (1990) 104 *Harvard Law Review* 43, 53; and KM Sullivan, 'Religion and Liberal Democracy' (1992) 59 *University of Chicago Law Review* 195, 216.

[49] Douglas Laycock was among the experts that drafted RFRA and supported it in congressional hearings; see D Laycock and OS Thomas, 'Interpreting the Religious Freedom Restoration Act' (1994) 73 *Texas Law Review* 209, 210–11 and D Laycock, 'Conceptual Gulfs in *City of Boerne v. Flores*' (1998) 39 *William & Mary Law Review* 743, 774–75. Ira Lupu was another expert who tried to alert Congress

Freedom Restoration Act (RFRA) in the House of Representatives and with only three dissenting votes in the Senate. RFRA provides that 'Government shall not substantially burden a person's exercise of religion even if the burden results from a rule of general applicability' and the rule must be 'the least restrictive means of furthering that compelling governmental interest'.[50] RFRA explicitly purported to 'restore the compelling interest test as set forth in *Sherbert v. Verner* … and *Wisconsin v. Yoder* … and to guarantee its application in all cases where free exercise of religion is substantially burdened'.[51] RFRA went as far as contradicting judicial experience by stating that 'the compelling interest test as set forth in prior federal rulings is a *workable test* for striking sensible balances between religious liberty and competing prior governmental interests'.[52] In short, in RFRA, Congress decided to position itself as an adversary of the Supreme Court. The Court had found its own jurisprudence wanting and had claimed that the legislator is better suited than judges to craft exemptions in the name of accommodation of religion; in RFRA, Congress openly defied the Court by finding, instead, that judges are better suited to the task and by curiously making the jurisprudential finding that the Court was wrong to think its own past precedents unworkable.[53]

VI. The *Hobby Lobby* Moment as the Turning Point for Social Acceptance of Religious Accommodation

In 1997, the Supreme Court held RFRA unconstitutional, but only as to its restrictions on state and local conduct, on grounds of federalism.[54] The statute's restrictions on federal government remained in place, however, and the Court later unanimously found that the members of a religious group called Uniao do Vegetal had a RFRA-based right to the sacramental use of hoasca, a hallucinogenic tea ingested as part of their communion sacrament.[55] In a bizarre twist of fortune, the close parallel between the hoasca and the peyote ceremonies enabled the Court to conclude that no compelling state interest could justify the federal prohibition of the hallucinogenic tea, inasmuch as the Federal Government had long ago created an exemption from the Controlled Substances Act in favour of the sacramental use of peyote.[56]

on the internal inconsistencies of the *Sherbert* line of cases but found his message unwelcome; see IC Lupu, 'The Failure of RFRA' (1998) 20 *University of Arkansas at Little Rock Law Journal* 575, 577–85.

[50] 42 USC.§ 2000bb-1(a)–(b).

[51] 42 USC § 2000bb(b)(1).

[52] 42 USC § 2000bb(a)(5) (emphasis provided).

[53] Eisgruber and Sager (n 21) 261.

[54] *City of Boerne v Flores*, 521 US 507 (1997). The decision, which rested on the claim that Congress had exceeded its 'enumerated powers' authorising it to legislate under the Federal Constitution, will not be analysed here.

[55] *Gonzales v O Centro Esperita Beneficente Uniao Do Vegetal*, 546 US 418 (2006).

[56] See above n 45.

After yet another round of political protests, the final congressional act of the accommodation drama came with the adoption of the Religious Land Use and Institutionalized Persons Act (RLUIPA) in 2000.[57] On the one hand, this statute broadened the definition of 'religious exercise'[58] and restored the *Sherbert* compelling state interest in favour of religious persons vis-à-vis state and local laws through a careful choice of constitutional bases for congressional action. On the other hand, it also considerably limited its scope to only two domains: restrictions on the religious exercise of prison inmates and restrictions on land uses of ecclesiastical institutions. As to prisoners, the case for RLUIPA can only be regarded as meritorious since in the great bulk of litigated cases, the courts have proven reluctant to challenge the judgements of prison wardens, who, generally, are unsympathetic to prisoners' requests for reasonable accommodation.[59] But as to land uses, the presumptive exemption from urbanism restrictions granted to every religious organisation (however mainstream and majoritarian or unfamiliar and minoritarian) unless the state can demonstrate that the burden imposed on the organisation is the least restrictive means to further a compelling state interest, does not sit comfortably with the aim to ensure equal treatment for the members of vulnerable religious minorities and secure the urbanism and environment interests of local communities.

However, the initially wide political consensus in favour of religious accommodation between the liberal left and the religious right, which was built after *Smith* in 1990 and until the enactment of RLUIPA in 2000, was eventually blown to pieces by *Burwell v Hobby Lobby Stores, Inc* (2014), the most recent Supreme Court decision concerning RFRA.[60] This case brought religious cultural wars to the forefront and completed the loop by turning even good faith initial proponents of RFRA against this statute, and even against the very notion itself of accommodation. The internal tension between the principle of equality and the carving out of exemptions from general laws, which was lurking from the beginning, now exploded in the public sphere.

Hobby Lobby involved a clash between two federal statutes, RFRA and the Patient Protection and Affordable Care Act (ACA) of 2010. In the US, where there is no system of universal social security coverage, most workers are insured by their employers' health insurance plans. The ACA required all businesses employing 50 or more employees to provide the latter with 'minimum essential coverage' as specified by regulations of the Department of Health and Human Services (HHS). The minimum coverage promulgated by the HHS 'contraceptive mandate' covered the 'Food and Drug Administration-approved contraceptive

[57] 42 USC §§ 2000cc–2000cc-5.

[58] Hereinafter, religious exercise is defined as 'any exercise of religion, whether or not compelled by, or central to, a system of religious belief,' which is to be 'construed in favor of a broad protection of religious exercise, to the maximum extent permitted by the terms of this chapter and the Constitution' (USC § 2000cc-5(7)(A)).

[59] Eisgruber and Sager (n 21) 269–70.

[60] *Burwell v Hobby Lobby Stores, Inc*, 573 US 682 (2014).

methods' and 'sterilization procedures' as forms of preventive care for female employees.[61] HHS exempted from the scope of its regulations 'religious employers' (ie, churches and their auxiliaries, associations of churches, and religious orders) as well as religious non-profit organisations that objected for religious reasons to the covered contraceptive services.[62] The cost of the covered contraceptive services for any female employees of exempted religious employers and non-profit organisations would not be covered by the employers; they would be provided by a government-sponsored alternative instead. Crucially, neither RFRA nor the ACA mentioned for-profit organisations as being eligible for religious accommodation.

The plaintiffs Hobby Lobby Stores and Conestoga Wood Specialties were for-profit corporations that commercialised non-sectarian products but were 'closely held' (had more than 50 per cent of the value of their outstanding stock owned by up to five individuals and did not provide personal services) and were managed according to the religious principles of the families controlling them.[63] A deeply divided Supreme Court accepted the RFRA-based claim for accommodation of the two plaintiff businesses. It decided that as applied to closely held for-profit corporations, the HHS regulations imposing the contraceptive mandate substantially burden the exercise of religion under RFRA, and that even though securing cost-free access to the challenged contraceptive methods can be accepted as a compelling state interest, the Government failed to show that the mandate is the least restrictive means of furthering that interest. The Court restrained itself to the statutory interpretation of RFRA and left outside its purview any constitutional issues concerning the Free Exercise Clause.

For the first time, the Court recognised a for-profit organisation's claim of 'religious belief' based on a literal interpretation of the Dictionary Act, which defines 'persons' to include corporations, and did not find any reason to differentiate between non-profit and for-profit organisations when it comes to matters of religious exercise.[64] This determination is the most controversial part of *Hobby Lobby*. For Justice Alito, who wrote the majority opinion, RFRA's 'sweeping' protection for religious liberty also includes the people who own and control closely held companies through the familiar legal fiction of a corporation as 'person'. It is worth quoting *in extenso* from Justice Alito's opinion:

> [I]t is important to keep in mind that the purpose of this fiction is to provide protection for human beings. A corporation is simply a form of organisation used by human beings to achieve desired ends. An established body of law specifies the rights and obligations of the people (including shareholders, officers, and employees) who are associated with

[61] Group Health Plans and Health Insurance Issuers Relating to Coverage of Preventive Services Under the Patient Protection and Affordable Care Act (77 Federal Register 8725).

[62] Some of these organisations believe that various forms of contraception amount to abortion, to which they are religiously opposed.

[63] Internal Revenue Service, *Corporations* (Publication 542, 2022) 3.

[64] *Burwell v Hobby Lobby Stores, Inc*, 573 US 682, 705–09 (2014).

> a corporation in one way or another. When rights, whether constitutional or statutory, are extended to corporations, the purpose is to protect the rights of these people.[65]

The prick of the religious burden thus pierces the corporate veil and stings the Greens and the Hahns (the families owing Hobby Lobby and Conestoga, respectively).[66] As to the non-differentiation between non-profits and for-profits, the Court held that while

> it is certainly true that a central objective of for-profit corporations is to make money, modern corporate law does not require for-profit corporations to pursue profit at the expense of everything else, and many do not do so. For-profit corporations, with ownership approval, support a wide variety of charitable causes, and it is not at all uncommon for such corporations to further humanitarian and other altruistic objectives.[67]

The time that the Supreme Court would hold unanimously the fact that a business was 'infused with a religious purpose' as legally irrelevant seems long past.[68]

The rest of the opinion flowed smoothly from these findings. The $2,000 per-employee penalty for corporations dropping minimum coverage was enough to show that the HHS contraception mandate substantially burdens the corporations' exercise of religion, especially if one accounts for

> the circumstances under which it is wrong for a person [the corporation's owners] to perform an act that is innocent in itself but that has the effect of enabling or facilitating the commission of an immoral act by another [the corporation's employees].[69]

The Court found it unnecessary to decide on whether there was any compelling state interest in the HHS contraceptive mandate since HHS was unable to show that the mandate was the least restrictive means of furthering the alleged compelling interest. Since HHS itself has, at its disposal, an approach that is less restrictive than requiring employers to fund contraceptive methods that violate their religious beliefs (namely an accommodation for non-profit organisations with religious objections) it would suffice to also extend this accommodation to for-profit organisations with religious objections,[70] under which women would still be entitled to all approved contraceptives without cost-sharing.[71]

Hobby Lobby was met with indignation both within the Supreme Court and in society at large. Gone were the days when liberals and conservatives alike stood fully behind the notion of religious accommodation. In *Hobby Lobby*, Justice

[65] ibid, 706–07.

[66] The term 'corporate veil' expresses the fundamental legal concept that a corporation's managers or shareholders are not legally responsible for the corporation's actions. 'Piercing the corporate veil' thus refers to a situation in which courts put aside limited liability and hold a corporation's managers or shareholders personally liable for the corporation's actions.

[67] *Burwell v Hobby Lobby Stores, Inc.*, 573 US 682, 711–12 (2014).

[68] *Tony and Susan Alamo Foundation* (n 30).

[69] ibid, 724. It is interesting that Justice Alito cites, in this regard, three Jesuit morality manuals. ibid, 724, fn 34.

[70] ibid, 728–32.

[71] ibid, 693; *cf* also on this issue Justice Kennedy's concurrence (ibid, 736–39).

Ginsburg's dissent talked about a 'decision of startling breadth' and effectively lambasted the Court's understanding of religious exemptions, writing that 'the Court holds that commercial enterprises … can opt out of any law (saving only tax laws) they judge incompatible with their sincerely held religious beliefs', and that 'compelling governmental interests in uniform compliance with the law, and disadvantages that religion-based opt-outs impose on others, hold no sway, the Court decides, at least when there is a "less restrictive alternative"'.[72] The main point of contention was whether a corporation qualifies as a 'person' capable of exercising religion. Justice Ginsburg challenged the majority's unprecedented view of for-profit religion by making the commonsense assertion that 'the exercise of religion is characteristic of natural persons, not artificial legal entities'.[73] She made a particularly strong point by insisting on a principled distinction between religious organisations and for-profit corporations. Furthering the autonomy of religion organisations through accommodation strengthens individual religious freedom as well, since such organisations exist to foster the interests of the persons adhering to the same religious faith. This is not the case of for-profit organisations, since their workers are not commonly drawn from one religious community; indeed, the law forbids any religion-based criterion for the selection of the workforce in for-profit corporations.[74]

With this basic distinction in mind, allowing claims of religious accommodations to business corporations (even though RFRA or ACA themselves are silent on such an option) is tantamount to imposing the religious beliefs of a closely held corporation's managers or shareholders upon their workers, and, in this case, more particularly upon their female employees. The loop is now complete. With *Hobby Lobby*, it became quite evident to all that the notion of accommodation of religion through the granting of exemptions from generally applicable laws only is constitutionally benign when it serves to protect the rights of vulnerable minorities from the whims of the economically and socially powerful. Even though Justice Ginsburg tried to salvage RFRA per se from the aggressive interpretation of the *Hobby Lobby* Court,[75] the crux of the matter is that this emblematic federal statute was comfortably used, because of its wide breadth, not as a shield against state oppression of religious autonomy, but as a sword for powerful corporations to force their religious beliefs on their employees.[76]

[72] ibid, 739–40.

[73] ibid, 752.

[74] ibid, 753–54.

[75] ibid, 747: 'the Court sees RFRA as a bold initiative departing from, rather than restoring, pre-*Smith* jurisprudence'.

[76] Several experts hastened to conclude that RFRA was in fact unconstitutional as violative of the Establishment Clause; see, eg, FM Gedicks and RG Van Tassell, 'RFRA Exemptions from the Contraception Mandate: An Unconstitutional Accommodation of Religion' (2014) 49 *Harvard Civil Rights-Civil Liberties Law Review* 343.

VII. The European Court of Human Rights' Reluctance to Recognise Religious Accommodation

Kristin Henrard has convincingly shown that the ECtHR is very hesitant about developing any kind of duties of reasonable accommodation in Europe.[77] Even though the ECtHR has accepted that the prohibition of discrimination also encompasses duties of differential treatment, in *Thlimmenos v Greece*, and has used accommodation language when it comes to protecting people with disability, in *Glor v Switzerland*, neither of the two possible grounds for such duties (the prohibition of discrimination and the protection of fundamental rights) has actually served much to devise judicial measures of accommodation.[78] This general reluctance to identify duties of accommodation is even more pronounced in the case of religious accommodation: neither the *Thlimmenos* rationale of state duties of differential treatment on the grounds of religion nor the effective enjoyment of Article 9 ECHR freedom of religion have been sufficient to recognise and effectively approve religious-based accommodation claims. The main factor for this minimalist judicial stance seems to be the lack of a sufficient European consensus on matters other than the protection of the rights of the disabled and prisoners, both of which enjoy a strong basis in international law.[79] This lack of an adequate degree of consensus in the Council of Europe goes hand in hand with a broad margin of appreciation for Member States in matters of state–religion relations, leaving little room for the Court to manoeuvre in designing measures of accommodation of religion.[80] Practically, the ECtHR prefers to leave to the state's discretion any accommodations that would noticeably affect the visibility of religions in the public sphere, presumably because it considers state–religion relations as being part of the state's national constitutional identity.[81]

In this self-restrained context, the four consolidated *Eweida and others* cases created expectations some years ago of seminal importance. Indeed, *Eweida* was a significant breakthrough because the ECtHR reversed the traditional line of reasoning of the former European Commission on Human Rights, which had held, in several decisions, that the possibility of resigning from a job and changing employment meant that there was no interference with an employee's religious

[77] Henrard (2016, n 2) 965–69.

[78] *Thlimmenos v Greece*, App No 34369/97, 6 April 2000; *Glor v Switzerland*, App No 13444/04, 30 April 2009.

[79] As to the disabled, there is worldwide recognition of their rights by the UN Convention on the Rights of Persons with Disabilities of 30 March 2007, whereas as for prisoners, there is a European consensus on the need for accommodation of their religious practices reflected in the Council of Europe European Prison Rules 22.1 and 29.2 of 2006.

[80] Henrard (2016, n 2) 969–78.

[81] K Alidadi, 'Reasonable Accommodations for Religion and Belief: Adding Value to Article 9 ECHR and the European Union's Anti-Discrimination Approach to Employment?' (2012) 37 *European Law Review* 693, 703.

freedom (jurisprudence known as the 'freedom to resign'). The ECtHR stated, for the first time, that it would apply a balancing and proportionality test:

> Given the importance in a democratic society of freedom of religion, the Court considers that, where an individual complains of a restriction on freedom of religion in the workplace, rather than holding that the possibility of changing job would negate any interference with the right, the better approach would be to weigh that possibility in the overall balance when considering whether or not the restriction was proportionate.[82]

Nevertheless, the Court's task of determining whether the measures taken at national level are justified in principle and proportionate was not clarified in *Eweida* because the concrete factors in the balancing process were not clearly articulated. The ECtHR, rather, contented itself with a standardised and quite inoperative reference: 'regard must be had in particular to the fair balance that has to be struck between the competing interests of the individual and of the community as a whole, subject in any event to the margin of appreciation enjoyed by the State'.[83] One can conclude that the ECtHR did not really engage with the doctrine of reasonable accommodation, its rationale, or its inherent limits; its ad hoc balancing process remains rather shallow and mostly untheorised.[84] This lack of conceptual density is obvious when it came to justifying a different treatment for otherwise similar situations in compliance with Article 14 of the ECHR. According to the Court, the scope of the margin of appreciation enjoyed by a state 'will vary according to the circumstances, the subject-matter and the background'.[85] In fact, only in the first of the four *Eweida* cases was reasonable accommodation granted to the applicant, who had complained that UK law failed adequately to protect her right to manifest her Christian religion by allowing her employer (British Airways) to proscribe the visible wearing of a cross around her neck. In that case, the ECtHR was explicit as to the rights and interests at stake and as to their relative weight in the ad hoc balancing process:

> Ms. Eweida's cross was discreet and cannot have detracted from her professional appearance. There was no evidence that the wearing of other previously authorised items of religious clothing, such as turbans and hijabs, by other employees, had any negative impact on British Airways' brand or image. Moreover, the fact that the company was later able to amend the uniform code to allow for the visible wearing of religious symbolic jewelry demonstrated that the earlier prohibition was not of crucial importance.[86]

Most importantly, the accommodation of Ms Eweida's religiously motivated desire to wear a visible cross over her work uniform did not encroach on the

[82] *Eweida* (n 8), [83].
[83] ibid, [84].
[84] M Hill, 'Religious Symbolism and Conscientious Objection in the Workplace: An Evaluation of Strasbourg's Judgment in *Eweida and others v UK*' (2013) 15 *Ecclesiastical Law Journal* 191, 200–03.
[85] *Eweida* (n 8) [88].
[86] ibid, [94].

interests of others.[87] In the three other joint cases, though, the Court disposed of the claims for accommodation by simply relying on the wide margin of appreciation of the state without actually balancing the respective interests, thus glossing over the freedom to manifest one's religious beliefs in the workplace.

All in all, in Europe, only a hesitant step forward has been taken towards the recognition of accommodation on the basis of religion. The general unwillingness of the ECtHR to satisfy such claims is clearly associated with the lack of a convincing European consensus on religious matters and with the existence, in most cases, of a significant potential impact of such accommodations on the interests of others.[88] Therefore, even after *Eweida*, the ECtHR still remains unready to accept claims for accommodation of religion other than on an ad hoc basis, and only in cases where the particular matter is uncontroversial.

VIII. Conclusion

According to an 'assimilationist' conception of religion, a democracy is justified in providing accommodations to religious persons in the name of equality, only if certain roughly similar types of accommodations for other social categories have also been granted for the satisfaction of their particular needs. Under this strictly egalitarian viewpoint, there should be nothing normatively weightier about religiously based claims than any other claims for particularistic accommodations vis-à-vis general legislation. However, such a conception is reductionist since it denies to religious persons, as a matter of principle, any religiously grounded diversification vis-à-vis the general law, even though they enjoy a fundamental right to their freedom of religious exercise, including a right against indirect discrimination.

This line of thought led to the originally benign anti-assimilationist idea underlying accommodation, that accommodation is the optimal solution a pluralist democracy can contrive for the diversification in the treatment of religiously based claims in order to fully protect the right to freedom of religion for vulnerable minorities. But ironically, in the US, the evolution of both federal legislation and Supreme Court case law (especially after the controversial *Hobby Lobby* ruling) has shown that the idea of accommodation has paved the way for an 'integralist' conception of religion. In the integralist understanding, religion is seen as a normative phenomenon permeating the entire public sphere and all domains of people's lives.[89] It is a style of religious commitment that is comprehensive and

[87] ibid, [95]. This did not apply in the second joint case of the Christian nurse Ms Chaplin, whose chain and cross could conceivably cause injury to patients if someone pulled on it or if it came into contact with open wounds.

[88] Henrard (2016, n 2) 983.

[89] KD Wald, 'Religion and the Workplace: A Social Science Perspective' (2009) 30 *Comparative Labor Law and Policy Journal* 471.

thus inseparable from other social institutions, including the most secularised ones (the for-profit corporation and the marketplace itself). The proliferation of businesses such as Hobby Lobby, with their interweaving of religious views into corporate decisions about what benefits to support or oppose, has all but shattered the traditional picture of the corporation as entirely separate from its owners or shareholders as to its liabilities. Once the right of religious accommodation is also given to for-profit corporations, the traditional picture of the marketplace as an identity-neutral and amoral public space, strictly separated from the private spaces of home and religious temples, and a sanctuary from societal cultural wars, is also shaken.[90] This development cannot but be alarming for political liberalism since it denotes a religion that no longer respects the line between the public and the private spheres and a fragmented society where practically all social or legal norms are contested and open to renegotiation in an endless 'war of gods'.[91]

Ultimately, this development goes to show that the concept of accommodation is neither innocent nor harmless and should be treated with extreme care. This is exactly the point where two political and legal cultures with different backgrounds, paradoxically converge. The outcry against accommodation as a sword for powerful corporations to force their religious beliefs upon their workers in America, and the jurisprudential reluctance to recognise (or tailor) measures of accommodation in Europe, both go in the direction of a prudent restriction of both the regulatory scope and the normative strength of this potentially explosive theoretical tool.

[90] RJ Colombo, 'The Naked Private Square' (2013) 51 *Houston Law Review* 1.

[91] M Weber, 'Science as a Vocation' in HH Gerth and C Wright Mills (eds), *From Max Weber: Essays in Sociology* (Oxford, Oxford University Press, 1946) 149.

14

Divine Command and Religious Liberty: A Theological Reflection on Islamic Constitutionalism

MAHAN MIRZA

There is no single form of government that scripture and tradition clearly spell out as 'Islamic'. The Muslim world consists of Muslim heartlands where Muslims reside in the overwhelming majority, of places where they were once a majority but are now a minority, of countries where their population hangs in the balance between majority and minority, and of young fledgling communities in a so-called diaspora propelled by the forces of globalisation. The polities of Muslim countries range from monarchies to religious and secular democracies.[1] Islamic political philosophy has historically adapted to shifting political realities.[2] Accordingly, the scholarly tradition has recently begun to provide guidelines for Muslims on how to live as permanent minorities in non-Muslim lands.[3]

The prophet Muhammad was the undisputed religious and political leader of the Muslim community and its non-Muslim allies (collectively called an *ummah*) during his lifetime.[4] For the predominant Sunni tradition, the prophet Muhammad passed away without designating a successor. One hadith informs Sunnis that 'scholars are the heirs of prophets', privileging the collective body of scholars as the locus of authority.[5] Scholars derive legitimacy by their ability to interpret revelation for the guidance of the community. In Shi'a Islam, by contrast, the prophet designated an heir in whose hands authority ultimately rests, and in whose progeny it is to be passed down through the generations. The Sunni/Shi'a

[1] D Philpott, *Religious Freedom in Islam: The Fate of a Universal Human Right* (Oxford, Oxford University Press, 2019).

[2] G Böwering, P Crone and M Mizra (eds), *Princeton Encyclopedia of Islamic Political Thought* (Princeton, Princeton University Press, 2012).

[3] I Zahalka, *Shari'a in the Modern Era: Muslim Minorities Jurisprudence* (Cambridge, Cambridge University Press, 2016).

[4] K Jomaa, *Ummah: A New Paradigm for a Global World* (New York, SUNY Press, 2022).

[5] Jami' al-Tirmidhi, available at sunnah.com/tirmidhi:2682.

schism, originating in the first decades of Islam, developed into mature legal and theological sects over the centuries. The relationship between religious scholars and political leaders has been contested and renegotiated across time and place.

Neither Sunnism nor Shi'ism enjoy complete internal unity. Differences result from divergent interpretations of scripture in the case of Sunnis, and, in the case of Shi'as, from the added complexity of identifying correct genealogies for rightful succession. Much of the Islamic scholarly tradition is an exercise in managing reasonable disagreements.[6] Despite a range of disagreements, these various traditions of Islam nonetheless overlap considerably in both form and substance, relying, as they naturally do, on a common narrative on the biography of Muhammad, overlapping reports about his life and words, and the exact same text of the Qur'an.

Islam's history of managing and living with disagreements provides a natural resource for the religious freedom conversation today, even though Muslims have not always exemplified religious freedom in their own societies, especially when assessed by contemporary standards. The past is not necessarily prologue for the present, but it can provide inspiration that generates new configurations suitable for present needs.

Arguably, one of the most fruitful resources from Islamic thought for religious freedom is the theological position known as 'voluntarism' or 'divine command', which holds that God is not bound by the morality humans arrive at independently through philosophic deliberation. The theological problem was framed in ancient philosophy by Socrates: 'The point which I should first wish to understand is whether the pious or holy is beloved by the gods because it is holy, or holy because it is beloved of the gods.'[7] Divine Command adopts the latter position, or, stated another way: the good is known by what God commands.

Far from being irrational, Divine Command is the outcome of a rational position that absolute moral truths are not apodictically discoverable. According to this position, Human claims to having arrived at moral standpoints that are universal are nothing other than arrogation of conjecture to the status of objective reality.

Divine Command came to play a central role in Islamic theology, primarily identified with the Ash'ari/Maturidi schools of thought. Across these schools, and even within them, Divine Command is not monolithic, with scholars employing 'reason' to varying degrees to interpret revelation, elicit divine intent, and corroborate, restrict or particularise scriptural imperatives.[8] The methodological linchpin in Divine Command theology is to avoid consciously projecting one's own preferences into the interpretive process, even though the subjective self remains omnipresent in actual practice.

[6] J Walbridge, *God and Logic in Islam: Caliphate of Reason* (Cambridge, Cambridge University Press, 2010), esp ch 8: 'The Institutionalization of Disagreement'.

[7] Plato, *Euthyphro*, available at classics.mit.edu/Plato/euthyfro.html.

[8] R Harvey, *Transcendent God, Rational World: A Māturīdī Theology* (Edinburgh, Edinburgh University Press, 2021).

From a philosophical point of view, Divine Command reasoning is resonant with feminist and postmodern ethics: moral consensus is a fleeting inter-subjective phenomenon that shifts from hither to thither. There is no such thing as a universal moral perspective. What separates Divine Command from postmodernism is its anchor to revelation. For believers, intentional reference to scripture leads to a kind of inter-subjective consensus (known formally as *ijmā'*) among scholars, which provides the moral guidance necessary in a particular time and place.[9]

Ironically, critics often tend to identify theological voluntarism or Divine Command theory with the fideism that brings out the worst in religion: violence and intolerance. If things are good not because they can independently be known to be good by human reason, but only because God tells us they are good, the argument goes, human beings will suppress their own moral instincts to blindly do whatever they think God is telling them to do.[10] This argument misses at least two key points.

The first point the argument misses is the tempering aspect of operating in a scholarly network. Positions that are morally repulsive are naturally isolated as aberrations that stand against more widespread consensus. The second point that the argument misses is more vital to the topic at hand: individual religious freedom. The relativising of human reason permits a kind of radical freedom: every individual believer is free to give their best shot at moral reasoning. Interpreters are free to either strengthen consensus, reshape consensus or stand against consensus. There is no universal position from a human vantage point; there are only arguments offered by fallible human beings embedded in dynamic social realities. One good faith effort to seek 'the good' is as good as another.

While acts of worship, private morality and religious devotion cannot be compelled, public morality is the purview of law that is regulated by rulers or state institutions. People may hold whatever private position they like, but they are not free to enforce whatever laws they like. That is true for every society (religious or secular) that values the rule of law. A public/private distinction has historically been an important feature in Islamic political thought.[11]

Those who do not believe in this or that revelation (revelation ultimately being an 'a-rational' anchor) cannot be held to the moral standards that revelation sets for believers, since knowledge of the morality that proceeds from it rests on a prior belief in its truth. This is perhaps one way to understand the Qur'anic phrase 'there is no coercion in religion (*dīn*)'.[12] Laws that regulate public life for the welfare of all, however, are a different matter. While they may be directly or indirectly

[9] A Hasan, *The Doctrine of Ijma in Islam: A Study of the Juridical Principal of Consensus* (Islamabad, Islamic Research Institute, 1978).

[10] Sensitivities around such a reception of Divine Command prompted the 'Common Word' initiative: www.acommonword.com.

[11] Böwering, Crone and Mirza (n 2) 430–31.

[12] Qur'an 2:256. All translations are from S Hossein Nasr et al (eds), *The Study Quran* (New York, HarperCollins, 2015).

influenced by revelation, they are ultimately open to public deliberation. Despite the enduring presence of dissenting views, laws that regulate human–human relations are distinct from laws that address human–divine relations.

Whereas Divine Command approaches to theology can serve as a guarantor for religious freedom, appeals to universal moral positions grounded in notions of natural law can be inimical to religious freedom. Islamic history bears testimony: when the Abbasid Caliph Ma'mum (r 813–833) attempted to establish Mu'tazila theology in his realm (by some accounts because of a dream in which he met Aristotle) he initiated a violent inquisition (*miḥna*) against his opponents.[13] The Mu'tazila show affinity to a kind of natural law reasoning, where the good is knowable independently of revelation.[14] If God is good, the argument goes, then God is bound by the good that is knowable to humans through philosophy, and people who disagree are simply flawed reasoners who stand against both God and morality. The irony is that Divine Command theology can be less inflexible than Natural Law philosophy/theology when it comes to tolerating others who arrive at different moral positions.

Calls for 'an Islamic enlightenment' are based on a misreading of Divine Command, that its mainstreaming was a tragic wrong turn in Islamic intellectual history. In other words, a turn to Divine Command is exactly 'what went wrong'. It closed Muslim minds, arrested the advance of science, and brought upon the modern Islamic world a crisis of governance, authoritarianism and terror. A return to the road not taken of Islamic 'rationalism', for critics, is the only thing that can save Muslims, and consequently, the rest of the world.[15]

While it is impossible to deal with this thesis in detail here, there are strong reasons to push back on it. For one, the mainstream theology of the 'Twelver' Shi'as, unlike mainstream Sunnism, adheres to the rationalist theology of the Mu'tazila. They did not take a so-called wrong turn. Nevertheless, the Iranian branch of Twelver Shi'as have developed revolutionary models of theocratic governance in recent history. On the other hand, it has been suggested that the 'anti-rational' strand of Muslim theology, which I associate here with Divine Command theology, is precisely what permitted the exact sciences to flourish in the classical period.[16] Lastly, empirical studies of terrorism suggest that the primary driver of violence is geopolitics, not theology, and the primary actors in global terrorism are individuals who stand against (not with) scholarly consensus.[17]

[13] Böwering, Crone and Mirza (n 2) 255–26.

[14] A Emon, *Islamic Natural Law Theories* (Oxford, Oxford University Press, 2010). See also response by R Koujah, 'A Critical Review Essay of Anver M. Emon's *Islamic Natural Law Theories*' (2015) 14 *UCLA Journal of Islamic and Near Eastern Law* 1.

[15] M Akyol, *Reopening Muslim Minds: A Return to Reason, Freedom, and Tolerance* (New York, St Martin's Publishing, 2021).

[16] M Mirza, 'Believing is Seeing: The Universe in the Eyes of Bīrūnī and Ibn Sīnā' in J Elias and B Orfail, *Light Upon Light: Essays in Islamic Thought and History in Honor of Gerhard Böwering* (Leiden, Brill, 2019) 366–82.

[17] RA Pape and JK Feldman, *Cutting the Fuse: The Explosion of Suicide Terrorism & How to Stop It* (Chicago, University of Chicago Press, 2010).

There are ample resources for religious freedom in Islam beyond the theological framing suggested here.[18] Daniel Philpott, for example, in his work on *Religious Freedom in Islam*, offers us 'seven seeds of freedom': the verses of the Qur'an; the life of the prophet Muhammad; a legacy of tolerance in Islamic history; the development of liberal Islam among contemporary believers; the emergence of Muslim religious freedom advocates; favourable legal developments in Muslim majority states; and the precedent of secularism in Islamic legal thought.[19]

A noteworthy criticism of Divine Command (the elephant in the room, so to speak) is: what if the God we are talking about is capricious, such that fidelity to scripture can only lead to forms of consensus that unbelievers would consider abhorrent? This argument, while interesting, is antithetical to religious freedom. It is ultimately saying is that some religions are essentially bad. Consequently, they should not be afforded full religious freedom because they threaten the rest of us.[20]

Asma Uddin engages this argument in her first book, *When Islam is Not a Religion: Inside America's Fight for Religious Freedom*. 'The fear is,' she writes, 'that Muslims will use religious freedom to "destroy" and "take over" America.' Because of this fear, which is called Islamophobia or anti-Muslim racism, some critics attempt to classify Islam as a political ideology, which can be restricted in the name of preserving democracy or safeguarding national security.

Such criticisms are ultimately an indication of the inability to deal with difference. The simple fact is that all religions offer conceptions of the good that extend into the public sphere. What holds for Islam is no less valid for any religion. Religions make political demands on us.[21] The challenge is how to fairly regulate these demands to maximise freedom and flourishing for all. Disqualifying some religions from the field defeats the purpose. We should be able to presume that a plurality of believing people, who ground their positions in scholarly terms that come to acquire broad consensus, will not arrive at moral positions that are unequivocally beyond the pale for religious outsiders. If we proceed otherwise, then the very idea of pluralism stands in peril.

At times, the crossover of religious belief from the private to the public is helpful, as in the case of US Senator Mitt Romney, who, in explaining why he voted in favour of impeaching President Donald Trump, said: 'I swore an oath before God to exercise impartial justice. I am profoundly religious. My faith is at the heart of who I am. I take an oath before God as enormously consequential.'[22] At other times, the crossover is unhelpful, as in the case of President George W Bush, who, in

[18] M Akyol, *Why, as a Muslim, I defend Liberty* (Washington DC, Cato Institute, 2021).
[19] Philpott (n 1) 178–205.
[20] A Uddin, *When Islam is Not a Religion* (Cambridge, Pegasus Books, 2019).
[21] C Smith, *Religion: What it is, How it Works, and Why it Matters* (Princeton, Princeton University Press, 2017).
[22] 'Full Transcript: Mitt Romney's Speech Announcing Vote to Convict Trump' *The New York Times* (5 February 2020), available at www.nytimes.com/2020/02/05/us/politics/mitt-romney-impeachment-speech-transcript.html.

justifying a preemptive war against Iraq, said: 'The liberty we prize is not America's gift to the world; it is God's gift to humanity.'[23]

In a provocative but compelling paper, Asifa Qureshi argues that Islamic scriptural sources function very similarly to constitutions.[24] Titled 'Interpreting the Qur'an and the Constitution', the paper identifies parallel modes of reasoning across two legal traditions (the Islamic and the American) specifically plain meaning literalism, historical understanding originalism, and reasoning in reference to underlying purpose and spirit. 'When it comes to ways of thinking about textual interpretation,' she argues, 'Muslim and American jurists following a given method often will have more in common with each other than with those of an opposite methodology in their own society.' All traditions have internal tensions; our shared humanity provides us with common cognitive skillsets that apply both within traditions and across traditions.

The line between private religiosity (the realm of religious freedom) and public morality (the realm of law with the coercive power of the state) is elusive for all traditions. That holds true as much for democratic societies as it does for theocratic ones. Islamic political thought has historically provided a significant arena for public policy for the welfare of citizens that is not derived directly from scripture. 'The Islamic Secular,' as Sherman Jackson calls it:

> [I]s neither governed nor adjudicated through the concrete indicants of revelation or their extension as recognized in Islamic legal methodology (*uṣūl al-fiqh*). It remains Islamic, however, in its imperviousness to the impulse, first articulated by Hugo Grotius in the seventeenth century, to proceed 'as if God did not exist' (*etsi Deus non daretur*).[25]

In other words, 'the Islamic secular' is a realm in which the subjective beliefs of policymakers informally inform the secular realm of public policymaking. Needless to say, only a citizenry with a coherent set of beliefs that are embraced in a general cultural consensus will permit such a polity to function seamlessly. Societies that are fragmented culturally will have less of a chance of functioning well politically, even if they have mature democratic institutions in place, a fact that is in plain sight today in advanced and stable democracies.[26]

As President George Washington said in his farewell address to his fellow Americans: 'With slight shades of difference, you have the same religion, manners, habits, and political principles.'[27] He could not make that speech today. All societies

[23] 'Text of President Bush's 2003 State of the Union Address' *The Washington Post* (28 January 2003), available at www.washingtonpost.com/wp-srv/onpolitics/transcripts/bushtext_012803.html.

[24] A Quraishi, 'Interpreting the Qur'an and the Constitution: Similarities in the Use of Text, Tradition, and Reason in Islamic and American Jurisprudence' (2006) 28 *Cardozo Law Review* 67.

[25] S Jackson, 'The Islamic Secular' (2017) 34 *American Journal of Islamic Social Sciences* 1.

[26] P Friesen, et al, 'American Democracy at Risk: A Global Comparative Perspective' Keough School of Global Affairs (October 2020), available at www.keough.nd.edu/publications/american-democracy-at-risk-a-global-comparative-perspective.

[27] G Washington, 'Washington's Farewell Address to the People of the United States' Senate Document No 106-121, available at www.govinfo.gov/content/pkg/GPO-CDOC-106sdoc21/pdf/GPO-CDOC-106sdoc21.pdf.

have safeguards to preserve their core identity. In the case of the US, the presidency is reserved for a naturally born citizen, born on US soil, and the punishment for treason is death. Likewise, in some countries where Islam occupies pride of place in the constitution, the head of state can only be a Muslim, and the punishment for apostasy is death.[28]

Given this comparative background, we may now ask: are there essential differences between Islamic and European conceptions of society, governance and rights that are constitutionally irreconcilable with each other? Are European values universal? Must faithful Muslims compromise their religious freedom to conform to European universality? Given competing notions of what it means to be European or Islamic, there are no straightforward answers to these questions.

If Islamic teachings can be interpreted liberally, such that no substantive differences remain between them and European norms, there is nothing further to discuss. However, for a large number of traditional Muslims, tensions remain. According to Muhammad Fadel, 'the tension between normative Islam and the international human rights movement is real'.[29] Normative Islam, for Fadel, represents the broad-based consensus of scholars who follow traditional methods for interpreting scripture.[30] If European values as expressed in the European constitution can be taken as a proxy for international human rights norms, then the conflict between normative Islam and Europe is just as real.

Fadel highlights three areas of conflict to by way of illustration: slavery, women's rights and *ḥudūd* punishments. His proposed method for reconciliation is to seek political overlap, not theological agreement, by separating the metaphysical implications of norms from their legal effects. Fadel argues that it is possible to find overlapping consensus in substance between normative Islam and modern Europe at the level of law and politics, if not at the level of theology or philosophy.

Take the issue of slavery. Although Islamic norms have historically permitted slavery, it has never been an obligation to own slaves, nor has it ever been a sin to manumit slaves. On the contrary, the manumission of slaves has been universally held as an act of virtue and can also serve as an act of penance. If a government bans slavery, it is not commanding Muslims to sin, but only normalising virtue. Viewed this way, the banning of slavery may be considered perfectly acceptable as part of the temporal order established by the ruler, so long as the ruler refrains from requiring citizens to condemn the possibility of ever owing slaves as a universal evil across time and time and place.

The issue of women's rights is more complicated, but it can be dealt with in a similar manner. While normative Islam does not advance the absolute equality of gender in society, particularly in the institution of marriage, it nonetheless maintains absolute equality of all human beings as individual subjects accountable

[28] E Powell, *Islamic Law and International Law: Peaceful Resolution of Disputes* (Oxford, Oxford University Press, 2020). See Table 2.1 therein for a list.

[29] MH Fadel, 'The Challenge of Human Rights' (2008) 5 *Seasons* 59.

[30] See Amman Message (2004): ammanmessage.com.

to God. That being said, there is nothing in European law that prevents Muslims from behaving according to the legal norms of their traditions, so long as those norms are freely practiced and self-regulated.

Accordingly, men who believe it is religiously permissible to physically discipline their wives may continue to do so, even in Europe, if both parties voluntarily and privately accept such behaviour. If they disagree among themselves, they may seek counselling or arbitration through family, elders or religious institutions. However, if one party chooses to formally object through the courts, then the law of the land will apply. Should that happen, we might come to discover very little daylight between secular European and normative Islamic reasoning when it comes to adjudicating domestic violence.

According to *The Study Quran*, 'Islamic law prohibits injurious violence against one's wife, and some schools of Islamic Law consider it a legitimate reason for which a woman can seek divorce.'[31] The law further stipulates that striking (should it come to that) must not leave so much as a mark. Considering that the Prophet Muhammad never struck any of his wives and expressly disliked the practice, the legal prohibition of domestic violence is at the very least not un-Islamic.

Take the case of *ḥudūd* punishments. A *ḥadd* (singular of *ḥudūd*, literally meaning 'limit') punishment is one that is prescribed by God. *Ḥudūd* punishments include amputation of the limbs, flogging, lapidation and even death for crimes like highway robbery, fornication, adultery and murder. In public opinion (for up to as many as 90 per cent of Malays) the implementation of *hudūd* is the sole standard for a state to qualify as truly Islamic.[32] The Qur'an offers glad tidings to those who carefully guard the limits (*ḥudūd*) prescribed by God.[33]

The European Constitution bans cruel punishments. Torture and capital punishment are 'explicitly prohibited'.[34] For Europe, the *ḥudūd* are thus to be unequivocally categorised as unconstitutional. Muslims who believe that *ḥudūd* must be implemented per Divine Command will find their religious freedom stifled in Europe (a freedom that is in turn also guaranteed by the same Constitution).[35] We are thus in a situation where two constitutional rights (some would say two universal human rights) are at odds: freedom on the one hand; and prohibited acts on the other. How might these be reconciled?

Sharia scholar Mohammad Hashim Kamali offers one possible solution. He invites us to view the *ḥudūd* not as literally prescribed mandates, but rather as scripturally prescribed limits that are not to be transgressed.[36] In other words,

[31] Hossein Nasr et al (n 12) 208.

[32] F Abdul Rauf, *Defining Islamic Statehood: Measuring and Indexing Contemporary Muslim States* (London, Palgrave Macmillan, 2015) 33.

[33] Qur'an, 9:112.

[34] European Constitution at 22, available at www.europeanconstitution.eu/wp-content/uploads/2019/05/European-Constitution-Full-Text.pdf.

[35] ibid, 15.

[36] Abdur Rauf (n 32) 34.

there is nothing wrong with prescribing less severe punishments for crimes that require a *ḥadd* punishment. Kamali maintains that according to the Sharia the problem would be to go beyond the limits, not to stop short of the limits. It is entirely within a ruler's prerogative to prescribe lesser punishments, so long as the limits that have been set by God are not transgressed.

Fadel opts for a different approach. Each act, and consequently each punishment, he clarifies, has two dimensions: moral and legal. The moral belongs to God; the legal to the ruler. The moral dimension either incurs sin or wins divine favour and is therefore *religious*. The legal dimension involves interpersonal relations and public welfare and is therefore *political*.

The ruler (in our case the state) has discretionary power in the political realm. Individual believers, however, should have the freedom to act in the moral realm. The state is free to regulate the political, so long as believers are not commanded to sin. On the flipside, believers who, seeking penance, freely choose more severe penalties for crimes they have committed, should have the freedom to exercise that right. In this solution, advocates of European universalism and normative Islam need not impose their metaphysical commitments on each other. Instead, they may seek a political rapprochement that genuinely acknowledges pluralism.

To be sure, with rare exceptions, normative Islam aligns to a very high degree with European ideals. This alignment is captured nicely by the Egyptian scholar Muhammad' Abduh (d 1905), who, on returning from a visit to Europe, reportedly said: 'I went to the West and saw Islam, but no Muslims; I got back to the East and saw Muslims, but no Islam.'[37] This quote has inspired the Islamicity Indices project that ranks the countries of the world according to Islamic values and principles of governance. Western democracies, not Muslim-majority countries, consistently rank the highest in these indices.[38]

To quote Fadel at length:

> [H]uman rights law is about governance and about the limits on the means that states can use to further their policies. The general political goals of the human rights movement – ensuring that states exercise their secular powers in a way consistent with the basic dignity of all persons – are broadly consistent with the aspirations of the vast majority of Muslims. However, the human rights movement risks losing the support of Muslims and the followers of other traditional religions if it adopts absolute and transcendental moral language. Muslims believe that only God is the source of transcendental value, and even though Muslims and the human rights community will find much common ground at the practical level, Muslims will rightly object to what they consider false metaphysical claims. But while Muslims must be particularly sensitive to the erroneous metaphysical doctrines of many human rights advocates, they should not believe that because some theories of human rights include metaphysical principles that

[37] H Askari, Ho Mohammadkhan and L Mydin, *Reformation and Development in the Muslim World: Islamicity Indices as Benchmark* (London, Palgrave Macmillan, 2017) 5.

[38] See islamicity-index.org/wp.

> are inconsistent with Islamic theology, they must inevitably reject human rights law in order to remain faithful to their theological doctrines.[39]

Is a rapprochement between Enlightened Europeans and traditional Muslims possible where each side agrees to bracket its ultimate commitments to make multiculturalism work? The imbrication of religion and politics in all societies requires rethinking for deep pluralism. Even as Muslims must continue to rethink their inherited traditions in new contexts, Europe must continue to rethink its universalism.

In his magnum on *Religion in Human Evolution*, Robert Bellah traces the history of religion from its earliest stages in deep history until the Axial turn about 2,000 years ago.[40] Drawing on a range of theorists in anthropology, psychology, science and history, Bellah identifies three thresholds in religious evolution: ritual, whose origins can be found in the behaviour of higher animals; mythology, which is only possible with the birth of language; and theory: 'The theoretical breakthrough in each axial case led to the possibility of universal ethics, the reassertion of fundamental human equality, and the necessity of respect for all humans, indeed for all sentient beings.'[41] Bellah's final insight is that the universal ethics that emerged from each Axial case (whether Chinese, Greek, Indian or Semitic) was a particular kind of universalism that can never really be separated from its culture of origin.[42] At the end of a very lengthy text, Bellah leaves us with the following cautionary note:

> [S]o the final lesson of this chapter and this book for our present situation in a world of multiple traditions is that theory that has come loose from its cultural context can assume a superiority that can lead to crushing mistakes … To assume that 'we,' particularly if we mean by that the modern West, have universal truths based on revelation, philosophy, or science that we can enforce on others, is the ideological aspect of racism, imperialism, and colonialism.[43]

Is it possible for Europe to rethink its universalism as it welcomes the stranger into its borders? That is the real question to ask when considering the citizenship of devout Muslims within Europe. As humanity transitions into a shared global civilisation, the question is equally salient in reverse.

[39] Fadel (n 29) 75.
[40] R Bellah, *Religion in Human Evolution* (Cambridge, Belknap Press, 2011).
[41] ibid, 608.
[42] See also I Wallerstein, *European Universalism: The Rhetoric of Power* (New York, The New Press, 2006).
[43] Bellah (n 40).

PART IV

Securitisation and Islamophobia

15

Muslims in Europe: Religious Freedom and Security

AGUSTÍN MOTILLA

I. Introduction

This chapter[1] aims to synthesise the multiple ways in which the presence of the Islamic religion affects Europe. It would be no exaggeration to say that the dialectic between Islam and European society is one of the main problems presented by the religious phenomenon in the present century, just as, in the past, the legal status of the Catholic Church was the subject of intense controversy (consider the German *KulturKampf*, the French Third Republic, the Spanish Second Republic, and the controversy surrounding the religious cults or sects of the 1980s and 1990s).

II. Different Perspectives of Islam in European Societies

All of this indicates the multiple points of view regarding Islam, beyond its nature as a monotheistic religion with different traditions and cultures. Three of these viewpoints, all of which certainly have a relevant impact on religious freedom, are relevant to the matters discussed in this chapter.

First, in most European Union (EU) countries (leaving aside the secular existence of minorities of Muslims of Turkish origin (in Greece and Bulgaria) or Tatar origin (in Poland, Lithuania, and Finland), Islam is the majority religion of the immigrants who arrived in the 1960s and 1970s (in Germany, or, mostly, in France and Great Britain) or in the 1980s and 1990s (in the rest of the EU). Their different customs, difficulties in using the language of the country in which they settled, or state of poverty and marginalisation, have made their social integration more difficult. They are seen as different, 'strange' people.

[1] The text is based mainly on the paper given on 21 September 2021, at the Annual Conference of the European Consortium for Church and State Research 'Islam and Human Rights in the European Union', held in Thessaloniki.

Second, there is the tendency of conservative Islam towards fundamentalism and theocracy, which is present in the proliferating Salafi religious movements and also in the politics of states of such international weight as Saudi Arabia (in Sunnism) and Iran (among Shiites).

Third, one can see the desire of certain Islamic states to control their nationals abroad and use them, if necessary, in their foreign policy as a tool to create pressure. A case in point is the way in which the Moroccan Government allowed children and adolescents to invade Ceuta in 2021 in retaliation for Spain's permitting a leader of the *Polisario Front* to be treated in a Spanish hospital. Another is Turkey, which, through its public institution *Diyanet*, is very active in countries like Germany or Bulgaria. These are paradigmatic cases, to which can be added the policy of diffusing fundamentalist Islam through the spread of 'petrodollars', practised by Saudi Arabia and other countries of the Persian Gulf.

III. Societal Situation of Islam in the European Countries

Certainly, Islam in Europe is much more than a religion. Islam has the dogmatic content of a monotheistic, perhaps little developed, religion that constitutes an authentic *Weltanschauung*: morals, traditions and laws all inspire the very being and the actions of the *umma* (community) of believers. However, apart from the dogmatic aspects of the religion, there is the fact that many Muslims are immigrants (whose social, legal and economic position leads them to marginalisation), as well as the fundamentalist drift of this religion, and the desire of dictatorial or authoritarian states (such as Saudi Arabia, Turkey and Morocco) to influence the internal politics of European states through their nationals.

Faced with this situation, the different European states have adopted a type of response depending on the social composition of Muslims in each country. There are a great variety of social compositions, but they can be classified into four different groups:

1. *States with very little Islamic immigration*. These nations have a low percentage of Muslim immigrants, very recently arrived in the country (particularly through the policy of assignment of immigrants fleeing armed conflicts in Syria and Yemen). The Czech Republic and Sweden are examples of this group.
2. *Countries in which an historical Islamic minority coexists with recent Muslim immigrants*. For example, in Finland or Lithuania where Tatars were members of the Soviet or Russian occupying armies. Similarly, in Greece, Hungary and Bulgaria, Turks settled during the long rule of the Caliphate. It should be noted that in these countries the historical Islamic minority is, generally, well integrated. They have a legal status that guarantees their rights and freedoms and do not constitute an element of social or political conflict.

3. *States that have recently received significant Muslim immigrant population.* These states, without having a significant minority of Muslims throughout their history, received a large number of Muslim immigrants, mainly during the 1960s and 1970s (as in Germany and Belgium) or the 1980s or 1990s (as in Italy and Spain), from Turkey, Morocco or, more recently, Middle Eastern or sub-Saharan countries. This situation has led to serious problems of integration, as well as terrorist attacks perpetrated by jihadist groups. There, measures adopted to end marginalisation are accompanied by security policies that seek to prevent terrorism. Religious freedom is limited by these actions aimed at guaranteeing public order.
4. *States that possessed colonial empires that ruled over large populations of Muslims during the nineteenth and twentieth centuries.* Very early on, these countries welcomed immigrants from their colonies as blue-collar workers. Countries such as the UK and France have the largest Muslim populations in Europe, settled for more than a century. These countries have also suffered the worst acts of jihadist terrorism on their soil. It is not surprising that they have an extensive and long tradition of measures relating to integration and public security.

IV. Response of European States Confronting Islam

We can see that the answers to the issue of Muslim integration in Europe, conditioned by the social situation in each country, can be grouped into four categories that range from low to high levels of intervention on the part of the state in questions relating to the status of Islam and the religious freedom of the Muslims.

Those states with assimilated historical minorities or with a minor presence of Muslim immigrants tend not to adopt special measures: they guarantee a common status for all recognised denominations and the general protection of the right to religious freedom (this group includes Finland, Sweden, Lithuania, the Czech Republic and Portugal).

States with large Muslim populations that deal with integration and security problems tend to maintain a general or a specific regime that guarantees Muslim communities an acceptable status of freedom, while also adopting measures for public security and the fight against terrorist jihadism that affect some aspects of Muslim religious freedom (as in Germany, Italy, Spain and the UK, amongst others).

Finally, there are some states that, in some way, consider Islam incompatible with national principles and values. For this reason, these states adopt various policies that discourage their presence in the country; or that seek to assimilate them, through coercive actions, to their supposed values of national identity.

In the case of France (whose policy has influenced other countries such as Belgium and the Netherlands), the state uses public policy to try to protect the secular values of the republic in the face of religious 'communitarianism' and the self-marginalisation of Islam. Laws such as those prohibiting the Islamic headscarf in school or the burqa in public places, seek to put an end to visible symbols that are the product of this communitarianism. Or, in an effort that to create a 'French Islam' that accepts republican values, President Macron has recently proposed the Law to Reinforce National Principles. These are measures taken in addition to the security measures adopted to prevent terrorism.

At the other extreme, and generally promoted by right-wing anti-Islamic parties, the nationalist policies of states such as Bulgaria, Poland and Hungary can be mentioned. The value system of the Christian tradition of these countries are especially reaffirmed, into which, from their perspective, Islam does not fit well. The refusal by Poland and Hungary to accept the quotas of Muslim immigrants accorded to them by the European Commission is justified on these grounds.

In my view, the current policy of Orbán in Hungary, or that carried out by Kaczynski in Poland, presupposes a certain confessionalism on the part of the state, which, albeit latent, is inconsistent with the fight against discrimination and the safeguarding of religious freedom which underpin the European institutions.

V. Islam, Religious Freedom and Security in Europe

Within the general framework of the regulation of the religious freedom of Muslims by states with a significant Muslim presence (a framework characterised as being somewhere between religious freedom and security) this chapter will refer later to some relevant aspects of the exercise of Muslim beliefs.

An especially sensitive issue for Muslim communities settled in Europe is the construction of mosques or prayer centres. It is in these places of worship that religious meetings are held, Islam is taught, and aid to families in need is channelled. In most countries with heavy Muslim immigration, the planning and construction of mosques has caused social problems. The mosques do not have access to funds for renovating or conserving buildings of cultural interest since the majority of them have been built in recent times (eg the small amount received by the British Council of Muslims for this purpose, and the 2005 Belgian law withdrawing aid to Islamic mosques). Thus, they depend mostly on private donations.

There is an obvious reticence when the mosque is financed by foreign countries (particularly Saudi Arabia) that retain ownership of them. In France, the Reinforcing the Republican Principles Act aims to better control these donations to limit the alleged ideological influence of foreign states on the organisation of Muslim communities. In the past, some countries, such as the Netherlands, turned to public funding in the construction of Islamic places of worship, given the pressing need resulting from the immigrant population. In other countries, such as France, funding was limited to the maintenance of buildings already in existence. This benefits established churches but not new religions. That is why it was a wise move to call for a wider interpretation of aid to the Islamic '*associations culturelles*' which would permit partial funding by municipal authorities for construction and maintenance.

One also must not forget the importance of the surveillance of mosque activities to control the Muslim population. It has been especially intense in countries such as Great Britain, Germany and France. This includes control of mosque-goers and the funds the mosques receive and even adopting the extreme decision of closing some mosques. Fornerod emphasises that the Marseilles mosque *As Sounna* was closed by a prefectural decree because 'the place disseminates ideas inciting hatred and discrimination contrary to republican principles, likely to provoke the committing of acts of terrorism'.[2]

Mosques have also been used as an example of stereotypical expressions of an ideology aimed at undermining Western values (just as the woman's headscarf has become a symbol of gender discrimination). Minarets are seen as trying to change the skylines of the European landscape where, historically, church towers dominate the horizon. Headscarves and minarets are the visualisation of a rampant Islam, of the 'Muslim tide' attempting to change democracy, pluralism, human rights and the secularisation of the state with the aim of imposing the medieval rules of law. These ideas are behind the Swiss ban on minarets, proposed by a far-right, anti-Islamic party and approved by voters in the 2009 referendum.

VI. Security Measures Through Public Promotion of Islamic Activities

Other aspects of the religious freedom of Muslims, like measures which can be found to guarantee free exercise and the ideological control of Islam in the West (related directly or indirectly to security), are dealt with through public promotion and economic subsidies. These include government financing of the training of imams. The concern of governments regarding the education and preaching carried out in the mosques and prayer centres has proved to be directly related to terrorist attacks. For example, the 2017 massacre in Barcelona was directed by the imam of the mosque of the village of Ripoll (Girona), who was the leader of the terrorist cell where several young people with Moroccan roots were radicalised.

This concern has led to the possibility of creating schools or colleges where imams can be trained using legal and economic aid provided by the government, through agreements with Islamic representatives. In Holland, Belgium and Finland, public authorities have found a way to both prevent a rise in radical Islam and encourage the social integration of Muslims by offering Bachelor's and

[2] A Fornerod, *Islam and Human Rights in the European Union: France* (manuscript presented to the European Consortium for Church and State Meeting held in Thessaloniki, 23–25 September 2020) 10.

Master's degrees in Islamic Theology at public universities. In France, while the *laicité* regime of the 1905 Law prohibits public funding of any religious teaching, the non-application of the Law in the *Alsacia-Mosselle* region is used to fund a school of Islamic theology for the training of future imams. The aim in constituting a French Council of Imams sponsored by the Government is to distance Islamic communities from foreign states and prevent the dissemination of radical-fundamentalist messages as well.

Closely related to the imams' concern is the problem of Muslim communities' representation in the country. France and Belgium use public funds to organise the elections of Muslim representatives who then work with the Government. Fostering this working relationship with the French Council for the Muslim Faith (the institutional representation of Islamic communities in France) has been a personal commitment of the Minister of the Interior. However, the Council 'is regularly undermined by internal disagreements and its representativeness is often questioned by Muslims themselves'.[3]

Certain doubts about these policies should be highlighted. Their compatibility with the right to religious freedom, autonomy of religious denominations, and neutrality of public powers (values at the very core of liberal democracies) must be questioned. One must remember the European Court of Human Rights' jurisprudence in the Greek cases (*Serif* and *Agga*) or Bulgarian cases (*Hassan* and *Chauch*) because, quoting the Strasbourg Court's jurisprudence, 'any attempt to control religious denominations through the appointment or destitution of their leaders by the public authorities of the State is considered an act against pluralism and democratic society and, so, against article 9 of the European Convention'.

VII. Religious Chaplaincy and Islamic Teaching

Another issue that worries European governments and which falls somewhere between respecting the right to religious freedom and the guarantee of public safety, is the appointment of people who will carry out the work of religious assistance or the teaching of Islam in schools.

Regarding religious chaplaincy in public institutions (especially in the armed forces, prisons and hospitals) and the teaching of religion in schools, the prevailing tendency is the non-existence of financing of personnel on the part of the public administration. In the first case, that of religious chaplaincy, Islamic chaplains paid with public funds are either few in comparison with those of traditional churches (as is the case in Great Britain and France) or, in other countries, the law does not provide for these chaplains as it does in the case of Christian chaplains (as is the case in Italy, Malta, Slovenia and Poland). The same conclusion can be reached

[3] ibid, 3.

in the case of Islamic religion teachers paid for by the state. In those cases, when this service is provided for by government law, the difference between the funding which goes to traditional churches and that which goes to Islamic communities, as well as the difference in the number of teachers for the respective religions, is considerable.

These differences could be justified in terms of the number of followers, or the number of children studying Islamic religion, who request aid or education. In Spain, for example, there must be more than 10 students in the same year requesting Islamic religion courses for the state to pay teacher salaries. Nevertheless, it is surprising that in Spain, a country with nearly a million Muslims, the state only pays for some teachers in Ceuta and Melilla. At times, this can be explained by the fact that certain obstacles are created by the education authorities themselves. For example, in Madrid, although there are 8,000 Muslim schoolchildren registered, the schools do not inform the parents of their right to Islamic religious education, and the requests for this education are not communicated to the administrative authorities in charge of funding. In Catalonia, despite the number of children and teenagers who are enrolled, the *Generalitat* has not hired any teachers of the Islamic religion. However, for the 2020–21 academic year the Catalonian Government has begun a pilot project to offer Islamic religion classes in some public schools in Barcelona, Girona and Tarragona. Given the current state of public opinion after the terrorist attacks in Madrid in 2004 and Barcelona in 2017, it is not seen as 'politically correct' that Islam should receive public funding in this way.

Security measures are also being planned in the cases of elections of individuals providing religious assistance or teaching Islamic religion classes. Regarding religious assistance in prisons, in most of the countries of the EU the prison's prior authorisation of the imam who is to provide such religious assistance is required. In education, generally, the states are vigilant with regard to the content of courses and teachers.

In Spain, the public foundation *Pluralismo y Convivencia* (Pluralism and Living Together) financed the publication of the textbook '*Descubrir el Islam*' (Discovering Islam). It is the first textbook on the Islamic religion written in the language of an EU country, but public authorities are also allowed to oversee its content.

In some countries, the election of Islamic religion teachers is intertwined with foreign policy. One example can be seen in Germany. As Muslim associations are defined by the regional or national origin of their members, the largest Muslim Association, DITIB, is controlled by the Turkish Directorate of Religious Affairs, the *Diyanet*. German authorities insist on the independence of German schools from foreign state interference. So, some Lander, like North Rhine-Westphalia, have introduced Islamic Advisory Councils to decide on the religious content and the teachers who will teach Islam. The Land is represented in these Councils, and also controls the Muslim representation, the right to nominate requires an agreement between the Land and the Muslim Association and the agreement may only be concluded with Muslim Associations that meet certain requirements, such as independence from another state. In any case, the teaching is carried out by teachers who have been trained in the German language and under German state supervision.

VIII. Food Regulation

Lastly, in food regulation issues, most countries allow animals to be sacrificed, while observing sanitary regulations, by exsanguination without any previous blow to the head to reduce suffering, in accordance with religious ritual. This may be carried out by the person designated by the Islamic authorities. Nevertheless, there are also countries where, for the sake of animal welfare and to prevent suffering, slaughter is prohibited without previous stunning (for example, in Belgium's Flemish Region, Finland and Sweden) and, as national reports underline, with the Muslim communities' consent.

Generally speaking, in public establishments (prisons, military bases, educational centres) efforts are made to provide food that is adequate according to Islamic religious precepts. Therefore, the enforcement of the ruling is usually left to the discretion of the prison administration, with Muslim inmates having no subjective right to demand it.

IX. Conclusion

In conclusion, adapting to the presence of Islam, considered in all its dimensions, remains one of the major challenges facing European society. As occurred in the past with the status of the Catholic Church in the countries of central or southern Europe, or the measures adopted regarding cults or religious sects, the position of Muslims, today, constitutes a true touchstone of the breadth of the exercise of religious freedom in a country. Broadly speaking, European countries regulate the issue by trying to reconcile security and religious freedom. There is no doubt that the policies of control and surveillance of Muslims have affected and continue to affect the autonomy of Islamic communities.

In particular, the policies situated at opposite extremes tend to criminalise acts and manifestations of society (which have been considered by international organisations as a legitimate exercise of religious freedom) and raise doubts regarding their compatibility with the principles and values of pluralism, human rights and the rule of law, which are pillars of European society. On one hand, there are those that impose, as a social principle, the absolute neutrality of individuals before options of religious content, for the sake of equality in civic values. In this regard, the United Nations Special Rapporteur for freedom of religion and belief has warned 'against the use of "doctrinal secularism," which risks reducing the space for religious or belief pluralism in practice'.[4] On the other hand are those countries that, invoking historical cultural values from their past, reject Islam as a whole, as incompatible with the West. This leads to make three final remarks.

First, the statement that Islam is absolutely incompatible with Western democratic values, basing it on the Quran texts, or that Islam has radical and fundamentalist tendencies, is only a partial view that reveals prejudice. All other religions could, for that matter, be declared incompatible with Western values as well. One can find many examples of violence and intolerance in the Bible, such as the death sentences for homosexuals or adulterers. These ideas are clearly not acceptable in modern Western society. In addition, modern doctrines of a pacifist Islam, which defends human rights, are often unknown. They have evolved by adapting the sacred texts to the current conditions, just as Judaism and Christianity have done.

Second, the importance of religion (particularly Christianity) as a historical and cultural element of European society should be distinguished from the values and principles on which pluralist democracies are based. Among these values is religious freedom, which, due to its scope, extends to the exercise of all religions and agnostic or atheistic beliefs as well as expressions of freedom of conscience.

Third, measures aimed at integrating Muslims into the living-together model (based on secularisation, human rights and fundamental liberties) should prevail. Of course, it is fair to demand that Islamic communities should accept the rules of law of each country. Nevertheless, quoting Todorov's statement,

> the possibility of practising their own culture without discrimination does not prevent them from being loyal to the country they are living in … one common law does not mean one culture … If we dispossess human beings of their particular culture, they would simply cease to be human beings.[5]

Religion is the distinctive feature of Islamic culture. So, safeguarding religious practice within the framework of European values must be a priority for public authorities, not only as a guarantee of religious freedom but also cohesion and civil peace. The criminalisation of Islam will foster exclusion and ultimately violence. The most reasonable way to achieve the peaceful integration of Muslims into European society is through dialogue with Islamic communities to moderate their religious practices and prevent Muslims from feeling like they are second-class citizens.[6]

[4] www.ohchr.org/EN/Issues/FreedomReligion/Pages/ReportStateReligionRelationships.aspx, § 89.

[5] T Todorov, *El miedo a los bárbaros. Más allá del choque de civilizaciones* (tr N Sobregués) (Barcelona, Galaxia Gutemberg, 2008) 196–97.

[6] See the reasoning of EU discourses on this issue, summarised in A Motilla, 'Problemas y retos de la inmigración islámica en Europa; la posición de la Unión Europea' (2011) 9 *Revista Electrónica del Departamento de Derecho de la Universidad de la Rioja* 7, 14.

16

The Legal Treatment of Islamophobic Speech in Europe

LINA PAPADOPOULOU

I. Setting the Scene: The Social, Conceptual and Legal Framework

A. Islamophobic Speech: The Relevance and Topicality of its Legal Treatment

Three aspects of historical, technological and social developments in Europe have made the topic discussed in this chapter more acute than it was a couple of decades ago: first, an increase in the number of Muslims; secondly, the post-secular society,[1] in which religion reappears in the public sphere not least because of the public emergence of Islam; and thirdly, Web 2.0, with the advent of digital platforms and social media.

Indeed, until recently, Europe was almost exclusively a 'Christian fortress'. In certain political ideologies, and even constitutional interpretations, this empirical reality becomes a normative ideal. However, Christianity is no longer either the exclusive reality or a constitutional normative ideal. Migration flows from other continents, mainly Asia, increased in the last decades of the twentieth and the first decades of the twenty-first century, with a record influx during the last 10 years.[2] The Muslim population is also increasing in size within Europe – more than any

[1] J Habermas, Notes on Post-Secular Society(2008) 25 *New perspectives quarterly* 17ff.

[2] From 2012 to 2019 the number of refugees declared to the UNHCR rose from 10.5 to 17.2 million (most of them coming from Syria), while between 2014 and 2016, 48% of the 6.7 million of asylum-seekers were registered in Europe. From 2015 to 2019, the population of non-European immigrants to Europe increased from 35 to 38 million approximately; see European Commission, 'European Political Strategy Centre, 10 trends shaping migration' (2017); International Organisation for Migration (IOM), 'World Migration Report 2020' (Geneva, 2019) 85. In 2020, the population of non-European migrants in Europe exceeded 40 million; see IOM, 'Migration and migrants: Regional dimensions and developments' in M McAuliffe and A Triandafyllidou (eds), 'World Migration Report 2022' (Geneva, IOM, 2021) 37.

other religious group as a percentage – and it will continue to do so, even disregarding the exceptionally high flows of asylum-seekers and migrants.[3] At the same time, second- and third-generation immigrants are becoming citizens of European states. This leads to an increase in religious diversity.[4]

The peaceful and harmonic coexistence of diverse religious communities is undermined, especially due to the actions of two ostensibly opposed but consequently converging poles. On the one hand, xenophobic groups and far-right-wing political parties adopt an aggressive type of nationalism and nativism. They cultivate authoritarian trends in society, which take on the form of phobic racism. As long as the economic – and, currently the energy – crisis looms, the 'natives' find scapegoats in the faces of culturally different immigrants. This explains and, perhaps, gives rise to intense anti-Muslim hate speech. Moreover, the element of violence is rather implicit in the history of monotheistic religions, some aspects of which might even glorify it.[5] On the other hand, small sections of the Muslim community radicalise their believers and cause terrorist attacks in urban centres around the Western world.[6] In this respect, 9/11 was a turning point. For example, reactions in Muslim countries against the Danish cartoons depicting the Prophet Muhammad[7] were just a prelude to the violent and inhumane criminal acts against the creators of the French magazine *Charlie Hebdo* and jihadist terrorist attacks resulting in individual or mass loss of human life most notably in Paris (November 2015), Brussels (March 2016), Nice (July 2016) and Manchester (May 2017).[8] These attacks were similarly bolstered by the two opposing poles: on the one hand, racist generalisations and stereotypical presentations of the Muslim community; and on the other hand, by the lack of universal and unconditional condemnation of the attacks by that same community, which lacks a centre of leadership capable of communicating an unconditional message of disapproval. These violent incidents further reinforce the aforementioned phobias, while at

[3] See Pew Research Center, 'Europe's Growing Muslim Population' (29 November 2017), available at www.pewresearch.org/religion/2017/11/29/europes-growing-muslim-population.

[4] See European Commission, Directorate-General for Research and Innovation, 'Pluralism and religious diversity, social cohesion and integration in Europe, Insights from European research' (European Union, 2011).

[5] L Woolf and M Hulsizer, 'Intra- and Inter-Religious Hate and Violence: A Psychosocial Model' (2003) 2 *Journal of Hate Studies* 5.

[6] C Allen and JS Nielsen 'Summary report on Islamophobia in the EU after 11 September 2001' (Vienna, EUMC, 2002).

[7] F Rose, the culture editor of the Danish newspaper Jyllands-Posten, in his article 'Why I Published Those Cartoons' (19 February 2006) *The Washington Post* (available at www.washington-post.com/archive/opinions/2006/02/19/why-i-published-those-cartoons/f9a67368–4641-4fa7-b71 f-843ea44814ef), explained, after the events, his decision to publish the cartoons saying that: 'When I visit a mosque, I show my respect by taking off my shoes. I follow the customs, just as I do in a church, synagogue or other holy place. But if a believer demands that I, as a nonbeliever, observe his taboos in the public domain, he is not asking for my respect, but for my submission. And that is incompatible with a secular democracy.'

[8] See, Europol, 'European Union Terrorism Situation and Trend Report' (2021).

the same time, multiplying and intensifying racist phenomena, including the ever-increasing spread and intensity of sweeping anti-Muslim hate speech.

These phenomena exacerbate religious differences or, in any case, clothe political ideologies or racist discrimination in a religious mantle. At the same time, they also signal identity conflicts, causing rifts in the ideal-typical perception of citizenship, ie the status of a citizen within the nation-state and within the European Union, regardless of more specific cultural characteristics. By extension, these phenomena also affect both political and constitutional theory and constitutional law, as they raise questions at a doctrinal level concerning the sovereignty of the constitution and the fundamental principles of our social coexistence, as these have evolved and been shaped since the Enlightenment. Sometimes, however, these phenomena also call into question the very 'coexistence with equal freedom', which is also the ultimate 'end', the purpose that the constitutional institutions (must) serve.

Consequently, religiously intolerant discourse is encountered at ever-increasing frequency and goes hand-in-hand with racism, in the broad sense, as 'neo-racism', which is not based on anthropological, biological origin and divisions, but constitutes a 'cultural racism', rooted in ethno-cultural differences or particularities. This neo-racism is marked by belief in the inferiority of the target group based not only on race but also religion.[9] The latter reappears on the public sphere without the need to be 'translated' to secular values and ideals. Religious difference is politicised, instrumentalised and turned to a fertile breeding ground for neo-racism and nativism. Consequently, both Islamophobia and the ever-present anti-Semitism are growing rapidly.[10]

Islamophobic speech – always present in traditional media (newspapers, TV and radio) – has been radically enhanced in the blogosphere.[11] The internet, as a new 'public communication network'[12] and public – yet privately owned – place

[9] Woolf and Hulsizer (n 5) 9.

[10] According to an FRA survey, 'Experiences and perceptions of antisemitism – Second survey on discrimination and hate crime against Jews in the EU' (10 December 2018), 40% of Jews in the EU fear being physically attacked, while another 2017 survey found that 27% of Muslims had experienced incidents of intolerant harassment in the past 12 months, with this rising to 31% for Muslim women who wear headscarves in public. See FRA, 'Antisemitism – Overview of antisemitic incidents recorded in the European Union 2011–2021' (3 November 2022), available at: fra.europa.eu/en/publication/2022/antisemitism-overview-2011–2021.

[11] O Nwabuzo and L Schaeder, 'Racism and Discrimination in the Context of Migration in Europe' (Brussels, European Network Against Racism Shadow Report, 2016) 15. According to a report drafted by ex-Facebook employees, experts on statistics, approximately one out of 1,000 posts (or five million out of the five billion posts daily) violates the company rules concerning hate speech. See R Mac and C Silverman, 'After the US Election, Key People Are Leaving Facebook and Torching the Company In Departure Notes' (11 December 2020) BuzzFeedNews, available at www.buzzfeednews.com/article/ryanmac/facebook-rules-hate-speech-employees-leaving; G Rosen, 'Community Standards Enforcement Report, November 2020' (Meta, 19 November 2020), available at about.fb.com/news/2020/11/community-standards-enforcement-report-nov-2020.

[12] Art 2(d), L 108/3: 'public communications network. means an electronic communications network used wholly or mainly for the provision of publicly available electronic communications services'.

of information and communication and exchange of ideas, is not as amenable to regulation as traditional media are. Communication platforms and social media are bringing about a structural transformation of this space and of the so-called 'marketplace of ideas', allowing an exponentially greater number of individuals and groups to express themselves and be heard directly and unmediated without substantial obstacles. Thus, online service providers, digital platforms and social media now function – parallel to traditional media, if not mainly themselves – as 'gatekeepers', both in terms of content as well as users-producers, who can spread their views through such media. At the same time, this new medium is a fertile ground for hate speech[13] due to its decentralised architecture in its 2.0 incarnation. The relatively inexpensive technological ability to spread thoughts and congregate with like-minded users, the anonymity or pseudonymity that the internet provides, and its unmediated egalitarianism have resulted in an increase in online hate speech in terms of volume and intensity. It has also been found that online intolerant speech has a negative effect not just on the persons and groups it targets but also on those who speak out in favour of freedom, tolerance and the fight against adverse discrimination, and can cause silence (the 'chilling effect') and inhibit democratic dialogue on digital platforms.[14]

B. Islamophobia: A Definition

'Islamophobia' as a neologism emerged at the end of the last century[15] and was developed as a political concept in order to raise awareness and understanding in society concerning the growing hostility towards Islam and Muslims. Nowadays, albeit widely used, 'Islamophobia' remains an underexplored and controversial term. One of the most widely used definitions comes from the UK All Party Parliamentary Group (APPG) on British Muslims, which defined it as a type of racism 'that targets expressions of Muslimness or perceived Muslimness'.[16] Although various markers of 'Muslimness' may be deployed (including religious symbols and clothing), religion is also usually conflated with race. Their combination, without further reference to specific acts or omissions, reveals that, in most cases, Islamophobia is indeed more akin to racism than fear (phobia). The visual identifiers of being Muslim prompt expressions of racism by the perpetrators, who, in this way, exhibit aggressiveness more so than fear.

Consequently, it can hardly be disputed that, firstly, Islamophobia is a reality throughout Europe, as it targets a religious minority within a 'Christian fortress'

[13] B Perry and P Olsson, 'Cyberhate, The Globalization of Hate' (2009) 18 *International Review of Law, Computers & Technology* 185.

[14] European Commission, 'Code of conduct on countering illegal hate speech online' (2016), available at ec.europa.eu/justice/fundamental-rights/files/hate_speech_code_of_conduct_en.pdf.

[15] See, Runnymede Trust, 'Islamophobia: A Challenge for Us All' (1997).

[16] All Party Parliamentary Group on British Muslims, 'Islamophobia defined: The inquiry into a working definition of Islamophobia' (2018) 11.

and, secondly, that there is a resonance with other expressions of 'phobias', be it latent racism, like anti-Semitism, or other 'phobias' against minority groups of different nature, such as transphobia.[17] Nevertheless, it is submitted[18] that there is a dichotomous relationship 'between the contestation attributed to Islamophobia as a political – and public – concept and Islamophobia as a 'real' and tangible discriminatory phenomenon'. The contestation of the former relies not only on its definitional vagueness,[19] but also on accusations that it exaggerates the existing phenomenon it describes. Moreover, proscribing expressions of 'Islamophobia' altogether may lead to silencing any legitimate criticism of Islam, as the term (like other phobias, such as homophobia, transphobia, etc) can be ideologically misused and abused to prevent people from expressing their legitimate concerns.

'Islamophobic speech', which this chapter is concerned with, as an expressive manifestation of Islamophobia, shares the vagueness of the latter. Its use in quotation marks aims at underlining its inability to express its nature and content with legal accuracy. There is a need to 'translate' this amorphous term into legal categories that are better known and well defined in European legal systems. Without such specification, the term will remain an empty receptacle susceptible to misuse.

In a 2008 report, the European Commission for Democracy through Law (the 'Venice Commission') distinguished three types of regulation of anti-religious speech: (1) the restriction of blasphemy; (2) the restriction of religious insults; and (3) the restriction of religious hate speech.[20] Following this schema, a tripartite distinction of 'Islamophobic speech' should be introduced. First, Islamophobic speech *stricto sensu*, ie the expression of fear or a phobia that Islam will prevail in European societies combined with the belief that this will lead to unwanted political changes incompatible with liberal democracy and/or that it will undermine Christianity. Second, aggressive Anti-Muslim hate speech as a specific manifestation of general hate against Muslims or those perceived to be Muslim. Third, blasphemous speech and defamation of Islam, its Prophet and symbols. This speech tends to criticise and even mock Islam as a religion. However, in order to find the right place in the legal system for these different sorts of speech, we must first take a closer look at an issue that has been discussed *ad nauseam*: the constitutional framework for free speech which forms the basis for any further responses to the main question on the proper legal treatment of the three categories of 'Islamophobic speech'.

[17] I Zempi and I Awan, *Islamophobia: Lived Experiences of Online and Offline Victimisation* (Bristol, Policy Press, 2016).

[18] C Allen, *Reconfiguring Islamophobia, A Radical Rethinking of a Contested* Concept (London, Palgrave Macmillan, 2020) 8.

[19] ibid, 6.

[20] See Venice Commission, 'Blasphemy, insult and hatred: finding answers in a democratic society, Science and technique of democracy, No. 47' (Council of Europe Publishing, 2008); See I Leigh, 'Damned if they do, damned if they don't: The European Court of Human Rights and the protection of religion from attack' (2011) 17 *Res Publica* 55, 57.

C. Basic Assumptions Concerning the Freedom of Expression on which this Paper Relies

The notion of freedom is generally considered, both in Hobbesian and Utilitarian philosophic thought, as having a negative meaning (as lack of coercion).[21] The 'freedom principle' constrains the state's ability to limit individual freedom by proscribing specific acts and behaviours. More specifically, freedom of speech was one of the first (together with economic and religious freedoms) rights to be recognised. Its special position in the constellation of rights is attributed to its acknowledgment as not only a negative liberty, and as such an end in itself, like most rights, but also to its inextricable link, as a means to an end, to the ideals and imperatives of the Enlightenment, both collective – parallel to the personal – autonomy, ie democracy, and the relentless pursuit of truth, beyond and even opposed to established religious authorities and dogmas (particularly those of the Catholic Church at the time). That is why, in his essay 'What is Enlightenment?', Immanuel Kant defines the latter as 'the human being's emancipation from its self-incurred immaturity'. He further associates this emancipation with religious freedom and free expression in the public space.[22] Therefore, freedom of expression is, historically and conceptually, concomitant with religious freedom, understood also as *freedom from* coercive dogmatic thinking. Consequently, speech can only be limited when it directly prevents the state from serving its main purpose of safeguarding individual freedom, since freedom is the fundament and objective of the social contract.[23] Along the same lines, Spinoza considers a statement that can harm another person as an act and not as simple expression,[24] which can therefore be limited.

Any privileged positioning of free expression in constitutional thought is to be attributed to mainly consequentialist arguments, which emphasise its positive function as a means to achieve other goals and values, rather than merely as an end in itself.[25] On the contrary, the non-consequentialist arguments based on a principled approach focus on the right itself and are directed from rights-based strategies.[26] Thus, the special positioning of the right to free speech is due to the fact that it serves the pursuit of truth – a consequentialist argument already found in John Stuart Mill's *On Liberty*), the achievement of personal plans and collective

[21] I Berlin, *Four Essays on Liberty*, (Oxford, Oxford University Press, 1969) 122.

[22] I Kant, *Beantwortung der Frage: Was ist Aufklärung?* (originally published, 1784) 481. Similarly, Spinoza, *Tractatus Theologico-Politicus*, ch XX uses examples connected with religion to clarify his thesis on freedom of expression.

[23] Spinoza (ibid) 231; E Pitts, 'Spinoza on Freedom of Expression' (1986) 47 *Journal of the History of Ideas* 21, 27.

[24] Pitts (ibid) 28.

[25] *cf Whitney v California* 274 US 357 (1927) (Brandeis J concurring).

[26] R Dworkin, 'Is there a right to pornography?' (1988) 1 *Oxford Journal of Legal Studies* 177, 178. DK Badamchi, 'Justifications of freedom of speech: Towards a double-grounded non-consequentialist approach' (2014) 41 *Philosophy and Social Criticism* 907.

autonomy, ie, democracy, which is predicated on the free exchange of ideas and popular participation.[27] This explains why freedom of speech is considered not only a civil but also a political right[28] and, moreover, possesses an objective dimension as a principle lying at the foundation of every liberal-democratic polity.

If these end goals justify the distinguished positioning of the right to free speech, it can be inferred that, when not in service of these goals, freedom of expression falls to the level of other civil rights. In these cases, its possible limitations are correspondingly connected with those instances where speech bluntly undermines its aforementioned objectives. Such types of speech would then be defamation of a specific person and hate speech (undermining the chances of the specific person or the members of the target group to achieve their own life plans); fake news (directly and intentionally negating the truth); direct incitement to violence; and undermining the prerequisites of liberal democracy and the fundaments of the ECHR (such as pro-Nazi speech) and the endorsement or undermining the significance of genocides (such as Holocaust denial[29]). On the contrary, defamation of religion or blasphemy do not challenge democracy or truth unless someone accepts the divine truth of a specific religion as such, which would altogether uproot the *ratio* of free speech, as presented above.

The above (necessarily) brief presentation of the historical and philosophical roots of the right to free speech also predestines and forms its legal design. In the ECHR, the right to freedom of expression is enshrined in Article 10, which is similar to Articles 8, 9 and 11 in structure: the first paragraph recognises the fundamental right, while the second paragraph lays down formal and substantive requirements for limitations. Similarly, the European Court of Justice has long recognised the protection of free speech[30] as reflecting common constitutional traditions of the Member States and international treaties to which they are signatories, and the right is now enshrined in Article 11 of the EU Charter of Fundamental Rights. Notwithstanding its significance, not only is freedom of expression not an absolute right, but it is also not a 'privileged' or 'primary'[31] right. This privileged position might be the case in the USA, where the right enjoys enhanced protection both in black letter law and in constitutional tradition and case law. However, there are many who think that this ought to be the case also in Europe, despite the fact that

[27] A Meiklejohn, 'The First Amendment is an Absolute' (1961) *The Supreme Court Review* 245; C Yong, 'Does freedom of speech include hate speech?' (2011) *Res Publica* 385, 389; *cf* Badamchi (ibid) 8, who includes citizens' participation, together with autonomy, in the non-consequentialist arguments. This would only be convincing if participation were considered as a self-serving objective, outside of the functioning of democracy.

[28] Indicatively, *Handyside v United Kingdom* § 49 A no 549/72 (1976) EHHR, §49; *Otto-Preminger-Institut v Austria*, 13470/87, 20.09.1994, §49.

[29] See *Pastörs v Germany* [5th Section], 55225/14, 03.10.2019.

[30] Indicatively see C-245/01, *RTL Television GmbH v NLM*, 23.10.2003; C-368/95 – *Vereinigte Familiapress*, 26.06.1997; C-112/00, *Eugen Schmidberger, Internationale Transporte und Planzüge v Austria*, 12.06.2003.

[31] *cf* S Kentridge, 'Freedom of Speech: Is it the Primary Right?' (1996) 45 *International and Comparative Law Quarterly* 253.

neither in the aforesaid supranational bills of rights nor in any national European Constitution does there exist a hierarchy of rights favouring free speech over, for instance, equality or dignity.

On the contrary, freedom of expression is, in the ECHR, associated with duties and responsibilities, which, according to the ECtHR, depend on the conditions under which the person acted and the means used.[32] In other words, any limitations are imposed by states following an evaluation on the basis of the content and context of the speech (eg, broadcast over the radio or TV[33] or the internet[34]), so as to judge the possible influence of the speech. In other words, when it collides with other rights, freedom of speech needs to be balanced and weighed against other constitutionally recognised goods and rights, in order for the legislature, the executive, and the judiciary to discover in which direction the scales tip.

The ECtHR has indeed found[35] that, amongst the 'duties and responsibilities', in the context of religious opinions and beliefs, there is

> an obligation to avoid as far as possible expressions that are *gratuitously offensive* to others and thus an infringement of their rights, and which therefore do not contribute to any form of public debate capable of furthering progress in human affairs.

This wording by the Court, as reasoned as it may be, gives rise to more questions than answers. Is any blasphemy and defamation of religion, any speech insulting the religious feeling of others and hate speech alike 'gratuitously offensive' and should it be considered as such, thus allowing proscription by the state? Or should there be a differentiation between these three different types of speech, although all of them can be considered 'Islamophobic', when they target Islam and Muslims? Should these types of speech, based on constitutional evaluations, be equalised and free or criminal offences, or should we differentiate between them on the basis of considerations relating to constitutionally protected goods and societal values? This chapter takes the latter view, even if it somewhat strays from the complex and sophisticated jurisprudence of the ECtHR.

[32] *Handyside* (n 28); *Vereinigung Bildender Künstler* v Austria, §26 A no 68354/01, (2007) EHHR [1st Section].

[33] *Jersild v Denmark*, §31 A no 15890/89 (1995) EHRR. *Otto-Preminger* (n 28) §49: 'As the Court has consistently held, freedom of expression constitutes one of the essential foundations of a democratic society, one of the basic conditions for its progress and for the development of everyone. Subject to paragraph 2 of Article 10 (art. 10-2), it is applicable not only to "information" or "ideas" that are favourably received or regarded as inoffensive or as a matter of indifference, but also to those that shock, offend or disturb the State or any sector of the population. Such are the demands of that pluralism, tolerance and broadmindedness without which there is no "democratic society"' (see, particularly, the *Handyside v the United Kingdom* judgment of 7 December 1976, Series A no 24 at 23, [49]).

[34] *Delfi AS v Esthonia* § 134, A no 64569/09 [Grand Chamber], (2015) EHRR.

[35] *Otto-Preminger* (n 28) (emphasis added).

II. Differentiated Legal Treatment for Different Types of 'Islamophobic Speech'

A. Prohibited Speech Acts: Hate Speech

There are four main answers to the question of which acts the state can legitimately criminalise without arbitrarily and excessively violating personal autonomy, either generally or as the latter is exemplified in more specific fundamental rights such as freedom of expression. Criminal sanctions may be legitimately imposed in order to prevent harm to others (the harm principle), offence to others (the offence principle), self-harm (legal paternalism), and victimless immoral conduct (legal moralism).[36] The first rationale can be traced back to John Stuart Mill and the well-known 'harm principle', while the other, originating with twentieth-century political and social philosopher Joel Feinberg, supplements and widens the harm principle by adding the 'offence principle' to it. In other words, what is being accepted here is that, when it comes to restrictions of a fundamental right and, in this case, freedom of expression, the 'harm principle' should be adopted rather than the 'offense principle'.[37] The 'harm principle' can hardly be rationally disputed. However, the 'devil' lies in the elaboration of the concept of harm. Even the most ardent supporters of freedom of speech rarely challenge the criminalisation of moral agency in crimes, such as incitement, libel, defamation or verbal abuse. Hate speech, however, remains disputable as to whether it causes harm to the individuals belonging (or taken to belong) to the group targeted. It is no surprise that the philosopher Jeremy Waldron's famous book, where hate speech remains free and protected speech, is titled *The Harm in Hate Speech*. Feinberg defines harm as not only a thwarting of someone's interests but also, at the same time as a violation of their rights. According to a different view, however, hate speech is not different from blasphemy or religious defamation, as both these categories of acts are merely viewed as offences and 'mere' offences should not warrant state interference with personal liberty.[38]

[36] J Feinberg, *The Moral Limits of the Criminal Law, vol. I: Harm to Others* (Oxford, Oxford University Press, 1984) 13.

[37] The 'offence principle' as a criterion for justifying criminal prohibitions has been proposed by J Feiberg, *The Moral Limits of the Criminal Law, vol 1: Harm to Others* (ibid); and *vol 2: Offense to Others* (Oxford, Oxford University Press, 1985) 5: 'Offensive behavior as such is no kind of menace, but at its worst only severely irritating nuisance'.

[38] eg F Haiman, *Speech and Law in a Free Society* (Chicago, University of Chicago Press 1981) 6, who develops a civil-libertarian approach to free speech, after overtly stating his pre-hermeneutical choices and ends that his analysis serves, them being the 'self-expression and self-fulfillment of the individuals' but not the social order.

What is peculiar about 'hate speech'[39] is that it comprises[40] expressive acts with which the internal hatred felt by the speaking subject for a person or a group of persons is externalised. This hate is not due to specific personal experiences of the perpetrator or behaviours of the target, but because of a specific identity characteristic of the latter (such as race, religion, colour, gender, sexual orientation or gender identity, disability, etc). According to the Council of Europe:[41]

> The term 'hate speech' shall be understood as covering all forms of expression which spread, incite, promote or justify racial hatred, xenophobia, anti-Semitism or other forms of hatred based on intolerance, including: intolerance expressed by aggressive nationalism and ethnocentrism, discrimination and hostility against minorities, migrants and people of immigrant origin.

Therefore, hate speech is publicly uttered speech designed to spread and promote,[42] incite or justify hatred against specific, historically oppressed groups, and it can be spread either in person or online.[43] Empirically and logically speaking, the target group is usually a minority and certainly vulnerable and historically in a disadvantaged position within the given society. The prohibition of this specific form of speech is based on the assumption of the categorisation of expressive acts into those that contain and spread ideas and those that are more akin to an act, and which can therefore be punished as such, given that criminal law is primarily directed at punishing actions that cause harm.[44] The strength of hate speech

[39] *Hassrede* or *Volksverhetzung* in German, the latter being historically connected with the Nazi propaganda by Hitler's National Socialist German Workers' Party.

[40] As rightly pointed by T McGonagle, 'The Council of Europe against online hate speech: Conundrums and challenges' (Council of Europe expert paper, 2013) 3, although the term 'hate speech' has been extensively integrated into international and national legal texts, there is not yet a commonly accepted definition.

[41] Council of Europe, Committee of Ministers, 'Recommendation No R (97) 20 on the Committee of Ministers to Member States on "Hate Speech"' adopted by the Committee of Ministers on 30 October 1997 at the 607th meeting of the Ministers' Deputies. See also European Commission against Racism and Intolerance, 'General Policy Recommendation No 15 on Combating Hate Speech' adopted on 8 December 2015: 'namely, the advocacy, promotion or incitement of the denigration, hatred or vilification of a person or group of persons, as well any harassment, insult, negative stereotyping, stigmatization or threat of such person or persons and any justification of all these forms of expression – that is based on a non-exhaustive list of personal characteristics or status that includes 'race,' colour, language, religion or belief, nationality or national or ethnic origin, as well as descent, age, disability, sex, gender, gender identity and sexual orientation. See also Council Framework Decision 2008/913/JHA of 28 November 2008 on combating certain forms and expressions of racism and xenophobia by means of criminal law, L 328, 6.12.2008, 55–58.

[42] M Rosenfeld, 'Regulation of Hate Speech' in V Amar and M Tushnet (eds), *Global Perspectives on Constitutional Law* (Oxford, Oxford University Press, 2009) 181, 'designed to convey or promote hatred on the basis of race, religion, or ethnic origin'.

[43] CR Carlson, 'Exploring Legal Responses to Hate Speech in the United States' (2020) 32 *University of Baltimore Journal of Media Law & Ethics* 32, 35.

[44] Z Chafee, *Free Speech in the United States* (Cambridge, Harvard University Press, 1948) 149–50. See, however, H Franklyn, *Speech and Law in a Free Society* (Chicago, University of Chicago Press, 1981) 21, who insists that every kind of speech contains ideas and is being accepted by a similarly minded audience. Thus, if we agree to punish some kinds of speech, we have to do it not because they are more like acts, but because we have concluded that it is justified to prohibit them under specific circumstances.

to *incite* violence, hate or discrimination makes it function more like an act. Furthermore, hate speech of all shades aims, in its mildest version, to silence the people who are its target, ie it offends the freedom of expression of the specific people, while in its worst version it aims to exterminate them. Thus, hate speech is now recognised as a pervasive social problem,[45] driving some digital platforms and social media themselves to self-regulation.[46]

Because of the above, it is now recognised that hate speech attacks human dignity and equality or, under another approach, public order. Given that it is difficult to exclude any of the above principles, ie values and goods, it would be more accurate to accept that hate speech attacks and undermines peaceful coexistence, the *vivre ensemble* in a liberal democratic society.

It should, however, be clarified that all offensive speech does not necessarily constitute 'hate speech' in the technical sense of the term, although hate speech is always offensive. Hate speech is, rather, a subcategory of offensive speech, which, when directed against Islam or Muslims can be termed as 'Islamophobic hate speech'. While hate speech is and should remain punishable, other aggressive speech is not and should not necessarily be prohibited. This is because aggressive speech does not in any case attack any goods that are and should be protected more than the free expression.

More specifically, Nicholas Hatzis defines the nature of offence as a 'constellation of unpleasant feelings stirred up when our expectations to be treated in a particular way are disappointed', resulting in mental pain due to the conflict between our inner reality and the outside world.[47] This is a broad definition that includes forms of speech and expression quite distant from the definition of hate speech and, thus from any thought of prohibition, let alone criminalisation. Hence, Hatzis rightly observes that the category of offensive speech must be differentiated from speech that promotes hatred, as these are morally different types of speech and it is wrong to borrow arguments from discussion of hate speech in order to support restrictions on aggressive expression.[48] Hate speech, on the other hand, possesses special characteristics both quantitatively, in terms of degree of aggressiveness, as well as qualitatively.

[45] See ECRI, 'General Policy Recommendation No 5 (revised) on preventing and combating anti-Muslim racism and discrimination' adopted on 16 March 2000 and revised on 8 December 2021 (Strasbourg, 1 March 2022), available at www.coe.int/en/web/european-commission-against-racism-and-intolerance/recommendation-no.5; M Williams and M de Reya, 'Hatred Behind the Screens: A Report on the Rise of Online Hate Speech' (Mishcon Academy, 2019) 10.

[46] A Kantor, 'Measuring Our Progress Combatting Hate Speech' (Meta, 19 November 2020), available at about.fb.com/news/2020/11/measuring-progress-combating-hate-speech. Similarly, YouTube announced (YouTube Community Guidelines enforcement) that it removed 47 million hateful comments between September and December 2020 and 43.6 million between January and March 2021, while Facebook and Instagram removed 22.1 million posts between July and September 2020.

[47] N Hatzis, *Offensive Speech, Religion, and the Limits of the Law* (Oxford, Oxford University Press, 2021) 3.

[48] ibid. To the same direction, see also DK Badamchi, *Dimensions of Free Speech, An Exploration of a New Theoretical Framework* (London, Springer, 2021) 119.

In the case at hand in this chapter, the target of hatred is Muslims; or even those perceived to be Muslims because of their skin colour and external appearance, ethnic or national origin, or status as immigrants or asylum-seekers. Due to this intersectionality of discrimination and hatred, Islamophobic speech is very often also xenophobic and racist *stricto sensu*.[49] The concerning aspect of criminalising hate speech is the fact that it brings about sanctions upon the person articulating it without any tangible harmful effects. This raises the question of what the harm in hate speech is. Criminalising hate speech seems to be antithetical to the trend in the western world to decriminalise offences against religions and religious symbols, such as blasphemy and defamation of religion.

'Islamophobic' speech includes all such types of speech acts, ie both anti-Muslim speech full of hatred and incitement to hate, discrimination or violence, and blasphemy against Islam and defamation of it. It can also include other, more harmless, declarations of political ideas or prejudices, what could be termed as 'Islamophobic speech *stricto sensu*'. This may indeed express somebody's fear vis-à-vis the possibility of Islam prevailing in a country, as one might equally express one's fear of or dislike for Christianity or a political regime, eg, communism or neo-liberalism, prevailing in the political sphere. This second kind of Islamophobic speech cannot be criminalised as it falls under the protection of freedom of thought and political expression as a *sine qua non* prerequisite of liberal democracy. Deconstructing all religions, ideologies, faiths or political ideas and proposing ones different to those already established is a necessary condition for the advancement and progress of political society as a whole. It goes without saying that this liberty should apply to all religions, both the state and/or prevailing religion(s) and minority religions. Equally, 'islamophobic speech' that falls under the category of blasphemy and defamation of religions should also, much like attacking any other religion, a prevalent or a minority one, be free and unprohibited.

Anti-Muslim hate speech, on the other hand, targets Muslims based on and because of their faith and adherence to the specific religion, rather than the religion per se. It also attacks persons who, for example, due to the colour of their skin are taken to be Muslims, even though they might not be, or even the advocates of religious equality and non-discrimination. It is a very aggressive kind of speech, aiming at silencing every member of its target group, making them invisible, inciting discrimination and hatred against them, and excluding them from social life and the public sphere. This kind of speech not only violates equal freedom of speech and religion, but also undermines democracy, as it discriminates on the basis of religion. If the added value and enhanced protection of free speech can be attributed to the fact that it is not only an individual right, but also a prerequisite for democracy, then hate speech as a vector for undermining democracy and violating equal dignity and citizenship cannot enjoy such enhanced protection. It

[49] *cf* F Kübler, 'How much freedom for racist speech? Transnational aspects of a conflict of human rights' (1998) 27 *Hofstra Law Review* 336, 367; J Weinstein, *Hate Speech, Pornography, and the Radical Attack on Free Speech Doctrine* (Boulder, Westview 1999) 127–35.

needs to be balanced against other fundamental rights, such as equal treatment, religious freedom, and human dignity. Therefore, it can be prohibited and criminalised when it is overtly aggressive or when considerations of proportionality allow for that assessment.

B. Defamation of Islam and Blasphemy

At the international level, there is a shift of legal interest from the legal prohibition of defamation (or insult) of religions or blasphemy, accompanied by a tendency to abolish these crimes of opinion, to providing legal protection to persons against discrimination and threats of violence on grounds relating to their religious or general beliefs. This shift means that the legal good in question is no longer protection of religion per se but protection of believers. This differentiation is of decisive importance in two respects: firstly, from the point of view of the legal doctrine on the subject at hand, as it relates to the protected legal good and the characteristics that allow an expression to fall under the spectrum of prohibited 'Islamophobic speech'; and secondly, from a constitutional-philosophical perspective regarding the concept and characteristics of constitutional democracy and the neutrality displayed by the state (and what kind of neutrality this ought to be).

The difference between Islamophobic *hate* speech, on the one hand, and all other 'Islamophobic speech', on the other, lies in the fact that, in the former case, the victims are human beings rather than abstract symbols, beliefs or ideas. In the latter case, some believers might indeed experience shock, indignation, moral outrage or revulsion, their sentiments might be truly hurt, but this is due to their moral/religious conscience having been attacked by the speech and communicative act of others within the domain of the exchange of ideas. However, the believers' right to religious freedom (including religious equality and freedom of being discriminated against based on their religious beliefs) has not been violated as long as the same principles and impartial judicial practice applies to all religions. This differentiation has two interconnected bases. First, religions as such, as is the case with any other belief systems, should not be protected from criticism or even ridicule, since that would be impede the free development of the citizenry's personality, the exchange of ideas, and the possibility of progress and search for the truth or a better social setting. Second, one's sentiments and feelings of being offended due to the speech acts of others need *not* be protected by the law.[50]

Offence is thus a totally subjective notion: the same words or symbolic acts would cause totally different reactions among different subjects, while the *harm*

[50] See also European Commission for Democracy through Law (Venice Commission), 'Report on the Relationship Between Freedom of Expression and Freedom of Religion: The Issued of Regulation and Prosecution of Blasphemy, Religious Insult and Incitement to Religious Hatred', Study 406/2006, adopted by the Venice Commission at its 76th Plenary Session, 17–18 October 2008, paras 64–68.

caused by hate speech is characterised by a more enhanced objectivity or, better said, intersubjectivity. Although there might be some persons not harmed when the minority or historically discriminated group they belong to becomes the target of incitement to hatred and violence, most of them would. For example, the phrase 'get X group out of the country' would equally incite discrimination and hatred against any named group. Conversely, a blasphemous picture depicting an erotic scene between Jesus Christ and Mary Magdalene or a 'satanic verse' against the Prophet Muhammad would probably cause emotional pain to certain Christians and certain Muslims respectively but would not undermine their equal dignity or citizenship status. Inter-subjectivity should be considered a crucial element, in addition to differentiating between insulting the beliefs and insulting the believers.

C. Islamophobic Speech *Stricto Sensu*

While blasphemy against Islam and hate speech against Muslims are subcategories of Islamophobic speech, not all Islamophobic speech constitutes blasphemy or hate speech. What remains can be named 'Islamophobic speech *stricto sensu*' because it entails nothing else but a rational or irrational fear (phobia). This is speech that expresses the speaker's fear in the face of a less or more imagined scenario of Islam prevailing in the (non-Islamic) country in which they live, or their own lives being adversely affected through the expansion of Islam (or religion more generally) in Europe. This kind of speech insults Muslims as equally as any criticism of left- or right-wing political ideology would insult its respective proponents, or as equally as any criticism of neo-liberalism as inhume, or of traditional Christian values as backward-looking could stir unpleasant emotions among their respective adherents. This *stricto sensu* Islamophobic speech is protected, as it contributes to the exchange of ideas and democratic dialogue. Similarly, the expression of fear in the face of a scenario where the majority of the population would become homosexual, or of the belief that homosexuality is a sin – when expressed by a religious minister, for example – is definitely 'homophobic' and insults homosexuals and maybe hurts their emotions; it cannot, however, be proscribed by the state, as long as it does not constitute hate speech, as defined above (incitement to hatred, violence or discrimination).

This argument implies that feelings, religious or other, as such, are not and cannot be protected by law due to their highly subjective and volatile character. Their protection is not –and should not be considered to be – part of the right to freedom of religion (or political pluralism, private life, etc). In other words, one's right to hold and express their religious beliefs, to exercise their rituals and not be discriminated because of them does not include a right that others should not express different opinions, beliefs or ideas, or even ridicule one's own system of beliefs or ideas. In this respect, the law should offer protection to the believer from insults, not their beliefs, be they religious, political, philosophical, biotheoretical or of any other nature. Thus, speech hurting the feelings should be immune from legislative control.

This answer relies on three considerations. First, if feelings were to be protected, they should be protected against not only speech but also, even more, against acts. This would indeterminately and excessively limit general freedom, as there are countless acts (including speech acts) that would hurt the feelings of many people. For instance, electoral results, denial of expressions of love and marriage proposals, failures in exams or interviews and many more such experiences hurt the feelings of people every day. Social and political life would be completely impossible if feelings were to be legally protected. Second, protection of feelings would radically undermine legal certainty, as a component of rule of law and penal law specifically. As feelings are, above all else, subjective, an individual would not be in a position to know whether somebody else's feelings would be hurt by their acts. In turn, this would mean that one could easily even pretend that their feelings have been hurt in order to silence somebody else. If feelings were to be balanced against each other, this would result in the exchange of ideas, political dialogue, criticism and even personal relationships becoming impossible. An insult of feelings signals a subjective attitude and does not in itself justify restriction, whereas hate speech creates or contributes to the creation of objective conditions of discrimination and exclusion.[51] Islamophobic speech that is critical of, or even aggressively rejects, Islam may be politically undesirable or culturally unethical, but it does not necessarily constitute hate speech. Similarly, fierce, even aggressive, rejection of homosexuality (eg, by religious ministers, whether Muslim, Christian or other) does not in any case constitute 'hate speech', although it is homophobic.

III. Conclusion

Islamophobic speech is a very broad category comprising a variety of speech acts ranging from the expression of sentiments or political opinions and anti-Islamic defamation or blasphemy, on one hand, to prohibited anti-Muslim hate speech, on the other. If political debate, however intense, can contribute to the flourishing of democracy, hate speech, which is by definition neo-racist and anti-democratic, aiming to destroy the rights and freedoms of others, is an obstacle to and undermines (liberal) democracy. As a result, in these cases, the ECtHR correctly applies Article 17 ECHR to proscribe very aggressive hate speech by excluding it from the protective field of Article 10 ECHR as an abusive exercise of the right to freedom of expression.[52]

Consequently, while Islamophobia can constitute a useful category in political discussions and functions as a political marker to identify the expressions

[51] Badamchi (n 48) 123.

[52] See the Commission's decisions: *Glimmerveen and J Hagenbeek v The Netherlands*, A no 8348/78 and 8406/78, 11.10.1979; *Kühnen v Germany*, A no 12194/86, 12.05.1988, DR 56, 205; *BH, MW, HP and GK v Austria*, A no 12774/87, 12.10.1989, DR 62, 216; *Ochsenberger v Austria*, A no 21318/93, 02.09.1994; *Walendy v Germany*, A no 21128/92, 11.01.1995, DR 80, 94; *Remer v Germany*,

of uneasiness about coexistence with growing Muslim minorities and aggression against them and as a problem that needs to be politically tackled, 'Islamophobic speech' as a unitary species that includes all three different types of speech indicated above might have an obscuring effect as a legal category. This is because it can either lead to limitations of speech broader than those appropriate for a liberal democratic society, or, on the contrary, it can backfire and be abused by far-right-wing political forces in their attempt to justify anti-Muslim hate speech. Both these dangers need to and can be anticipated if the exact legal categories are used both in public discourse and especially in legal debates.

A no 25096/94, 06.09.1995, DR 82, 117; *Honsik v Austria*, A no 25062/94, 18.10.1995, DR 83-A, 77; *Nationaldemokratische Partei Deutschlands, Bezirksverband München-Oberbayern v Germany*, A no 25992/94, 29.11.1995, DR 84, 149; *Rebhandel v Austria*, A no 24398/94, 16.01.1996; *Nachtmann v Austria*, A no 36773/97, 09.09.1998. Also the ECtHR's judgments, *Witzsch v Germany*, A no 41448/98 [4th Section], 20.04.1999; *Schimanek v Austria*, A no 32307/96 [1st section], 01.02.2000; *Garaudy v France*, A no 65831/01 [4th Section], 24/06/2003; *Norwood v UK*, A no 23131/03, 16.11.2004.

17

Security and Liberty in the Shadow of Islamophobia in Europe

MERILIN KIVIORG

I. Introduction[1]

In March 2022, the United Nations (UN) General Assembly proclaimed 15 March as the International Day to Combat Islamophobia and called for strengthened international efforts to foster a global dialogue on the promotion of a culture of tolerance and peace at all levels, based on respect for human rights and the diversity of religions and beliefs.[2]

The European Union (EU) representative pointed out during discussion of the resolution that the bloc is strongly opposed to all forms of hostility and violence. However, he expressed concern with the approach of singling out one religion as it risks undermining this universal approach. Along similar lines, the representative of France supported the protection of all religions and beliefs, since the creation of an international day to combat Islamophobia does not address concerns to fight against all forms of discrimination. He voiced his regret that his delegation's proposals to endorse the freedom of religion and belief (for everybody) were not taken on board. In his view, all discrimination should be condemned with equal vigour.

Clearly there are politics in play when human rights are discussed at the UN. The resolution was initiated primarily (albeit not solely) by majority Muslim countries and the above concerns were expressed by representatives of majority Christian countries.[3] This sectarian 'tug of war' does not really contribute to the

[1] This chapter is written with support from the Estonian Research Council grant PRG969 'Russia and Consolidation of Regional International Law in Eurasia'.

[2] UN, 'General Assembly Unanimously Adopts Texts on Combating Islamophobia, Protecting Rangelands, Tackling Difficulties for Widows, Bicycles as Public Transportation', press release (15 March 2022), available at press.un.org/en/2022/ga12408.doc.htm; International Day to Combat Islamophobia, UNGA Res no 76/254 (15 March 2022).

[3] The draft resolution was proposed by: Afghanistan, Albania, Algeria, Azerbaijan, Bahrain, Bangladesh, Benin, Brunei Darussalam, Burkina Faso, Cameroon, Chad, Comoros, Côte d'Ivoire,

protection of human rights and freedom of religion or belief generally in any of these countries (whether majority Muslim or Christian). Perhaps this was one of the reasons why, in the end, neither of the representatives opposed the adoption of the resolution. Moreover, the UN General Assembly previously had adopted several more general resolutions on the matter.[4] It is also important to note that the text of the debated 2022 resolution was much wider in its scope than its title suggests. Among other things, it expressed concern over the rise in instances of discrimination, intolerance and violence directed against members of many religious and other communities in various parts of the world, including cases motivated by Islamophobia, anti-Semitism, Christianophobia and prejudices against persons of other religions or beliefs.[5]

While there is a value in combating generally all phobias, discriminations and intolerances, there is also value in a specific focus. There is a tendency in human and state behaviour to target specific groups of people, including on grounds of their religion, belief or ethnicity. A general struggle with discrimination may sometimes dilute attention from the most serious issues and does not necessarily consider specific social or local factors, or the history of adverse treatment of these groups. That is why, within the limited scope of this chapter, the above-mentioned considerations determine its focus on Islamophobia.

This chapter starts from three premises: (1) Islamophobic attitudes translate into legal practice that affects both the way we understand the scope of liberties and security in a broader sense (human security); (2) law, or a legal approach, is poorly equipped to deal with the problem of Islamophobia; and (3) security is important for the protection of fundamental freedoms including the freedom of religion or belief (FoRB), and protecting these freedoms is important for security. The latter is akin to the Organization for Security and Co-operation in Europe's (OSCE) comprehensive security approach. The OSCE has pointed out the vital connection between FoRB and security in one of its latest guidelines: 'sustainable security is not possible without full respect for human rights'.[6] In OSCE terms, security is understood as comprehensive, cooperative, equal, indivisible and

Djibouti, Egypt, Gabon, Gambia, Guinea, Guinea-Bissau, Guyana, Indonesia, Iran (Islamic Republic of), Iraq, Jordan, Kazakhstan, Kuwait, Kyrgyzstan, Lebanon, Libya, Malaysia, Maldives, Mali, Mauritania, Morocco, Mozambique, Niger, Nigeria, Oman, Pakistan, Qatar, Saudi Arabia, Senegal, Sierra Leone, Somalia, Sudan, Suriname, Tajikistan, Togo, Tunisia, Turkey, Turkmenistan, Uganda, United Arab Emirates, Uzbekistan and Yemen. UN Digital Library, 'International Day to Combat Islamophobia: Draft Resolution' available at digitallibrary.un.org/record/3964504?ln=en.

[4] eg 'Combating intolerance, negative stereotyping, stigmatisation, discrimination, incitement to violence and violence against persons, based on religion or belief' UNGA Res no 75/187 (16 December 2020); 'Freedom of Religion or Belief' UNGA Res no 75/188 (16 December 2020); 'Declaration on the Elimination of All Forms of Intolerance and of Discrimination Based on Religion or Belief' UNGA Res 36/55 (25 November 1981); and 'International Day Commemorating the Victims of Acts of Violence Based on Religion or Belief' UNGA Res 73/296 (28 May 2019).

[5] 'International Day to Combat Islamophobia' UNGA Res no 76/254 (15 March 2022).

[6] OSCE Office for Democratic Institutions and Human Rights, 'Freedom of Religion or Belief and Security: Policy Guidance' (Warsaw, 2019) 7.

grounded in human rights. The approach is not only about physical security, but has several complementary dimensions (politico-military, economic and environmental, and human) which are each viewed as being of equal importance.[7]

Starting from these premises, this chapter examines the implications of Islamophobia from the perspective of international human rights law with primary focus on the observations of the UN human rights treaty monitoring bodies (primarily the Human Rights Committee and the Committee on the Elimination of Racial Discrimination) regarding the matter in selected EU countries during their treaty monitoring cycles.[8] In that respect, this chapter will analyse the degree of fulfilment of countries' positive obligations under international human rights law to maintain neutrality and impartiality regarding religion and belief, as well as their obligations to avoid discrimination and combat stereotyping and Islamophobia.[9] It will also place those observations into the larger context of current social statistics on attitudes towards Islam in Europe. Two specific contexts where Islamophobia has been particularly in evidence today will be briefly highlighted in this chapter: the COVID-19 pandemic and migration. This chapter will suggest that there is a considerable room for improvement regarding compliance with international human rights treaties. Although EU countries are parties to a majority of the main UN human rights treaties, there is a lack of comprehensive research on the implementation of these treaties.[10] This is because the regional human rights system under the Council of Europe and implementation of EU law has received more prominence than the UN framework with respect to human rights implementation.[11]

[7] ibid, 9.

[8] The Human Rights Committee supervises implementation of the International Covenant on Civil and Political Rights (ICCPR). The Committee on the Elimination of Racial Discrimination (CERD Committee) monitors the Convention on the elimination of All Forms of Racial Discrimination (CERD).

[9] States' negative obligations refer to a duty not to act or refrain from action that would hinder human rights. Positive obligations require national authorities to act; that is, to take necessary measures to safeguard a right or, more precisely, to adopt reasonable and suitable measures to protect the rights of the individual. See eg D Shelton and A Gould, 'Positive and Negative Obligations' in D Shelton (ed), *The Oxford Handbook of International Human Rights Law* (Oxford, Oxford Univeristy Press, 2012) 562–83.

[10] The main human rights treaties are as follows: the International Convention on the Elimination of All Forms of Racial Discrimination; the International Covenant on Economic, Social and Cultural Rights; the International Covenant on Civil and Political Rights; the Convention on the Elimination of All Forms of Discrimination against Women; the Convention on the Rights of the Child; the International Convention on the Protection of the Rights of All Migrant Workers and Members of their Families; the Convention on the Rights of Persons with Disabilities; and, the International Convention for the Protection of All Persons from Enforced Disappearance.

[11] In fact, there seems to be a global shortage of relevant research. Major effort was made in 1999 and 2022 to gather relevant data in selected countries from different regions globally. See C Heyns and F Viljoen (eds), *The Impact of the United Nations Human Rights Treaties on the Domestic Level* (The Hague, Kluwer Law International, 1999); C Heyns, F Viljoen and R Murphy (eds), *The Impact of the United Nations Human Rights Treaties on the Domestic Level* (Leiden, Brill, 2023, forthcoming).

II. The Socio-Legal Context

There are numerous definitions of Islamophobia which are all influenced by different theoretical approaches such as racism, prejudice studies and decolonial perspectives. There is no agreed definition of Islamophobia in international law generally or international human rights law specifically. However, there are some working definitions. For example, Awan and Zempi put forward the following definition in their 2020 briefing paper for the UN special rapporteur:

> A fear, prejudice and hatred of Muslims or non-Muslim individuals that leads to provocation, hostility and intolerance by means of threatening, harassment, abuse, incitement and intimidation of Muslims and non-Muslims, both in the online and offline world. Motivated by institutional, ideological, political and religious hostility that transcends into structural and cultural racism which targets the symbols and markers of a being a Muslim.[12]

They define Islamophobia as a new form of racism, cultural racism. While the 'old' racism was based on a belief of biological superiority, this 'new' racism is based on notions of religious and cultural superiority. In this sense, Islamic religion, tradition and culture are seen as a 'threat' to 'European values and identity', while 'visible' or perceived Muslims are viewed as 'culturally dangerous' and threatening the 'Western way of life'.[13]

The 2020 European Islamophobia report points out that Islamophobia operates by constructing a static 'Muslim' identity, which is attributed in negative terms and generalised for all Muslims. However, 'Islamophobic images are fluid and vary in different contexts, because Islamophobia tells us more about the Islamophobe than it tells us about the Muslims/Islam.'[14] In this sense, the report does not see Islamophobia as an exclusively Muslim problem, but rather as a problem of the structural and systemic racism that characterises a whole society: 'Islamophobia not only directly devalues the lives of otherized people, but questions the humanity of a society that pretends to stand for the equality of all humans.'[15]

Considering the above, it can be argued that rigid definitions, especially legal definitions of Islamophobia are not necessarily useful or desired. Contexts vary and Islamophobic attitudes may manifest themselves in various forms and places.[16] However, a working definition to understand the complexity of this specific phobia

[12] I Awan and I Zempi, 'A Working Definition of Islamophobia: A Briefing Paper for the UN special Rapporteur on Freedom of Religion or Belief. Preparation for the report to the 46th Session of Human Rights Council' (November 2020), available at www.ohchr.org/sites/default/files/Documents/Issues/Religion/Islamophobia-AntiMuslim/Civil%20Society%20or%20Individuals/ProfAwan-2.pdf.

[13] Awan and Zempi have developed the definition keeping in mind primarily British context. However, they do extend their definition to apply in a wider European context.

[14] E Bayrakli and F Hafez (eds), 'European Islamophobia Report' (Leopold Weiss Institute, 2020) 10.

[15] ibid, 11.

[16] See also, for a comprehensive account on Islmophobia, K Najib, *Spatialized Islamophobia* (London, Routledge, 2022).

may be useful. It is also helpful for legal professionals to be aware and mindful of the multiple forms it can take.

According to the Second EU Minorities and Discrimination Survey in 2017, 76 per cent of Muslim respondents felt strongly attached to the country they live in. This data also shows, contrary to some popular beliefs, that Muslims are loyal to the countries they live in. As pointed out by the Director of the European Union Agency for Human Rights (FRA) Michael O'Flaherty: 'Our survey results make a mockery of the claim that Muslims aren't integrated into our societies. On the contrary, we see a trust in democratic institutions that is higher than much of the general population.'[17]

Unfortunately, the statistics also show that Islamophobia persists. According to the same survey, 31 per cent of Muslim respondents seeking work had felt discriminated against over the preceding five years and 42 per cent who had been stopped by the police over the previous year said this happened because of their migrant or ethnic minority background.[18] The report found that, on average, one in three Muslim respondents faced discrimination and prejudice in the previous year and 27 per cent had experienced a racist crime.[19] The survey also concluded that, despite the adoption of relevant directives at the European level, 17 years after adoption of these directives, many people with immigrant or ethnic minority backgrounds face discrimination in various circumstances and many still do not know their rights or where to turn to report such incidents.[20]

Some categories of people may also be more vulnerable to Islamophobic attacks and discrimination. The 2021 report by the European Network Against Racism (ENAR) points out that Islamophobia can especially impact women:[21] their religious identity becomes visible when they wear the hijab, and consequently they face constant and continuous discrimination including verbal and, in some instances, physical abuse in everyday encounters in the street.[22] Visibly Muslim women are also more vulnerable on the job market and possibly to intersectional discrimination.[23] According to the European Commission against Racism and Intolerance (ECRI), in many cases, intersectional discrimination further worsens the situation, for example for Black Muslims or Muslim women, or women with a migrant background.[24]

[17] FRA, 'Muslims in the EU: High levels of trust despite pervasive discrimination' press release (21 September 2017), available at fra.europa.eu/en/news/2017/muslims-eu-high-levels-trust-despite-pervasive-discrimination.

[18] FRA, 'Second European Union Minorities and Discrimination Survey: Main Results' (2017).

[19] ibid.

[20] Council Directive (EC) 2000/78 on Employment Equality [2000] OJ L195/16; Council Directive (EC) 2000/43 on Racial Equality [2000] OJ L 180/22; FRA (n 18).

[21] ENAR, 'Suspicion, Discrimination and Surveillance: The Impact of Counter-terrorism Law and Policy on Racialised Groups at Risk of Racism in Europe' (2021) 8 available at www.enar-eu.org/wp-content/uploads/suspicion_discrimination_surveillance_report_2021_executive_summary.pdf.

[22] ibid.

[23] Case C-157/15 *G4S Secure Solutions* [2017] ECLI:EU:C:2017:203; Case C-804/18 and C-341/19 *WABE and MH Müller Handel* [2021] ECLI:EU:C:2021:594.

[24] ECRI, 'Annual Report of ECRI Activities Covering the Period from 1 January to 31 December 2020' (March 2021) 13.

Some specific circumstances have also contributed to the rise of Islamophobia, such as European migration crises and the COVID-19 pandemic.[25] The UN Special Rapporteur, for example, pointed out that representatives of four European states have publicly rejected Muslim refugees or migrants in their societies, amid accusations of preferential treatment for Christian refugees.[26] Recently, even in the context of migration resulting from the Russian war against Ukraine, one can see potentially Islamophobic attitudes. For example, an independent survey in Estonia showed that the 'ideal migrant/refugee' is a 'Christian fluent English-speaking female doctor who intends to go back to Ukraine as soon as the war is over.'[27]

The 2021 ENAR report points out that, at its inception, the EU's counter-radicalisation policies focused exclusively and explicitly on Muslims and Islam. The report suggests that in placing suspicion and scrutiny on Muslim identities and religious practices it enabled discrimination:[28]

> As Member States adopted, developed and implemented their counter-radicalisation policies and action plans, supported by EU coordination and sharing of best practice, they replicated and reinforced a focus on Muslim religious identities and practices. At the same time, the development of pre-emptive offences that criminalise actions that occur before there is any plan to commit an act of terrorism underpins and legitimises prosecutions that rely heavily on evidence of associations and identities that are deemed dangerous.[29]

The data from the ENAR's research suggest that these developments have contributed to a securitised suspicion of Muslim religious practices and expressions of religious identity, making them a source of fear and anxiety, that trigger further investigation by police or other state officials.[30]

There are concerns that stereotypes and generalisations about Muslims are informing counter-terrorism measures in Europe that restrict liberties for all and negatively impact Muslim communities. For example, a 2021 OSCE report points out that 'despite OSCE commitments emphasizing that terrorism must not be identified with any ethnicity, nationality, religion or belief, in practice there are concerns that counter-terrorism efforts often have a disproportionate or even exclusive focus on specific groups, frequently Muslim communities'.[31]

The UN Special Rapporteur on Contemporary Forms of Racism, Racial Discrimination, Xenophobia and Racial Intolerance, E Tendayi Achiume, reported

[25] I refer here to the 2015 European migration crisis and the 2021 humanitarian crisis on Poland–Belarus border.

[26] Special Rapporteur on Freedom of Religion or Belief (A Shaheed), 'Countering Islamophobia/anti-Muslim Hatred to Eliminate Discrimination and Intolerance Based on Religion or Belief' (Human Rights Council, 2021).

[27] T Jüristo, 'Milline on ideaalne põgenik' (SALK, 29 July 2022).

[28] ENAR (n 21) 6.

[29] ibid.

[30] ibid.

[31] OSCE/ODHIR, 'Democracy and Human Rights in the OSCE, The OSCE Office for Democratic Institutions and Human Rights Annual Report' (2021) 30.

also that the rise of neo-Nazi movements and other practices contribute to fuelling contemporary forms of racism, racial discrimination, xenophobia and related intolerance.[32] Similar concerns were pointed out by the Special Rapporteur on Freedom of Religion or Belief, who emphasised that conspiracy theories drawing on xenophobic and racist narratives about Muslims are also propagated online by far-right groups. They are designed to influence attitudes towards policies meant to promote immigration and inclusion, or to ascribe blame for challenges facing a society; such theories include fabrications that immigrant Muslim populations are going to 'outbreed' native populations and are widespread in Europe.[33]

The COVID-19 pandemic shifted the attention and priorities of people and societies from migration and terrorism to health problems. Nevertheless, examples of Islamophobic attitudes in European countries were pointed out by several rapporteurs to the 2020 European Islamophobia Report (for example in Greece, Hungary, Ireland and Italy).[34] The evidence gathered during the compilation of the Office for Democratic Institutions and Human Rights' (ODIHR) annual hate crime data also indicates that violent acts against particular groups and communities continue to be a concern across the OSCE region.[35] Already existing types of racism, xenophobia, and additional forms of intolerance emerged as pandemic-related acts of intolerance and discrimination. Some minority communities were negatively portrayed by the general public, ranging from ordinary citizens to high-level politicians and policymakers, and the media.[36] The COVID-19 pandemic has led to a proliferation of baseless conspiracy theories and scapegoating with a corresponding negative impact on the minority communities affected.

Today, European focus has shifted again since the Russian invasion of Ukraine on 24 February 2022. The dynamics of that war may also have long-term consequences on how societies form their attitudes, law and policy towards different religious or belief communities, and how they understand security and liberty.

Serious threats to security do exist and need response (including legal response and prevention); however, generalisations about certain groups or individuals

[32] UN/HRC, 'Special Rapporteur on Contemporary Forms of Racism, Racial Discrimination, Xenophobia and Related Intolerance' (2018), available at www.ohchr.org/en/special-procedures/sr-racism; UN/HRC (E Tendayi Achiume), 'Combating Glorification of Nazism, neo-Nazism and other Practices that Contribute to Fuelling Contemporary Forms of Racism, Racial discrimination, Xenophobia and Related Intolerance' (2022) available at www.ohchr.org/en/documents/thematic-reports/a77512-combating-glorification-nazism-neo-nazism-and-other-practices.

[33] Special Rapporteur on Freedom of Religion or Belief (n 26) 6.

[34] See eg, Bayrakli and Hafez (n 14) 414, 438, 457, 476, 492. For example, the report noted that a widely watched news programme in Germany used Islamophobic semiotics to blame returning Kosovar travellers for 'bringing back' the virus. It also noted that similar arguments were used in other European countries with a considerable Kosovo-Albanian population such as Switzerland and Finland.

[35] However, one needs to keep in mind that the OSCE membership is wider than just the EU. Thus, the data also reflects on the countries that do not necessarily sign up for democratic values, such as Russia.

[36] OSCE/ODIHR, 'OSCE Human Dimension Commitments and State Responses to the Covid-19 Pandemic' (2020) 128, available at www.osce.org/files/f/documents/e/c/457567_0.pdf.

must still be avoided.[37] For example, the report of the Special Rapporteur on the Promotion and Protection of Human Rights and Fundamental Freedoms while Countering Terrorism points out that states' overbroad definitions of 'terrorism', 'extremism', and 'violent extremism' lead to abuses.[38] The report showed that violations of derogable and non-derogable rights are particularly experienced by religious groups, minorities and civil society. Along similar lines, the OSCE comprehensive concept of security underlines the fact that effective counter-terrorism measures and human rights are not competing but mutually reinforcing objectives: 'sustainable security requires the protection of human rights. Ensuring security and protecting life is, in itself, a human rights commitment'.[39]

III. FoRB and Security in the UN Treaty Monitoring Bodies

All EU countries have signed and ratified a majority of the main UN human rights treaties including the International Covenant on Civil and Political Rights (ICCPR) and the International Convention on the Elimination of All Forms of Racial Discrimination (CERD).[40] All states are obliged to participate in regular reporting under all the human rights treaties they are members of and every convention has its own supervising committee that receives its applicable report when submitted. During the treaty monitoring cycles, in addition to reports from states, the treaty monitoring committees review various reports (including shadow reports by NGOs and information provided by specialised agencies) to produce concluding recommendations or observations about the situation in a specific country. In addition, states must submit to periodic review by the UN Human Rights Council, which periodically monitors countries' overall human rights situations.

It must be noted that the human rights treaty committees are comprised of independent experts. For example, both the Human Rights Committee (HRC), which supervises implementation of the ICCPR, and the Committee on the Elimination of Racial Discrimination (that supervises CERD) are each composed of 18 independent experts who are persons of 'high moral character and recognized

[37] See eg, M Kiviorg (ed), *Securitisaton of Religious Freedom: Religion and Limits of State Control* (Granada, Editorial Comares, 2020).

[38] UN/HRC, 'Human Rights Impact of Policies and Practices Aimed at Preventing and Countering Violent Extremism: Report of the Special Rapporteur on the Promotion and Protection of Human Rights and Fundamental Freedoms while Countering Terrorism' (2020).

[39] OSCE/ODIHR, 'Policy Brief: Border Management and Human Rights. Collection, processing and sharing of personal data and the use of new technologies in the counter-terrorism and freedom of movement context' (2021) 8.

[40] International Covenant on Civil and Political Rights (adopted 16 December 1966, entered into force 23 March 1976) 999 UNTS 171 (ICCPR); International Convention on the Elimination of All Forms of Racial Discrimination (adopted 21 December 1965, entered into force 4 January 1969) 660 UNTS 195 (CERD).

competence in the field of human rights'. The UN Human Rights Council, however, is an intergovernmental body, including members whose human rights records are questionable.[41] Thus, focusing on specific treaty committees' concluding observations should, in principle, paint a more adequate picture of the situation in a country. It needs to be noted that there are sometimes delays in states' reporting, and consideration of reports (including shadow reports) may take a substantial amount of effort and time in the treaty committees. The system is by no means perfect and there are occasional mistakes.[42] However, all reporting cycles are followed by follow-up procedures that oblige states to report on specific measures taken on expressed points of concern, and remaining problems will be carried forward in the 'list of issues' for the next cycle of reporting.

It is also important to note that although UN human rights treaties are legally binding on parties, the concluding observations, recommendations and views adopted by committees regarding individual communications are not. This could be one of the reasons that regional systems have attracted more scholarly attention. The regional systems are still considered to be more effective because decisions of the European Court of Human Rights and the European Court of Justice are legally binding and thus are perceived to carry more weight. However, UN documents do have an authoritative character and can provide a very good idea of how states relate to their obligations under the binding conventions. Implementation and reporting under multiple UN human rights conventions paints a comprehensive picture of the problems or concerns at hand.

Both the CERD Committee and HRC have expressed concerns about the treatment of Muslims in numerous EU countries. Some reoccurring themes stand out more than others; for example, intersectional discrimination, especially against women. In contrast to their European counterparts, UN treaty monitoring bodies have consistently called on states to revise their bans on the burqua, niqab or other religious symbols that may exacerbate the marginalisation of Muslim women.[43]

This chapter focuses more on hate speech and security of the Muslim religious community and individuals. The counter-terrorism measures disproportionately affecting Muslims will also be mentioned. The following will solely discuss concluding observations where hate speech and security issues regarding Muslim

[41] There are 47 members in total. Membership in 2022 includes, for example, China, Uzbekistan and Sudan.

[42] M Kiviorg, 'Estonia' in Heyns, Viljoen and Murphy (n 11).

[43] eg HRC, 'Concluding observations on the fifth periodic report of the Netherlands' (CCPR/C/NLD/CO/5, 18 July 2019) para 58; HRC, 'Concluding observations on the sixth periodic report of Belgium' (CCPR/C/BEL/CO/6, 1 November 2019) para 17; CERD, 'Concluding observations on the combined twenty-second to twenty-fourth periodic reports of the Kingdom of the Netherlands' (CERD/C/NLD/CO/22-24, 24 August 2021) para 25. In that respect also note that the HRC has decided to take a different approach to hijab bans than its European counterpart, the European Court of Human Rights. See *Hudoyberganova v Uzbekistan*. HRC Comm No 931/2000, CCPR/C/82/D/931/2000, 5 November 2004. Also see discussion of this case in M Kiviorg, 'International Obligations and Internal Tensions: Individual Religious Autonomy and Gender Equality in Russia and Central Asia' (2022) 20 *The Review of Faith & International Affairs* 47.

communities or individuals have been explicitly pointed out. For the sake of accuracy, it will also look at concluding observations and follow-ups from no earlier than 2018. European states have done a large amount of good work in dealing with Islamophobia. The concluding observations primarily focus on problematic aspects rather than positive aspects regarding implementation of conventions.

A. Hate Speech

Before coming to the Committees' reports, one needs to note that according to the 2020 European Islamophobia Report, most European states do not record Islamophobic incidents as a separate category of hate crime.[44] The report notes that from the EU countries, Bulgaria, Croatia, Estonia, Hungary and Malta do not record hate crimes at all and others, such as Finland, Greece and Italy, do not specify anti-Muslim hate crimes. The report also suggests that in those countries where the data is collected, it still may not give a full picture.[45] As noted by the report, this data collection is necessary to help understand and prevent specific local problems related to specific phobias and mistreatment.

For example, in its 2021 Concluding Observations on Finland, the HRC points out a concern about the persistence of intolerance, prejudice, hate speech and hate crimes against vulnerable and minority groups, including Muslims.[46] It recommends that the state improve relevant data collection, take effective measures to prevent both online and offline hate speech, firmly and publicly condemn such speech, and intensify efforts aimed at addressing the problem. Similar concern was expressed and recommendations given by the CERD Committee in its 2021 observations regarding Belgium.[47] The Committee also pointed out that Belgium's existing registration system does not allow for distinguishing between or identifying specific cases of ethno-religious hatred such as antisemitism, Islamophobia, anti-Gypsyism, Afrophobia or anti-Asian hatred. The Committee noted that the largest proportion of racist hate crimes in Belgium are ethno-religious in nature.[48]

Similar concerns were expressed by the CERD Committee in 2019 about Lithuania. It noted strong prejudices and negative sentiments prevailing in Lithuania towards members of vulnerable and minority groups, in particular

[44] Bayrakli and Hafez (n 14) 18. Recording hate crimes seems to be problematic overall. Concluding observations of many UN human rights treaty monitoring bodies (ie the HRC, CERD Committee and CEDAW Committee) often indicate that there is a problem in countries recording their specific hate crime. There seems to be also a question of how one legally defines and separates different categories of hate crime based on different phobias people may have. There is also problematic legal difference between incident and a crime.

[45] ibid, 19.

[46] HRC, 'Concluding observations on the seventh periodic report of Finland' (CCPR/C/FIN/CO/7, 23 March 2021) para 14.

[47] CERD Committee, 'Concluding observations on the combined twentieth to twenty-second periodic reports of Belgium' (CERD/C/BEL/CO/20-22, 29 April 2021) para 17.

[48] ibid.

migrants, Muslims and Romas.[49] The analogous accusations were also made by HRC in 2020 about Portugal.[50] In the case of Portugal, the HRC also pointed out the low number of complaints and lack of information on convictions and penalties imposed, which is covered by the Portugal's statistical secrecy policy. The observation about the low number of complaints also seems to confirm the findings of the above-mentioned Second EU Minorities and Discrimination Survey. The 2019 CERD Committee observations on Hungary add another dimension to this. The Committee reminded Hungary that a low number of complaints does not necessarily signify the absence of racial discrimination. However, 'it may signify the existence of barriers to the invocation of the rights in the Convention domestically, such as a lack of trust among victims in the State's justice institutions and authorities'.[51]

In its 2018 Concluding Observations, the CERD Committee expressed concern about the continued reports of racist hate crimes and hate speech against Muslim ethno-religious minority groups (especially Muslim women in Sweden) and stereotypical representation of Muslims in the media and by politicians.[52] The Committee praised Sweden for efforts to ameliorate its data-collection methods and address under-reporting; however, it remained concerned about the high number of reported hate crimes and the continuation of racist violence there. A particular concern was expressed about reports of arson attacks against mosques and reception centres for asylum-seekers. The Committee also noted the gap between the number of reported cases of hate speech and hate crimes, and the number of investigations, prosecutions and convictions of perpetrators.[53]

In a 2019 follow-up, the Committee found Swedish efforts to address issues only partly satisfactory, noting that Sweden did not indicate the specific measures taken to guarantee the security of property belonging to Muslim ethno-religious minority groups. In the Committee's view, Sweden did not take adequate and concrete measures to ensure funding and affordable insurance for the safety of mosques and other common property. The Committee considered the response of Sweden partially satisfactory and encouraged the state to strengthen its efforts to fully implement its recommendations.[54]

In 2022, the HRC detected persistent racist hate speech used against migrants, refugees, Muslims, Jews and other ethnic and religious minorities in the

[49] CERD Committee, 'Concluding observations on the combined ninth and tenth periodic reports of Lithuania' (CERD/C/LTU/CO/9-10, 9 May 2019) para 11.

[50] HRC, 'Concluding observations on the fifth periodic report of Portugal' (CCPR/C/PRT/CO/5, 27 March 2020) para 14.

[51] CERD Committee, 'Concluding observations on the combined eighteenth to twenty-fifth periodic reports of Hungary' (CERD/C/HUN/CO/18-25, 8 May 2019) para 12.

[52] CERD Committee, 'Concluding observations on the combined twenty-second and twenty-third periodic reports of Sweden' (CERD/C/SWE/CO/22-23, 10 May 2018) para 18.

[53] ibid, para 10.

[54] CERD Committee, 'Consideration of the follow-up report submitted by the Government of Sweden' (CERD/100th session/FU/MJA/ks, 13 December 2019).

Netherlands by politicians and high-level public officials, through social media and at public events (such as football matches). The Committee pointed out that hate speech has not only led to significant harm to the rights or reputations of persons and groups of persons subjected to it but has also contributed to hate crimes and a growing climate of intolerance.[55]

Problems in relation to racist hate speech are also explicitly pointed out in the 2019 CERD Committee observations on Poland. The Committee was concerned about the prevalence of racist hate speech against minority groups, including Muslims, Roma, Ukrainians, people of African and Asian descent, Jews, migrants, refugees and asylum-seekers, which fuels hatred and intolerance and incites violence towards such groups.[56] The Committee pointed out that leading public figures, including politicians and media officials, are frequently the source of such offensive statements or 'fail in their responsibility to strongly denounce hate speech'.[57] The same concern was pointed out in the 2019 concluding observations of the HRC regarding the Czech Republic. The HRC was particularly concerned that senior officials in the Czech Republic encouraged the public perception of migration as a threat to public security and that the media had been used to instil fear of migrants and asylum-seekers and strengthen stereotypical prejudices based on ethnicity or religion. While praising the state for adopting measures to address racism and hate speech, the Committee was concerned about the reported high level of hate speech against Muslims.[58] The prevalence of hate speech targeting Muslims in political discourse, in the media, on the internet and even in government-sponsored campaigns was also mentioned in the 2019 HRC observations about Hungary.[59]

The restrictions due to the COVID-19 pandemic have also been mentioned in some newer reports from the committees. However, those reports address the issue more generally, for example, expressing concern about protection of vulnerable groups, refugees and asylum-seekers, though not necessarily explicitly mentioning Muslims. The 2021 report by the Special Rapporteur on Freedom of Religion or

[55] HRC, 'Concluding observations on the fifth periodic report of the Netherlands' (CCPR/C/NLD/CO/5, 18 July 2019) para 15.

[56] The war perpetrated by Russia against Ukraine and the mass exodus from Ukraine have changed this perspective. However, longer-term consequences of the migration remain to be seen.

[57] CERD Committee, 'Concluding observations on the combined twenty-second to twenty-fourth periodic reports of Poland' (CERD/C/POL/CO/22-24, 20 August 2019) para 15. Similar to some other concluding observations, it insisted that the state prohibit and punish those for participation in organisations that openly promote racial hatred in the state, 'in particular those that openly espouse affinity with the ideology and publicly display the symbols of Nazism, fascism or totalitarianism'. It also pointed out the 'extremely low percentage of offences of hate speech and hate crimes that are reported, despite the recorded increase in the incidence of such crimes'. CERD Committee, 'Concluding observations on the combined twenty-second to twenty-fourth periodic reports of Poland' (CERD/C/POL/CO/22-24, 20 August 2019) para 19.

[58] HRC, 'Concluding observations on the fourth periodic report of the Czech Republic' (CCPR/C/CZE/CO/4, 1 November 2019) para 16.

[59] HRC, 'Concluding observations on the sixth periodic report of Hungary' (CCPR/C/HUN/CO/6, 29 March 2018) para 17.

Belief, however, explicitly points out some examples of Islamophobia. For instance, he observes that in the UK, internet users alleged that Muslim communities were responsible for the spread of COVID-19. Additionaly he found that 'Encrypted chat platforms, including WhatsApp and Telegram, have also been used to spread Islamophobic disinformation, particularly during the COVID-19 pandemic.'[60]

B. Security Concerns

Many reports critique the vague definitions of terrorism and extremism in states' laws and highlight the ways in which they are open to abuse. For example, vague definitions are indicated in the 2021 HRC observations about the Finnish Criminal Code.[61] The same was pointed out in the 2018 HRC concluding observations about Bulgaria.[62] The Special Rapporteur on Freedom of Religion or Belief, in his report on Islamophobia, noted that over the previous two decades, Muslim individuals and communities bore the brunt of the use and abuse of counter-terrorism measures. He highlighted reports, including those of the HRC and CERD Committee, indicating that national security and counter-terrorism measures have disproportionately and discriminatorily targeted Muslims and that many such measures had been adopted with little transparency, contained sweeping definitions of 'terrorism' and had been implemented with poor oversight. In this context he referred to France, Austria, Sweden and the Netherlands from within the EU countries.[63]

Issues regarding the focus of investigations are also often pointed out as a problem. In 2018, the CERD Committee expressed concern about reports that the Terrorism Act in Sweden disproportionately targeted Muslims, while crimes committed by other groups, such as neo-Nazis, were not investigated as terrorism.[64] This seems to be in line with the findings of the above-mentioned 2021 ENAR report suggesting that when Member States adopted, developed and implemented counter-radicalisation policies, they replicated and reinforced a focus on Muslim religious identities and practices.[65] Related underlying issues have been pointed out in the Report of the Special Rapporteur on freedom of religion or belief. He noted that several countries disproportionately focus on negative angles for news stories involving Muslims, such as reporting on their perceived failure to integrate,

[60] Special Rapporteur on Freedom of Religion or Belief (n 26) 11. Analogous findings were also pointed out in the 2021 report of the Institute for Freedom of Faith and Security in Europe. H Rose, 'Pandemic Hate: COVID-related Antisemitism and Islamophobia, and the Role of Social Media' (IFFSE 2021).

[61] HRC, 'Concluding observations on the seventh periodic report of Finland' (CCPR/C/FIN/CO/7, 23 March 2021) para 10.

[62] HRC, 'Concluding observations on the fourth periodic report of Bulgaria' (CCPR/C/BGR/CO/4, 29 October 2018) para 33.

[63] Special Rapporteur on Freedom of Religion or Belief (n 26 above) 7–8.

[64] CERD Committee (n 57) para 19.

[65] ENAR (n 21) 6.

and that more media attention is often paid to attacks committed by Muslims than attacks committed by far-right extremists.[66] Interestingly, in the case of Sweden, the CERD Committee recommendations were not followed up by the state or the Committee itself.[67]

One specific issue that emerges from reports regarding counter-terrorism measures is the repatriation of children in armed conflict zones. For example, this is specifically mentioned in the HRC observations about Finland. In that respect, the Committee specifically points to al-Hol refugee camp in Syria.[68] The rights of children are also addressed in the latest reporting cycle of Bulgaria, where the HRC notes the lack of sufficient protection against prosecution of teenage children forcibly recruited into terrorist groups.[69] The rights of children in the context of counter-terrorism is a broader topic that deserves a separate paper as such issues have also been picked up by the Committee on the Rights of the Child that supervises the implementation of the Convention on the Rights of the Child.[70]

While dealing with counter-terrorism measures, many concluding observations draw states' attention to data collection and profiling. For example, the HRC recommended that Belgium amend its legislation by expressly prohibiting ethnic profiling and ensuring the effective implementation and monitoring of the prohibition.[71] The follow-up state report did not indicate any specific effort on behalf of Belgium to act on this recommendation.[72] Similar concern about profiling was expressed in the 2022 CERD Committee concluding observations on Denmark. The Committee noted the likelihood that an arrest does not lead to a conviction and that the rate at which charges for a crime are subsequently dropped are higher for persons of an ethnic minority background as compared with persons of Danish ethnic origin. In the Committee's view, this means that the police might well act in haste to presume persons of ethnic minority background commit crimes. The Committee recommended a clear prohibition of racial profiling. It also recommended putting in place operational guidelines for police and other law enforcement officers to prevent and combat racial profiling as well as other policy measures to combat racial profiling.[73]

The 2020 report and recommendations by ENAR and a collective of NGOs highlighted the issue more generally in the EU during the COVID-19 pandemic.

[66] Special Rapporteur on Freedom of Religion or Belief (n 26) 5.

[67] CERD Committee, 'Consideration of the follow-up report submitted by the Government of Sweden' (CERD/100th session/FU/MJA/ks, 13 December 2019).

[68] HRC (n 61) para 10.

[69] HRC (n 62) para 33.

[70] Convention on the Rights of the Child (adopted 20 Nov 1989, entered into force 2 September 1990) 15773 UNTS 3 (CRC).

[71] HRC, 'Concluding observations on the sixth periodic report of Belgium' (CCPR/C/BEL/CO/6, 1 November 2019) paras 15–16.

[72] HRC,' Information Received from Belgium on the Follow-up to the Concluding Observations on its Sixth Periodic Report' (CCPR/C/BEL/FCO/6, 31 January 2022).

[73] CERD Committee, 'Concluding observations on the combined twenty-second to twenty-fourth periodic reports of Denmark' (CERD/C/DNK/CO/22-24, 30 November 2021) para 20.

The report noted that while EU Member States enforced the lockdown measures, the enforcement had a disproportionate negative impact on Muslim men, who were depicted as less observant of the public policies and assumed to be suspicious and dangerous.[74]

IV. Conclusion

There is an anxiety and tension in Europe and beyond; the social and political situation and atmosphere are rapidly changing and it has become increasingly more complex to explain the processes that take place. Tensions have flared up as a result of several factors, notably terrorist threats to physical security, migration, and the rise of far-right movements and populism. The COVID-19 pandemic added another layer of insecurity and, among other things, stoked intolerance towards minority communities. Today, there is a major war raging in Europe that has its own impact on security and liberty, including freedom of religion or belief.

As previously discussed, serious threats to security exist and need addressing (including, through legal remedies, policies and prevention), however, generalisations about certain groups or individuals must be avoided. There is a vital connection between human rights and security: 'sustainable security is not possible without full respect for human rights'.[75] In that respect one also needs to take note of the detailed reports regarding deficiencies in the EU's and its Member States' efforts to tackle security issues with emphasis on Muslim religious identities and practices.

There needs to be a consensus on Islamophobia not being an exclusively Muslim problem, but rather a problem of the structural and systemic racism that characterises a whole society. Islamophobia not only directly devalues the lives of otherised people, but questions the humanity of a society that claims to uphold equality for all.[76]

States do have legally binding positive duties to implement human rights conventions, including the CERD and ICCPR. However, as indicated by the treaty monitoring bodies and various surveys, there are significant deficiencies in that implementation. Law, or a legal approach, may also not be sufficiently equipped to deal with the problem of Islamophobia in all its complexity. Hence the treaty monitoring bodies' recommendations that often go beyond the strictly legal measures that states need to take on board to comply with international human rights conventions.

[74] ENAR, 'Addressing Islamophobia: A response to the Covid-19 crisis and broader inequalities' (2020).

[75] OSCE Office for Democratic Institutions and Human Rights (n 6) 7; OSCE/ODIHR (n 39) 8.

[76] Bayrakli and Hafez (n 14) 11.

18

The European Debate on Restrictions on Foreign Funding of Islam

ZOILA COMBALÍA

I. Introduction

The growing presence of Islam in Europe is raising the question of the legitimacy of the restriction or legal control of foreign funding to Muslim communities due to the possible use of such funding as a vehicle for political control or a channel for the promotion in Europe of a form of Islam which, if not violent, is at least radical and far removed from European values.

The Australian Government was one of the first governments to question such funding channels when, in 2007, it rejected a Saudi request to transfer funds to the Islamic Society of South Australia. In the same vein, the Norwegian Government refused aid from Saudi Arabia for the construction of a mosque in Oslo in 2010, citing the lack of religious freedom in that country. Since then, many European countries have announced measures to curb foreign funding of Islam, mainly from Gulf countries and Turkey, but also sometimes from the Maghreb. However, to date, the only Western country to have passed legislative measures directly preventing the foreign funding of Islam has been Austria, which did so through the law of 25 February 2015 regulating the legal status of Islam in the country (*Islamgesetz*).

This is a complex issue because, although it seems necessary to adopt measures to prevent funding that is used for political or ideological control purposes and results in the radicalisation of Muslim communities in European countries, at the same time it is necessary to maintain respect for the principle of equality and non-discrimination between religious communities, without fostering a generalised suspicion of Islamic communities or of economic aid from third countries for legitimate activities, such as the practice of worship.

As a manifestation of the concern about the possible harmful use of foreign financial aid to European Islam, mention can be made of the various reports prepared in different countries to study this issue and propose the most appropriate measures to alleviate the abuse. This chapter will briefly describe the content of some of these reports, as well as the Austrian law restricting such funding. It will then analyse the 2018 Resolution of the Parliamentary Assembly of the Council of Europe that outlines guidelines and recommendations on how to address this issue, consistent with respect for human rights. In relation to this, after a brief reference to the Belgian, Spanish, Italian and German cases, this chapter will analyse the reports published in the Netherlands, France and Great Britain.

II. Reports from Various European Countries on the Foreign Financing of Islam

A. Belgium

In Belgium, the House of Representatives addressed the issue of foreign funding of Muslim communities following the terrorist attacks perpetrated in the country on 22 March 2016, specifically examining the issue of funding by Middle Eastern countries.

In March 2018, the Belgian Federal Government took the decision to terminate the 1967 agreement that entrusted the concession of the Grand Mosque of Brussels to Saudi Arabia for a period of 99 years. The decision followed a recommendation of the commission of inquiry into the terrorist attacks, aimed at putting an end to the interference of foreign states in Belgian Islam. The commission of inquiry, chaired by Patrick Dewael, recommended this rupture, stressing that the Cinquantenaire Mosque was characterised by its defence of a very rigorous vision of Islam, inspired by Saudi Wahhabism. A 2015 State Security note questioned some sermons and courses that 'intrinsically promote the rejection of all those who are not Salafists and may therefore lead to a higher degree of radicalization', although no direct link to terrorism was established.

B. Spain

In Spain, the National Intelligence Center (CNI) prepared a report on this issue in 2011. According to the newspaper *El Pais*, which had access to the text even though it was not made public, the CNI document analyses with concern the funding granted by Saudi Arabia, Kuwait, Qatar, the United Arab Emirates, Libya and, above all, Morocco, to Muslims in Spain, who numbered 1.2 million people at that time.[1] The Spanish secret Service warned that:

[1] Recently, according to the Report of the Observatorio Andalusí of 21 December 2021, the number of Muslims in Spain could be 2,250,486. *cf* 'Observatorio Andalusí, 'Estudio demográfico de la población musulmana' (UCIDE, 2023), available at observatorio.hispanomuslim.es/estademograf.pdf.

> The consequences of the financing lead in negative attitudes to coexistence, such as the appearance of ghettos and parallel societies, Islamic courts and police outside the current legality, the lack of schooling for girls, forced marriages, etc .... There is not enough control of the financial flows which, in the form of donations and aid from other countries, are given to the Islamic community in Spain.[2]

Since the reports on the situation of religious freedom in Spain prepared by the Advisory Commission on Freedom of Religion, under the Ministry of the Presidency (formerly under the Ministry of Justice), it has been proposed on several occasions that the system of funding through tax allocation available to the Catholic Church should be extended to other faiths that request it, including the Islamic Commission of Spain.[3] Although this would not prevent foreign financing, it would undoubtedly reduce it considerably.

C. Italy

In Italy, concern has been expressed regarding certain foreign financing of Islamic entities and mosques based there, more specifically funding from Qatar. This concern led to a question (with request for a written answer) to the European Commission by the Italian Member of Parliament Lorenzo Fontana (a member of Lega Nord). The text of the question was as follows:

> Over the past few years, Qatar has been investing heavily in Italy's mosque infrastructure. A new controversy has arisen in Italy as a result of the Union of Islamic Communities and Organisations (UCOII) wanting to buy the historic Villa Basilewsky and convert it into a mosque. Costs are believed to be around EUR 30 million. According to media reports, the project is being co-financed by Qatar. Qatar is viewed as highly controversial by scholars, politicians and experts when it comes to the funding of Islamic centres because many religious organisations in the Emirate are said to have close ties with the Muslim Brotherhood, as does the UCOII. This is giving rise to concerns that radicalisation is taking place through the channel of mosques funded by Qatar. 1. Does the Commission know about this project? 2. Is the Commission aware of any other projects in Italy for Islamic centres funded from Qatar? 3. Does the Commission share the opinion that Islamic centres in Italy funded from Qatar can lead to radicalisation?[4]

[2] I Cembrero, 'El CNI alerta de que seis países musulmanes financian al islamismo' *El País* (31 July 2011) available at www.elpais.com/politica/2011/07/31/actualidad/1312140952_655494.html.

[3] *cf*, for example, Z Combalia, J Mantecón, R García, JM de Portugal and J Rossell, 'Informe anual sobre la situación de la libertad religiosa en España en 2017' (Ministerio de Justicia, Madrid, 2018), available at www.mpr.gob.es/mpr/subse/libertad-religiosa/Documents/InformeAnual/InformeAnual_2017.pdf. The Spanish state allocates to the Catholic Church a percentage of the income tax (0.7%) of taxpayers who have expressly declared in their personal income tax return a willingness for it to do so. In the absence of such a declaration, the corresponding amount is allocated to other purposes of social interest.

[4] L Fontana, 'Question for written answer E-000840/2017 to the Commission: Rule 130', available at www.europarl.europa.eu/doceo/document/E-8-2017-000840_EN.pdf.

The response states the following:

> National policy related to foreign financing of religious institutions and cultural centres is the responsibility of individual States and is regulated by national law. In line with Article 17(1) of the Treaty on the Functioning of the European Union, the Union does not prejudice the status under national law of churches and religious associations in the Member States. With regard to risks of radicalisation in this context, in the wider framework of the European Agenda on Security, in June 2016, the Commission adopted a communication on the prevention of radicalisation leading to violent extremism, which includes strengthening cooperation with third countries facing similar challenges. The EU and the State of Qatar conduct a regular dialogue in the framework of the Gulf Cooperation Council and bilaterally, including on radicalisation and extremism.[5]

As a result of the intention of some Saudi Arabian institutions to join the Board of Directors of *La Scala di Milano*, along with the consultation on this issue, other consultations were introduced on the initiatives regarding the funding from some Arab countries, including Saudi Arabia, for Islamic places of worship in Italy which, if the funding went ahead, could easily come under the influence of wahhabism. The response of Matteo Salvini, then Minister of the Interior, on this issue was as follows:

> In this context, special attention is being paid to the sources of financing of the various places of worship, which we are monitoring one by one. On this front, the information activity of the Intelligence Department and the preventive activity of the Police Forces are being developed. To date, fortunately, no link has emerged between the financing provided to Islamic associations by foreign States and terrorism-related crimes. The Ministry of the Interior, however, is obviously aware of the need to maintain the capacity of our info-investigative apparatus at the highest level, and this, beyond question, is what it does on a daily basis. Our goal is to come up with concrete initiatives, also at the regulatory level, on which I am personally working, obviously open to the contributions from this Parliament, to regulate the activities of mosques and places of worship, while also tracing the relate funding. The objective of the Government is also to refer to the creation of a register of ministers of worship and to the definition of appropriate instruments that allow a more effective control action, including the closure of radical associations and irregular places of worship. It is evident, in fact, also in the light of the current international context, that some places of congregation in the past and perhaps also in the future may become centers of recruitment and be infiltrated by religious extremism.[6]

D. Germany

In Germany, in December 2016, two federal intelligence agencies, the Federal Intelligence Service (FIS or *Bundesnachrichtendienst*) and the Federal Office for

[5] Available at www.europarl.europa.eu/doceo/document/E-8-2017-000840-ASW_EN.pdf.

[6] 'Question for immediate reply, addressed to the Minister of the Interior, 3-00609' (12 March 2019), available at www.camera.it/leg18/410?idSeduta=0141&tipo=stenografico.

the Protection of the Constitution (*Bundesamt für Verfassungsschutz*), produced a report (*Zwischenbilanz*) for the Government on how the Gulf States exported their religion to Germany. The report, which was partly leaked to the press, addressed the long-term influence strategy of these states in Germany and included references to the issue of funding.

On 12 December 2016, the *Süddeutsche Zeitung* newspaper, along with broadcasters NDR and WDR, publicised a suspicion that, according to the FIS and the Federal Office for the Protection of the Constitution, several religious organisations from Saudi Arabia, Kuwait and Qatar were promoting salafism in Germany. The aim of the missionary activities promoted by these states, including the construction of mosques and training centres as well as the dispatch of imams, was, allegedly, to spread a fundamentalist variant of Islam.

On the other hand, with regard to Turkey, the main 'sponsor' of Islam in Germany, it should be noted that the German Government withdrew from the general budgets of 2018 and 2019 the items of subsidies to the Association of Turkish Muslim Mosques (DITIB), which are spread throughout the country and in which preaches a network of about 970 imams sent by the Administrative Council of Religious Affairs of Turkey (Diyanet) with each imam serving the Association for a period of five years. The Association has repeatedly rejected the offer of German imams trained at the universities of Münster, Osnabrück and Tübingen. The Association has been the source of several controversies, most recently when it came to light that in several of its mosques (at least in those of Herford, Mönchengladbach and Ulm) schoolchildren were dressed in military uniforms and given Turkish flags to recreate war scenes of nationalist exaltation. It is estimated that, through different government programmes, dependent on various ministries, the DITIB received funds amounting to around six million euros between 2014 and 2017.

Analogous to what has been proposed for Spain with the tax allocation, in Germany it has been proposed that a religious tax be applied to Muslim communities, similar to the one applied to other churches in the country, which would allow German Islam to be self-financed without depending on foreign aid. However, so far this has not been possible due to the difficulty of the Islamic communities in complying with the necessary requirements to establish themselves as a public corporations, mainly through the registration of their members.[7]

[7] 'In the absence of a similar tax, mosques in Germany are reliant upon donations, raising concerns about possible financing by foreign organisations and governments, which has sometimes prompted questions about the promotion of fundamentalist ideologies. For example, there has been growing concern about the influence of the Turkish-Islamic Union for Religious Affairs (DITIB), an arm of the Turkish Government based in Germany. Several voices have spoken in favour of introducing a religious tax for Muslim communities. According to *Deutsche Welle* (DW), 'a lawmaker from Germany's other ruling party, the center-left Social Democrats (SPD), agreed that a mosque tax could help Islam in Germany become more independent. The SPD's domestic policy chief Burkhard Lischka agreed that it was a topic "worthy of discussion"'. The founder of a progressive Berlin mosque, Seyran Ates, supported the measure, telling DW that Islam in Germany 'has a huge influence from outside, from foreign countries'. She added that German Muslims 'have to stand up themselves. They have to take care

E. The Netherlands

Following the controversy generated in the Netherlands[8] by donations to Dutch mosques from entities sponsored by Middle Eastern governments, the Dutch Parliament commissioned an initial study focused on assessing whether a reliable estimate of the extent of foreign funding of Islam is possible. It entrusted the task to RAND-Europe, which completed its work with the publication of an extensive and rigorous report whose main conclusion was that there is hardly any reliable data on the subject.

The starting point is that there is no register and no obligation to report foreign donations. For historical reasons, mosques in the Netherlands have been established as associations (*verenigingen*) or as foundations (*stichtingen*), taking advantage of the flexibility of these legal forms and the ease with which they can be established. Although there is an important tradition of donations from the community itself, larger projects require external contributions, especially considering there is no public funding for religious activities in the country. Therefore, there is no doubt that some Dutch Islamic institutions receive funds from abroad.

On the other hand, the report emphasises that almsgiving plays a fundamental role in Islam; in fact, *zakat* is one of its five pillars. Although other religions also attach importance to almsgiving, European countries are donors rather than recipients of aid so there is no record of non-Islamic churches or religious communities in Europe receiving significant funding from abroad.

There is hardly any documentation to show the extent of foreign aid; moreover, information on financial transactions is not public and the accounting transparency of Islamic institutions is generally poor. However, there are official links between certain Dutch mosques and some foreign governments (for example, with Turkey through Diyanet) or with international organisations such as *Milli Görüş*.

The report also noted that it was not possible, with the data available to it, to assess the role that such foreign funding plays as a possible instrument of control of Islam in the Netherlands or vehicle for the penetration of behaviour in conflict with democratic values. Obtaining reliable information would require intelligence services to act or get an investigation order, which the authors of the document did not recommend, given the costs and legal doubts that would generate. Moreover, the report points out, foreign funding (and even influence) is not a priori an illegal matter.

In light of their findings, the report concluded with recommendations aimed at enhancing the financial transparency of Islamic institutions but still avoiding

about their own religion here in Germany. So Muslims in Germany should do something for Islam in Germany'. 'Germany Mulls Introducing "Mosque Tax" for Muslims' DW (26 December 2018), available at www.dw.com/en/germany-mulls-introducing-mosque-tax-for-muslims/a-46866041.

[8] See, S Hoorens et al, 'Foreign financing of Islamic institutions in the Netherlands: A study to assess the feasibility of conducting a comprehensive analysis' (Rand Corporation, 2015), available at www.rand.org/t/rr992.

unnecessary invasive investigations. For example, it argued that the obligation to report donations exceeding certain amounts could be encouraged, even if the donor, amount or destination of the funds are kept confidential. They found that greater transparency would positively impact trust in Islamic institutions.

F. France

In France, the Senate commissioned two reports related to the subject in hand. Those reports are addressed in turn below.

a. Report No 345 on the Financing of Places of Worship

This report analyses, in general terms, the problems that the ban on the public funding of places of worship in the 1905 law generates for religious minorities as some groups, having grown rapidly in recent decades, encounter difficulties in having places of worship, which is not conducive to the integration of these communities in France.[9] The conclusion of the report is that, although it seems desirable to maintain the legislation in force, it would be appropriate to improve information, especially to local authorities, about the exceptions allowed by law. The report includes a number of proposals in this regard.

As regards the financing of Muslim places of worship by foreign states, after considering the data provided by the embassies, the report considers that this financing is 'very little compared to the demands required by the Muslim faithful in France'.[10] Amar Bendjama, the Algerian ambassador to France, indicates that the relatively modest aid for the construction of mosques is mainly aimed at showing the support of the country of origin for the communities settled in France, as well as encouraging donations from local communities.

b. Report on the Organisation, Place and Financing of Islam in France and its Places of Worship

More specific, insofar as referring to Islam, is this second report,[11] dated 5 July 2016, written by Senators Corinne Féret (Pres), Nathalie Goulet and André Reichardt. The objective was pointed out by Senator Bariza Khiari as follows:

> [W]e must be able to fight against the instrumentalization of religion for political purposes, without stigmatizing Muslims and giving everyone the means to exercise

[9] M Hervé, 'Report 345' (17 March 2015), available at www.senat.fr/rap/r14-345/r14-3451.pdf.
[10] ibid.
[11] C Féret, N Goulet and A Reichardt, De l'Islam en France à un Islam de France, établir la transparence et lever les ambiguïtés, Rapport d'information n° 757 (2015–2016), 5 July 2016, available at www.senat.fr/rap/r15-757/r15-757.html.

> their own religious practice with dignity, without compromising secularism … The law must protect the faith, as long as the faith does not seek to impose the law. Muslims in France must be considered full citizens, not marginalized citizens.

Throughout the report, the rapporteurs start from four premises: a) the intangibility of the 1905 law, interpreted as neutrality and not as militant separatism; b) the relatively recent appearance of the Muslim cult in the French religious landscape, which places it in a phase of settlement; c) the observation that the concordat practice of Alsace-Moselle favours a fruitful dialogue between public authorities and confessions, but does not offer the appropriate legal instruments to respond to the current problems of Islam in France; and d) the determination not to apply to the Muslim cult proposals that are valid for other confessions but are not effective in the case of Islam.

On these assumptions, the report addresses seven points.[12] Here we will refer only to those which are more directly related to the issue of the foreign financing of Islam. First, with regard to the compatibility of the preaching of imams in France with the values of the Republic, the role played by foreign states in their appointment and training must be questioned. The report notes that most of the imams are foreigners (only 20–30 per cent have French nationality). Almost all of the imams work as volunteers and only one-third of them are paid (either full or part time).

Leaving aside the occasional case of imams who enter the country temporarily to help during Ramadan and who do so on short-term visas, according to the Ministry of the Interior, three countries are the main suppliers of imams to France. Those countries are Turkey (151 imams), Algeria (120 imams) and Morocco (30 imams). Thus, in total, there are 301 imams (for the 2,500 places of worship in France) financed by foreign states.[13] They enter the country under various statuses. In some cases, they do so as teachers of the language and culture of the country of origin (ELCO) or, especially in the case of those financed by Turkey, as social workers.[14] All this is done within the framework of agreements signed with the Ministry of the Interior and the Ministry of Foreign Affairs, which shows the existence of a double discourse when, in the Government, the need to restrict the influence of third countries on Islam in France is alluded to.

The foreign imams who are invited in application of Conventions have to fulfil a series of requirements, such as the learning of the language, upon which the concession and renewal of visas is conditional. In addition, the Government has highlighted the advantage that, since they are paid directly by the states of

[12] These points are: 1) the Muslim community; 2) the training of imams and chaplains; 3) the financing of Muslim worship; 4) the halal industry; 5) the representative interlocutor of the Muslim faith for the public authorities; 6) private Muslim education; and 7) local authorities and the Muslim religion.

[13] In Germany, for example, the Turkish State funds about 970 imams.

[14] The Teaching of the Language and Culture of Origin (ELCO) is a system designed in France in 1977 to allow children of immigrant parents to maintain a link with their country of origin. The classes are taught by teachers recruited, paid and supervised by the countries of origin. These are optional courses given within the public school system.

origin, the imams are controlled by these states, which is a guarantee against radicalisation. However, the drawback is that these imams generally do not master the French language and do not understand the social and cultural context of the country, resulting in their being distant from the faithful, particularly the younger ones, who were born in France.

Mosques that do not have an imam paid by a foreign state appoint their own; these imams are usually unpaid, although some have a full- or part-time salary. Apart from imams working in mosques, there are those who provide religious assistance in public institutions such as hospitals, prisons and the army who, in this case, are financed by the French state.

The conclusion of the report is that there is a pressing need for competent religious leaders, with authority in religious matters, trained to prevent radicalisation and develop a counter-narrative to combat extremism. The 'consular' imams undergo their training in their countries of origin, while those who study in France mainly attend two centres: the European Institute of Human Sciences and the Al-Ghazali Institute, attached to the Grand Mosque of Paris, both of which are experiencing difficulties in the performance of their tasks. There is also an agreement with Morocco to host 40 French students at the Mohammed VI Institute in Rabat. In any case, it should be borne in mind that the state cannot make the exercise of the imamate conditional on a certain level of training, either religious or secular.

After addressing the issue of imams, the report focuses directly on the second issue: the sources of financing for the construction or operation of mosques. In the absence of public funding, resources come from donations (some from abroad) although it is noted that the main source of funding is provided by the faithful of the community itself (as is the case with other denominations). The difference is that Muslim worship has a greater need for the construction of places of worship, due to its recent presence and rapid expansion, which implies that it must ask its followers for more financial help than other faiths, while, generally, it is a population with fewer financial resources. In addition to this financing channel, there is funding from foreign states (although it is scarce and relatively concentrated in a few states and places of worship) often in large emblematic mosques.

As for the countries that provide funding, Turkey channels its aid through the dispatch of imams rather than through donations to communities or mosques. Morocco grants aid, both for the construction or support of mosques and to pay 30 imams practising in France.[15] Algeria's financing is mainly carried out within the framework of an agreement with the Grand Mosque of Paris. In the case of Saudi Arabia, the ambassador noted that his country 'participated in the financing of

[15] The Moroccan Embassy notes that, for example, the aid in 2016 amounted to six million euros. Regarding the mosques in whose construction or restoration Morocco participated, the ambassador mentions those of Saint Etienne, Strasbourg, Evry and Mantes-la-Jolie. The Kingdom of Morocco directly owns the Evry mosque.

eight French mosques: the aid ranged from 200,000 to 900,000 euros per project, in total, 3,759,400 euros'.[16] In addition, Saudi Arabia pays the salary of some 14 imams working in mosques in France who are not of Saudi nationality; these funds are not subject to a bilateral agreement. The foreign donations that arouse the greatest suspicion are those made by private donors. In this regard, it should be noted that several Gulf countries, in particular Bahrain, the United Arab Emirates and Saudi Arabia have recently developed strict regulations in terms of the control and transparency of donations made by private individuals abroad.

Regarding the third issue, the report highlights the fact that communities managing a place of worship can, under the 1905 law, incorporate as a religious association and then benefit from some tax advantages not available to other associations. However, many Islamic communities do not register because they combine the purposes of worship with cultural or social care purposes, and because, in addition, as common associations they have fewer administrative and accounting obligations if their income does not exceed certain amounts.

The report notes the failure of the project to centralise the financial resources of Islam by establishing, by the decree of 31 May 2005, the Foundation for the Works of Islam in France, recognised as a public utility institution on 25 July of that year, whose main mission was to finance the construction and management of places of worship, in agreement with the local authorities of the municipalities concerned. The aims of this centralisation of resources were, on one hand, to put an end to the mosque's financial dependence on the countries of origin and, on the other hand, to promote greater transparency in the financing of Islam in the country. However, the problems of representation of French Islam, composed of sectors at odds with each other, have hindered the effectiveness of this tool. The document made some proposals to reactivate the Foundation so that it could become operational and meet the challenge of transparency and the need to control foreign funding.

Fourth, the report concludes by pointing out that although the relatively recent establishment of Islam in France is linked to successive waves of immigration, the link between Muslim immigrants and their countries of origin remains strong and is reflected through imam financing, the organisation of the halal sector, or the national representation of Muslim communities. The document identifies these links and suggests ways of bringing about a transition towards a French Islam adapted to the context of the country, compatible with the values of the Republic, and supported by the community itself, which requires a renewal of representation, training of imams in France (including secular cultural training) and greater transparency in funding, especially from abroad. The text concludes that France was, for a long time, a country renowned for its knowledge and teaching of Arabic language and culture, and would be honoured to regain the position it once held, in particular by creating university chairs in Islamology and supporting research in those fields.

[16] Available at www.senat.fr/rap/r15-757/r15-7579.html.

G. The United Kingdom

a. *Funding of Extremism, Including Foreign Funding*

On 30 November 2015, then Prime Minister David Cameron commissioned a report by the Home Office on the nature, extent and source of funding for Islamist extremist activity in the UK, including overseas sources. On 12 July 2017, the Secretary of State for the Home Department, Amber Rudd, in a written statement on the presentation of the report to Parliament, stated that, for security reasons, the document was not being published in full. However, she highlighted its four main conclusions.[17]

First, the submission notes that the main source of aid to Islamist extremist organisations in the UK comes from small, anonymous donations, mostly from domestically based individuals. Donors are sometimes unaware of the full agenda of these organisations. Although for a small number of extremist organisations, foreign funding is an important source of income, this is not the case for most. Second, some extremist organisations present themselves as charitable organisations to enhance their credibility, using Islam's emphasis on alms (*zakat*) and charitable activities. Third, as an effective tool to prevent the financing of extremism, regulation with an emphasis on transparency is recommended. Fourth, the support received from abroad has enabled some individuals to be trained in institutions that teach a highly conservative Islam and supply Islamic institutions in the UK with materials and preachers of this ideology. Some of these individuals have evolved towards extremism.

After a careful study of the report, the Government stated that it would continue with public awareness campaigns to encourage people to learn about the activities and objectives pursued by the organisations to which they donate money, but declared its intention to increase control over charities to prevent abuses committed under their protection. The Charity Commission would henceforth ask charities to declare their foreign sources of funding.

b. *Foreign-Funded Islamist Extremism*

This study highlights the fact that foreign funding of Islamist extremism in the UK comes primarily from Iran and the Gulf countries, especially Saudi Arabia, which, since the 1960s, has sponsored the export of wahhabism to Muslim communities in the West.[18] This funding takes the form of donations to mosques and Muslim educational institutions, which have hosted extremist propaganda and imams. In

[17] A Rudd, Written Statement to Parliament (HCWS39) (12 July 2017), available at www.questions-statements.parliament.uk/written-statements/detail/2017-07-12/hcws39.

[18] T Wilson, 'Foreign Funded Islamist Extremism in the UK' Research Paper No 9 (The Henry Jackson Society, 2017), available at henryjacksonsociety.org/wp-content/uploads/2017/07/Foreign-Funded-Islamist-Extremism-final.pdf.

some cases, this aid has also taken the form of scholarships for the training of British Muslim leaders in Saudi Arabia. In the UK, although it has been decided not to legally prohibit the foreign funding of Islam, work is being done to adopt measures that will lead to greater transparency in such funding.

III. Prohibition of Foreign Funding of European Islam: The Austrian Law on Legal Relations with Islam of 2015

Although the issue of the foreign funding of Islamic communities is a common concern for Western European countries, so far only Austria has introduced restrictive legal measures. In 2015, it enacted a federal law on the legal status of Islam, replacing a 1912 law, which had been in force since the time of the Habsburgs.[19] It is clear that the situation and challenges the Islamic presence generates in Austria today are very different from those prevailing at the beginning of the last century, so an update of the legal framework was necessary.

The Muslim population in Austria is currently around 570,000 people (seven per cent of the population). Their presence stems mainly from immigration that began in the 1960s from Turkey and the former Yugoslavia. The aim of the new law is to promote the integration of Muslims in Austria so they do not have to choose between their religious or citizenship identity. Although, unlike other European countries such as Spain or Italy, the specific status of Islam in Austria was not formalised in a bilateral law (but in a unilateral one) the law-making process was carried out in agreement with the religious authorities. Thus, when the process was launched in 2012, the State Secretariat for Integration, together with the president of the Islamic Religious Community in Austria (*Islamische Glaubensgemeinschaft in Österreich* or IGGÖ), created a platform for dialogue with seven working groups and the participation of numerous experts. Despite this, the final text of the law, supported by the deputies of the government coalition of Social Democrats and Christian Democrats, was heavily criticised by local Muslim organisations, which alleged discrimination against other denominations.

The law deals with the main issues that cooperation with Islamic communities raises for the public authorities. It recognises the autonomy of these communities and regulates the acquisition of legal personality and the protection of Islamic denominations. It provides for the right of the confession to submit proposals on matters that concern them to legislative and administrative bodies and establishes the obligation that the rules affecting their faith should be communicated to them

[19] Federal Act on the external legal relations to be adopted by Islamic religious societies (BGBl. I Nr 39/2015) (Islamgesetz 2015); came into force 30 March 2015; available at ilo.org/dyn/natlex/natlex4.detail?p_lang=en&p_isn=101856&p_country=AUT&p_count=1019.

within a reasonable timeframe. It guarantees Islamic religious assistance in public institutions (such as hospitals, prisons and the armed forces) and states that the ministers in charge of providing this assistance must have the appropriate training and experience, and be authorised by the Islamic religious community. It provides protection for dietary requirements and religious holidays, as well as cemeteries and burials. It upholds Austria's commitment to ensure academic education for religious leaders; thus, Muslims aspiring to be imams will be able to study at the University of Vienna in cooperation with the religious communities. The law states that religious doctrine, institutions and customs may not contradict legal regulations and that the religious entity must maintain a positive attitude towards society and the state. These groups face the possibility of losing legal recognition if their attitude changes or public security and order are threatened.

Among the matters dealt with, the prohibitions on Islamic communities receiving foreign funding were particularly controversial. In this regard, the law states, in Article 6.2, that religious communities and their members must procure the necessary means for their usual activity aimed at satisfying the religious needs of their members in their own country. The main objection raised to this provision is that a similar prohibition does not apply to other religious communities, primarily Jewish and Orthodox Christian communities, which also maintain ties with foreign states.

It should be noted that the law does not prevent all foreign financial assistance; it only prevents continuous or stable financial assistance. That is, one-off allocations such as those deriving from an inheritance, are not excluded, but the administration of such assets is required to take place in Austria. The legal restrictions on foreign funding (including the ban on hiring foreign imams in Austria as of 31 March 2016) primarily affect Turkey: in 2015, 60 of the 300 Muslim imams working in Austria were Turkish and received their salary from the Turkish Diyanet.

IV. Resolution 2237 (2018) of the Parliamentary Assembly of the Council of Europe on 'Regulation of Foreign Funding of Islam in Europe Aimed at Preventing Radicalization and Islamophobia'

These laws show there is concern in some European countries about the foreign financing of Islam in Europe due to the implications for national security, domestic Islamic integration, the viability of coexistence and the safeguarding of European values. However, it is necessary to consider that the treatment of this issue must be approached with the same values that it is intended to safeguard, that is, with respect for freedoms and fundamental rights and the non-discrimination of Muslims or Islamic communities. In this regard, particularly worthy of mention is Resolution 2237 (2018) of the Parliamentary Assembly of the Council of Europe on the 'Regulation of foreign funding of Islam in Europe aimed at preventing radicalisation and Islamophobia'.[20]

The Parliamentary Assembly assumes that the right to receive donations, regardless of their origin, is inherent in religious activities and, therefore, Member States must ensure that restrictions or suspicions in this area are not generalised. According to the Resolution, the foreign funding of religion is not only not a problem but can contribute to greater openness and the promotion of interreligious dialogue.

However, there is no doubt that some foreign states abuse this tool and use support for certain religious communities as a means to exert political influence, promote Islamic nationalism among the beneficiary communities, or spread radical Islam. On this point, the Assembly refers to its Resolution 1743 (2010) on 'Islam, Islamism and Islamophobia in Europe', where it notes that:

> [S]ome Islamic organizations active in Member States have been initiated by governments abroad and receive financial support and political guidance from those governments. The objectives of such organizations are hence not religious. National political expansion into other States under the guise of Islam should be brought to light … Therefore, Member States should require the transparency and accountability of Islamic as well as other religious associations, for instance by requiring transparency in their statutory objectives, leadership, membership and financial resources.[21]

Based on the above, the Assembly made four recommendations. First, it recommended Member States put an end to any foreign funding of Islam used for national political expansion into other states under the guise of Islam. Second, it urged States to reject all attempts at interference in their territory by foreign organisations which aim to put in place a parallel society and not allow foreign funding to reach any organisations which undermine human rights and dignity and oppose living together as guaranteed by the principles of human rights, democracy and the rule of law. In particular, it urged States to prevent any foreign attempt to indoctrinate young people.[22] Third it urged Member States to ensure full compliance with the framework established by the European Convention on Human Rights and the case law of the European Court of Human Rights, the Venice Commission and the Assembly. This implies, in particular, that a general ban on all foreign funding is arguably unreasonable and not necessary in a democratic society, regulations introducing discrimination between different religious groups on religious grounds must be banned, and any regulations governing funding should be proportionate.[23] Finally, it encouraged states to implement policies

[20] Resolution 2237 (2018) of the Parliamentary Assembly of the Council of Europe on the Regulation of foreign funding of Islam in Europe aimed at preventing radicalisation and Islamophobia, available at pace.coe.int/en/files/25040.

[21] Resolution 1743 (2010) of the Parliamentary Assembly of the Council of Europe on Islam, Islamism and Islamophobia in Europe, available at pace.coe.int/en/files/17880/html.

[22] ibid, at nº 6. 2.

[23] ibid, at nº 6. 3.

that increase transparency; for example, through annual financial reports clearly identifying the origin of any foreign funding and how it is used, including funding received through informal transfer systems, such as money brokers or *hawala* networks. It also recommended involving Muslim organisations in this promotion of transparency, through preventive actions vis-à-vis donors and the entities which receive the donations.[24]

In the event that any State adopts more drastic measures, such as a radical ban on foreign funding, the Assembly recalled the need to treat all religious communities equally and avoid placing the Muslim community under a generalised suspicion that could promote Islamophobia. The Assembly also pointed out that appropriate regulation of the financing of Islamic communities could produce positive side-effects for integration, for example, by fostering the emergence of representatives to liaise with the public authorities.

The Assembly's Recommendation stated that, in the face of a rudimentary and literalist Salafist theology, a breeding ground for radicalisation and even violence, the answer would come from an enlightened Islam. In this regard, it noted with satisfaction the widespread trend in several European states to improve the level of training of imams which the Assembly believes could curb the importation of imams trained abroad.[25] Consequently, they urged Member States to support courses that promote an Islam compatible with the European value of coexistence and to dedicate means to this end and support initiatives, including the establishment of European Faculties of Theology open to Islam.

The Assembly highlighted recent studies that show that the integration of Muslims in various European countries has grown in recent years, strengthening the bond they feel with their countries of residence. This does not prevent many from observing their religious practices and requirements and, on occasion, from continuing to maintain ties with their countries of origin or those of their ancestors. It also notes that they continue to be victims of Islamophobia on a significant scale.

Referring to paragraphs 3, 13 and 20 of Resolution 1743 (2010) and Resolution 2076 (2015) on freedom of religion and coexistence in a democratic society, the Assembly urged Member States to consider these specific characteristics or requirements of their religion and increase efforts to combat Islamophobia, since, while foreign funding may, as noted, be conducive to radicalisation,

[24] ibid, at nº 6. 4.

[25] The question of the legitimacy of imposing a certain secular training to practise as an imam has been raised in France. In French public universities there have been several attempts to establish a postgraduate degree in Islamic sciences, which has encountered various difficulties. Thus, the French tradition is reluctant to accept religious studies in public universities. In addition, there are different sensitivities among Muslims and difficulties in recruiting suitable faculties. There are several university degrees in civic education in the country. By a Decree of 2017, their obligatory nature was established for chaplains who are appointed and remunerated by the state; however, it was understood that beyond the personnel hired by the state, it is not possible to oblige a minister of worship to be in possession of a certain degree in order to exercise religious functions.

radicalisation is also, not least, fostered by Islamophobia. Finally, the Assembly invited Member States to implement the Action Plan adopted by the Committee of Ministers on 'The fight against violent extremism and radicalisation leading to terrorism', while at the same time noting the importance the plan accords (in its preventive proposals) to measures which encourage living together on an equal footing in culturally diverse democratic societies.

V. Conclusion

In short, it is clear that the studies carried out in connection with the European concern about the possible negative effects of the foreign financing of Islam show, in general, the disadvantages that would derive from a general legal prohibition of such financing. The reports and documents lean, rather, towards the adoption of measures aimed at increasing transparency in the financing received by the Islamic communities, as well as the promotion of positive preventive measures, especially by promoting the training of imams that are respectful of European values and the country's culture. If in some cases, like in Austria, a legal restriction on foreign funding is enacted, care should be taken to not damage the values and rights it aims to protect, and especially not to generate a generalised suspicion of Islam that would have repercussions on the increase of Islamophobia, thus hindering democratic coexistence.

19

Islamophobia, Xenophobia and Religion in the European Union: A Quantitative Analysis

ANASTASIA LITINA AND KONSTANTINOS PAPASTATHIS

I. Introduction

The growth of the radical right within the European Union (EU) and the instrumental role attributed to religion for its agenda brought the place of religion in nativist politics to the fore. Overall, it was argued that Christianity is represented as a core feature of European/national identity and cultural belonging, and as such a 'basis for defining (non) "nativeness"'.[1] Its instrumental transformation into 'a civilizational and identitarian "Christianism"' aims to construct an ingroup–outgroup distinction by stigmatising Islam as a corrupting element for the European/national value system, stereotypically representing Muslims as a threat to national homogeneity and state security, being by definition 'terrorists'.[2] In short, Christianity is employed as a criterion for excluding Islam; thus forming a frame not necessarily related to religious belief or values, but to an imagined sense of shared belonging.[3] However, while the relationship between religion and

[1] C Mudde, *Populist Radical Right Parties in Europe* (Cambridge, Cambridge University Press, 2007) 19.

[2] R Brubaker, 'Between Nationalism and Civilizationism: the European Populist Moment in Comparative Perspective' (2017) 40 *Ethnic and Racial Studies* 1191.

[3] See N Marzouki, D McDonnell and O Roy (eds), *Saving the People: How Populists Hijack Religion* (London, Hurst, 2016); M Minkenberg, 'Religion and the Radical Right' in J Rydgren, *The Oxford Handbook of the Radical Right* (Oxford, Oxford University Press, 2018) 523–60; M Minkenberg, 'The Radical Right in Europe: Cultural Shifts and Religious Nativism' in J Haynes (ed), *The Routledge Handbook of Religion, Politics and Ideology* (London, Routledge, 2022), 91–105; DN DeHanas and M Shterin, 'Religion and the Rise of Populism' (2018) 46 *Religion, State and Society* 177; J Kešić and JW Duyvendak, 'The Nation Under Threat: Secularist, Racial and Populist Nativism in the Netherlands' (2019) 53 *Patterns of Prejudice* 441; F Höhne and M Torsten (eds), *Religion and Neo-Nationalism in Europe*, (Baden-Baden, Nomos, 2020); A Hennig and M Weiberg-Salzmann (eds), *Illiberal Politics and Religion in Europe and Beyond: Concepts, Actors, and Identity Narratives* (Frankfurt, Campus, 2021).

nativism has been extensively studied from a qualitative perspective, its empirical elaboration has not attracted broad scholarly interest. This chapter aims to help to fill this lacuna through exploring the individual attitudes to Islamophobia and xenophobia at a micro level and how they are related to religious affiliation and practice in the western, central and eastern EU countries.

To this end, the chapter addresses the following questions:

1. What is the relationship at a micro level between religiosity, anti-immigrant attitudes and Islamophobia? Does religiosity correlate positively or negatively to Islamophobia and immigration?
2. Is there a pattern in behaviour of the religious in relation to their church affiliation? Do Catholics and Protestants have different attitudes vis-à-vis nativism (the so-called confessional cleavage)?

Section II of this chapter presents the data and research strategy we employed. Section III explores question 1 above, namely the interplay between religiosity and anti-immigration/islamophobia-elated attitudes. Section IV explores the findings of question 2 above; and section V elaborates on the possible confessional pattern. Finally, section VI, the conclusion, summarises the findings and refers to possible extension of this research.

II. Data, Empirical Strategy and Selection

To address the research questions, this chapter employs data from five rounds of the European Values Study (EVS) dataset, a cross-sectional dataset that captures and quantifies the social and political values of people from several countries around the world from 1981 to 2021. Using this dataset, this chapter undertakes OLS regressions to conditionally correlate a measure of church attendance (as a proxy for the degree of religiosity) with anti-immigration and Islamophobia-related attitudes. The idea behind using all available rounds of EVS is to capture the broader picture of religious nativism, considering these issues not just as a short-term question, but as being at the core of policymaking for many decades.

For analysis, we measure the independent variable of frequency of religious attendance, derived from the EVS question: 'Independently of marriages and funerals, how often do you attend religious services?' Respondents choose a value between 1 and 8, with 1 denoting 'more than once a week'; 2 denoting 'once a week'; 3 denoting 'once a month'; 4 denoting 'only on special holy days/Christmas/Easter'; 5 denoting 'other specific holy days'; 6 denoting 'once a year'; 7 denoting 'less often than once a year'; and 8 denoting 'never/practically never'. Therefore, higher values indicate lower religiosity. To capture nativist attitudes, our dependent variable is constructed by measuring anti-immigrant and Islamaphobic responses to the following questions:

1. On this list are various groups of people. Could you please mention any that you would not like to have as neighbours? Respondents choose between: Immigrants/foreign workers.

2. Do you agree, disagree, or neither agree nor disagree with the following statements? When jobs are scarce, employers should give priority to people of this country over immigrants. Respondents choose between: Agree/disagree.
3. Immigration policy preference: How about people from other countries coming here to work? Which one of the following do you think the Government should do? Respondents choose between: Let anyone come/As long as jobs available/Strict limits/Prohibit people from coming.

To measure Islamophobia, we used the question: On this list are various groups of people. Could you please mention any that you would not like to have as neighbours? Respondents have the option to choose Muslims as an answer.

In order to factor in various socioeconomic differences, we controlled for additional individual variables of the respondent such as age, gender, education level and employment status. Last, we introduced a survey wave fixed effects, in order to capture the role of potential time-specific shocks. Standard errors are clustered at the country level. It is important to note that our findings indicate correlations and not causality.

III. Findings

Before proceeding to the analysis, it should be made clear that this chapter does not aim to measure whether European societies are nativist or not, but whether religion drives people to have more or less xenophobic and Islamophobic attitudes than the more secular segments of the social whole. That being said, the empirical findings indicate that, on average, more religious people tend to express a preference for not having foreign or Muslim neighbours and tend to agree with employers giving priority to native workers. On the other hand, there is no significant effect of supporting the implementation of a stricter immigration policy (Figure 19.1).

Figure 19.1 Western and Eastern Europe

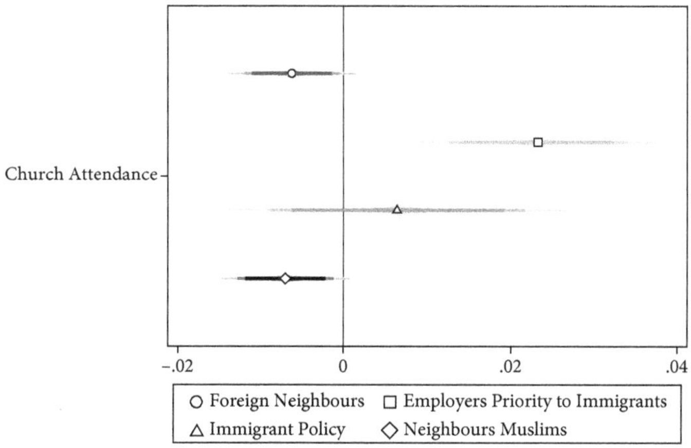

However, if we control separately for each European country, the picture changes since many countries partly or completely deviate from the general trend. There is also a category of countries where the religious/secular divide has no effect whatsoever on political attitudes. The countries in this category are: Romania (Figure 19.2), Switzerland (Figure 19.3), and Latvia (Figure 19.4).

Figure 19.2 Romania

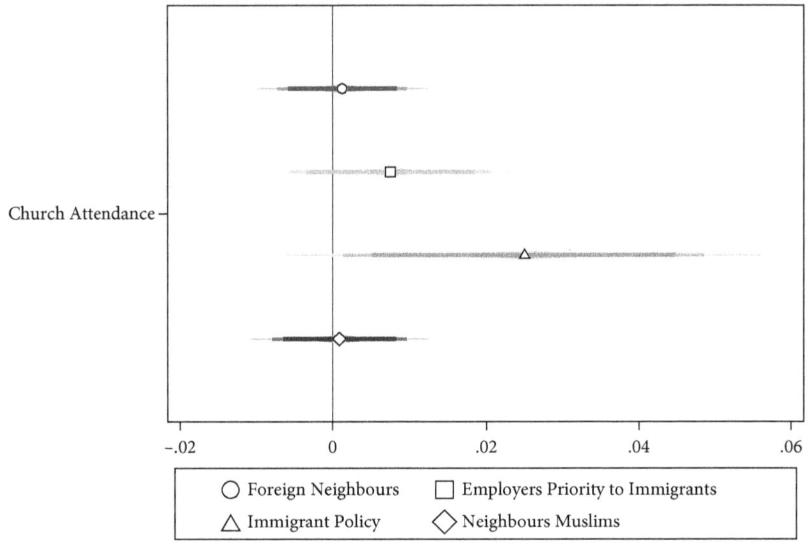

Figure 19.3 Switzerland

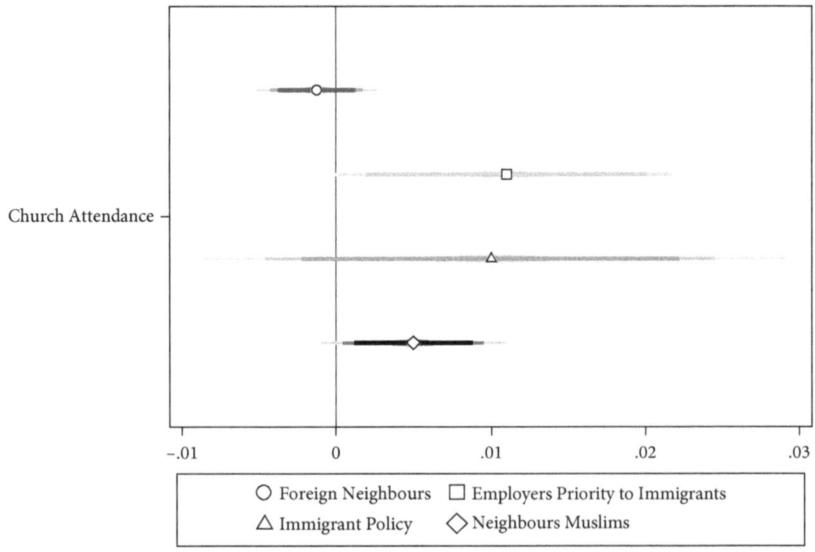

Figure 19.4 Latvia

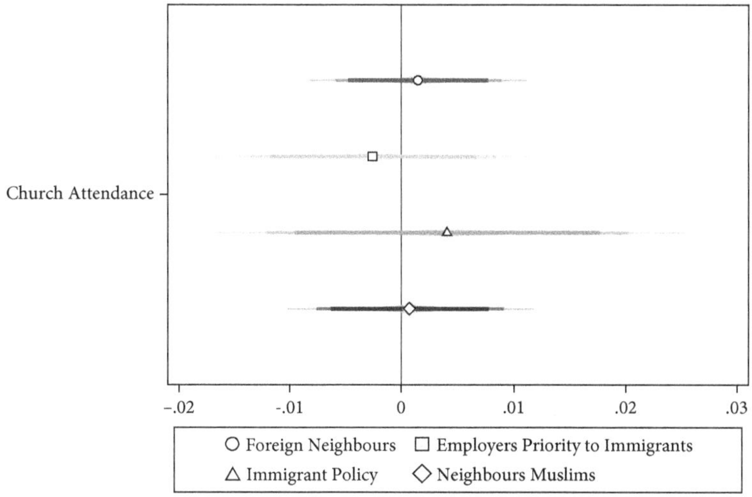

The second category is countries where the religious/secular divide plays a minor role in the formation of political attitudes. For instance, religiosity is positively correlated with one of many nativist variables or has a very little effect on some of them. Those countries are the following.

Starting with Hungary (Figure 19.5), stronger religiosity is associated with stronger nativist attitudes with respect to employment, and negative attitudes towards Muslim neighbours. The Netherlands (Figure 19.6) manifests similar results with respect to foreign and Muslim neighbours.

Figure 19.5 Hungary

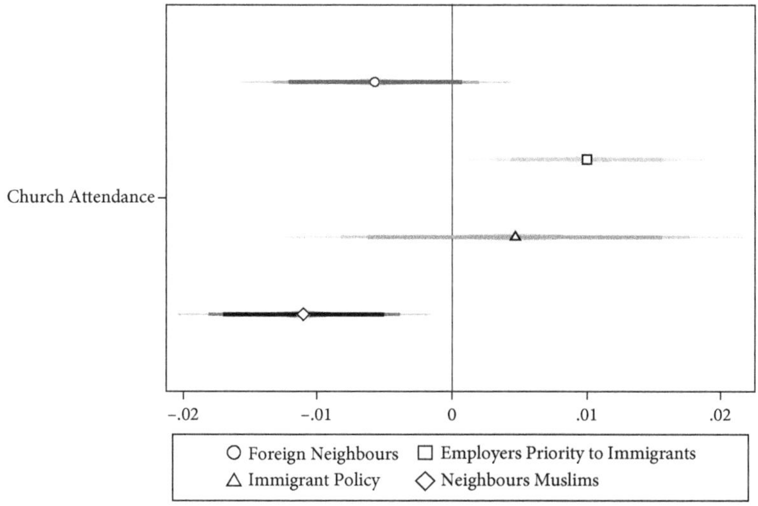

Figure 19.6 The Netherlands

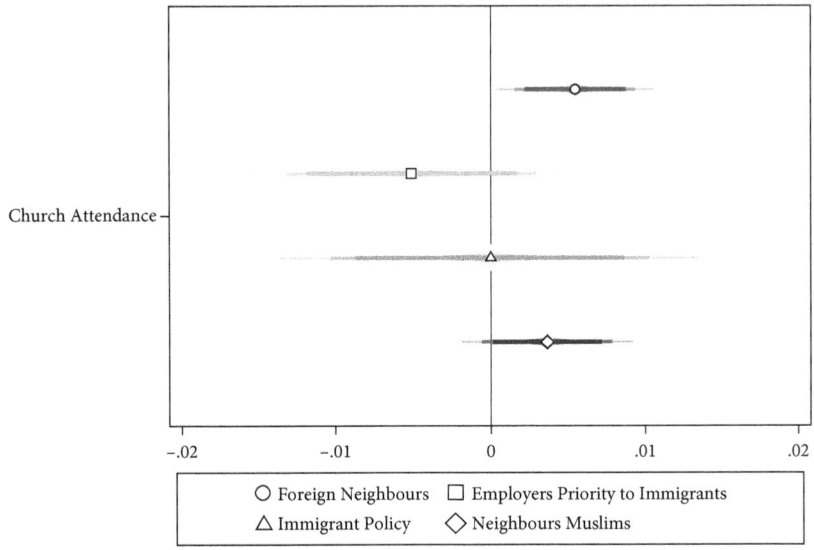

In the Czech Republic (Figure 19.7), the more secular people are, the more nativist of an outlook they have. In particular, the more likely they are to mention that they do not want foreign neighbours or Muslim neighbours, and the stricter the immigration policy they desire. On the other hand, the religiosity cleavage has no effect regarding the idea that priority should be given to natives.

Figure 19.7 Czech Republic

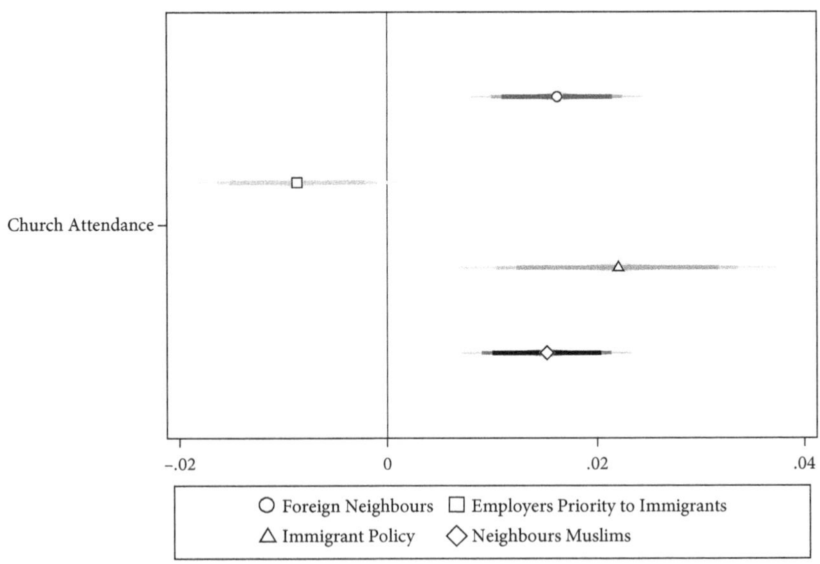

In Finland (Figure 19.8), the more secular people become, the less they are likely to state they do not want foreign neighbours, and the more likely they are to state that they do not want Muslim neighbours. On the other hand, in Finland, the degree of religiosity has no effect on the way society forms its view on immigration policy.

Figure 19.8 Finland

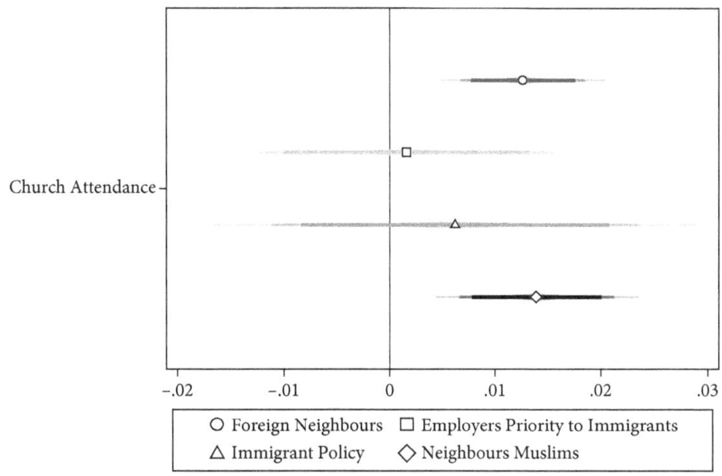

Overall, as regards Germany (Figure 19.9) the more secular people become: a) the less they are likely to mention that they do not want foreign neighbours; b) the more they disagree with the statement that employers should give priority to immigrants; and c) the more they are likely to mention that they do not want Muslim neighbours.

Figure 19.9 Germany

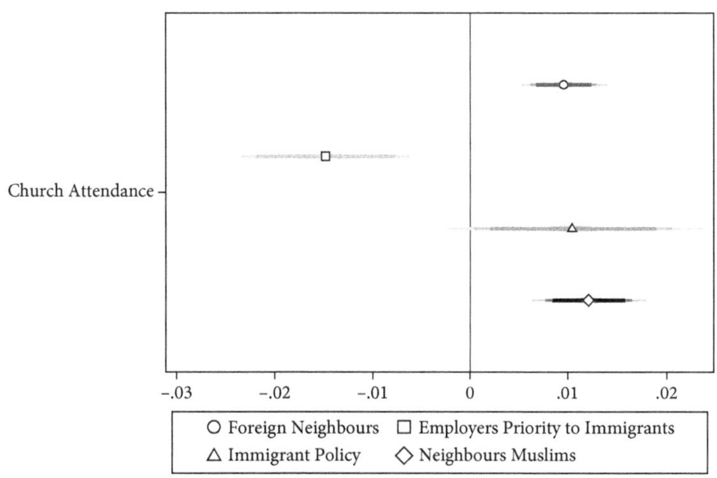

Overall, Italy follows the European paradigm (Figure 19.10). The only exception is related to immigration policy, where the more secular people become, the stricter the immigration policy they desire.

Figure 19.10 Italy

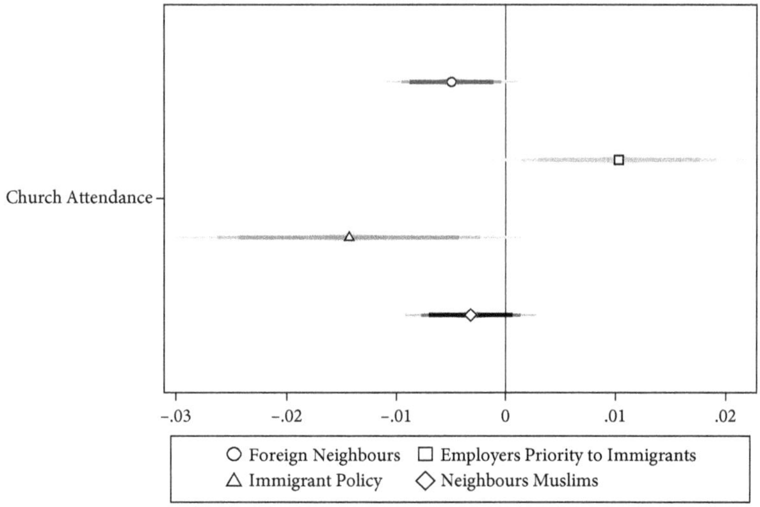

Slovakia (Figure 19.11) is different from the other countries in this category since higher levels of religiosity are positively related to higher levels of Islamophobia (the more religious they are, the more likely they are to mention they do not want Muslim neighbours).

Figure 19.11 Slovakia

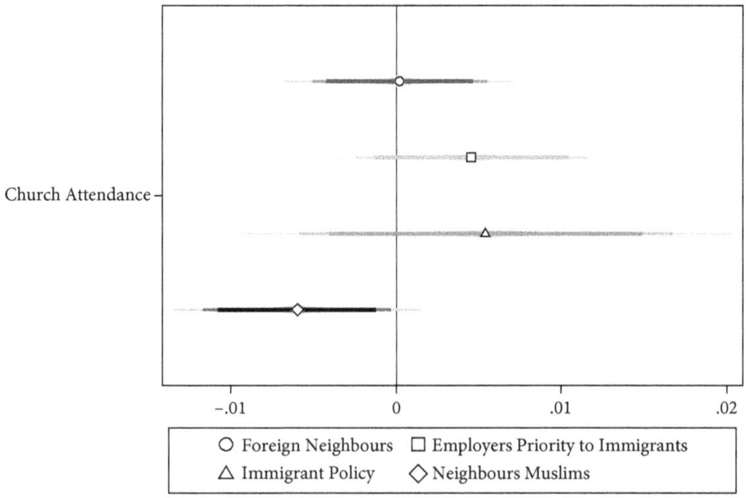

Lithuania also generally follows the European paradigm (Figure 19.12), with the exception that the more religious people become, the more likely they are to mention that they do not want foreign neighbours. Norway, on the other hand, is the opposite (Figure 19.13). The more secular people become, the more likely they are to mention that they do not want foreign and Muslim neighbours.

Figure 19.12 Lithuania

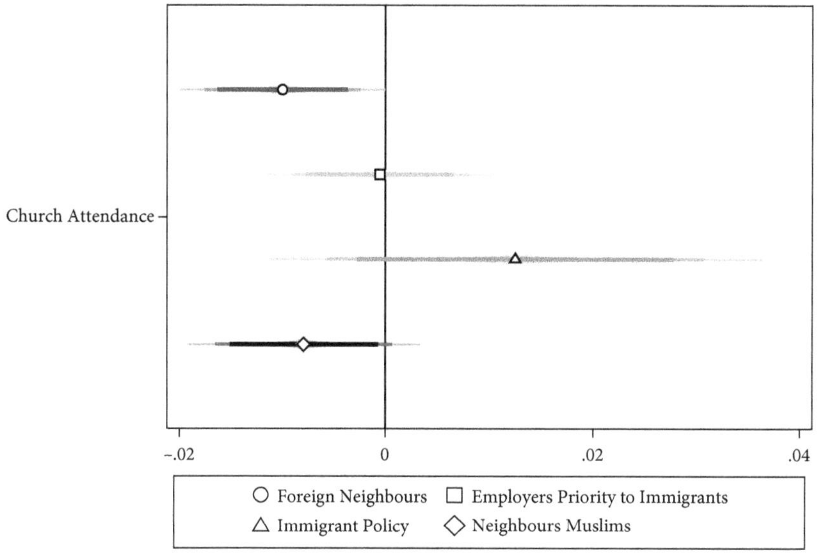

Figure 19.13 Norway

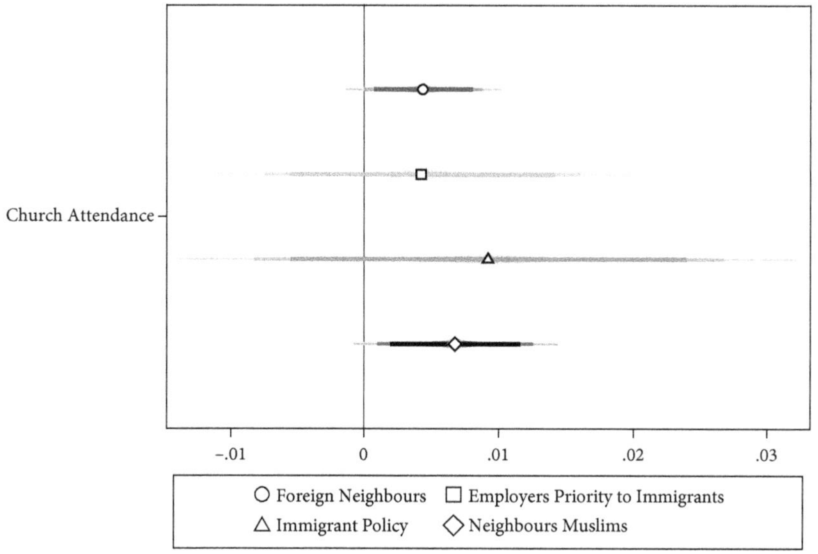

Poland (Figure 19.14) and Slovenia (Figure 19.15) are also exceptions. They deviate from the European pattern over the disagreement of the more secular people with the statement that priority should be given to natives. For Poland, there is also a tendency to avoid Muslim neighbours. Slovenia manifests similar attitudes in all categories except for that of avoiding foreign neighbours. On the other hand, Sweden (Figure 19.16) is the exact opposite: the more religious people, not the secular ones, seem to agree with those statements.

Figure 19.14 Poland

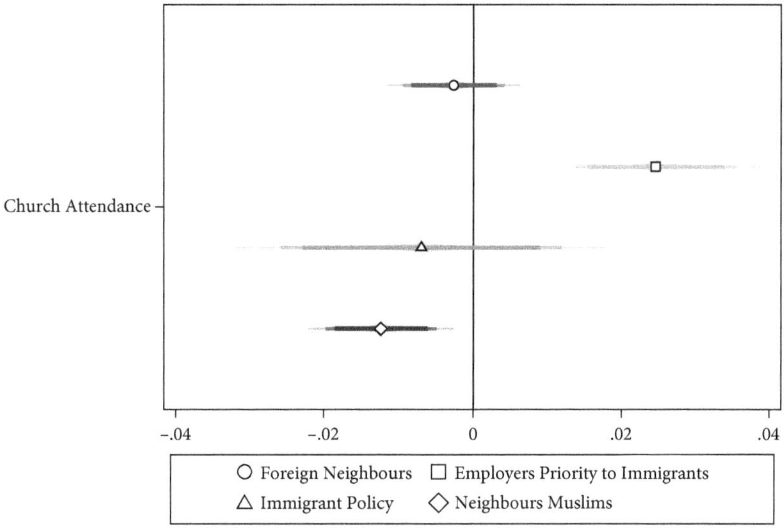

Figure 19.15 Slovenia

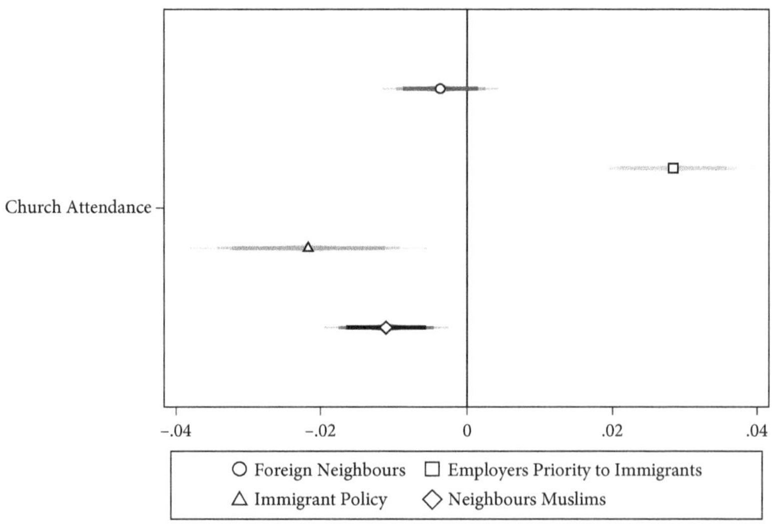

Figure 19.16 Sweden

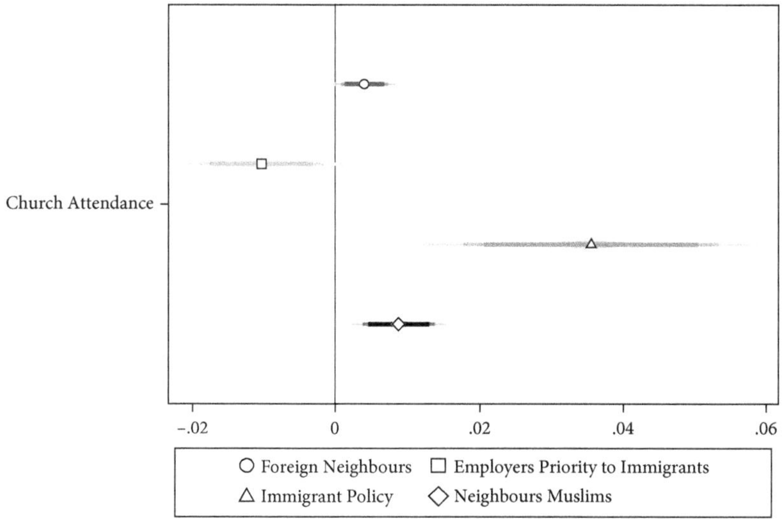

Spain (Figure 19.17), the outlier of the European paradigm, is in a category on its own, since the religious/secular divide is completely reflected regarding nativism. Specifically, greater religiosity is positively associated with anti-immigrant attitudes, since the more secular people are: a) the less likely they are to state they do not want foreign neighbours; b) the more likely they are to disagree with the statement that priority should be given to natives; and c) the less strict an immigrant policy they desire.

Figure 19.17 Spain

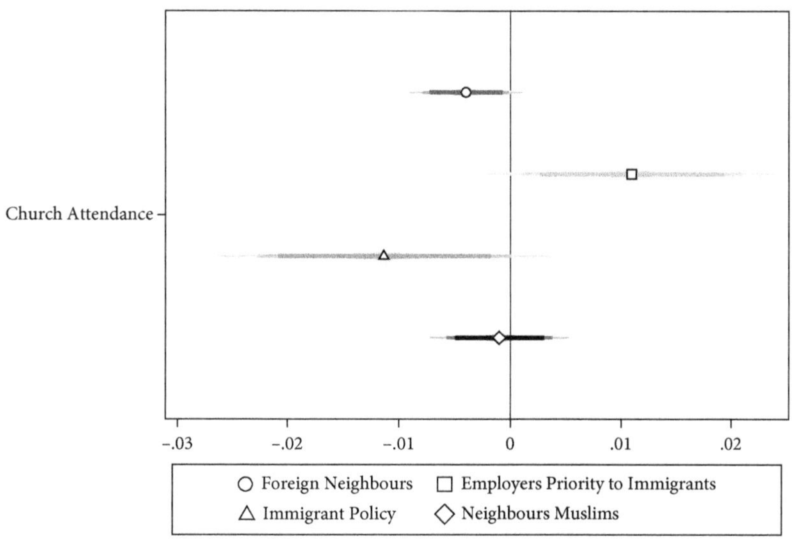

IV. The Confessional Cleavage

As regards question 2 in section I above – the possible existence of a confessional cleavage between Catholics and Protestants in relation to xenophobia and islamophobia – the results show that religion has no significant effect on the political attitudes under investigation. On the one hand, among the Roman Catholic countries (Italy, France, Spain, Poland, the Czech Republic, Slovenia, Slovakia, Hungary, Lithuania) (Figure 19.18), we found the religiosity factor to be in effect. In particular, the more religious people become: a) the more likely they are to state they do not want foreign neighbours; b) the more likely they are to disagree with the statement that priority should be given to natives; c) the less strict an immigrant policy they desire; and d) the more likely they are to state they do not want Muslim neighbours.

Figure 19.18 Roman Catholic countries

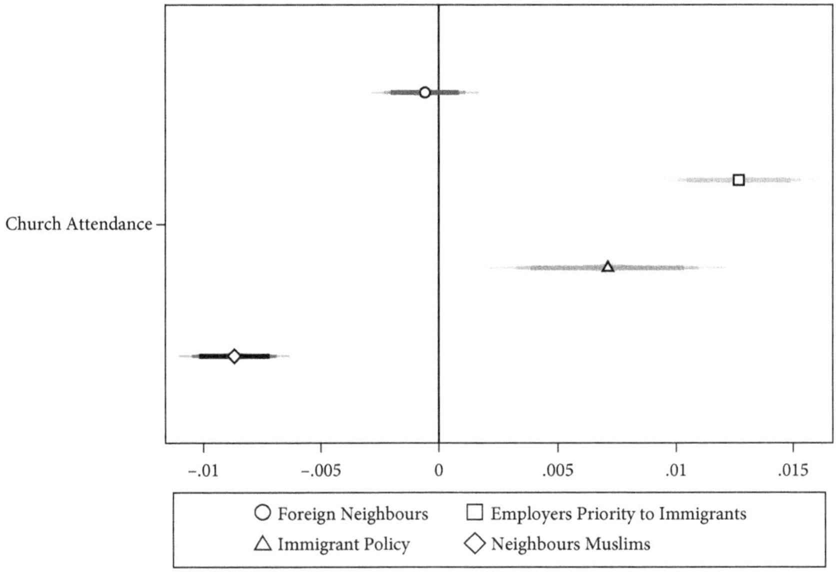

On the other hand, in Protestant countries (Finland, Sweden, the Netherlands and Norway) (Figure 19.19) the religiosity effect in particular is not strong, since the more religious people become: a) the less likely they are to state they do not want foreign neighbours; b) there is no effect as to whether they disagree with the statement that priority should be given to natives; c) there is no effect on their views as to which immigrant policy they want; and d) the less likely they are to state that they do not want Muslim neighbours.

Figure 19.19 Protestant countries

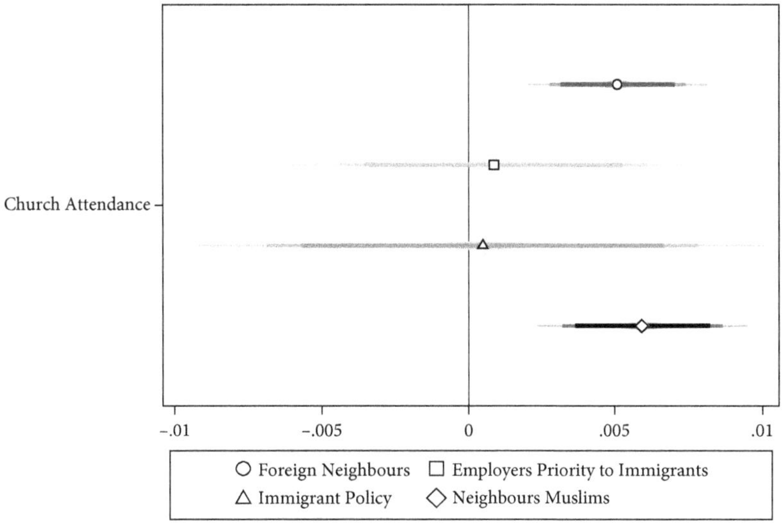

These findings do indeed demonstrate a divergence in political attitudes among Catholics and Protestants, confirming the confessional cleavage. However, when we examine Catholics and Protestants across the EU as a whole, the results are conclusively homogenous; religiosity does not correlate with nativism. For the Muslim population, the correlation is present but somewhat weaker (Figure 19.20B). In short, there is not a substantial confessional divide as regards the religiosity effect in relation to xenophobic or Islamophobic attitudes (Figures 19.20A, 19.20C and 19.20D).

Figure 19.20A Orthodox

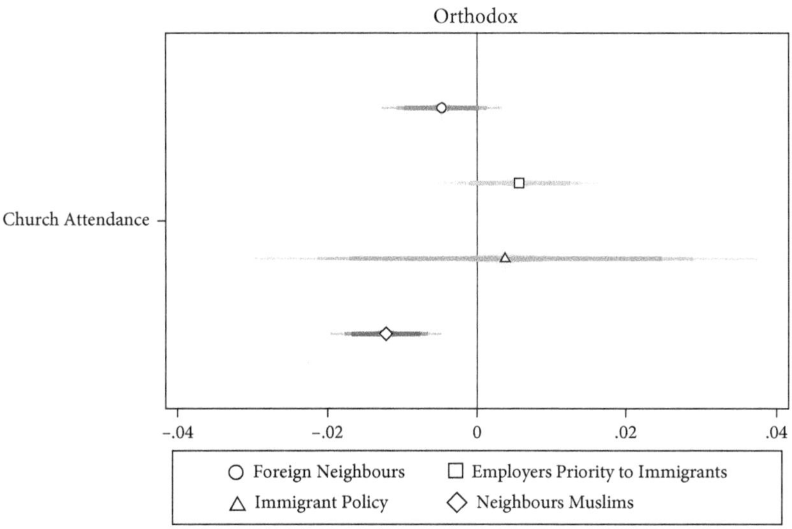

Figure 19.20B Muslims

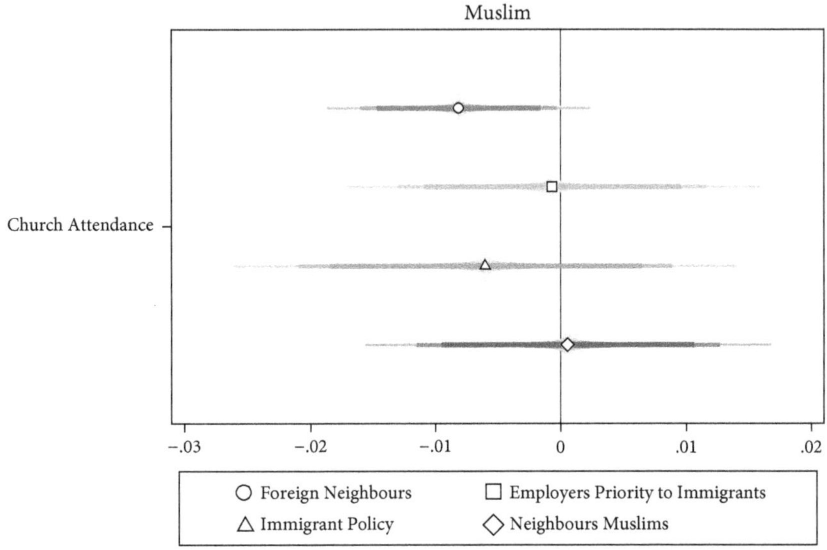

Figure 19.20C Catholics

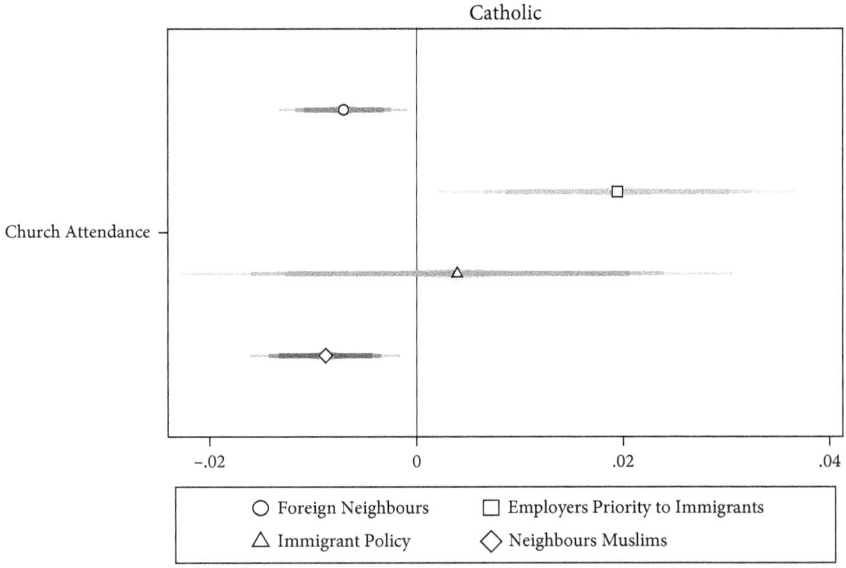

Figure 19.20D Protestants

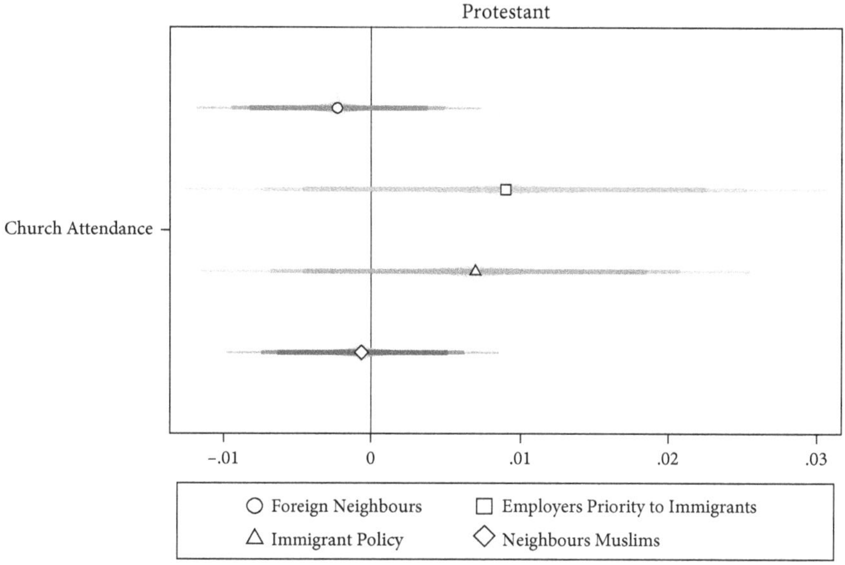

V. Conclusion

This chapter has endeavoured to elaborate from a quantitative perspective the interplay between religion and nativist attitudes. To this end, we studied, at a micro level, the possible positive or negative effect of religiosity on anti-immigrant attitudes and Islamophobia. Moreover, we examined the possible existence of a confessional divide in relation to xenophobia (whether Catholics or Protestants as religious cultures differ in their stance vis-à-vis nativist attitudes). We conclude that there is not a uniform pattern among Western and Eastern European countries on anti-immigration and Islamophobia, though the religious body of each one does hold a different political attitude. In short, the potential interplay of the two factors should be studied on a case-by-case basis.

Another overall conclusion is that the religious body in most of these countries does not differentiate from the secular sections of society regarding the questions under investigation. Consequently, religiosity either has no effect whatsoever on anti-immigration or exerts, in some countries, a partial influence in relation to one or two aspects of the nativist context.

Moreover, the chapter suggests there is not a homogenous Roman Catholic or Protestant attitude vis-à-vis immigration and Islam, but the religious bodies from countries of the same creed follow different paths. In effect, the stereotypical identification of Catholic or Protestant religious bodies with either a pro- or anti-nativist attitude is not confirmed. When we examine Catholics and Protestants across the

EU as a whole, the two religious bodies manifest differences with respect to nativist attitudes. This would suggest that a Spanish Catholic can potentially differ both from their French and Italian counterparts as well as from a Swedish or Dutch Lutheran. In any case, further research and stronger identification is necessary to further clarify the political behaviour and discourse of the religious milieu within a given country. This chapter has endeavoured to make a contribution towards locating the presence or absence of these hypothesised correlations.

INDEX

abortion, 20
agency and autonomy of women, 101–3, 109, 110
Albania:
ECHR values, 24
Muslim population, 58, 59, 64–65
assimilation policies, 67–68, 87, 99, 185–86, 201–2
old and new Islam, 71
schools, 120, 121
Austria, 5, 7, 89
burqa ban, 50
cultural racism
schools, 118–19
funding of Muslim religious societies, 90
integration policies, 74–75, 86, 89
restrictions on foreign funding, 241–42, 252–53, 256
targeting of Muslims, 237
theological training, 90–91
autonomy of religious denominations, 7–8, 11–12, 95, 182, 204

Belarus, 62
Belgium, 45, 68, 81–82, 201
burqa ban, 49
counter-terrorism measures, 238–39
headscarf ban, 77
integration policies, 86, 91, 201–2, 203–4
populist activism, 10
promotion of Muslim activities, 203–4
recording of hate crimes, 234
religious slaughter, 80, 153, 161, 206
religious symbols and clothing, 49, 77
restrictions on foreign funding, 242
blasphemy against Islam, 6–7, 9–10, 213, 215, 217, 220, 221–22, 223
Bosnia and Herzegovina, 41, 45, 50
Muslim population, 58, 59, 64–65
Bulgaria, 64, 67, 152, 202, 204, 237
burqa ban, 50
Muslim population, 199–200, 200
recording of hate crimes, 234
burqa bans:
conflicting Islamic and European values, 5, 49–50, 53–54, 202
SAS v France, 148–49

Cairo Declaration on Human Rights in Islam 1990, 24–25, 50–51
Charter of Fundamental Rights of the EU (CFREU), 18, 25, 29, 76, 79–80, 154, 157–58, 160, 215
children:
balancing education and respect for religion, 8–9, 112–13
freedom of religion
children's self-determination, 113–15
see also schools
Christian legacy in Europe, 1, 18–19
decline, 19–21
circumcision, 27
citizenship rights, 5, 37, 38, 41, 42, 45, 67, 70, 71, 77–78, 118, 121–22, 211, 220–21, 252
clothing, 27
see also burqa bans; headscarf bans
commitment to fundamental rights, 88–90, 231–32
Committee on the Elimination of Racial Discrimination, 227, 232–33
compelling state interest test (USA), 170, 172, 173–76, 176–77, 178–82
see also reasonable accommodation
conflicting loyalties, 11–12
balancing education and respect for religion, 8–9, 112–13
consolidation of national funding for faiths, 90–92, 203–4
constitutional morality, 3–4, 17, 19–21, 30
coronavirus, 20, 227, 230, 231–32, 236–37, 238–39
Council of Europe, 18, 79
constitutional morality, 20
hate speech, 218

Parliamentary Assembly of the Council of Europe (PACE)
anti-Sharia sentiment, 50–51, 129
compliance with human rights obligations, 24–25, 50–51, 129, 242
restrictions on foreign funding, 253–56
see also European Convention on Human Rights
Court of Justice of the EU (CJEU):
freedom of religion, 80–81
procedural rights, 28
religious slaughter cases, 12–13, 153, 156–58
additional stunning prior to the killing, 161–64
avoidable pain and suffering, 159–61
bindingness of judgments, 165
equal treatment argument, 163
organic food production labelling, 155–56
systems restraining bovine animals, 159
temporary slaughterhouses, 153–55
Croatia, 64
hate speech, 234
Cyprus, 64
Muslim population, 58, 65
Czech Republic, 61
hate speech, 236
Muslim population, 63, 200, 201
religious/secular divide, 262, 268

defamation of Islam, 213, 215, 216, 217, 220, 221–22, 223
democracy, 4–5, 20, 137
Islamic constitutionalism, 23–24
liberal democracy, 10–11, 17, 21–23, 28–29, 30
freedom of expression, 213, 214–15, 220–21, 223
reasonable accommodation, 185
secularism principle, 148
universality of democracy, 21–23
Denmark, 5, 60
burqa ban, 50
counter-terrorism measures, 238
regulation of Islam, 123–25, 137
criminalisation of hate speech, 131–35
criticisms of, 135–36
justifiable limitations of religious freedom, 129–31
religious slaughter, 158–59
targeted oppression, 7
diversity within Islamic community, 34–35, 85–86, 187–88
lack of organisation, 86–88
"specificity" of the Muslim faith, 86
Divine Command approaches to theology, 188–89
Islamic constitutionalism, 193
moral and legal punishment, 195–96
slavery, 193
women's rights, 193–94
misinterpretation of approach, 190–93
divorce, 20, 194
family law pluralism, 103–7
Muslim Arbitration Tribunal, 106
Sharia councils, 53, 104–7
women's experiences, 107–9

economic migration, 36
education:
balancing rights and freedoms, 113–15
educative rights and duties of parents, 115–17
intercultural education, 121
respect for religion, 8–9, 112–13
see also schools
equality and difference:
feminist theory, 100–3
Estonia, 61–62, 63, 230
hate speech, 234
EU law, 17, 75, 80–81, 165, 227
see also Charter of Fundamental Rights of the EU; Court of Justice of the EU
European Commission on Human Rights:
religious accommodation, 183–84
European constitutionalism, 13–14
"constitutional morality, 19–21
Islam, relationship with, 17
Islamic constitutionalism, relationship with, 23–25
judicial systems, 28–29
religious foundations, 18–19
decline, 19–21
societal impact of, 21
value of human person, 20
European Convention on Human Rights (ECHR), 17
Cairo Declaration on Human Rights in Islam, relationship with, 24–25
First Additional Protocol, 26, 29
obligation to respect human rights (Art. 1), 142

prohibition of discrimination (Art. 14), 26
reasonable accommodation, relationship with, 183
right to freedom of thought, conscience and religion (Art. 9), 11–12, 29
religious clothing, 142–43
right to a fair trial (Art. 6), 28
right to respect for private and family life (Art. 8), 143
right to effective remedy (Art. 13), 28
procedural rights, 28
European Court of Human Rights (ECtHR), 3–4
reasonable accommodation, 183
Eweida and others v UK, 183–85
prohibition of discrimination, relationship with, 183
religions and states, relationship between, 79–80
religious freedom, 79–80
European values:
bias against Islam, 53–55
human rights foundation, 3–6
Islamic values compared, 5–6, 43–44, 53–55
burqa bans, 49–50
headscarf bans, 47–49
old versus new Islam, 6
secularism, 44–47
Sharia courts, 52–53
Sharia law, 50–52
political-legal values, 44, 53–55
religious-cultural values, 44, 53–54
precedence, 54–55
secularised state, 4

family law:
legal pluralism, 103–4
divorce and Sharia councils, 104–7
family structure and roles, 115–16
female genital mutilation, 27
feminist theory, 100
equality and difference
autonomy, 103
feminism, multiculturalism and religion, 101–2
liberalism, 100–1
post-colonial feminist theory, 103
sexual equality and women's agency, 101
Finland:
counter-terrorism measures, 238
hate speech, 234
Muslim population, 199, 200, 201
old versus new Islam, 60, 61, 67
religious slaughter, 159, 206
religious/secular divide, 263, 268
theological training, 203–4
food regulation, 206
religious slaughter cases, 12–13, 153, 156–58
additional stunning prior to the killing, 161–64
avoidable pain and suffering, 159–61
bindingness of judgments, 165
equal treatment argument, 163
organic food production labelling, 155–56
systems restraining bovine animals, 159
temporary slaughterhouses, 153–55
France:
burqa bans, 49, 50, 77–78, 79–80, 144
Ebrahimian v France, 150
El Morsli v France, 145
SAS v France, 148–49
colonialism, 38–39, 58, 60
cultural racism in schools, 118–19
Ebrahimian v France, 150
El Morsli v France, 145
laïcité, 5
liberalism, 77–78
Muslim population, 37, 60, 85, 199, 201
populist policies, 10, 77–78, 89
religious slaughter, 153, 161
religious/secular divide, 268
restrictions on foreign funding, 247–50
SAS v France, 148–49
secondment of Imams, 91
secular state doctrine, 45, 68, 93, 101, 146, 201–2, 202–3
security measures, 202–3, 203–4, 237
freedom of expression, 214–15
ECHR, 215–16
see also hate speech
funding of Islamic activities, 90–92, 203–4
restrictions on foreign funding, 241–42
Austria, 252–53
Belgium, 242
Council of Europe, 253–56
France, 247–50
Germany, 244–45
Italy, 243–44
Netherlands, 246–47
Spain, 242–43
United Kingdom, 251–52

gender equality, 4–5, 94, 104, 125
burqa cases, 49–50
headscarf cases, 47–49, 54
Germany:
burqa ban, 50
citizenship rights, 78
Islamic law and Sharia, 103–4
liberalism, 78–79, 93–94
Muslim population, 58, 60, 63, 199, 200, 201
public morals, 128
religious/secular divide, 263
restrictions on foreign funding, 244–45
schools and school textbooks, 118–19, 205–6
state religious neutrality, 45
surveillance of mosque activities, 203
theological training, 91
Greece:
confessionalism, 79
hate speech, 234
hegemony of religion, 68
infringement of religious freedom, 26–27, 204
Muslim population, 22–23, 58, 64–65, 199, 200
Sharia, 24–25, 27

hate crimes:
international law, 234–37
Office for Democratic Institutions and Human Rights
annual survey, 231
hate speech, 9–10
criminalisation, 131–35
harm principle, 217
legal moralism, 217
legal paternalism, 217
offence principle, 217
definition, 218–21
international law, 234–37
Islamophobic speech distinguished, 221
see also freedom of expression; Islamophobic speech
headscarf bans:
conflicting Islamic and European values, 47–49
ECtHR case law, 141–46
Ebrahimian v France, 150
Hamidović v Bosnia and Herzegovina, 150
Leyla Şahin v Turkey, 147–48
SAS v France, 148–49
history and historical narrative, 31–32
constraints of, 32–33
diversity within Islamic heritage, 34–35
religious fundamentals, 35–36
heritage distinguished, 33–34, 35–36
immigrants, perception of, 36–38
inter-religious coexistence, 40–41
human rights:
old versus new Islam, 69
rights of Muslim communities, 85–88, 94–95
commitment to fundamental rights, 88–90
consolidation of national funding for faiths, 90–92
unification of organisation/representation, 92–94
see also individual conventions and international bodies
Human Rights Committee, 227, 232–33
Human Rights Council, 126, 232–33
justifiable limitation of freedom of religion, 126
security concerns, 237–39
Hungary, 61–63, 82
hate speech, 234, 236
Muslim population, 200, 202
populism, 10, 75–76, 202
racial discrimination, 235
religion/secular divide, 261, 268

identity:
balancing social integration and religious identity, 3, 21–22, 38–40, 98–99, 107–9, 257–58
belonging, 41, 71, 82, 97–98, 109, 257–58
multiculturalism, 105, 108
multiple identities of children, 120
religious-cultural values, 44, 48–49, 54, 228–30
immigration:
citizenship and faith, relationship between, 36–37
economic migration, 36
political refugees, 36–37
post-colonial migration, 60–61
post-war migration, 36
pre-war migration, 36
radicalism, 37–38
inheritance rights, 26, 108

integration of Muslim citizens, 40–41, 201–2
assimilation policies, 67–68, 87, 99, 185–86, 201–2
old and new Islam, 71
schools, 120, 121
multiculturalism, 40, 42, 77, 100, 105, 108, 111–12, 115, 121, 196
old and new Islam, 67
schools, 117, 118
interculturalism, 9, 119–20
social inclusion, 121
International Covenant on Civil and Political Rights (ICCPR), 232–33
justifiable limitation of freedom of religion, 126–27
international human rights, 3, 193
Islamophobia, 9, 227, 228, 239
intolerance, 9–13
see also burqa ban; headscarf ban; Islamophobia
Ireland, 60
hegemony of religion, 68
Muslim population, 58
Islam:
European perspectives on, 199–200
growth of, 1–2
social composition of Muslims, 200–1
see also individual entries
Islamic constitutionalism:
Divine Command approaches to theology, 193
moral and legal punishment, 195–96
slavery, 193
women's rights, 193–94
European constitutionalism, relationship with, 23–25
Islamic values:
European values compared, 5–6
old versus new Islam, 6
citizenship, 70
human rights, importance of, 69
institutional position of minority communities, 68–69
"minoritisation" of Islam, 67–68
national and religious ideologies, 69–70
post-colonial European countries, 60–61
post-communist/socialist European countries, 61–64
post-Ottoman European countries, 64–65
Islamophobia, 9–13, 212–13
attempts to combat, 225–26
Catholic versus Protestant countries, 268–71
international law, 228–32
religious/secular divide, impact of
no impact on political attitudes, 260–61
some impact on political attitudes, 261–67
see also hate speech
Islamophobic speech:
legal treatment of, 209–12, 223–24
blasphemy, 221–22
criminalisation, 131–35
defamation of Islam, 221–22
hate speech, 217–21
Islamophobic speech *stricto sensu*, 222–23
see also blasphemy; defamation of Islam; hate speech
isolationist policies of Muslim organisations in Europe, 38–40
Italy, 48–49, 52, 54
burqa bans, 50
divorce, 20
hate speech, 234
infringement of religious freedom, 26–27
Islamic teaching, 204–5
Lautsi and Others v Italy, 150–52
Muslim population, 201
religious/secular divide, 264, 268
restrictions on foreign funding, 243–44, 252

judges, 17
balancing rights and freedoms, 29
courts, 29
European constitutionalism, 28–29
independence, 21
judicial review, 17
liberal democracy, 29

Kosovo, 41, 50, 58–59, 64

Latvia, 61, 63, 260, 261
law and politics, 70–71
citizenship, 70
human rights, importance of, 69
institutional position of minority communities, 68–69
"minoritisation" of Islam, 67–68
national and religious ideologies, 69–70
legal accommodation of Islamic practices, *see* **reasonable accommodation**
legal pluralism:
family law, 103–4, 108

liberal constitutionalism:
rising anti-Islamic policies, 77–81
limitations to religious freedom:
Denmark, 123–25, 137
criminalisation of hate speech, 131–35
Danish Constitution, 129–31, 135–36
discrimination issues, 135–36
international standards, 125–28
margin of appreciation, 128
necessity and proportionality, 127–28, 133–34
prescribed by law, 127, 131
protection of public order and morals, 128, 129–31, 134–35
Lithuania, 61, 62–63, 152, 199, 200, 201
hate speech, 234–35
religious/secular divide, 265, 268
Luxembourg, 60, 88

Malta, 60, 152, 204–5
hate speech, 234
"minoritisation" of Islam, 67–68
Monaco, 152
morality clauses:
criminalisation of hate speech, 135
religious freedom, relationship with, 12
mosques, 202–3
multiculturalism, 40, 42, 77, 100, 105, 108, 111–12, 115, 121, 196
old and new Islam, 67
schools, 117, 118
Muslim women, *see* **women**
"Muslimophobia", 9–13
Muslims in politics, 6–7

nativist attitudes, 258–59, 271–72
Catholic versus Protestant countries, 268–71
religious/secular divide, impact of
no impact on political attitudes, 260–61
some impact on political attitudes, 261–67
Netherlands, 60, 77–78
burqa bans, 59
hate speech, 235–36
Muslim population, 261, 262, 268
populism, 10
restrictions on foreign funding, 246–47
security concerns, 237
state religious neutrality, 45, 201–2
neutrality principle:
religious neutrality of the state, 19, 23, 25–28, 30, 45, 68, 79–81, 95, 204, 221, 227
North Macedonia, 41, 58, 64
Norway:
burqa ban, 50
religious/secular divide, 265, 268

old versus new Islam:
assimilation policies, 71
citizenship, 70
European values and Islamic values compared, 6
Finland, 60, 61, 67
human rights, importance of, 69
institutional position of minority communities, 68–69
"minoritisation" of Islam, 67–68
multiculturalism, 67
national and religious ideologies, 69–70
post-colonial European countries, 60–61
post-communist/socialist European countries, 61–64
post-Ottoman European countries, 64–65
"othering" Muslim communities, 4
political polarisation, 73–74
populism, 74–77

parental responsibility:
educative discretion of parents
freedoms and rights of children, 113–15
peaceful coexistence, 2–3, 6–9, 117–18, 146, 219
Poland:
Muslim population, 58, 62–63, 67, 199
populism, 75, 82, 202
religious/secular divide, 265–66, 268
political polarisation, 73–74
see also populism
political refugees:
citizenship and faith, relationship between, 36–37
radicalism, 37–38
populism:
political polarisation, 73–74
rise of, 10–11, 74–77, 81–82
Portugal, 234–35
post-colonialism and Muslim immigration, 60–61
post-communism/socialism and Muslim populations, 61–62
economic migration, 63–64
ex-Soviet Union countries, 62–63
post-Ottoman countries and Muslim populations, 64–65

prohibition of discrimination (Art. 14 ECHR), 26, 184
proportionality:
criminalisation of hate speech, 133–34, 220–21
limitations of religious freedom, 127–28, 130, 135–36, 137, 143, 157, 172, 184
religious slaughter, 157–58
proselytism:
implicit proselytism
religious symbols and clothin, 146–47
public order limitation clauses, 11–12, 26–27, 124–25, 127–28, 129–31, 137
criminalisation of hate speech, 134–35, 136, 219
religious freedom, relationship with, 12, 134–35, 201

quantifying/defining Islam and Muslims, 58–60
post-colonial European countries, 60–61
post-communist/socialist European countries, 61–64
post-Ottoman European countries, 64–65

reasonable accommodation:
assimilationist policy, relationship with, 185
backlash
Employment Division v Smith, 176–77
compelling state interest test (USA), 170, 172, 173–76, 176–77, 178–82
ECtHR, 183
Eweida and others v UK, 183–85
prohibition of discrimination, relationship with, 183
equality of treatment, 172–73
Islamic practices, 12, 167–68
philosophical foundations
US religious autonomy and freedom, 169–70
prohibition of discrimination, relationship with, 183
Religious Freedom Restoration Act (USA), 177–78
Burwell v Hobby Lobby Stores, Inc, 179–82
reservations, 173
US case law, 185–86
backlash, 176–77
Burwell v Hobby Lobby Stores, Inc, 179–82
Employment Division v Smith, 176–77
Frazee v Illinois Department of Employment Security, 172
Goldman v Weinberger, 175
Hobbie v Unemployment Appeals Commission, 172
Lyng v Northwest Indian Cemetery Protective Association, 175–76
Sherbert v Verner, 170, 174
strict scrutiny standard, 170
Thomas v Review Board, 171
United States v Lee, 174–75
Wisconsin v Yoder, 170–71
religious/secular divide:
no impact on political attitudes, 260–61
some impact on political attitudes, 261–67
religious freedom:
Art. 9 ECHR, 11–12
infringements, 26
balancing European constitutionalism, 25–28
children's self-determination, 113–15
equality of Muslims, 25–26
interpretative challenges, 26
full guarantee of, 18
limitations, 123–25, 137
criminalisation of hate speech, 131–35
Danish Constitution, 129–31, 135–36
international standards, 125–28
see also Denmark; limitations to religious freedom
morality clauses, relationship with, 12, 134–35
mosques, 202–3
public order limitation clauses, relationship with, 12, 134–35
security, relationship with, 202–3
religious nativism, *see* **nativist attitudes**
religious neutrality of the state, 19, 23, 25–28, 30, 45, 68, 79–81, 95, 204, 221, 227
religious pluralism, 6–7, 8, 19, 79–80, 111–12, 117, 119, 167
religious slaughter:
Belgium, 80, 153, 161, 206
CJEU judgments, 12–13, 153, 153, 156–58
additional stunning prior to the killing, 161–64
avoidable pain and suffering, 159–61
bindingness of judgments, 165
equal treatment argument, 163
organic food production labelling, 155–56
systems restraining bovine animals, 159
temporary slaughterhouses, 153–55

Denmark, 158–59
Finland, 159, 206
France, 153, 161
proportionality, 157–58
Sweden, 158–59, 206
Switzerland, 164
religious symbols and clothing:
conflicting Islamic and European values, 53–54
burqas, 49–50
headscarves, 47–49, 147–50
schools, 119–20
ECtHR case law, 141–46
Ebrahimian v France, 150
Hamidović v Bosnia and Herzegovina, 150
Lautsi and Others v Italy, 150–52
Leyla Şahin v Turkey, 147–48
SAS v France, 148–49
implicit proselytism, 146–47
religious freedom (ECHR Art. 9), 142–43
voluntary submission to restrictions, 146
Romania, 67, 260
rule of law, 3, 6, 13, 17–18, 21, 23–24, 28, 30, 124, 137, 206–7, 223, 254
good governance, 137
Russia:
government-controlled Islam community system, 68
invasion of Ukraine, 21–23, 230, 231–32
Muslim population, 59, 61–62, 64, 200

San Marino, 152
schools:
balancing rights and freedoms, 113–15
educative rights and duties of parents, 115–17
food restrictions, 119–20
inter-religious coexistence, 117–20
physical education, 119
problematic subjects, 119
religious education, 117–18
freedom of religion, 118–19
history of religion, 118
stereotypes, 119
religious symbols and clothing, 119–20
respect for religion, 8–9, 112–13
secularism:
conflicting Islamic and European values, 44–46
secularism versus secularisation, 46–47
democracy, 148
growth of, 1–2
religious/secular divide
no impact on political attitudes, 260–61
some impact on political attitudes, 261–67
secular state doctrine, 45, 68, 93, 101, 146, 201–2, 202–3
security concerns, 206–7
international law, 237–39
national funding of Islamic activities, 90–92, 203–4
religious chaplaincy, 204–6
theological training of Imams, 90–92, 203–4
Serbia, 41
Sharia councils in the UK, 7–8
divorce, 52–53, 104–7
women's experiences, 107–9
Sharia courts:
conflicting Islamic and European values, 52–53
Sharia law, 24–25, 26–27
conflicting Islamic and European values, 50–52
inheritance rights, 26
Slovakia, 63, 264, 268
Slovenia, 78, 204–5, 266, 268
social inclusion, 70
balancing integration and religious identity, 3, 21–22, 38–40, 98–99, 107–9, 257–58
intercultural education, 112, 121
Spain, 52, 68, 86
burqa ban, 50
citizenship, 252
colonialism, 38–39, 40
Islamic teaching, 205
Muslim population, 201
religious/secular divide, 267, 268
restrictions on foreign funding, 242–43, 245
schools and textbooks, 118–19
"specificity" of the Muslim faith, 86
state neutrality, *see* **neutrality principle**
Sweden, 45, 103–4
hate crimes and hate speech, 235, 238
Muslim population, 200
religious slaughter, 158–59, 206
religious/secular divide, 266, 267, 268
security concerns, 237

Switzerland:
religious/secular divide, 260
religious clothing, 146–47
religious slaughter, 164
schools, 77–79

theological training, 90–92, 203–4

Ukraine, 62
invasion of Ukraine, 17, 21–23, 230, 231–32
UN Commission on Human Rights:
justifiable limitation of freedom of religion, 126
UN Convention on the Elimination of All Forms of Racial Discrimination (CERD), 227, 232–33
hate speech, 236
security concerns, 237–39
UN Convention on the Protection of the Rights of All Migrant Workers and Members of their Families:
justifiable limitation of freedom of religion, 126
UN Convention on the Rights of the Child (UNCRC), 113
justifiable limitation of freedom of religion, 126
security concerns, 237–39
UN General Assembly, 126, 225–26
justifiable limitation of freedom of religion, 126
unification of organisation/representation of Muslim faith, 92–94
United Kingdom, 7, 8, 38–39
multiculturalism, 77
Muslim population, 58
religious clothing, 5
restrictions on foreign funding, 251–52
Sharia councils, 53, 103–4
divorce, 104–9
state religion, 45

United States:
compelling state interest test, 170, 172, 173–76, 176–77, 178–82
see also reasonable accommodation
reasonable accommodation
backlash, 176–77
Burwell v Hobby Lobby Stores, Inc, 179–82
Employment Division v Smith, 176–77
Frazee v Illinois Department of Employment Security, 172
Goldman v Weinberger, 175
Hobbie v Unemployment Appeals Commission, 172
Lyng v Northwest Indian Cemetery Protective Association, 175–76
philosophical foundations, 169–70
Religious Freedom Restoration Act, 177–78, 179–82
reservations, 173
Sherbert v Verner, 170, 174
strict scrutiny standard, 170
Thomas v Review Board, 171
United States v Lee, 174–75
Wisconsin v Yoder, 170–71

voluntarism, *see* **Divine Command**

Westphalian state, 18–19
women, 7–8, 97–98
divorce
Sharia councils, 104–7
women's experiences, 107–9
feminist theory, 100
autonomy, 103
equality and difference, 100–3
feminism, multiculturalism and religion, 101–2
liberalism, 100–1
post-colonial feminist theory, 103
sexual equality and women's agency, 101
legal pluralism, 98–99
Sharia councils
women's experience, 107–9

www.ingramcontent.com/pod-product-compliance
Ingram Content Group UK Ltd.
Pitfield, Milton Keynes, MK11 3LW, UK
UKHW020246290926
15470UKWH00002B/770

9 781509 966950